brief contents

PREFACE xv

ABOUT THE AUTHORS xvii

ACKNOWLEDGEMENTS xviii

CHAPTER 1 ELECTRONIC COMMERCE, INFORMATION SYSTEMS AND THE ROLE OF TECHNOLOGY 1

CHAPTER 2 MODELS FOR ELECTRONIC COMMERCE 43

CHAPTER 3 THE TECHNOLOGY OF BUSINESS TO CONSUMER ELECTRONIC COMMERCE 75

CHAPTER 4 DEVELOPING AND IMPLEMENTING ELECTRONIC TRADING SYSTEMS 116

CHAPTER 5 BUSINESS TO BUSINESS INFRASTRUCTURE 149

CHAPTER 6 BUSINESS TO BUSINESS INTEGRATION 177

CHAPTER 7 ELECTRONIC PAYMENT SYSTEMS 212

CHAPTER 8 TECHNOLOGY OF SECURE ELECTRONIC TRADING 243

CHAPTER 9 DEVELOPING A SECURITY POLICY FOR ELECTRONIC COMMERCE 273

CHAPTER 10 THE IMPACT OF LAW AND ETHICS ON TRADING USING ELECTRONIC COMMERCE 300

CHAPTER 11 MANAGING THE TECHNOLOGY OF INTERNET BUSINESS 329

CHAPTER 12 THE FUTURE OF E-COMMERCE TECHNOLOGIES 361

GLOSSARY 379

INDEX 390

contents

PREFACE   xv

ABOUT THE AUTHORS   xvii

ACKNOWLEDGEMENTS   xviii

CHAPTER 1 **ELECTRONIC COMMERCE, INFORMATION SYSTEMS AND THE ROLE OF TECHNOLOGY**
(Elaine Lawrence)   1

Introduction   2
    History of e-commerce   2
    A history of computing, the Internet and the World Wide Web   4
The advent of electronic commerce   8
    An overview of EDI   8
    The digital economy   9
    M-commerce   9
Types of electronic commerce   10
    Business to consumer (B2C)   11
TECHNICAL INSITE: A BUSINESS OF ONE   12
TECHNICAL INSITE: COOPERATIVE BUSINESS TO BUSINESS MODELS   13
    Business to business (B2B)   13
    Consumer to business   15
    Consumer to consumer   15
    Government to government (G2G)   15
    Government to business (G2B) and government to consumer (G2C)   15
Terminology for the new age of business   16
    The Internet   16
    Intranets   16
    Extranets   17
    Ultranets   18
    Hypertext transfer protocol   19
    Transmission control protocol/Internet protocol   19
    Bluetooth   19
TECHNICAL INSITE: MOBILE DEVICES AND THE BLUETOOTH TECHNOLOGY   20

Uniform Resource Locators   20
Browsers   21
Client/server architecture   21
Java   21
Search engines   22
How the Internet works   22
Architecture of the World Wide Web   27
Email   30
Information systems and Internet commerce   31
E-commerce as a management tool   32
TECHNICAL INSITE: TECH-WISE CEOs: FROM THE GEEK AS BOSS   33
How this book is organised   35
Summary   36
KEY TERMS   36
CASE STUDY   37
QUESTIONS   40

CHAPTER 2   **MODELS FOR ELECTRONIC COMMERCE** *(Craig Parker)*   43
Introduction   44
Online advertising models of e-commerce   44
Advertising-supported model   45
Web portals   47
Yellow Pages model   49
Company-based models of e-commerce   50
Online subscription model   50
Online fee-for-service model   52
Online fee-for-transaction model   53
B2C virtual communities   53
Virtual storefront model   54
Inter-organisational models of e-commerce   57
Electronic procurement model   58
Multi-organisational electronic service delivery model   59
Supply chain management model   60
TECHNICAL INSITE: E-COMMERCE REQUIRES INTELLIGENT SUPPLY CHAINS   62
Third party models of e-commerce   63
Electronic malls   63
B2B virtual communities   64
Internet auction model   64
Internet exchange model   66

TECHNICAL INSITE: APPLICATION INTEGRATION WITH EXCHANGES   68
Summary   69
KEY TERMS   69
QUESTIONS   70
CASE STUDY   70

CHAPTER 3

THE TECHNOLOGY OF BUSINESS TO CONSUMER ELECTRONIC COMMERCE
(Richard Braithwaite)   75

Introduction   76
The basic web computing model   76
    HTML   77
    JavaScript   79
    HTTP   82
TECHNICAL INSITE: A HANDS-ON INTRODUCTION TO HTTP   84
    TCP/IP   84
Extending the web computing model to perform transactions   86
    Forms   88
    Sending data via HTTP   90
    The common gateway interface   91
State information   96
    Cookies   96
    Embedding session information in a URL   97
    Hidden fields   97
Programming the web model   98
    Perl   99
    PHP, Active Server Pages and ColdFusion   99
    Java   105
    ActiveX   107
TECHNICAL INSITE: B2C TECHNOLOGY IN ACTION   109
Security of B2C transactions   110
Summary   111
KEY TERMS   112
QUESTIONS   112
CASE STUDY   113

CHAPTER 4

DEVELOPING AND IMPLEMENTING ELECTRONIC TRADING SYSTEMS
(Elaine Lawrence)   116

Introduction   117
System development methodologies — background   118
    Objects and components   119

te
of
bu

ELAINE LAWRENCE

STEPHEN NEWTON

BRIAN CORBITT

RICHARD BRAITHWAITE

CRAIG PARKER

John Wiley & Sons Australia, Ltd

First published 2002 by
John Wiley & Sons Australia, Ltd
33 Park Road, Milton, Qld 4064

Offices also in Sydney and Melbourne

Typeset in 10/12 pt New Baskerville

National Library of Australia
Cataloguing-in-Publication data

Technology of internet business.

   Bibliography.
   Includes index.
   ISBN 0 471 42186 3.

   1. Internet. 2. Business — Communication
   systems. 3. Business — Computer network
   resources. 4. Electronic commerce — Planning.
   I. Lawrence, Elaine.

004.678

Cover image and images used in internal design:
© Digital Vision 2001

Printed in Singapore by
CMO Image Printing Enterprise

10 9 8 7 6 5 4 3 2 1

Web development methodologies	119
Joint application development	120
Going on line	121
Dynamic systems development method	122
TECHNICAL INSITE: THE SUPERIOR SOFTWARE FOR WINDOWS (SSW) SYSTEM DEVELOPMENT METHODOLOGY	123
Rational unified process	125
TECHNICAL INSITE: E-SOFTWARE DEVELOPMENT	125
New business models	127
Mobile commerce models	128
TECHNICAL INSITE: FUTURE MOBILE E-BUSINESS SCENARIOS	128
Interactive television models	128
Collaborative e-business models	129
TECHNICAL INSITE: LIVELINK: A WORLDWIDE COLLABORATIVE WEB MODEL	129
Client/server model	130
Internet business technologies and standards	130
Internet inter-ORB protocol	132
Database management systems	133
Data warehousing	134
Database integration	134
Oracle's solution	135
JavaBeans	135
TECHNICAL INSITE: BUILDING A VIRTUAL STORE	136
Project management: methods and issues	138
Rapid application development (RAD)	140
Definitional framework for RAD	141
Auditing e-commerce	142
Summary	143
KEY TERMS	143
QUESTIONS	143
CASE STUDY	144
CHAPTER 5 BUSINESS TO BUSINESS INFRASTRUCTURE *(Stephen Newton)*	149
Introduction	150
The B2B transformation	150
XML	151
DOM	152
DTDs and XML schemas	152
XSL	153
XLINK and XPOINTER	154

XPATH	154
Benefits of XML	154
XML/EDI	155
XML/EDI trading system	158
ebXML	159
TECHNICAL INSITE: XML AND B2B INFRASTRUCTURE	159
The Extranet	162
What is an extranet?	162
Benefits of the extranet	164
Extranet architecture	165
Extranet security	166
Securing the extranet transaction — the role of encryption and authentication	166
TECHNICAL INSITE: A QUESTION OF SECURITY	167
The Virtual Private Network (VPN) extranet	169
What is a VPN?	169
VPN extranet technology	171
Summary	172
KEY TERMS	172
QUESTIONS	172
CASE STUDY	173
CHAPTER 6 **BUSINESS TO BUSINESS INTEGRATION** *(Stephen Newton)*	177
Introduction	178
Enterprise application integration (EAI)	178
Why EAI?	178
EAI technologies	179
Integration architecture explained	180
Middleware technology	181
TECHNICAL INSITE: EAI SOFTWARE	182
Application technology	183
Cataloguing	183
Order processing	184
Payment system	184
Work flow management	185
Content management	185
Personalisation	187
EAI checklist	187
TECHNICAL INSITE: CORPROCURE — B2B E-PROCUREMENT	188

Supply chain integration (inter-enterprise)   190
    Traditional supply chain inefficiencies   191
    Supply chain management techniques   191
Three models for supply chain integration   191
TECHNICAL INSITE: USING THE VMI MODEL   193
Managing the human factor   195
    The virtual organisation   195
EAI return on investment   199
    EAI: a significant investment   199
    Increased revenue   200
    Capital cost reduction   201
    Process simplification   201
    Inventory management   201
    Why is business to business ROI different?   202
TECHNICAL INSITE: NEW AGE ROI   202
    E-business ROI guidelines   204
Summary   205
KEY TERMS   205
QUESTIONS   205
CASE STUDY   206

CHAPTER 7   **ELECTRONIC PAYMENT SYSTEMS**
(Brian Corbitt, Elaine Lawrence and Stephen Newton)   212

Introduction   213
B2C electronic payment systems   213
    Credit cards on the Internet   213
    How credit cards work on the Internet   214
TECHNICAL INSITE: TRIPLE C: CYBERSPACE CREDIT CARDS   216
EFTPOS   217
Electronic cheques   217
E-wallets   218
Digital cash and prepaid cards   219
Other digital currency products   221
Smart cards (stored value cards)   223
    Types of SVCs   227
    Advantages and risks of SVCs in business   227
B2B electronic payment systems   228
    Electronic funds transfer and EFTPOS   228

Electronic Data Interchange   229
    Traditional EDI   229
    Communications channels   229
    Direct link EDI   230
    Private networks   230
    Value-added networks   230
EDI standards   231
    Benefits of traditional EDI   232
    Shortcomings of traditional EDI   233
Internet EDI   234
TECHNICAL INSITE: HUB AND SPOKE MODEL
  A PRACTICAL APPROACH TO WEB-BASED INTERNET EDI   234
Internet EDI components   236
    Back-end database system   236
    Translator   236
    Mail repository   236
    Web server   237
    Adapter   237
Open buying on the Internet (OBI)   237
Summary   238
KEY TERMS   239
QUESTIONS   239
CASE STUDY   240

CHAPTER 8   **TECHNOLOGY OF SECURE ELECTRONIC TRADING**
(Brian Corbitt, Elaine Lawrence and Stephen Newton)   243

Introduction   244
Why security is important   244
Types of attacks   244
    Denial of service and distributed denial of service   245
TECHNICAL INSITE: WESTERN UNION WEB SITE HACKED   245
    Viruses   246
    Dealing with viruses   247
    Trojans, vandals and spam   248
Human security issues   248
TECHNICAL INSITE: COMPUTER FORENSICS   249
Elements of computer security   249
    Confidentiality and privacy   249
    Security safeguards   250
    Accountability   250

Encryption and authentication   250
    Secret-key (symmetric) encryption   250
    Triple DES   251
    Public-key (asymmetric) encryption   251
Digital signatures   254
    Steps showing how digital signatures work   254
Digital certificates   255
    The X.509 certificate standard   256
Elements of Internet security   256
    Secure Sockets Layer (SSL)   257
    S-HTTP   257
    Secure Electronic Transaction (SET)   258
    Cryptolope   258
Network security technology   258
    Firewalls   258
    Access control lists   261
    Passwords   261
TECHNICAL INSITE: CHANGING PASSCODES   263
Threat-mitigation techniques   263
Summary   265
KEY TERMS   265
QUESTIONS   266
CASE STUDY   266

CHAPTER 9   DEVELOPING A SECURITY POLICY FOR ELECTRONIC COMMERCE
(Brian Corbitt and Elaine Lawrence)   273

Introduction   274
Trust and electronic commerce   274
    What is trust?   274
TECHNICAL INSITE: ELECTRONIC TRANSACTIONS BILL TO PROVIDE VITAL LEGAL
   FRAMEWORK FOR E-COMMERCE   276
    The management of trust in e-commerce   278
    Anonymity   279
    Data mining   280
    SET and trust   280
    Trust and e-commerce relationships with government   281
    When trust fails   282
Trust seals   282
TECHNICAL INSITE: THE TRUSTe STORY   284
TECHNICAL INSITE: SECURITY BEGINS WITH POLICY   285

Developing a security policy 286
  Developing a security requirements report 286
TECHNICAL INSITE: BANK DATA SAFE AS HOUSES 288
  The policy development process 290
  Acceptable network and computer use 290
  Physical access 291
  Legal policies 291
  Internet access 291
  Virus and denial-of-service attack policies 291
TECHNICAL INSITE: SECURITY MEASURES
  THE GOOD, BAD AND FRUSTRATING 292
  Penalties and security breaches 293
Policy implementation process 293
  Auditing 294
  Managing security policy implementation 294
Summary 295
KEY TERMS 296
QUESTIONS 296
CASE STUDY 296

CHAPTER 10 | **THE IMPACT OF LAW AND ETHICS ON TRADING USING ELECTRONIC COMMERCE**
(John and Elaine Lawrence) 300

Introduction 301
Legal issues surrounding online transactions 302
TECHNICAL INSITE: FROM SHRINKWRAP TO CLICKWRAP 302
Control of Internet content 304
Privacy 306
TECHNICAL INSITE: LITTLE WEB BUG IS WATCHING YOU 306
Cookies 307
TECHNICAL INSITE: TREASURY'S WEB SITE 'BREACHED PRIVACY LAWS' 308
Monitoring employees 309
Intellectual property 310
  Copyright 311
  Digital watermark technology 311
TECHNICAL INSITE: OF NAPSTER, GNUTELLA, MP3, INTERTRUST AND WEBNOIZE 312
Patents 314
Trade marks 315
Criminal activities 316
Online banking and taxation issues 317
Hackers and crackers 317
  Combating hackers and crackers 318

Domain names	319
Jurisdiction	319
Defamation	320
TECHNICAL INSITE: JUDGE REFUSES BANK'S PLEA TO CLOSE 'DEFAMATORY SITE'	321
Ethics	322
Summary	323
KEY TERMS	323
QUESTIONS	324
CASE STUDY	324

CHAPTER 11

MANAGING THE TECHNOLOGY OF INTERNET BUSINESS
(Brian Corbitt)

	329
Introduction	330
Web adoption and its significance for managing organisations	330
An e-savvy strategy for e-commerce	335
Managing technology	338
Strategy development	338
Leadership issues	340
Managing the infrastructure (planning and installation of e-commerce technologies)	340
TECHNICAL INSITE: ONE FOR ALL, ALL FOR ONE: STUDY OF CEREBOS FOODS	343
Developing more integrated solutions	347
TECHNICAL INSITE: CUT RATE CALLS	348
Emerging trends in managing Internet commerce technologies	350
Summary	354
KEY TERMS	354
QUESTIONS	355
CASE STUDY	355

CHAPTER 12

THE FUTURE OF E-COMMERCE TECHNOLOGIES
(Elaine Lawrence)

	361
Introduction	362
Pervasive e-business	362
Ubiquitous computing	363
Miniaturisation and mobile commerce	363
Nanotechnology	364
Assemblers	364
Self-replicators	364
What this could mean in the e-business world	365
TECHNICAL INSITE: THE NANOTECHNOLOGY OF CYBER CRIME	365

Twenty-first-century software   366
    Mobile wallets   366
    Geolocation software   366
    User interface   366
    Collaborative computing software   366
Interactive television   367
Communications   367
TECHNICAL INSITE: FAST ACCESS TO THE INTERNET OVER COPPER WIRES   369
Internet2   369
    Automobile internet   370
Teleworking   371
Bandwidth trading   371
E-publishing   373
TECHNICAL INSITE: E-PAPER AND E-INK   374
Bluesky forecast   374
Summary   375
KEY TERMS   375
QUESTIONS   375
CASE STUDY   376

GLOSSARY   379

INDEX   390

preface

Electronic business over the Internet has undergone exponential growth over the past seven years. Information technology is driving this economic growth, yet from early 2000 many companies began to experience difficulties as organisations shifted to the Internet's high change/high speed environment. It has been a heady ride and many e-businesses have fallen by the wayside. Nonetheless, three startup Dot Com companies, Amazon, eBay and Yahoo!, are now among the world's best-known brands. These three pioneers have software at their core — they innovate with it, they buy out other software companies to obtain exclusive use and they use software to replace people. Many large corporations now recognise that the Web can assist them to realise efficiency improvements, cost reductions and increased business opportunities leading to improved profits. In this textbook the authors examine how the e-commerce market has matured over these years. Following an information system/information technology approach, this text explains the processes and network infrastructure associated with e-commerce and the varied commercial transactions executed over the Internet.

A key theme of the text is to bridge understanding between business and information systems/technology so that students can communicate effectively in a professional environment. Topics covered include the establishment of secure trading systems, electronic payments systems, business to business (B2B) systems, business to consumer (B2C) systems and management of technological systems. To help explain the working of web programming languages such as HTML, JavaScript and XML, sample code is included. The project management involved in building large Internet businesses (both B2C and B2B) is also considered in order to help readers to understand the unique problems associated with developing large web-transactional B2C and B2B web sites at e-speed. Rapid Application Development and the use of new techniques such as Extreme Programming are discussed. The complex interplay of technology and the law in the global marketplace is developed, as is the impact of future technology on Internet commerce. With e-companies' growing interest in measuring customer behaviour, e-metrics (or web analytics) is examined. Also addressed are such important business/technology issues as customer relationship management, knowledge management, content management, profiling and personalisation systems.

In writing this book we have used the virtual collaborative consulting model for authoring with our authors in Sydney, Melbourne and New Zealand and our editors in Brisbane. Our team comprises computer science and information systems academics, practising e-business consultants and a lawyer.

Technology of Internet Business situates the study of Internet commerce within a national and international framework in order to illustrate many of the emerging trends and innovations. Special features integrated into the text include:

- clearly identified learning outcomes
- technical insites with thought-provoking content for promoting class discussion. Accompanying questions are generally worded so as to accommodate change and innovation over the next few years.
- discussion and research exercises at the end of each chapter
- case studies with discussion and research questions and exercises
- further reference material directing students to additional resources
- a key terms list in each chapter, facilitating quick reference and study
- a full glossary of technical terms.

Instructors who adopt the text will also be provided with password-protected access to a companion web site, maintained by the authors in collaboration with John Wiley, to keep readers abreast of changes with timely updates. This web site (see www.johnwiley.com.au), offers:

- PowerPoint slides for each chapter
- an Instructor's Manual with multiple-choice questions for each chapter and sample solutions for the case studies and technical insites.

The authors hope that this book will complement, update and expand on our previous business-oriented text, *Internet Commerce: Digital Models for Business*, second edition, and that both lecturers and students will find this text and the associated web site a valuable adjunct to their study of the technology that supports Internet business.

about the authors

Elaine Lawrence

Elaine Lawrence, DTech, MBIT, Grad Dip Commercial Computing, BA, CCNA, CCAI, MACS, is a senior lecturer in the Faculty of Information Technology at the University of Technology, Sydney, where she specialises in e-business and computer networking. She has extensive experience teaching e-commerce and is well known through her writing and research activities. She co-authored, with Brian Corbitt, the award-winning textbook *Internet Commerce: Digital Models for Business*. Elaine is a founding member of the Internet/intranet consulting company Cyber.Consult.

Stephen Newton

Stephen Newton is the principal consultant at eStrategies, a private company that specialises in providing business to business advice and project management to a business and government client base. He has completed a Master's in Computer Science, specialising in e-commerce at the University of Technology, Sydney.

Brian Corbitt

Brian Corbitt is Professor of Management Information Systems and Head of the School of Management Information Systems at Deakin University. His research specialisations are in e-commerce policy and in implementation of strategic systems in organisations utilising e-business systems. Applications in South-East Asia, Australia and New Zealand provide the focus for that research.

Richard Braithwaite

Richard Braithwaite is a lecturer in the Department of Information Systems, Deakin University, where he teaches courses on e-commerce security and emerging technologies.

Craig Parker

Craig Parker, BSc (CompSci), PhD, MACS, is a senior lecturer in the School of Management Information Systems, Deakin University, and is the Director of Deakin's Master of Electronic Commerce program. His research interests are in small business and regional community use of e-commerce, and in the development of e-commerce teaching tools such as Web-TRECS.

acknowledgements

The authors would like to thank the team at John Wiley & Sons who helped in the production of this book — in particular, project editor Jem Bates and publishing editor Darren Taylor. We are also grateful for the insightful comments and advice from the reviewers — notably, Gary Millar, of Mincom; Peter Chomley, RMIT University; Linda Dawson, Monash University; John Van Beveren, University of Ballarat; and Bruce Low, Southern Cross University.

The authors and publisher wish to thank the following for permission to reproduce material covered by copyright.

Figures
1.6: this web page is the property of autobyte1.com. inc., and is reproduced herein with its express permission; 2.1: OZEMAIL Pty Ltd; 2.2 YAHOO! Australia and NZ; 2.3: screenshot reproduced with permission. Copyright of Telstra Corporation Limited. Map reproduced with permission of UBD. Copyright Universal Press Pty Ltd. EG08/01; 2.4: reproduced with permission of Proquest Information and Learning Company; 2.5: John Wiley & Sons, New York; 3.5, 3.6: reproduced with permission of Netscape; 4.1, 8.3: reprinted by permission of Pearson Education Limited; 4.3: Adam Cogan/Superior Software for Windows; 5.4: XML/edi Group www.XMLedi-Group.org; 6.3: webMethods, Inc.; 6.6: from *The Corporation of the 1990s: Informational Technology and Organizational Transformation*, edited by Michael Scott Morton, copyright 1991 by The Sloan School of Management. Used by permission of Oxford University Press, Inc.; 6.8: WEB page image courtesy of Milacron Marketing Co; 6.9–12: reproduced with permission of Orica Chemnet; 7.1: reproduced with permission of XAMAX Consultancy Pty Ltd www.xamax.com.au; 7.2: Trintech.com; 7.3, p. 216: reprinted with permission from Discover Bank; 7.5: screenshot reproduced with permission of EPX; 7.7: Compaq/MilliCent © Compaq Computer Corporation; 7.8: HERTZ Australia Pty Ltd; 7.9: Telstra Corporation Limited; 7.11 (top left): Queensland Transport, (top and below right): National Australia Bank Ltd, (below left): MBF; 7.17: from Chung, Dietrich, Gottemukkala, Cohen & Chen, May 1999, *Proceedings of the 19th IEEE Workshops on Electronic Commerce and Web-based Applications*, IEEE Computer Society Press; 8.4: reproduced by permission of Microsoft Press. All rights reserved; 9.1: Mastercard International; 9.2: reproduced with permission of the author; 9.3: VeriSign, Inc.; 9.4: reproduced with permission of TRUSTe; 10.2: screenshot © InterTrust Technologies Corporation; 10.3: from www.patentwizard.com. By permission of Michael S. Neustel, Patent Attorney. Neustel Law Offices, Ltd; 11.1: Compass World IT Strategy Census 2000. Reproduced with permission; 11.2, 11.3, 11.6: by permission of McGraw Hill Companies; 11.5, 11.9: JADE; 11.11: screenshot reproduced with permission of Ford Motor Company Ltd; 11.12, 11.13: Enterprise Ireland; 12.2: Telegeography, 1730 Rhode Island Ave, Washington DC 20036. Reproduced with permission.

Text
Tables 1.1, 1.8, 6.7: reprinted by permission of Pearson Education Limited; table 2.1: reprinted with permission of Course Technology, a division of Thomson Learning; pp. 33–4: © The Economist Newspaper Limited, London. 11 January 2001; pp. 37–40: © 2000 Time Inc. Reprinted with permission; table 6.1: reproduced with permission;

CHAPTER 1

ELECTRONIC COMMERCE, INFORMATION SYSTEMS AND THE ROLE OF TECHNOLOGY

Learning objectives

You will have mastered the material in this chapter when you can:

- define electronic commerce, Internet commerce and mobile e-commerce
- distinguish between the Internet and the World Wide Web
- appreciate the history of computing, the Internet and e-commerce
- comprehend the impact of the World Wide Web on the Internet and on business
- give practical examples of the digital economy
- identify the rapid changes taking place in e-commerce and Internet commerce
- understand the role of the enabling technologies behind e-commerce
- identify the relationship between information systems development and Internet business
- appreciate the need for technically literate chief executive officers.

'Technology strategy is now part and parcel of business strategy and it is one of those things that, like international experience, cannot be mastered from a distance.'

The Economist, 11 January 2001. Reprinted in the Weekend Australian as 'The rise of the gifted geek', 20–21 January 2001, p. 56.

INTRODUCTION

At the start of the twenty-first century, there are mounting signs that the Internet is becoming all-pervasive in the business world. Large multinational companies are embracing the technology to forge giant global alliances with not only their partners but also their competitors — for example the Ford, General Motors and DaimlerChrysler car parts exchange alliance called Covisint.[1] Levi Strauss has developed a brand management model on its company intranet[2] that is available to any Levi Strauss marketer in the world. Dell Computers has developed a customer extranet for the employees of its largest corporate customers. Jack Welch, the chairman of General Electric, has enthusiastically embraced web technology for his company. He comments, 'We have learnt that digitizing is the easiest part. E-business was made for GE and the E in GE now has a whole new meaning.'[3]

However, it is not only the large players who are benefiting from the Web. The business-of-one model — that is, a business comprising a single person — is possible because of the Internet. Engineers, architects and authors can now work from home, interacting with virtual teams over the Internet to complete their projects. The case study on the software development company TP Information Systems (TPIS) on page 12 illustrates how a software engineer was able to successfully market his program to a global market.

HISTORY OF E-COMMERCE

There are many names to identify doing business electronically, such as electronic commerce (e-commerce), eCommerce, iCommerce, Internet commerce, e-business and digital commerce. In this book we will use the terms *e-commerce* and *Internet commerce* interchangeably. Increasingly, digital business is being carried out using mobile phones and **personal digital assistants** (PDAs) such as Palm Pilots. This business has been christened *m-commerce*. E-commerce can be defined as the buying and selling of information, products and services via computer networks today and in the future, using any one of the myriad networks that make up the Internet. However, Kalakota and Whinston (1996) point out that e-commerce has many definitions depending on the perspective from which you view it. These ideas have been summarised in table 1.1 (opposite).

Although the Internet was established in the 1960s in the United States, it was not until the 1990s that its commercial potential started to be realised. Prior to that, the Internet was an academic and research tool for government, educational and non-profit organisations that was subsidised by the government and kept strictly out of reach of the business community. In the mid-1980s the National Science Foundation (NSF) created a high-speed, long-distance telecommunications network into which other networks could be linked. (Other organisations now support this link.) By 1991 the NSF had dropped its restrictive usage policy and allowed many commercial sites. This development, along with the arrival of the World Wide Web, caused the business community to take notice of the Internet. The Web is a graphical hypertext environment that operates within the

Internet. It supports multimedia presentations, including audio, video, text and graphics. The protocol (a set of rules, procedures and standards) that underpins the Web is **Hypertext Transfer Protocol (HTTP)** and the protocol for doing business on the Web is **Secure Hypertext Transfer Protocol**, which provides a basis for secure communications, authentication, digital signatures and encryption.

TABLE 1.1	ELECTRONIC COMMERCE FROM FOUR PERSPECTIVES
PERSPECTIVE	**PURPOSE**
Communications	To deliver information, products/services and payments over the telephone, communication networks or other means
Business	To automate business transactions and work flows
Service	To cut service costs while improving the quality of goods and increasing the speed of service delivery
Online	To provide the capability of buying and selling products and information over the Internet and other online services

SOURCE: R. Kalakota and A. Whinston 1997, *Electronic Commerce: A Manager's Guide*, Addison-Wesley, Reading, MA, p. 3.

A new standard called **Extensible Markup Language (XML)** allows developers to customise tags such as <item-number>, <item-name> and <item-price>. Such a language will enable browsers and web servers to implement transaction processing tasks. Just as **Hypertext Markup Language (HTML)** (the programming language used to create a web page that permits information to be shared globally) allows for open text publishing, XML will bring open database publishing.[4] Extensible Style Sheet Language (XSL) provides the tools to describe exactly which data fields in an XML file to display and where and how to display them. Like any style sheet language, XSL can be used to create a style definition for one XML document or can be reused for many XML documents.[5]

Table 1.2 illustrates some of the major advantages of XML.

TABLE 1.2	BENEFITS OF XML
BENEFIT	**EXAMPLE**
Flexible way of expressing data	Sending data between client and server, transferring shared data among applications or storing on disk
Versatile way of presenting data	An XML-based purchase order could be highly detailed for a purchasing agent but presented in a simpler form for a consumer.
Allows for embedding data within HTML	The XML data can be updated without having to refresh the entire page.
Useful for end users	XML provides richer set of web applications for viewing, filtering and manipulating information on the Internet.

SOURCE: Microsoft Corporation 1998, 'XML: A Technical Perspective', http://msdn.microsoft.com/xml/articles/xmlwhite.asp#benefits.

These topics will be further explored in chapters 5 and 6.

Technology has been the driver of e-commerce developments. Since the development of the World Wide Web, an amazing number of new technologies and software applications have been released. These technologies have changed the way in which business can be done. Technology that is vital to e-commerce includes credit card processing, interactive advertising, traffic management, image transmission, audio and video streaming. For example, electronic publishing is revolutionising the way books and magazines are published. Stephen King published his novel *Riding the Bullet* on the Web and half a million copies were downloaded in two days. In April 2001 Time Warner launched its new iPublish.com unit dedicated to web publishing. MP3 technology has changed the way in which music is traded on the Web. **MP3** (MPEG-1 Audio Layer-3) is a standard technology and format for **compressing** a sound sequence into a very small file (about one-twelfth the size of the original file) while preserving the original sound quality when it is replayed.

Traditional businesses have been slow to respond to e-commerce. A survey (released in July 2000) of 70 of the world's top 150 airlines revealed a lack of board level responsibility for information technology, despite the fact that three-quarters of the airlines agree that IT can deliver competitive advantage[6] (see the case study on Impulse and Virgin Airlines in chapter 3). In Australia the big four banks were very slow to take up Internet banking — it was a small bank called Advance (now taken over by St George Bank) that took the lead. By the end of May 1999, nine of the 52 banks in Australia were providing transactional online banking services.[7]

A HISTORY OF COMPUTING, THE INTERNET AND THE WORLD WIDE WEB

The following table gives a brief timeline of the developments in computing over the past 60 years. It highlights important landmarks in the evolution of computing, the Internet and the World Wide Web.

TABLE 1.3	TIMELINE OF COMPUTER DEVELOPMENTS		
DATE	**COMPUTER/ INFORMATION SYSTEM**	**WEB SITES**	**NOTES**
1937	Atanasoff-Berry Computer	www.cs.iastate.edu/jva/ jva-archive.shtml	Established basis for development of electronic digital computers.
1943	Colossus, developed by Alan Turing	www.bletchleypark.org.uk	Used to break German military codes during the Second World War
1945	Stored program concept	http://ei.cs.vt.edu/ ~history/ VonNeumann.html	The stored program concept, developed by Dr John von Neumann, described how both data and stored programs could be held in memory (the basis for digital computers).

1946	Electronic Numerical Integrator and Computer (ENIAC)	http://inventors.about.com/science/inventors/library/weekly/aa060298.htm	The first large-scale electronic, digital, general computer
1947	Precursor of the transistor		Originally called a transfer resistance device, the transistor revolutionised computers.
1951	Universal Automatic Computer (UNIVAC 1)	www.public.asu.edu/~francis/comp/univac.html	A Remington Rand machine that was the first commercially available digital computer
1952	Description of symbolic notation for programming	www.cs.yale.edu/homes/tap/Files/hopper-story.html	A paper by Dr Grace Hopper, illustrating the idea of reusable software, described how to program computers using symbolic language rather than machine language.
1952–1953	IBM Model 650 released Development of Core memory	www.computer-museum.org/collections/ferrite_mem.html	A small ring or core of ferrite (a ferromagnetic ceramic) can be magnetised in either of two opposite directions. Such a core can be used for storing a bit of information. Core memory was invented in 1952 at MIT, and was for some time the most important memory device.[8] Followed by IBM 700 Mainframe
1957	IBM 305 RAMAC system Development of FORTRAN language (FORmula TRANslation)	www.digital.com/fortran	Uses magnetic disks for external storage FORTRAN, introduced by John Backus, is an easy-to-use, efficient programming language still used today in engineering circles.
1958–1959	Computers with built-in transistors IBM smaller desk-sized computers	www.pbs.org/transistor/background1/events/sscomputer.html	
1960	COBOL programming language introduced	www.CobolReport.com	Soon becomes dominant business computer language — still in use today
1965–1968	BASIC programming language Digital introduced PDP minicomputer IBM 8-inch floppy demonstrated by Alan Shugart of IBM	www.vb-web-directory.com	Dr John Kemeny led the development of this language — widely used on personal computers.

(continued)

TABLE 1.3 *(continued)*

1969–1971	ARPANET — the precursor of the Internet — is established. Fourth generation computers — up to 15 000 circuits on large-scale chips Development of microprocessor	www.isoc.org/internet-history	Marks the birth of the Internet — first used by academics and the military Dr Ted Hoff of Intel develops the microprocessor or programmable computer chip — the Intel 4004.
1975–1976	Altair, the first microcomputer Ethernet — the first local area network developed First Apple Computer	compnetworking.about.com/compute/compnetworking/msubethernet.htm www.asap.unimelb.edu.au/hstm/data/170.htm	Developed at Xerox Parc by Ian Metcalf, the Ethernet local area network allows computers to communicate and share software, data and peripherals such as printers. Affordable personal computer for enthusiasts developed by Steve Wozniak & Steve Jobs
1979–1983	Viscalc spreadsheet developed CompuServe and Source founded IBM Personal Computer released MS-DOS released Hayes smart modem released Electronic Data Interchange (EDI) developed in late seventies Electronic Funds Transfer (EFT)	www.bricklin.com/viscalc.htm http:///.zdnet.com/filters/printerfriendly/0,6061,221607784,00:html	This program, developed by Bob Frankston and Dan Bricklin, helped convince people that personal computers were useful. First online information services

Modems for personal computers become popular — 300 bps Business to business e-commerce |
| 1984–1989 | Development of Automated Teller Machines and telephone banking IBM PC–AT, Apple Macintosh, HP LaserJet printers for PCs Internet-based hypermedia enterprise at CERN, Switzerland National Science Foundation (NSF) created a high-speed, long-distance telecommunications network in US Cisco launched its first product | http://public.web.cern.ch/Public/ACHIEVEMENTS/web.html

www.cisco.com | E-commerce for the masses

Invented by Tim Berners-Lee — to become the WWW

Cisco routers now carry 85 per cent of the world's Internet traffic. |

1991–1994	1991 NSF dropped its restrictive usage policy and allowed in many commercial sites.	www.w3.org/History.html	Marc Andreessen creates the web browser called MOSAIC — later this leads to the development of Netscape Communications Corporation.
	Windows 3.1 released MOSAIC web browser released — leads to Netscape	www.microsoft.com	Microsoft's first foray into a graphical user interface
	Linux kernel developed	www.fsf.org	Linus Torvalds created Linux (like Unix operating system) — its distribution and enhancement takes place on the Internet.
1995–1997	Windows 95 released Java released Palm Pilot released	www.sun.com www.palmpilot.com www.pencomputing.com/index.html	Microsoft's Windows 95 operating system consists of 10 million lines of code. Sun releases its Java object-oriented programming language — its advantage is that it can run on a variety of computer platforms such as Windows, MacOS or Unix. US Robotics released this amazingly successful hand-held device, useful for mobile e-commerce.
	Windows NT 4.0 released Internet Explorer Digital Video Disc	www.microsoft.com encarta.msn.com/index/conciseindex/B5/OB532000.html	Microsoft's Windows NT becomes popular as developers find it simple to build and deploy business applications. Internet Explorer is Microsoft's free web browser
1998–1999	Windows 98		Microsoft's new operating system. The GUI is based on the look and feel of a browser.
	E-commerce booms	www.netcraft.co.uk/survey	The rise of the Dot Com economy — e.g. Amazon, e*Trade
	iMac released Microsoft Office 2000 *Department of Justice v Microsoft* antitrust suit Making computers Y2K compliant	www.apple.com	Apple Computer releases the iMac and a laptop that has wireless connectivity called AIRPORT. Microsoft ordered to split into two entities, appeals.
	Mobile eCommerce — WAP		Wireless Application Protocol
2000–2001	Free hardware and software offered by Internet service providers.		Early in 2000, the high-tech stock market fell — lots of Dot Com companies fail. Called the dot.bomb/techwreck/dot coma economy.
	Wireless Technology B2B e-commerce touted as being strong	www.mobilemcommerce.com	Rise of mobile e-commerce and business to business e-commerce

SOURCE: Adapted from G. Shelly, T. Cashman and M. Vermaat 2000, *Discovering Computers 2001: Concepts for a Connected World*, Course Technology, Cambridge, MA.

Electronic funds transfer (EFT), Personal Computer (PC) banking and Automated Clearing House (ACH) transactions are early versions of e-commerce that financial institutions successfully integrated into their service delivery systems.[9] EFT and **electronic funds transfer at point of sale (EFTPOS)** are electronic tools currently in use effectively to transfer the value of exchange process for goods or services or information. EFT is defined by Kalakota and Whinston as any transfer of funds initiated through an electronic terminal, telephone, modem, computer or magnetic tape so as to order, instruct or authorise a financial institution to debit or credit an account.[10] EFT utilises computer and telecommunication components both to supply and to transfer money or financial assets.

AN OVERVIEW OF EDI

Electronic Data Interchange (EDI) is essentially an electronic document facilitating, for example, EDI purchase orders, quotes, verification of delivery and authorisations. A clearing house collects the various EDI payment authorisations from customers and settles accounts once a day. It is used mainly over leased lines rather than the Internet. A buyer prepares an authenticated message, which permits the transfer of funds to a merchant. The message is sent to the merchant, who forwards it to the bank. The bank checks the validity of the message and credits the merchant's account. The bank then sends a message to an electronic clearing house indicating that a payment is due from the buyer's bank. Overnight the clearing house settles accounts among the participating banks. The buyer bank debits the buyer's account. This process is considered very expensive, so it is used mainly by large companies such as automobile manufacturers, large department store chains and oil companies.

EDI processes must have the following characteristics.

1. The exchange of information must be in a structured format so that the data are placed and found in predetermined places in the electronic message.
2. The format or structure of the information must be agreed upon by both the receiver and the sender.
3. The data must be machine readable. EDI does not involve the sending of data by fax from one organisation and then the rekeying of those data in the new place of operation.[11]

Internet EDI integrates existing legacy EDI systems with up-to-date e-commerce packages.[12] Business Systems Interoperation (BSI), Object Oriented EDI/Open EDI and Extensible Markup Language (XML) with EDI (XML/EDI) are examples of other attempts to ensure the relevance of EDI in the Internet commerce era. Further details on XML/EDI may be found at www.commerce.net/news/press/0821.html. EDI and Internet EDI are discussed in chapters 5 and 6.

THE DIGITAL ECONOMY

The entire Internet is accessible to users on what is essentially an unrestricted and equal basis — known as *ubiquity*. The user can go anywhere on the Net with a minimum of effort; there is no real technological reason for the user to start at a specific spot or web site. Because the Internet is interactive, exciting new forms of interactivity have developed. Software is distributed and tested on line, information is exchanged and modified more easily, data are stored on line — for example using docSpace (www.docspace.com, now owned by Critical Path) — and virtual organisations can operate more effectively through interacting globally at any hour of the day or night. The speed at which businesses can be established on the Internet places a great deal of emphasis on being first in a particular market category. Further, many Internet-based businesses have been developed as overlays of the existing infrastructure, which has reduced startup costs and deployment times.[13] However, early in 2000 many so-called **Dot Com** companies collapsed, prompting journalists and commentators to coin such names as the dot coma, dot bomb and tech wreck economy. In Australia, well-known failures included LibertyOne, dstore and eisa. The Gartner Group, however, believes that for many corporations the rise and fall of pure dot.coms will be seen as a 'phase' passed over in favour of long-term spending on improving connectivity and capturing revenue streams on the Web.[14]

Some larger older companies had been judged too slow and too concerned with their histories to compete effectively in the dot.com economy. The classic illustration of this was the slow reaction of Barnes and Noble to the rise of online bookseller Amazon. However, Barnes and Noble is now the second largest online bookshop on the Web. Older companies are now snapping up many of the failing dot.com companies. The media giant Bertelsmann AG, for example, bought out an ailing CDNow for $141 million dollars in 2000, and by the end of 2000 CDNow was the number three e-tailer in terms of the number of visitors.[15]

In fact, an economic revolution is occurring in every industry — from banking to selling groceries or cars, from planning weddings and birthday parties to managing farms and web servers, from routing container ships to making steel or selling postage stamps.

M-COMMERCE

Increasingly, digital business is being carried out using mobile phones and personal digital assistants (PDAs) such as Palm Pilots. This business has been christened *m-commerce* or *w-commerce*, for mobile e-commerce and wireless e-commerce. M-commerce or w-commerce is the buying and selling of goods and services through wireless hand-held devices such as cellular phones and PDAs.[16] The widespread use of cellular phones and PDAs, particularly among the younger generation and mobile workers, should ensure a large market. **Wireless Application Protocol (WAP)** is the emerging technology behind m-commerce that is common in Europe, where mobile devices are equipped with web-ready micro-browsers. WAP is a specification for a set of communication protocols to standardise the way that wireless devices, such as cellular telephones and radio transceivers, can be used for Internet access, including email and the World Wide Web.[17] Also, smart phones, using Bluetooth technology, offer fax, email and phone capabilities all in one, to make m-commerce acceptable to an increasingly mobile work force. Bluetooth is a computing and telecommunications industry specification that describes how mobile phones, computers and PDAs can easily interconnect with each other and with home and business phones and computers using a short-range wireless connection.[18]

The following areas are already utilising m-commerce:

- *financial services:* mobile banking for customers who use their hand-held devices to access their accounts and pay their bills — e.g. Swedish Postal Bank (PostBanken) and Citibank (Singapore); also brokerage services, in which stock quotes can be displayed and trading conducted from the same hand-held device[19]
- *telecommunications:* service changes, bill payments and account reviews can all be conducted from the same hand-held device; for example, 50 per cent of Portuguese mobile phone customers are anonymous pre-paid subscribers — they use ATM bill payment facilities to reload their mobile phone for more talk time[20]
- *service/retail:* gives consumers the ability to place — and pay for — orders 'on-the-fly'; pilot schemes in Scandinavia allow for consumers to use their mobile phones to pay for unattended car parking, soft drinks in vending machines and car washes[21]
- *information services:* delivery of financial news, sports figures and traffic updates to a single mobile device; for example, Dagens Industri has a pilot scheme allowing subscribers to receive financial data and trade on the Stockholm Exchange using Ericsson PDAs.[22]

TYPES OF ELECTRONIC COMMERCE

There are nine segments of e-commerce: business to consumer (B2C), business to business (B2B), business to government (B2G), consumer to business (C2B), consumer to consumer (C2C), consumer to government (C2G), government to business (G2B), government to government (G2G) and government to consumer (G2C). The e-commerce matrix is set out in table 1.4. Although an organisation may implement a solution in one segment of e-commerce, the same solution may also be applicable to other segments. For example, initially a business may create an online catalogue to fulfil an urgent business to business need, but later the business can expand or retool the same application to service other segments of their business, such as business to consumer and/or government to business.[23] B2B exchanges are considering shifting to **peer-to-peer (P2P) networks**,[24] where participants exchange information directly with one another, bypassing central exchanges. The basic technology for this paradigm shift is already available, as seen in Napster.com, Gnutella and other file trading systems, but it remains to be seen how quickly business embraces this technological change.

TABLE 1.4	THE E-COMMERCE MATRIX		
	BUSINESS	**CONSUMER**	**GOVERNMENT**
Business	B2B — GM/Ford, EDI networks	B2C — Amazon, Dell	B2G — tenders online, Eprocurement
Consumer	C2B — Priceline, Accompany	C2C — eBay, QXL	C2G/G2C — online voting
Government	Online tenders	Paying traffic fines, Victorian government (www.maxi.com.au)	G2G — state governments to federal governments

SOURCE: Based on 'The e-commerce matrix, in The E-Commerce Survey', *The Economist*, 26 February 2000, p. 6.

BUSINESS TO CONSUMER (B2C)

This segment is growing rapidly, as is demonstrated by the rise of online trading sites such as Schwab, eTrade and virtual bookstores such as Amazon. The growth of this sector has been extremely fast, and once it assumes critical mass real-world traders will find themselves experiencing problems. In the travel industry, margins are so thin that a loss of only 3 to 5 per cent of the market to the Internet would push large numbers of bricks-and-mortar travel firms out of business.[25] However, online travel agents may also face the same fate because of oversupply. A study by Bear Stearns of 1000 online travel sites predicts that only 20 per cent will survive in the longer term, principally the large and financial sound companies such as Travelocity.com and Expedia.[26]

FIGURE 1.1: The business to consumer site eTrade (www.etrade.com)

The following technical insite illustrates how the Internet enabled a software engineer to market his Windows NT password protection software globally.

technical
INSITE

A BUSINESS OF ONE
Password software offers big window of opportunity
BY TINA ELLIOTT

A YOUNG NSW programmer has developed security enhancement software for Microsoft Windows NT Server and sold it to more than 100 clients ranging from small organisations with 50 users to the Pentagon, the United States Army's IT managers and the US Air Force, which is rolling it out to users worldwide.

'I was surprised because I thought they would have had internally developed products,' said Mr Tonio Pirotta, director of TP Information Systems. 'Some [US defence] departments were in the process of developing these but mine came along and they said, "this is easier".'

Mr Pirotta wrote the first version of Password Policy Enforcer after reading some Microsoft developers' manuals on improving MS Windows NT system security.

The 27-year-old discovered a gap in the massive Windows NT market for protection against password cracking. After clearing the hurdle of not being a US product, there was six months' testing on PPE's stability, efficiency and security for military networks.

The attraction is not so much that the software was designed for the military, it's that no-one has had such a simple answer to a common problem for network managers in all sectors.

As the name implies, Password Policy Enforcer stops users choosing passwords that might compromise system security. In rejecting a password, Windows NT gives all the standard reasons but offers little direction. PPE gives more complex rules and detailed messages that reject a password for specific reasons, making it easy to pick the right password.

'Administrators find it very hard to get people to comply with a strict policy but simple passwords can be cracked in seconds,' Mr Pirotta said.

The big benefit is its ease of use and the time saved by help desk and general staff. In conjunction with a good security policy, PPE helps maintain better security. 'If you've got 500 or 5000 users [who] change their password every 30 days and Windows rejects their password, they could refer to a password policy or contact help desk and it's usually the help desk,' he said.

PPE licences are a few dollars or less per user. Clients in Australia, Europe and the US range from 50 to 120 000 users across finance, online business, telecommunications sectors, hardware and software vendors, health care and government agencies.

Sales so far have been through the company's web site, www.tpis.com.au, as Mr Pirotta has neither the time nor the budget for marketing. His involvement in the Federal Government's Commercialising Emerging Technologies (COMET) program aims to secure venture capital to fund growth.

PPE's target market of client-server systems is huge and growing. According to information technology researcher IDC, there were more than 3.8 million server shipments worldwide in 1998 and 1999, with each serving between five and 500 users on a system. Windows NT and Novell Netware are the two major operating systems for the world's client-server networks. Novell established an early lead and, in 1998, had about one third of the market, according to IDC. But Microsoft is acknowledged as having the fastest-growing share.

SOURCE: *Australian Financial Review,* 15 May 2000, p. 34.

EXERCISES

1. Do some research and find other examples of successful 'businesses of one' that have used the Internet to sell globally. Write a short report on your research results.

2. Check out www.tpis.com.au to see what developments have taken place since this article was written.

BUSINESS TO BUSINESS (B2B)

Businesses are becoming Networked Enterprises using the Web to hook up with suppliers, distributors, resellers, consultants and contractors. These collaborative networks, called extranets, have revolutionised the way many companies such as Cisco, Coles-Myer and General Electric do business. The following technical insite gives examples of such collaborative business models.

COOPERATIVE BUSINESS TO BUSINESS MODELS

BY FRANK CROSS

Two dominant B2B models appear throughout the literature. The first is the B2B business that builds its own Internet presence. Buyers will go to the company site to purchase and manage goods and services. The German global company Weidmuller is an example of this model. As the competition for the Weidmuller manufactured electronic parts heats up and the products shift towards being commodities, the customer service available through their web site differentiates Weidmuller from their competitors. The Weidmuller web site:

> lets Weidmuller's distributors buy from an online catalog listing the 10 000 electronic parts the firm sells in the U.S. . . . Weidmuller's distributors can tally purchases online based on pre-negotiated, customer specific prices. And distributors no longer have to call customer service representatives to check the shipping status of orders — that information is now available on the Web.[27]

The second and most dominant model in terms of sales strength, according to industry analysts, is the B2B exchange or online marketplace. 'Labeled **online marketplaces** (OLMs), these mostly venture-capital-funded start-ups are taking a radically new approach to link buyers and sellers and eliminating decades-old inefficiencies in the process.'[28] Examples of the new efficiencies Segal describes include NetBuy's virtual inventory, which is four times the size of the largest electronics components market distributor, and cuts long catalogue sifting and phone calls down to seconds. 'Instill, in the institutional food services market, has reduced the industry's 20% to 25% order-entry error rate to almost zero for its buyer members.' Segal characterises OLMs as follows:

- Rather than limiting themselves to selected manufacturers, OLMs increase liquidity and lower transaction costs by bringing together as many buyers and sellers as possible at one web site.

- OLMs are single-mindedly focused on rooting out industry inefficiencies by exploiting the unique features of the Internet: hypertext, graphics, real time database queries and low cost, standards based communication.

(*continued*)

- OLMs typically create a sense of 'community' by offering a wide range of services that complement the actual transaction, including discussion forums, industry news, job postings, data warehouses etc.
- OLMs rarely take title to products. [That is, an OLM site will generally not align itself to a product or service provider.]
- Most OLMs aim to maintain a high level of neutrality rather than, for example, favoring sellers over buyers or pushing one seller (brand) over another.[29]

Chemmatch.com is an example of the OLM B2B e-business model.

Chematch.com is a leading B2B Internet based marketplace for buyers and sellers of commodity chemicals, plastics and fuel products. Chematch.com's marketplace is centered around a real-time interactive trading exchange where members can anonymously bid, offer and negotiate online for the purchase and sale of chemical products.[30]

Chematch.com has 125 member organisations. The Chematch.com site is supplemented with an extensive information centre that provides members with industry news, forums and reference materials. Revenue is generated from 'commissions paid by each party for a completed transaction as well as from subscriptions to its information resource center'.[31] B2B OLM transactions are different from B2C transactions, where a click will complete a transaction. Given the scale of B2B transactions and the frequent associated contractual complexity, a click will generate a confirmation to the buyer and seller, and the 'negotiation is then taken offline, where parties finalize purchase orders and shipment terms',[32] as in the case of ChemConnect's World Chemical Exchange.

Where a B2C web site can simply accept credit card details, perhaps perform an online credit check and issue a receipt number, B2B is a far more complex proposition requiring greater investment if the returns on improved procurement and supply chain benefits described by IBM and Cisco earlier are to be realised. Integration of inventory systems to optimise procurement and integration of manufacturing and distribution systems to complete supply chain automation present far more complex IT development propositions. The OLM model also presents challenges such as 'receiving updated catalog information from multiple suppliers and providing personalized pricing to multiple buyers all at one site.'[33]

Some OLM model B2B organisations acknowledge these complexity barriers and motivate membership by helping members implement systems integration work through beta site programs. For example:

Buffalo Hospital Supply hasn't spent a nickel on technology or professional services to begin selling its products on the Internet. Medibuy.com has done all the systems integration work, including customizing contract pricing data for Buffalo's various customers.[34]

Medibuy.com Inc. is a San Diego B2B Health Care Exchange. OLM B2B exchanges are further motivating membership with the ability to provide detailed analysis of business transactions, such as Medibuy.com's detailed monthly reporting for buyers that can pinpoint high-volume suppliers, which 'hospitals can then target as candidates for contract renegotiation'.[35]

SOURCE: Adapted from Frank Cross 2000, 'Towards a RAD Approach to Electronic Business Project Management', MDP Project A, UTS, June, pp. 8–10.

EXERCISES

1. This article gives examples of rivals cooperating to do business in a collaborative fashion. This is often called 'co-operition'. Outline the advantages and dangers of such a way of doing business.

2. This article deals with the electronic, chemical and health industries. Do some research to find out if other industry sectors are working cooperatively via extranets, and write a short report on the example or examples you found.

CONSUMER TO BUSINESS

This type of e-commerce is epitomised by the web site www.priceline.com, which developed the Reverse Auction model where bidders set their price for items such as airline tickets or hotel rooms and a seller decides whether to supply them.[36]

CONSUMER TO CONSUMER

Originally, online auctions were used as a way for computer manufacturers to offload surplus material quickly. In the United States it was collectors of memorabilia and items such as 'Beanie Babies' and back issues of the *Saturday Evening Post* that propelled the growth of online auctions using the Auction model, such as eBay.com. (For more on Internet auctions, see pages 65–6.)

GOVERNMENT TO GOVERNMENT (G2G)

In Australia, with its system of a federal and state governments, the use of the Internet to communicate between governments is particularly relevant. The federal government web site at http://fed.gov.au contains links to all the state government sites. In 1999 the federal government released its plan to encourage its departments and agencies to procure electronically by participating in existing electronic trading communities and encouraging the development of new ones. In a discussion paper titled 'Moving to an Electronic Marketplace', the Office for Government Online (OGO) proposed supplementing the existing agency-based financial management systems that support procurement with a system in which 'the majority of agency purchases will be transacted from the desktop through electronic marketplaces on the internet'.[37]

GOVERNMENT TO BUSINESS (G2B) AND GOVERNMENT TO CONSUMER (G2C)

During the transition to the goods and services tax (GST) in July 2000 the Australian Taxation Office (ATO) relied heavily on the Internet. News about the changeover was available at the ATO's web site, www.ato.gov.au, and citizens and small businesses were able to apply for their Australian Business Number (ABN) over the Web.

Speeding tickets and traffic fines may be paid on line over the NSW Police Service's ePayments system for the Infringements Processing Bureau. The security of the payment system is supported by 128-bit encryption. ePayments is part of the first stage of the Infringements Management and Processing System (IMPS) Project, which includes a telephone-based, interactive voice response (IVR) service.[38] Over the next two years, subsequent releases of IMPS will see the replacement of the existing Traffic Penalties System with the establishment of an e-commerce portal for the IPB and the creation of new B2C and B2B projects. For details, visit www.infringements.nsw.gov.au.

TERMINOLOGY FOR THE NEW AGE OF BUSINESS

THE INTERNET

The **Internet**, a network of computer networks that has no central control or organisation, is changing the way people think about and do business. From its military, research and academic background, it has evolved into a serious business tool. The Internet is a worldwide system of computer networks — the mother of all networks — in which users at any computer can, with permission, get information from any other computer (and sometimes talk directly to users at other computers). It is a public, cooperative and self-sustaining facility used by hundreds of millions of people worldwide. Physically, the Internet uses a portion of the total resources of the currently existing public telecommunication networks. Technically, what distinguishes the Internet is its use of a set of protocols called TCP/IP (Transmission Control Protocol/Internet Protocol).[39]

The Internet is the largest computer network in operation in the world, having been developed in the 1960s and popularised in the 1990s. This popularisation occurred when the business and information exchange possibilities of the Internet were realised and specific drivers and search engines were developed to facilitate information exchange. This exchange has been enhanced with graphics, audio and video transmission, and interactive communication.

INTRANETS

Intranets are privately developed computer networks that operate within organisations. They rely on the standards and protocols of the Internet to operate, and invariably are protected by various forms of security to guard the internal operations of the user organisation. Intranets operate as separate networks within the operations of the Internet (see figure 1.2).

Some web developers (for example www.intranets.com) are allowing people to create intranets on the Web. At such a site you can create a private space on the Web that your group can easily access and where group members can share documents, calendars and event information. Educational institutions use intranets to set up virtual classrooms where students can interact with each other and their lecturers.

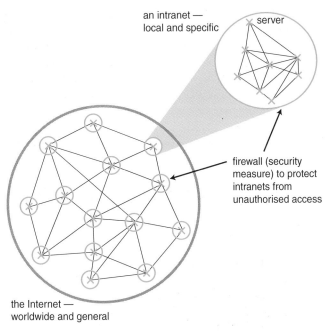

an intranet — local and specific

server

firewall (security measure) to protect intranets from unauthorised access

the Internet — worldwide and general

FIGURE 1.2: Intranets and the Internet

EXTRANETS

An **extranet** is a collaborative network that uses Internet technology to link businesses with their suppliers, customers or other businesses that share common goals. Extranets are usually linked to business intranets where information is either accessible through a password system or through links that are established collaboratively. They can also be private worldwide networks that operate on protocols that are either the same as the Internet or specifically developed for those networks. Unlike the Internet, these networks are not always in the public domain. SITA (Société Internationale Telecommunications et Aéronautique) is a company that runs a private network that operates throughout the world supporting the booking systems of most international airline systems and companies. This system is totally owned by the users and protected from public use by various security systems.[40] Such wide area networks (WANs) can span a large geographical area (across a state, a country or the world). Nodes on the network communicate using communication channels such as telephone wires or satellites. Local area networks (LANs) are normally restricted to one geographic region or department, such as the buildings on a university campus.

Other users of extranets include newsgroups, where new ideas or information are shared between companies or groups of companies. Training programs also can be shared and operated through extranets. SITA provides online training to customers and its own employees, using Lotus Notes software. **Groupware**, such as Lotus Notes and Microsoft Exchange, refers to programs that help people work together collectively while located remotely from each other. Groupware services can include the sharing of calendars, collective writing, email handling, shared database access, electronic meetings with each person able to see and display information to others, and other activities.[41] Sometimes this extends to shared catalogues that list all component parts or products that are of use to both suppliers and customers. Suppliers of aircraft parts, for example, would value being able to access Boeing's catalogues. However, the possibility of catalogues, booking systems and shared groupware being exposed to public access, or to capture by computer hackers, demands that attention be paid to appropriate security measures. These various networks, the Internet, intranets and extranets, perform different functions in e-commerce (see figure 1.3).[42]

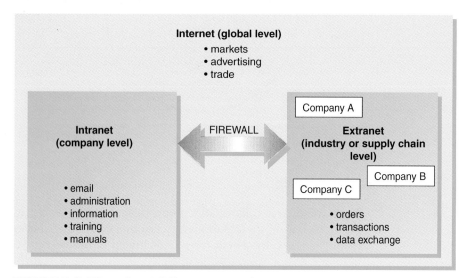

FIGURE 1.3: The role of different networks in e-commerce

ULTRANETS

Mako Katsumura[43] described what will be the ultimate world-wide network. Informally known as the **Ultranet**, it will exist once all of the relatively new Internet tools and methodologies mature into their next phase. The building blocks that will combine to form the Ultranet are:

- Java (see page 105)
- Internet Protocol version 6 (IPv6) (see page 86)
- Secure Electronic Transactions (SET) (see pages 220 and 280)
- Object-oriented database management systems (OODBMS)
- Extensible Markup Language (XML).

The prefix 'Ultra' is defined as 'going beyond what is usual or ordinary'. In his *JavaWorld* article, Matsumura uses the term Ultranet to refer to 'the mother of all networks', just like the Ultrasaurus was the ultimate giant dinosaur. If the Ultranet lasts as long as the dinosaur it will have been an 'ultra' success. The key to this ultimate network is the implementation of Internet Protocol version 6 (IPv6). IPv4 is already becoming limited by its addressing space. With IPv6 every device in the world can have an identity on the Ultranet. Tanenbaum (1996)[44] comments that IPv6 practically allows an IP address to be assigned to every molecule on the surface of the Earth.

HYPERTEXT TRANSFER PROTOCOL

Hypertext Transfer Protocol (HTTP) is the most basic protocol by which Hypertext Markup Language (HTML) resources are fetched across network connections.[45] This multimedia transport protocol is used in communications between browser clients and World Wide Web host computers. **Hypertext** is software technology that allows for fast and flexible access to information. Users browse and retrieve information by following links rather than by following a linear structure.

TRANSMISSION CONTROL PROTOCOL/INTERNET PROTOCOL

Transmission Control Protocol/Internet Protocol (TCP/IP) is the set of commands and communication protocols used by the Internet to connect dissimilar systems and control the flow of information. TCP allows users of the Internet to send and receive messages (e.g. email), find information, interact with other businesses and buy products, research personal details of people who have developed and placed personal material on a specific site (home pages), exchange business information or download software that can assist users to do more on the Internet. IP is a packet forwarding protocol that splits up packets automatically to send large messages across the networks, then reassembles them at their desintation.

BLUETOOTH

The **Jini Initiative** (from Sun Microsystems) is an architecture that enables all kinds of devices, such as desktop computers, personal digital assistants and mobile phones, to collaborate. **Bluetooth**™ Wireless Personal Area Networking (WPAN) technology creates a bubble of wireless connectivity for personal electronic devices.

When PCs and other devices are equipped with Bluetooth, personal digital assistants such as iPAQ Pocket PC and Palm Pilots will wirelessly update the calendar on office PCs, instead of using a cradle or cable attachment. Office arrangements will have greater flexibility because peripherals will not need to be within cable length of the PC.[46]

To illustrate some of these exciting developments, read the following technical insite on Bluetooth technology in which Paul May outlines some key points. Of course, much work will be needed to ensure that information can be delivered to wireless, handheld devices without unnecessary delay. Wireless Markup Language removes inessential graphics so that micro browsers work at high speed.

MOBILE DEVICES AND THE BLUETOOTH TECHNOLOGY

Bluetooth is a specification for short-range radio communications among mobile devices. Bluetooth enables devices to discover each other when they come within range and establish a networking relationship. Bluetooth is therefore conceptually similar to the dynamically adaptive Jini initiative. While Jini removes the need for devices to be explicitly installed on a network, Bluetooth allows devices to connect with each other in an ad hoc manner without the need for cabling. Jini can run over a Bluetooth network.

Bluetooth is more than a cable replacement option for devices in the same locale. It has integrated encryption and authentication functions, ensuring commerce transactions can be secured at the semantic level. Bluetooth also uses a transmission scheme that hops around a range of frequencies 1600 times per second, making it hard for any uninvited device to log a message. The power of a Bluetooth transmission is automatically choked back to the optimum requirement for any connection, which helps to insulate transactions from external monitoring.

SOURCE: P. May 2000, *The Business of Ecommerce from Corporate Strategy to Technology,* Cambridge University Press, Cambridge, UK, p. 164.

EXERCISES

1. What advantages do you see in this technology?
2. What are the advantages of personal digital assistants (PDAs) to an organisation?
3. Survey your colleagues to find out how many own a WAP-enabled or Bluetooth-enabled mobile phone or personal digital assistant such as a Palm Pilot. Report on its advantages and disadvantages.

UNIFORM RESOURCE LOCATORS

The unique address of a web page is called a Uniform Resource Locator, which may be typed into a text box at the top of a browser page. Below are some sample URLs.

TABLE 1.5	UNIFORM RESOURCE LOCATOR (URL) EXAMPLES	
TOOL	**SITE OR MACHINE NAME**	**DIRECTORY NAME AND/OR FILENAME**
file://	/CI/MOSAIC2/HTML	INTRO/index.htm
telnet://	138.25.78.8	(login library)
gopher://	info.anu.edu.au:70	/11/OtherSites/othergophers
news:	news.newusers.questions	
http://	kaos.erin.gov.au	/erin.html
ftp://	ftp.deakin.edu.au	/pub/pc-net/windows

SOURCE: E. Lawrence et al. 2000, *Internet Commerce: Digital Models for Business,* 2nd Edition, John Wiley & Sons, Brisbane.

TABLE 1.6	PROTOCOL MEANINGS AND USES	
PROTOCOL	**ACTION**	**PURPOSE**
file://	Retrieve local HTML and multimedia files	Useful for editing purposes
telnet://	Log onto and work on a remote computer	Checking out external libraries' resources
gopher://	Access text-based menu system	Searching and receiving documents
news:	Read messages from discussion groups	Communicating with wide range of people on topics of mutual interest
http://	Retrieve text and multimedia to a local computer	Linking a user's browser client to a web server
https://	Secure transactions	Encrypting credit card transactions
ftp://	Download files from remote computer	Downloading software, for example.

SOURCE: Lawrence et al. (2000).

Each URL defines the Internet protocol being used, the server on which the web site is stored or located and the path that will transmit the document. The Internet relies on what is called the Internet Protocol address to send data to a specific destination computer. This address is composed of four groups of numbers each separated by a full stop — for example, 138.25.8.1 is the identity of a mail server at the Faculty of Information Technology, at the University of Technology, Sydney. It is therefore possible to key in http://138.25.8.1 (the IP address) or alternatively http://webmail.mcs.uts.edu.au (called the domain name). IP addressing is covered in chapters 3 and 8.

BROWSERS

Web **browsers** are software packages that enable users to access and view web pages. Technically, a web browser is a client program that uses the Hypertext Transfer Protocol to make requests of web servers throughout the Internet on behalf of the browser user. **Netscape** Navigator used many of the user interface features of the original browser, Mosaic. Microsoft followed with its **Internet Explorer**. Today, these two browsers are highly competitive, with IE now in the lead position. **Lynx** is a text-only browser for Unix shell and VMS users. Another recently offered browser is Opera.[47]

CLIENT/SERVER ARCHITECTURE

Client/server refers to a pair of machines or a pair of role designations — a client requests services and a server provides them. For example, end-users at their personal computers request a web page from a server — say, a large computer housed at a university. A server may serve many clients and a client may use the services of many servers. This will be dealt with in more depth in later chapters.

JAVA

The programming language **Java** is used as a software development tool designed for use in the *distributed* environment that is the Internet. Java applets are small programs written in Java that are downloaded onto client machines, where they execute. Applets make it possible for a web page user to interact with the page. Details on Java are found in chapter 3.

SEARCH ENGINES

People 'surfing' the Web often use **search engines** to assist them find web pages and resources on the Internet. A search engine has three parts, which are described in table 1.7.

TABLE 1.7	SEARCH ENGINES AND HOW THEY WORK	
ITEM	**WHAT IT DOES**	**EXAMPLE**
A spider — sometimes called a 'crawler' or a 'bot'	Visits every page, or representative pages on every web site that allows searching, and reads it, using hypertext links on each page to discover and read a site's other pages	See www.altavista.com and its spider called Scooter. http://info.webcrawler.com/mak/projects/robots/faq.html
Catalogue	A program that creates a huge index or catalogue from the pages that have been read	www.google.com www.anzwers.com.au
Receiver	A program that receives a search request, compares it with the entries in the index and returns results to the surfer	WebFerret (from www.softferret.com) www.metacrawler.com

SOURCE: www.whatis.com, a property of Tech Target Inc.

An alternative to using a search engine is to explore a structured **directory** of topics. Yahoo, which allows users access to its search engine, is the most widely used directory on the Web. A number of web **portal** sites, which are designed to offer a variety of Internet services from one convenient location (e.g. www.ninemsn.com.au and http://garden.com), offer both the search engine 'keyword' and directory approaches to finding information.[48]

Resource definition format (RDF) is a highly flexible way of indexing collections of resources, similar to the manner in which card catalogues index the contents of a library.[49]

HOW THE INTERNET WORKS

The Internet operates within a structure that has existed to support other technologies, including telecommunications, and uses agreed standards and protocols. The Internet enables businesses to collect information, add value to information, conduct trade, and communicate with suppliers and customers. The Internet operates by taking data (such as an email message, a file, a document or a request for a file), dividing it into separate parts called packets and transmitting those packets along the best available route to the destination computer. Packet switching allows data packets to be sent over different routes to their destination. Once there, the data packets are reassembled into meaningful information. The software used for packet switching on the Internet is the communications protocols called Transmission Control Protocol/Internet Protocol (TCP/IP).

The Internet works within an infrastructure that covers all of the media necessary for moving information. This infrastructure includes private corporate networks, cable and satellite television and telecommunication networks (see figure 1.4).

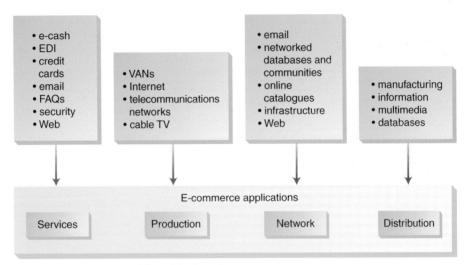

FIGURE 1.4: The building blocks of e-commerce

A number of existing telecommunication technologies support the Internet and facilitate e-commerce. Technologies for telephone connections form a worldwide network of cables, satellites and microwave dishes that allow the transmission of signals. The Internet transmits digital signals, which can readily use these existing telecommunication systems. In the past decade new physical networks have been established throughout the world to provide many new areas with access to cable television. The transmissions that flow over the Internet can also use these networks.

To use these physical telecommunication systems to gain access to the Internet, consumers, businesses or individuals need to be able to connect to one of the systems, either in the workplace or at home. The physical part of the Internet includes networks and communication lines owned and operated by many different companies and organisations. Large organisations such as universities or global companies often provide permanent, 24-hour, seven-days-a-week access for students and employees. Individuals might connect to the Internet via an online service, such as America Online. An Internet service provider (ISP), such as Davnet or Optusnet, is an organisation that has a permanent connection to the Internet and sells temporary connections to others for a fee. Such local ISPs connect to regional host computers operated by national service providers, such as Telstra or Optus. Regional host computers are connected to the major networks that carry most of the Internet communication traffic by high-speed communication lines called backbones, which could be compared to highways that connect major cities across the country.

There are four ways that businesses and individuals can connect to the Internet. Each method serves a different purpose and each would be suitable for businesses of different types and sizes.

On-demand, direct online connection to the Internet can be via either a modem or a LAN (for example an **ethernet** connection). Ethernet connections are a communications standard for transmitting data between computers. Most PC modems transmit data at between 28.8 Kbps and 56 Kbps. Cable modems can transmit at speeds of 500 Kbps to 2 Mbps. As the name suggests, a user can make this type of connection whenever a need to do so occurs. In a direct connection the machine connected has its own IP address and becomes part of the Internet itself. To make the connection, special Internet connection software, a modem and modem communications software are needed. Software packages for Internet connection are readily available from commercial computer stores and from ISPs.

An alternative online method of connecting to the Internet is by connecting to another machine that is connected directly to the Internet, and therefore is part of it. In this type of connection there is no need to purchase special software. Only a modem and modem communications software are needed. Such connections are not as flexible as direct connections and do not perform as many tasks.

An offline connection provides a user with access to the Internet whether or not he or she is connected. Information is downloaded and stored on a hard disk either by a user or by a user's agent when connected to the Internet. This downloaded information from the hard disk is then available to the user to access at any time. Special software is loaded onto a computer, which when connected to the Internet will allow material to be downloaded. This could be data transferred from one company to another or email messages sent in different time zones. This special software will allow replies written or sent in the offline period to be sent automatically once the machine is reconnected online to the Internet. This process is cheap but quite inflexible.

Supported connection to the Internet involves the use of more complex methods. The most common is connection by ethernet or by serial connections using SLIP and PPP protocols. These are discussed in the next section.

A protocol is a set of traffic rules, procedures and standards designed to allow the transmission of data and information. For successful transmission these rules have to be accepted. Across the Internet there has to be a uniform protocol or set of rules, otherwise computers would not be able to link to each other. In the process of communication on the Internet the protocol established allows two-way communication simultaneously (called the duplex mode for data transmission). This communication process is best illustrated by the Web and by telephone systems in operation in most places throughout the world. In some networks, including private networks where electronic data interchange (EDI) has been established, the links can be simpler. EDI transmission can be a simple one-way operation (called the simplex mode of data transmission) or it can be a transmission that allows data to be exchanged in both directions (the duplex mode). However, in most instances, transmission occurs in only one direction at a time. This is called the half-duplex mode of data transmission and illustrates how simply business communication and interaction can occur (see figure 1.5).

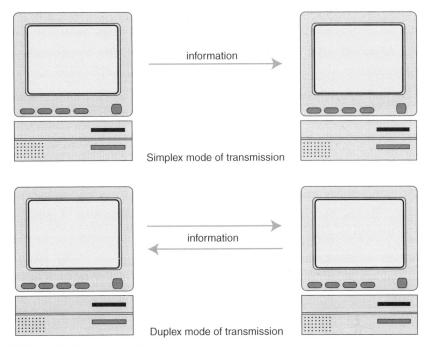

FIGURE 1.5: Simplex and duplex modes of data transmission

The most basic communications protocol of the Internet is the TCP/IP, which allows users of the Internet to:
- send and receive messages (email)
- find information, interact with other businesses and buy products
- find out personal information about people who have developed and placed this material on a specific site (home pages)
- exchange data (EDI) and business information
- download software that can assist the user to do more operations on the Internet.

Other protocols commonly used on the Internet include **Point-to-Point Protocol (PPP)**, **Serial Line Internet Protocol (SLIP)** and **Post Office Protocol (POP)**. The development of these types of protocol has enabled more complex operations to occur using the Web.

In the early days of development of the Internet most research institutions, government agencies and businesses were connected to smaller local area networks (LANs) within these organisations. The most common connection was via ethernet. There were few, if any, point-to-point links, which were most common in telecommunications systems prior to the development of the Internet. One of the reasons for this was the lack of a standard or protocol. PPP was developed to provide that standard and to manage IP addresses at a host server for the Internet. PPP permits a computer connected to a server via a serial line (such as a modem) to become a node on the Internet and enables anyone to connect to this computer from home, a business or a hotel room through a telephone connection. This link allows individuals or businesses to receive, send and store email, and browse the Web.

SLIP connects the user (business or individual) to the Internet and allows the user to use the Internet in the same way as PPP, except that SLIP permits the sending and receiving of files using only the TCP/IP protocol. (PPP also allows the user to transmit using other forms such as AppleTalk.) However, for most users of the Internet this is not an issue, since most individuals and businesses use TCP/IP only. PPP has been developed by many of the Internet service providers running commercial access to the Internet for individuals and small businesses. PPP enables service provider developers to establish an automatic login that provides the user with a password and automatic dialling of a telephone number to gain access to the Internet.

POP allows users to log into the electronic host, download messages to their computer and upload messages to the host for delivery over the network. In businesses, or through a service provider, there is a computer that receives all incoming email messages. A POP email program (such as Netscape Mail, Pegasus Mail or Eudora) downloads the email from the POP server to a local computer.

The most recent improvement in the attributes of the Internet has been the development of the World Wide Web. The Web allows the user to interchange and interconnect documents using hypertext. This process allows the user to create an interlinked, sometimes interactive process by which one document retrieved from the Internet can be used to establish a link to another document. This link is activated when the user clicks on a *hotlink* or *hyperlink* (a word, picture or feature highlighted within a document that triggers the link to another document located on another computer at another location. The protocol that enables these hotlinks is the Hypertext Transfer Protocol (HTTP). Figure 1.6 shows some examples of hotlinks or hyperlinks embedded in the text of a web page.

FIGURE 1.6: Hotlinks on the Autobytel web page

In the 1980s the International Organization for Standardization released the specifications of a standard generalised markup language (SGML). This protocol defined documents in plain text using tags embedded in the text to specify the definition. Hypertext markup language (HTML) is a form of SGML with a specified document-type definition. HTML is a programming language used to specify how a web browser (e.g. Netscape Navigator or Internet Explorer) will display a text file retrieved from a server. HTML allows the developer of a web page to define hyperlinks between that document and any others that the author might think are important to link together. HTML also allows the developer of a document on the Web to define any multimedia objects that are included in the document. HTTP was developed and adopted to enable consistent transmission of documents on the Web. It is a multimedia transport protocol. It does not process the packages of data it transmits, but rather it is a mechanism that allows users to search for information or data. Further, it allows databases to interact and information to be manipulated.

HTTP defines computer links to the Web when the computers support software that allows them to interact freely with other computers. Those that provide the links are called web **servers**. HTTP, and the ability of servers to support it, is what defines the Web and differentiates it from other networks. This protocol and the ability to support it also define the Web within the Internet. Web servers have become the places where home pages of all sorts have been developed and stored. The transmission of data within these pages relies on the simplicity and speed of HTTP.

In addition to the TCP/IP and HTTP protocols, the Internet uses other protocols such as:

- *file transfer protocol (FTP)*: allows the transfer of files between computers
- *Simple Mail Transfer Protocol (SMTP)*: enables mail transfer between computers within the organisation
- *Multipurpose Internet Mail Extensions (MIME)*: enables mail transfer in complex organisations.

Web servers are computers that run the HTTP process and are connected to a TCP/IP network. The web address that identifies other web sites and specific web pages is called a uniform resource locator (URL). It is a means of specifying a resource by incorporating the protocol, machine address, path and filename.

ARCHITECTURE OF THE WORLD WIDE WEB

The Web is based on a three-part architecture.
- HTML describes the contents of web pages on the Internet.
- HTTP provides the language that allows different servers and browsers to communicate.
- A **Common Gateway Interface (CGI)** is used by a web server to run a separate program that contains dynamic information, format it into HTML and send it on to the web server. For example, a web user at a virtual bookstore might enter some data, such as a book title, in HTML form on a web site. These data are sent to the web server, which uses the CGI interface

to get the appropriate book title from the database and return the information, formatted appropriately, to the user.

The modern Internet involves the interaction of a number of levels of providers and individuals. As can be seen from figure 1.7, individuals can connect (directly or via an intranet) to an ISP. The ISP is connected to an Internet access provider, which is connected to a national access provider. The national access provider is connected to a **very-high-speed backbone** (or spine) **network service (vBNS)**, the fastest communication lines on the Internet.

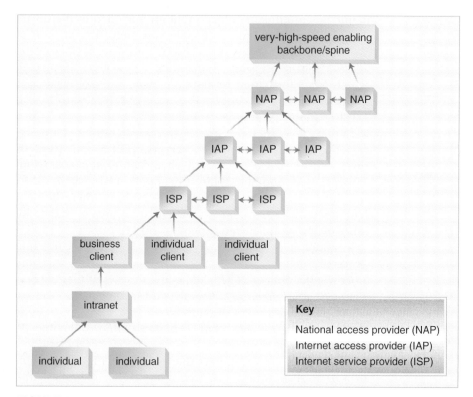

FIGURE 1.7: Architecture of the Web

These links use passwords and security protocols to allow access to the Internet. Access can be achieved in a number of ways, as shown in table 1.8. More basically, the structure of the World Wide Web allows a user to interact with various databases, collect information, and search for identity-specific and defined knowledge and information (see figure 1.8).

This structure enables users to access the Web for recreation purposes, for communication and, most important for us in the current context, for electronic commerce. It can support business to business e-commerce in the exchange of data (EDI), the billing and sending of accounts, the payment of accounts, electronic funds transfer and banking. The Web also provides companies with access to electronic catalogues for the supply of parts or complementary products.

The Web's structure also supports consumer to business e-commerce by providing companies with an opportunity to display their products, their services or their databases. They can sell data and, more important, sell processed information and knowledge. Consumers also can advertise and market products to other consumers.

A major attraction of the Web for business and consumers is ease of access. The consumer is not particularly concerned about which method of connection contact is used over the Internet. The purchase of a modem and a relatively cheap contract with an ISP enables e-commerce to begin.

TABLE 1.8	INTERNET ACCESS		
TYPE OF INTERNET ACCESS	**PROTOCOL**	**ACCESS SPEED**	
Dial-up (shell account): easy and inexpensive, but cannot use Netscape	Terminal emulation	9.6, 14.4 Kbps	
Dial-up IP: full access to Internet, but more complex to configure and set up	SLIP, PPP, CSLIP (compressed SLIP)	14.4 Kbps 56 Kbps	
Digital dial-up (ISDN): not widely available, and has problems with procurement and installation	PPP	64, 128 Kbps	
Leased line: high-speed dedicated link, but can be expensive if not used frequently	IP	56 Kbps 1.544 Mbps (T1)	
Cable modems	—	Up to 10 Mbps (customers share so throughput will be lower)	
Satellite (e.g. Satnet)	—	128 Kbps — may go up to 4000 Kbps	
DSL (digital subscriber line)	—	2 Mbps (high bitrate DSL)	
Wireless (e.g. Bluetooth, Airport)	—	720 Kbps–1 Mbps	

SOURCE: Adapted from Kalakota and Whinston (1997).

For small business, access is also relatively cheap, although the motivations for these companies actually to join up are somewhat more complicated and varied. Even with the ease of access to the Internet for small business, there are other technological hurdles to overcome if effective progress in this area is to be made.

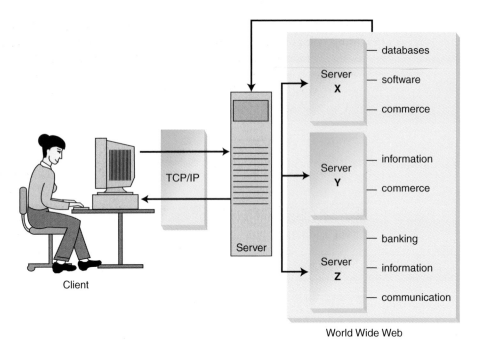

FIGURE 1.8: Structure of the Web

EMAIL

The most popular Internet application is email, which is the transmission of messages and files over a computer network. Billions of messages are sent around the world each day, and email has become a key driver behind the explosion of e-commerce. It is used to transfer company data orders, invoices, word-processed documents, spreadsheets and CAD files between business partners, saving much time and the expense of sending paper communications.

Email is becoming an essential element in virtually any information infrastructure. Sending an email to multiple recipients can distribute the message to an almost infinitely large number of people. This is an effective way of broadcasting important information to a wide spectrum of employees. Of course, email can also be targeted to specific individuals. **Attachments** may be added to email, allowing the inclusion of documents created in a number of word processing, database and spreadsheet packages. A sales presentation can be prepared in one part of an organisation, reviewed by another and modified by yet another before being presented.

All of this may take place across a large geographical area, and may occur easily within hours. The **Interactive Mail Access Protocol (IMAP)** allows for better control over the way messages are delivered. Instead of having all the new email messages delivered from the email server onto the user's computer in one go, IMAP gives the user greater flexibility in interacting with the inbox. The user may choose to download only the subjects of the new email messages, then select and download only relevant messages. IMAP also allows the user to see what files are attached to an email and then decide which ones to download. Obviously, this is ideal for users receiving email over slow connections such as a laptop computer connected to the Internet via a mobile phone.

An email address is a combination of a user name and a domain name — for example jerry@mcs.uts.edu.au, where Jerry is the username and mcs.uts.edu.au is the domain name. Figure 1.9 traces an email message from sender to recipient.

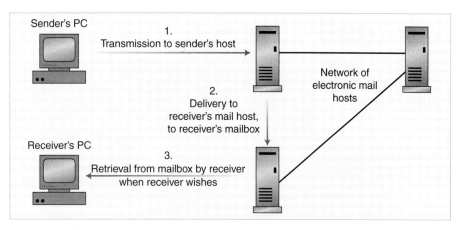

FIGURE 1.9: Internet mail

SOURCE: Ray Panko 1999, *Business and Data Communications and Networking*, 2nd Edition, Prentice Hall, New Jersey.

INFORMATION SYSTEMS AND INTERNET COMMERCE

The connection between information systems and Internet commerce, whether it be B2C, B2B, C2C, G2B or G2C, can be explained by examining the following definitions.

> IS (information system) is the collection of technical and human resources that provide the storage, computing, distribution, and communication for the information required by all or some part of an enterprise. A special form of IS is a management information system (MIS), which provides information for managing an enterprise.

> IS (information services) is a common name for an organization within an enterprise that is responsible for its data processing and information system or systems.[50]

Managing the change to electronic business models is a vital part of the process and many information technology methodologies need to be invoked. In this text we will consider the use of traditional systems development life cycle methodologies (these are outlined in figure 1.10). As well, new methodologies such as **Rapid Application Development (RAD)**, **Joint Application Development (JAD)**, extreme programming and prototyping will be investigated as aids to assisting in this change. In the following chapters the information technology and project management requirements for setting up e-commerce web sites will be examined.

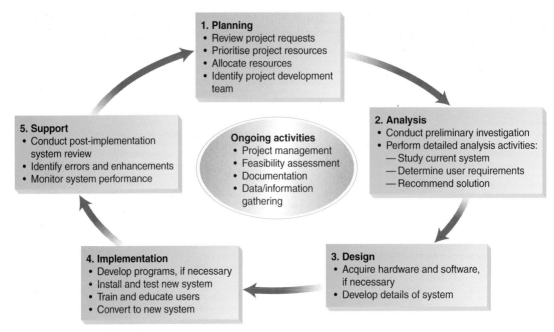

FIGURE 1.10: Traditional systems development life cycle
SOURCE: Shelly, Cashman and Vermatt (2000).

E-COMMERCE AS A MANAGEMENT TOOL

Unfortunately, many managers are not technically literate, and some of the rules that work in the real world do not necessarily work in cyberspace. Good managers traditionally look for a measurable return on investment, protect revenue streams and try to enhance the cost of entry into their market to keep the wolves at bay.[51] The Internet changes cost of entry and revenue streams; strategic online development is a matter of portfolio management, risk assessment and management.

Organisations need to develop and adopt strategies that enable them to cope with rapid change and the accelerating nature of information flows. Becoming an e-business means the organisation must adopt an ethos of perpetual transformation, which is often traumatic. Deborah Nelson, vice-president of marketing for support services for Hewlett Packard, illustrates the scale of the task when she comments that 'turning around a freighter is not easy'.[52]

In fact, internal business bureaucracies are the natural enemies of electronic commerce; if left unchecked, bureaucracy may stifle competition. E-commerce cuts today's bureaucracy out of the loop as routine transactions are automated.[53] According to Prins Ralston, ex-president of the Australian Computing Society, big companies should form an e-commerce subsidiary under separate management and draw people from both the parent company and outside sources. He calls this a new wineskin model.

The following technical insite shows that even chief executive officers now need to become technically literate.

TECH-WISE CEOs: FROM THE GEEK AS BOSS

TECHNOLOGY used to be something that CEOs left to a nerdy deputy. Now, like it or not, it is part of their job, which helps explain why Tom Glocer, a young American, is to be Reuters' next boss.

Once upon a time, chief executives were supposed to know it all, or to be wise enough to surround themselves with those who did.

It was part of their mystique: total command of the big picture combined with the ability to delegate technical details. Yet today's bosses find themselves spending their summers in technology boot camps in which 20-somethings show them how to send instant messages, steer search engines and download files.

Jack Welch and his deputies at GE, for instance, are practising reverse mentoring, inviting some nose-ringed youth to come in regularly and teach the old guys a techy trick or two. And at e-business conferences, old-economy bosses have recently been spotted taking notes (and, let's be honest, occasionally sleeping) in the seats that their designated tech deputies used to have to themselves.

Why do the giants of industry choose to humiliate themselves in this way when they could pay people to surf and otherwise understand technology for them? The short answer is that they have no choice: the chief executive is becoming more and more the chief information officer as well.

Technology strategy is now part and parcel of business strategy and it is one of those things that, like international experience, cannot be mastered from a distance.

There is, however, an alternative to teaching an old chief executive new tricks: pick a new one who already knows them. That is, in effect, what Reuters has done by its selection of Tom Glocer, a 41-year-old American,

to replace Peter Job, who is retiring in July.

Glocer, an unpretentious insider who formerly ran Reuters' American businesses, is no obvious nerd. He is a lawyer who joined Reuters seven years ago to work on mergers and acquisitions and quickly moved up the ranks.

Reuters is an odd combination of a financial-data provider, a 150-year-old newswire service and even a trading platform. It is rarely thought of as a technology company. Yet, as Glocer talks about the company, the inner geek in both of them is revealed.

Technological competence comes in three types. There are those who studiously try to keep up because they think they should. There are those whose day-to-day jobs require that they know their tools. And there are those who are instinctively attracted to technology, whose knowledge exceeds all reasonable professional requirements and sometimes verges on obsession.

Glocer is of the third type. While working for a New York law firm, he wrote simulation software that is still used to teach litigation techniques in law schools.

He has to stop himself in mid-interview from veering off on a wild tangent about the complexities of the Java sandbox. (Don't ask, but it has nothing to do with Indonesian beaches.) For Christmas, he gave those who report directly to him portable MP3 players with instructions to fill them with downloaded songs that best encapsulate the challenge for Reuters in 2001.

The assignment no doubt made them all the more deeply fond of the previous year's present of a simple crystal bowl.

(*continued*)

The fact is that Reuters is more of a tech firm than it first appears. Aside from its own software and communications infrastructure, which is huge, it owns about half of TIBCO, a leading e-business software firm, and it has nearly US$5 billion in other technology investments. It is starting to think of itself as a technology firm too.

Glocer describes its main advantage over such competitors as Bloomberg, Dow Jones and Thomson Financial as being not the strength of its news-gathering organisation, or the accuracy of its data, but the open platform nature of its technology infrastructure.

This is not Glocer's invention. It was Job who decided in the early 1990s to switch from selling services on custom-made Reuters terminals to selling them on generic PCs. At the time this was a daring bet that the efficiencies of a common standard would more than compensate for the inability to charge a premium for hardware.

Now the company is taking the whole notion one step further, embracing internet technology both internally and for its client services. This is considerably harder to get right.

During Job's tenure, Reuters was criticised for being slow to embrace the internet. Glocer, a creature of instant messaging and web interfaces, cannot imagine pursuing any other path.

Part of this is a matter of personality. But it is also no coincidence that Glocer is young and, to a lesser degree, an American and a non-journalist, both firsts in Reuters history. He is among the first from the generation that came of age with the PC to take over a big multinational.

Although many older executives have grasped the power of the internet age, and steered their companies to exploit it, most of them speak geek as a second language, rather than as the native tongue of one who has learnt it when young.

This is a subtle distinction but it can be enough to turn the uncertainty that too often falls back on consultants and endless analysis into the natural confidence to move quickly forward.

It's difficult to fake this stuff, Glocer says. You have to use it and to have a genuine understanding. The point, he says, is not for the chief executive to be a programmer, but for him to have tried enough technology at first hand to separate hype from reality.

The danger is that the boss might take this too far, losing sight of broader business goals in the whirlwind of technological change.

For all Glocer's technological affinity, Reuters retains a chief information officer and a chief technology officer to look after nerdy stuff. Tomorrow's bosses need to be more tech-wise than today's, but they also need reminding that technophilia is yet another temptation to be kept in check.

SOURCE: *The Economist*, 11 January 2001, found at www.economist.com. Reprinted in the *Weekend Australian* as 'The rise of the gifted geek', 20–21 January 2001, p. 56.

EXERCISES

1. Debate the proposals in the article under the statement that technological competence comes in three types.

2. Do some research to ascertain the standard of technological literacy of executives in major companies in your country. Write a short report on the results and recommend strategies that could be used to increase such literacy among executives.

HOW THIS BOOK IS ORGANISED

Electronic business over the Internet has grown exponentially over the past seven years. Information technology is driving economic growth and many companies are experiencing difficulties as organisations shift to the Internet's high change/high speed environment.[54] It has been a heady ride, with many e-businesses falling by the wayside en route. The fact remains, however, that three startup dot.com companies, Amazon, eBay and Yahoo!, are now among the world's best-known brands.[55] These three pioneers have software at their core — they innovate with it, they buy out other software companies to obtain exclusive use and they use software to replace people.[56] In this textbook the authors examine how the e-commerce market has changed over the past seven years. The text follows an information system approach, and details the processes and network infrastructure associated with e-commerce and the varied commercial transactions executed over the Internet.

A key theme in the text is the need to bridge understanding between business and information systems, so that students can effectively communicate and understand one another in a professional environment. Topics covered include the establishment of secure trading systems, electronic payment systems, business to business systems, business to consumer systems, and management of technological systems.

Chapter 1 introduces the reader to the history of e-commerce, outlines the various categories of e-commerce and the key technical terminology that will be further explained in later chapters. It introduces the idea of the implementation of e-business via a systems or software development approach, emphasising the need to get this e-business in place in a very short time frame.

Chapter 2 examines different types of business models for e-business — namely, the online advertising models, the company-based models, and the interorganisational and third party models.

Chapter 3 describes the major technologies behind business to consumer e-business. It describes how the basic web computing model can be extended to perform business transactions. It also describes different programming approaches for B2C applications and examines security issues behind B2C transactions on the Web.

Chapter 4 provides an overview of systems development methodologies and the arrival of web development methodologies. It shows how Rapid Application Development methods are being used by e-project managers. It covers database management systems and integration issues as well as Internet business technologies such as the Internet Inter-ORB Protocol.

Chapter 5 examines the technology behind the business to business infrastructure, paying particular attention to XML and ebXML. It provides an overview of extranet architecture and explains how to cope with specific security issues with extranets.

Chapter 6 looks at the technologies behind the integration of business to business e-business. It explains integration architecture and requirements. It also examines supply chain management issues and return on investment.

Chapter 7 examines the popular ways of paying for goods over the Internet — notably, credit cards — and also discusses the new digital cash systems. It examines the technologies behind electronic payment systems and reviews the technology behind electronic data interchange.

Chapter 8 addresses the need for security in computing networks. It examines the role of SSL, S-HTTP and SET in securing B2B and B2C payments on line.

Chapter 9 describes the steps to follow when developing a security policy for the networked economy. It examines the issue of trust in Internet commerce and discusses risk management techniques.

Chapter 10 examines the vexed issues of law and ethics as they relate to Internet commerce. It gives an overview of jurisdictional problems and identifies potential legal and technical solutions to various problems.

Chapter 11 addresses the management issues behind the adoption and implementation of electronic practices to business. It outlines techniques for handling outsourcing and application service providers.

Chapter 12 looks at the future of Internet commerce and explores some of the exciting new technologies that are being developed.

SUMMARY

This chapter has described the phenomenal growth of electronic business in the closing years of the twentieth century and the beginning of the twenty-first century. It provided a timeline showing the significant moments in the development of computer hardware and software, with particular emphasis on the arrival of the Internet and the World Wide Web, which are jointly responsible for having made electronic business available globally to both small and large players.

We introduced a range of fundamental key terms, and foreshadowed the importance of information technology development and project management methodologies in transforming businesses into e-businesses.

key terms

attachment
Bluetooth
browser
client/server
Common Gateway Interface (CGI)
compressing
directory
Dot Com
Electronic Data Interchange (EDI)
electronic funds transfer (EFT)

electronic funds transfer at point of sale (EFTPOS)
ethernet
Extensible Markup Language (XML)
extranet
file transfer protocol (FTP)
groupware
hypertext
Hypertext Markup Language (HTML)

Hypertext Transfer Protocol (HTTP)
information systems
Interactive Mail Access Protocol (IMAP)
Internet
Internet Explorer
intranet
Java
Jini Initiative
Joint Application Development (JAD)

Lynx	portal	server
MP3	Post Office Protocol (POP)	Simple Mail Transfer Protocol (SMTP)
Multipurpose Internet Mail Extensions (MIME)	Rapid Application Development (RAD)	Transmission Control Protocol/Internet Protocol (TCP/IP)
Netscape	resource definition format (RDF)	Ultranet
online marketplace (OLM)	search engines	very-high-speed backbone network service (vBNS)
peer-to-peer network (P2P)	Secure Hypertext Transfer Protocol	Wireless Application Protocol (WAP)
personal digital assistant (PDA)	Serial Line Internet Protocol (SLIP)	
Point-to-Point Protocol (PPP)		

EXERCISES

1. Go to the web sites of the following companies and prepare short reports on the e-business strategies recommended by:
   (a) IBM
   (b) SAP
   (c) Cisco.

2. Prepare a short report on peer-to-peer (P2P) networks and their likely impact on Internet commerce.

3. Prepare a short report on resource definition format and its impact on Internet commerce.

case study

DO YOU KNOW CISCO?

At this Westin Hotel Convention Center, just east of San José, California, a revival meeting is in progress. Cisco Systems' CEO John Chambers, 50, struts across the stage wearing a gray tweed suit and preaching the gospel of the network to a packed, 8000-strong congregation of the converted. We have made great strides, Chambers drawls in his West Virginian birch-beer-sweet voice, but we need to be ever vigilant, for around the corner, right outside this hall, lurks the enemy — Nortel, Lucent and start-up companies we've never heard of, jesters who would steal our cybercrown.

The audience, consisting of the truest of true believers — Cisco employees — is an easy sell. Chambers and Cisco have made at least 2500 of Cisco's 23 000 employees stock-option millionaires, which in turn has convinced the rest that they too will be millionaires. Investors have also got Cisco's brand of router religion, as the stock has split eight times and risen about 8000 per cent in the 10 years since it went public at $18 a share. One share of Cisco bought in 1990 is worth $14 000 today. The company, founded by John Morgridge as a technology-solutions company with a simple idea — hook-up networks — has ended up being the baby in the creche of the Internet revolution.

Cisco's principal products are routers — souped-up computers that sort the streams of information packets that whiz throughout the Internet. As it happened, routers turned out to be the indispensable heavy artillery of the digital revolution. As the Internet has grown, so too have the demands for bigger, faster, better routers. Today, Cisco manufactures gigabit routers that can handle a billion bits of information a second. Coming soon, as bandwidth requirements increase and Internet traffic doubles every 100 days — and as we consumers increasingly upload and download video, voice, music and data — Cisco will be ready with terabit (trillion) routers and more.

This confluence of technical expertise, market opportunity and ruthless efficiency has made Cisco the fastest company in history to reach $100 billion, $200 billion and, last month, $300 billion in market capitalization, leaving it the largest company in the world behind General Electric and Microsoft. Cisco has built dominant market share in a crucial high-technology industry — controlling 50 per cent of the $21 billion business-network market, where it has obliterated once formidable rivals like 3Com, Cabletron and Bay Networks. 'We definitely are in the sweet spot,' says Chambers of Cisco's prospects. 'The whole network business has become a home game for Cisco.' Think of it this way: in a wired world where we are just learning to walk, Cisco has become the biggest, best shoemaker on the planet.

In order to maintain Cisco's unprecedented growth rate, Chambers believes he has to remake the company into a great consumer brand. 'Three years ago, we didn't care if anyone knew who we were,' he admits. 'The decisions that mattered were made deep inside companies.' Today, making its brand as well known as Intel's or Hewlett Packard's is vital to Cisco's mission of building the New World Network.

Why the change? When it comes to information, homes are becoming much like offices — networks of linked devices connected to a server. In your home, PCs and TVs are linked via broadband Internet hookups such as cable modems or Digital Subscriber Lines (DSL) to the big server that is the Web. As everything from refrigerators (Cisco has just partnered with Whirlpool) to your furnace (Cisco and Samsung) gets Web-capable, each homeowner will become his own chief information officer, making on a household level the decisions corporate executives have been making for a decade: Who will wire the house? Who will power my network? Who will enable the myriad envisioned wireless household appliances?

Cisco anticipates the consumer-network market will be worth $9 billion and plans to take a dominant share, as it has done in 14 of the 15 markets in which it operates. That's why Cisco spent $60 million airing its 'Are You Ready?' television commercials and is emulating Intel's successful 'Intel Inside' campaign, which made megahertz a measure of computational power. 'In order to get to the next level, we need the consumer,' says Don Listwin, Cisco's executive vice-president.

The first product aimed at the household was launched last week at the Consumer Electronics Show in Las Vegas, where the company unveiled the Cisco Home Gateway. That's a DSL home-network hub that converts your phone jacks into broadband Ethernet ports. The company has even introduced a network version of Intel's megahertz gimmick to persuade consumers to upgrade and rewire their homes: PIQ, or Packet Intelligence Quotient. The

higher the PIQ, the faster data will zip around your house. Cisco is counting on consumers' rushing out to buy a new networking device, upgrading them from, say, PIQ 2 to PIQ 3. Did we mention that Cisco doesn't quite have the hang of this consumer business just yet?

It probably will, though. The culture of success is particularly virulent at Cisco. When you walk around the corporate campus in San José today, you get the feeling you are in a tiny, high-technology version of Switzerland, a neutral power — Cisco will partner with virtually any company and employ any promising technology — where the trains not only run on time, they arrive a few hours early. It's a campus of dozens of aqua and brown bunker-like buildings that seem to extend to the horizon, differentiated only by banners proclaiming, for example, that this particular building birthed *THE FIRST QUALIFIED DOCSIS-COMPLIANT HEAD-END ROUTER IN THE INDUSTRY.* 'It's a great place to work if you're an engineer,' says one. 'I can't think of why anyone else would work here.'

Actually, Cisco is run by a non-engineer. John Chambers sits amid the expanse of cubicles in an office as austere and tiny as an entry-level programmer's. His motto is, 'Never ask your employees to do something you wouldn't be willing to do yourself.' This culture of self-sacrifice and frugality means that Chambers and all top execs fly coach and have no reserved parking spaces. The same quest for efficiency has driven Cisco to make cutting-edge use internally of the networks it sells to other companies. Everything at Cisco — from health-insurance issues to softball schedules — is available on the Web. Already, Cisco makes 84 per cent of its sales over the Web, accounting in 1999 for about $9.5 billion in business-to-business e-commerce. To put that in perspective, mighty Amazon sold about $1.5 billion worth of products online.

Chambers is customer obsessed, a characteristic that will serve the company well as it moves into consumer markets. He discovered the dogma of customer service as a salesman at IBM and then saw firsthand the cost of losing customer focus when he joined mini-computer maker Wang in the late 1980s. As Wang's business eroded — in part because Wang didn't listen to customers — Chambers, the top sales executive, was forced to lay off 4000 workers. He vows never to do that again, even if it means keeping his company leaner and meaner than seems necessary. 'Laying off workers in a tough job market was the worst feeling in the world,' he says as he sips his fourth Diet Coke of the day. 'It made me physically ill.'

Even as the company has grown to become the king of the data network, it has remained, in many consumers' minds, a question mark. Ask most people what Microsoft or Intel do, and they'll tell you. But Cisco? 'I don't know,' says Harriet Sumner, 30, a customer-service manager for a computer-game company, 'but I own the stock.'

Chambers thinks it's important that people such as Sumner do know, especially now that Cisco wants to be successful in its other bold strategy: a march into the telecom business, where it will face a whole new level of well-entrenched competition. The $250 billion-a-year telephone-equipment business is where giants like AT&T's equipment-making spin-off, Lucent, and Canadian counterpart Nortel have built powerful, decades-long relationships with telephone companies and service providers. As voice and data networks converge — and data come to account for more than 90 per cent of network

traffic — Cisco has boasted that its networks, which are predominantly data or IP (Internet protocol) networks, will also become the leading voice networks.

Consumers, however, are still uneasy about IP telephone service. Do you really want your voice to be as unreliable as your Web connection? Cisco swears it has closed the gap and made its IP networks as reliable as voice networks. What would help, Cisco believes, is for consumers to come to believe in the Cisco brand to the point where they are exerting upward pressure on telephone companies and service providers to run Cisco networks. In other words, for Cisco to be able to apply a two-way squeeze from the corporate side and the consumer side so that your phone company will have no choice but to go with Cisco. 'Name recognition and branding are crucial to us,' says Chambers. 'We want the small business, the medium-sized business and even the consumer to want Cisco-powered networks.'

Cisco, in its history, has never gone after a market and failed. Lucent and Nortel, are you ready?

SOURCE: www.pathfinder.com/time/magazine/articles/0,3266,37170-1,00.htm.

Questions

1. Prepare a report on Cisco's online strategies, both as a business to business e-commerce company and as a business to consumer company.

2. Prepare a report on the Online Education system that Cisco has set up to prepare people for Cisco Certification.

SUGGESTED READING

Adam et al. 1999, *Electronic Commerce: Technical, Business and Legal Issues*, 2nd Edition, Prentice Hall, New Jersey.

Amor, D. 1999, *The E-business Revolution*, Prentice Hall, New Jersey.

Fellenstien, C. and Wood R. 2000, *Exploring E-Commerce: Global E-Business and E-Societies*, Prentice Hall, New Jersey.

Hoque, F. 2000, *e-Enterprise: Business Models, Architecture, and Components*, Cambridge University Press, Cambridge, UK.

Kalakota, R. and Whinston, A. 1996, *Frontiers of Electronic Commerce*, Addison-Wesley, Reading, MA.

Lawrence, E., Corbitt, B., Fisher, J., Lawrence, J. and Tidwell, A. 2000, *Internet Commerce: Digital Models for Business*, 2nd Edition, John Wiley & Sons, Brisbane.

May, P. 2000, *The Business of Ecommerce*, Cambridge University Press, Cambridge, UK.

END NOTES

1. Weinberg, N. 2000, 'B2B portals face their greatest test: reality', *Business Review Weekly*, 21 July 2000, p. 38.

2. Harvard Management Update 2000, 'Managers get caught up in a web of opportunities', as reported in 'What is e-commerce doing to your brand?', *Business Review Weekly*, 28 July 2000, p. 57.

3. Rudnitsky, H. 2000, 'General Electric finds a new way of working', *Business Review Weekly*, 28 July 2000, p. 58.

4. Lawrence et al. 2000.

5. Definition of XSL from www.whatis.com.

6. Head, B. 2000, 'Aviation e-commerce slow to take off', *Business Review Weekly*, 4 August 2000, p. 70. Survey commissioned by SITA, key supplier of computer and communications services to airlines.

7. Sathye, M. 1999, 'Growth of Internet Banking in Australia', Business Briefing, World Markets Research Centre, August 1999, p. 90, www.wmrc.com/busbriefing/BusBriefing/newpages/bbframes.html.

8. www.science.uva.nl/faculteit/museum/CoreMemory.html.

9. Rankin, Fiona 1999, 'The Evolution of Money in the Information Age: The requirements and implications of the new money commodities', Collecter99 Student Consortium Conference, Wellington, New Zealand, November 1999, www.collecter.org.

10. Kalakota and Whinston 1996, p. 298.

11. Lawrence et al. 2000, p. 115–7.

12. Adam et al. 1999, p. 21.

13. Adam et al. 1999, chapter 11.

14. Regan, K. 2000, Report: High-Speed Net Set to Transform E-Commerce Times, 17 October 2000, www.ecommercetimes.com/news/articles2000/001017-5.shtml.

15. Mahoney, Michael, 'Where Is CDNow, Now?', *E-Commerce Times*, 18 January 2001, www.ecommercetimes.com/perl/story/6804.html.

16. Definition from www.whatis.com.

17. Definition from www.whatis.com.

18. Definition from www.whatis.com.

19. Birch, D. 1999, 'Mobile Financial Services: The Internet Is Not the Only Digital Channel', World Markets Research Centre, Business Briefing on Electronic Commerce, August 1999, pp. 98–9. www.wmrc.com.

20. Birch 1999.

21. Birch 1999.

22. Birch 1999.

23. From the report *Mechanics of Becoming an Electronic Merchant* by Aseem Prakash, CEO of Interactive Knowledge On-Line, 10 August 1998, www.iko.com.au.

24. McAfee, A. 2001, 'P2P: Fairer Exchange', *Harvard Business Review*, as reported in *Business Review Weekly*, 9 February 2001, p. 78.

25. Anon 2000, 'E-Commerce — shopping around the Web', *The Economist*, 26 February 2000, p. 4.

26. Anon 2000, 'Glut of online travel companies', *Computimes New Strait Times*, 24 April 2000, p. 23.

27. Messmer, E. 2000, 'Firm taps B2B e-comm to boost customer service', *Network World* 17 (6), pp. 1, 92, 7 February 2000.

28. Segal, R. L. 2000, 'Online marketplaces: A new strategic option', *Journal of Business Strategy* 21 (2), pp. 26–9.

29. Segal 2000.

30. Chang, J. 2000, 'ChemMatch.com to go public as first commodity chemical B2B', *Chemical Market Reporter* 257 (11), pp. 1–11, 13 March.

31. Chang 2000.

32. Messmer, E. 2000, 'B2B Web sites not living up to hype yet', *Network World*, 17 (6), pp. 1, 79, 21 February.

33. Messmer 2000, 'B2B Websites'.

34. King, J. 2000, 'How to do B2B', *ComputerWorld* 34(a), pp. 48–9.

35. King 2000.

36. Sarno, T. 1999, 'Going, going, gone online', Icon, *Sydney Morning Herald*, 17 July, p. 6.

37. 'Federal Government reveals eProcurement Plan', *Ecommercetoday*, www.wcommercetoday.com.au, Issue 57, 26 August 2000.

38. 'NSW's online fines payment takes off', *Ecommercetoday*, www.wcommercetoday.com.au, Issue 100, 28 July 2000.

39. Definition of the Internet from www.whatis.com.

40. Lawrence et al. 2000, p. 50.

41. www.whatis.com.

42. Lawrence et al. 2000, chapter 3.

43. Matsumura, M. 1997, 'Ultranet, the next network', *JavaWorld*, November, www.javaworld.com/javaworld/jw-11-1997/jw-11-miko.html.

44. Tanenbaum, A. S. 1996, *Computer Networks*, 3rd Edition, Prentice Hall, New Jersey, p. 443.

45. May 2000, p. 161.

46. www5.compaq.com/products/wireless/wpan.

47. www.whatis.com.

48. www.whatis.com.

49. McAfee, A. 2001, 'P2P: Fairer Exchange', from *Havard Business Review*, reported in *Business Review Weekly*, 9 February 2001, p. 78.

50. Definitions from www.whatis.com.

51. Birmingham, A. 1999, 'Dispatches: Trick or Treat?' *Information Age: Australia's IT News Trends Monthly*, November, www.acs.org.au/infoage.html, p. 6.

52. Newton, S. 1999, 'Electronic Business: Critical Success Factors for Implementation — A Case Study of a Manufacturer of Electronic Parts', Graduate Student Symposium, Collecter99, Wellington, November.

53. 'The hand on the bulldozer controls', Rewire, Eric Wilson's E-commerce Manual, *Sydney Morning Herald*, 27 April 1999, p. 3.

54. Raths, D. 2000/2001, 'Agent of e-change: IT Management 2000', *Information Age*, December 2000/January 2001, p. 46.

55. Anon 2001, 'Internet Pioneers: We have lift off', *Economist*, 3 February 2001, p. 73.

56. Anon 2001, 'Internet Pioneers', p. 75.

CHAPTER 2

MODELS FOR ELECTRONIC COMMERCE

Learning objectives

You will have mastered the material in this chapter when you can:

- describe the different types of online advertising models of e-commerce and how they can be used to drive Internet users to an organisation's web site
- describe a range of company-based models of e-commerce and the types of industries for which each model is most applicable
- discuss the different ways in which two or more organisations can use e-commerce technologies to collaborate and to become more efficient and cost-effective
- describe the variety of Internet-based marketplaces now being established by organisations to enable multiple buyers and sellers to trade on line.

'The first determinant of a firm's performance is its business model. This is the method by which a firm builds and uses its resources to offer its customers better value than its competitors and to make money doing so.'

A. Afuah and C. L. Tucci 2001, *Internet Business Models and Strategies: Text and Cases*, McGraw-Hill Irwin, Boston, MA, pp. 3–4.

INTRODUCTION

We saw in chapter 1 that organisations worldwide are using e-commerce for purposes ranging from auctions to online stores. The biggest challenge for these organisations is determining the appropriate way in which to use e-commerce to improve customer satisfaction, operational efficiency and cost-effectiveness. One approach to this problem is for a company to understand the variety of e-commerce business models that have emerged on the Web and the most effective way to use them.

The e-commerce business models discussed in this chapter can be grouped into the following general categories:

- online advertising-based models, which provide many promotional opportunities for an organisation's web site so that it might be found on the Internet
- company-based models, which primarily support B2C relationships and often reflect the type of consumer trade occurring in the physical world (such as virtual stores)
- inter-organisational (B2B, B2G and G2G) models, which provide different ways in which organisations can trade or communicate with each other via the Internet
- third-party trading models, which are often developed to provide convenient, one-stop locations on the Web for businesses and/or individuals to find each other, conduct trade or just share ideas and business practices.

Each of the categories, and the models comprising them, will be explored in more detail in this chapter to explain how they work, what they are used for and the types of Internet technologies that support their operation, the last of which is the focus of this book and the remaining chapters.

ONLINE ADVERTISING MODELS OF E-COMMERCE

One of the challenges presented by the Web is attracting potential customers to a company's web site. This can be achieved in a number of ways, which include[1]:

- using traditional advertising approaches, such as television and radio advertising
- relying on offline branding, reputation or dominance in a market (such as Coca-Cola), so that customers might go directly to a web site
- distributing brochures and providing enticements to a company's existing customers to encourage them to use the web site
- using online advertising approaches.

This section will examine the last mentioned. More specifically, it will look at a number of online advertising models available to companies, typically offered by third party organisations, which can help attract potential customers to a company's web site.

ADVERTISING-SUPPORTED MODEL

Television, newspaper and radio organisations usually sell advertising space to companies during their free-to-air broadcasting of programs, so that companies can advertise their products and services. Potential customers are able to use these broadcasting services for free, but as a consequence users are exposed to advertising material. This is an example of an **advertising-supported model**.

Online versions of the advertising-supported model are also widespread and are often provided by web sites offering Internet searching capabilities, such as Google (www.google.com). **Internet search engines** specialise in building complex databases of web links, often comprising millions of web pages, which can be searched using keywords to find web sites providing the information, services or products of interest. Internet applications called web crawlers gather or find new web pages to be included in these databases by going to web pages currently in the databases and following the links on these web pages to any new web sites or web pages.[2] Details about new web pages are recorded in the database and might include the URL, keywords and page descriptions provided by the author, the full text of the web page and the language in which the page is written.

Some search engines on the Web index web pages quite differently. For instance, Google (www.google.com) rates the importance of a web page by the number of web pages linking to it and by the importance of these web pages that link to it.[3] This approach is intended to increase the relevance of search results, especially when it is combined with more conventional search engine techniques such as analysing the proximity of search terms to each other, because it will first list web pages that other users and web sites find important.

We can see, therefore, that Internet search engines are driven largely by databases that can be searched by entering keywords into web forms. Chapter 4 outlines this concept of web page and database integration in more detail, and chapter 3 describes how this integration is implemented using web programming.

Operators of this e-commerce business model are able to provide Internet search services for free because they sell advertising space to companies. Online advertising in search engines can take a number of forms, including:

- directory listings, where company home pages are categorised according to product/service types. Users can browse this directory and visit the web sites to investigate the company's product or service offerings.
- **banner advertisements**, which are small, rectangular billboard-style advertisements that are displayed on the search engine's web pages (see, for example, the 'Casino on the Net' advertisement in figure 2.1). Users can click on these banners and link (or *click-through*) to the company's web site (also known as **click-through advertising**).
- company links from the search engine home page, which are usually expensive (see the 'Shop Now' section in figure 2.1). High-profile Internet companies such as Amazon.com use this service because of the prominent exposure they receive on the search engine.

FIGURE 2.1: Search engines, banners and listings (www.ozemail.com.au)

Many companies use these forms of online advertising because the probability that their company link will be found on banners or in listings is much greater when compared with being found in a list of search results returned by a search engine. For example, most search engines will list approximately 10 hits or search results on each web page and, depending on the search terms used, might produce many thousands of hits. If a company's web site does not appear in the first 20 to 30 hits, there is little chance that the searcher will see it.

Some Internet service providers (ISPs), such as GoConnect (www.goconnect.com.au), also use the online advertising-supported model by providing free Internet connections. In exchange for this free service, users are shown online advertisements, which often appear in a separate window, while they are connected to the Internet. As with search engines, these free ISPs generate their revenue by selling advertising space. Users of this service cannot avoid the advertisements, because they must start a specific application that not only controls the user's access to the Internet but also controls the retrieval of the advertisements from the ISP's server.

Some shareware software providers, such as My GetRight (www.mygetright.com), also use this model to display advertisements while people use their software,[4] because these software developers find that users do not always pay the registration fee. When the shareware product is started, the software connects to the provider's server on the Internet in order to obtain the banner advertisements that are to be displayed on the user's computer.

The success of the online advertising-supported model depends in part on the number of visitors to the site or users of the free ISP service or software. Companies will not want to purchase online advertising space if the numbers of users are low, because the number of potential customers who will click on (that is, click-through) or who will see the advertisements will also be small.[5]

Some search engines that employ banner advertising attempt to increase click-through rates by matching banners to the particular search terms entered by the users. This can be achieved by storing keywords for each banner in the advertisement database, so that these keywords can be compared with the search terms entered by the user and a matching banner retrieved automatically from the database. This approach increases the relevance of the banner because it should relate to what the user is searching for and therefore may increase the chances of a click-through.

The advertising-supported model has been more effective for niche markets than it has been for general-interest web sites and search engines. For example, IT-related and specialist employment advertising sites are using this model successfully,[6] because these sites attract people with certain characteristics (such as age, income level and common interests). Companies can place advertisements on sites that will be more relevant to these target groups and, therefore, more likely to be of interest to the users.

The relative success of these specialist advertising-supported models can also be attributed to the recognition by these sites that Internet users tend to use the Web with a particular purpose in mind, in contrast to the passive nature of television.[7] Since Internet users are more likely to go to these specialist sites with a purpose (for instance looking for a job), they might take more notice of advertisements that are relevant to their activity.

There has been considerable debate about the effectiveness of banner advertisements. Many authors state that the average percentage of visitors who click-through has been as low as one per cent or less for about the past three years.[8] Meskauskas (2000)[9] states, however, that click-through rates for banner advertisements have not decreased below 0.05 per cent for more than one year, which is about the same success rate as is experienced by direct-response advertising in the physical world. Meskauskas therefore argues that this suggests banner advertising has reached maturity.

More advanced implementations of banner advertisements are starting to incorporate more **interactivity** into the banners so that users are not required to leave the site on which the banner is placed. Although few of these banner advertisements currently exist, it is anticipated that banners incorporating data entry and transaction capabilities (for example sending an order) will appear increasingly.[10]

WEB PORTALS

Most Internet search engines have now evolved into **web portals**, which are intended to serve as central points on the Web for users. More specifically, web portals try to position themselves as the first place web users will go when they start using the Web to carry out their activities, such as searching for information, services or products.[11] In addition to more conventional web searching facilities, web portals will also provide **value-added services**, including free email and information services such as news, sports, stock market, television and weather resources (see figure 2.2 for an example of these services), and product comparison services.[12]

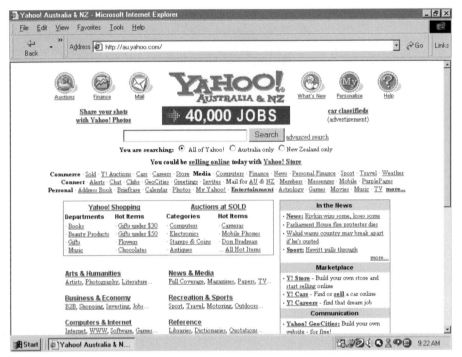

FIGURE 2.2: Web portals provide value-added services (www.yahoo.com.au)

Web portals are able to provide these services for free because their revenue is primarily generated by selling advertising space. The free services are intended to increase the number of users of the portal by providing these services in one location on the Web, and thus reduce the amount of searching or the number of separate web sites that users would otherwise need to visit.

A growing trend among many web portals is incorporating other e-commerce models (which are discussed later in this chapter) such as **Internet auctions**, **virtual communities** and **electronic malls**. This is often done by linking to other web sites that offer these models; however, more successful web portals such as Yahoo! (www.yahoo.com.au) have set up their own auctions and virtual communities to increase the likelihood that users will have everything they need at the one location in cyberspace.

Another value-added service many web portals have developed is customisation or, as it is also known, **personalisation**. For example, Yahoo! has set up facilities on its web site that include an online calendar, address book and web site bookmarks so that users can have their own personalised information on the Web. In addition, many web portals also allow users to design their own portal home pages by selecting hyperlinks they would like to appear on their personal home page.

This personalisation of web portals requires that the portal web site has a database that can store the personal settings of and information about the user. Portal web pages then retrieve this information from the database. Portal users also select a username and password, and are required to log in using their username and password to ensure that other users on the Web cannot get access to their personal information. Chapters 8 and 9 analyse this issue of security and privacy, and describe in more detail how it is achieved on the Web.

YELLOW PAGES MODEL

Internationally, traditional yellow pages, or business directories, take the form of paper-based books containing company advertisements and/or contact information. Company listings are categorised on the basis of the type of product or service they sell, and companies then pay for advertising space according to the type of advertisement (for example full page, banners or company listing).

The online **yellow pages model**, also a global development, is a web-based version of this approach, in which a database containing basic company information (such as company name, product or service type, physical location, telephone number and web site address) can be searched. More specifically, users are presented with an online form with fields for different types of search terms (such as the product or service), submit the data to the web site, after which the database is searched and the results are presented on web pages. This approach differs from the more generic advertising-supported model in that the only search results returned are lists of companies matching the search criteria, rather than a listing of matching web pages from the Internet. In other words, the search is focused on finding online companies rather than online pages or content.

Since the online business directory model provides a directory of organisations, with their details recorded in particular fields of a database (such as a field for the company name and a field for the locality code), searching can often be quite specific. For example, users might specify:

- their locality, so that search results are restricted to organisations located nearby
- a product or service, so that search results return only appropriate companies
- any restrictions that apply, such as displaying only those companies with a web site.

We can see, therefore, that online yellow pages are driven largely by databases that can be searched by entering keywords into web forms. Chapter 4 outlines this concept of web page and database integration in more detail, and chapter 3 describes how this integration is implemented using web programming.

Online business directories vary in their sophistication. For instance, Comfind (http://comfind.com) is an international site in which companies can provide a detailed specification of their products or services to help potential customers be more specific about their searches. These searches can also be limited to particular countries. Australian Yellow Pages® *OnLine* (www.yellowpages.com.au) provides visitors with online location maps to help them find the physical location of a company (see figure 2.3 for an example).

Providers of the yellow pages model typically allow only limited information about a company and its products or services to be stored. This means that companies are not able to differentiate themselves from other organisations on, for example, price, quality of service and speed of home delivery. Customers are also not able to see product or service comparisons, because they have to contact the company or go to its web site directly in order to find the more detailed information they need when making purchasing decisions. We have already seen in the web portal section above that some companies — such as http://shopping.altavista.com, which allows users to search for products and read a list of providers and their prices — are addressing this problem by offering comparison shopping.

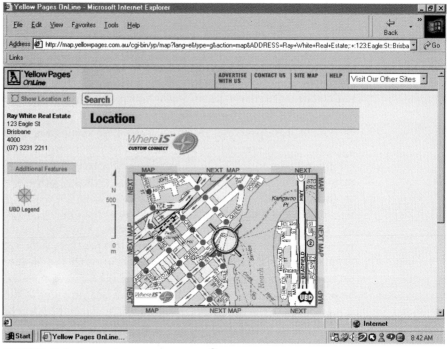

FIGURE 2.3: Australian Yellow Pages® *OnLine* location maps (www.yellowpages.com.au). Screenshot reproduced with permission. Copyright of Telstra Corporation Limited. Map copyright Universal Press.

COMPANY-BASED MODELS OF E-COMMERCE

It can be seen from the previous section that some e-commerce models allow organisations to promote their web sites. Another challenge for companies establishing a web site is generating sales from visitors and encouraging these Internet users to return. Company-based models of e-commerce that focus on this objective generally:

- present details about the company's products or services
- allow users to purchase these products or services on or off line
- provide customers with good quality online or offline after-sales service
- offer additional services that users will value, to encourage them to return on a regular basis to the firm's web site.

We will now examine the more common company-based models of e-commerce and the types of online facilities they provide to encourage return visits and to entice purchases.

ONLINE SUBSCRIPTION MODEL

Information providers, such as journal and encyclopaedia publishers, often adopt the **online subscription** model in which customers pay a subscription fee in order to access information on line.[13] The online subscription model is especially suited to information providers because articles, reports and other information can be provided electronically. This enables the providers to deliver current or updated information to subscribers without the associated physical distribution costs. For example, encyclopaedia publishers such as Encylopaedia Britannica (www.britannica.co.uk) can offer customers cheaper online alternatives to buying physical copies of yearbooks by giving subscribers access to the current information on their web site.

Subscribers can often conduct full-text searches of articles, in addition to printing and, in some cases, emailing facilities. For example, ProQuest (www.proquest.com) provides online access to article databases such as ABI Inform via its web site to subscribers — typically libraries and research centres. Authorised subscribers are given a username and password in order to log in to the service, after which they can use search tools to find relevant articles. These articles, which are retrieved from an electronic database, can be read on line, printed, received in text form by email and sometimes downloaded (see figure 2.4 for an example of a search for online articles).

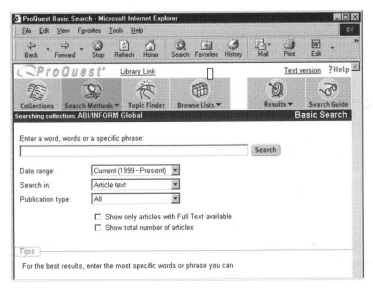

FIGURE 2.4: Online full-text article searches — www.proquest.com

An alternative to using usernames and passwords to authenticate valid users involves IP address-based access.[14] For example, ProQuest enables libraries, universities and other subscribers who might have large numbers of users to have access to the service determined by the IP address of the computers in the organisation. If the online ProQuest service recognises the IP address of the computer attempting to log in, it will enable direct access rather than requiring the user to provide a username and password. This is possible because all web browsers send their IP address to a web server in order to retrieve web pages, so that the ProQuest web server can check if an IP address is a subscriber. Chapter 3 provides an explanation of how web browsers and web servers exchange data such as IP addresses with each other, so that IP address-based access can be achieved.

A variation of the online subscription model of e-commerce is the experiment being undertaken by publishers and even authors to distribute books on line. For example, Stephen King has been trialling the online sale of instalments of a book called *The Plant*, which customers can download by instalment. King stipulated at the start of the experiment, however, that continued writing of the book and online publishing of the instalments would depend on at least 75 per cent of people who download each instalment paying for it. While the initial stages of the trial were successful,[15] fewer than half the readers were paying for the fourth instalment.[16] King has stopped the publication of *The Plant* so that he can concentrate on other projects,[17] but he plans to continue at a later date.[18]

We can see from this trial that a significant challenge for online publishers and authors is protecting their **intellectual property** and receiving payments or royalties to which they are entitled. Internet technology does not currently stop people from downloading and distributing copies for other people to read without payment. It must be emphasised, however, that this problem also exists in the physical world as a result of photocopiers — albeit to a lesser extent! The issue of intellectual property in the context of e-commerce is explored further in chapter 10.

ONLINE FEE-FOR-SERVICE MODEL

Organisations such as education institutions, web site developers and accounting firms use the **online fee-for-service model** of e-commerce to offer their services remotely to customers.[19] For example, education institutions are increasingly using the Web to offer online applications, enrolments and course materials (also known as distance education), so that students can study with them from any physical location. Web site developers often use this model to provide customers with remote web design and development services. The Web has therefore enabled or forced many service industries to compete not just in their own locations, but also on a national and global basis in the case where these services can be provided remotely.

The online fee-for-service model does not rely just on the Web for the delivery of material (in the case of education institutions) and the provision of information about the services. Effective online interaction between customers and the service providers is also critical. Although this has often been achieved using email, other online technologies can also be used, such as:

- computer conferencing, in which customers and service providers communicate using online discussion groups. This approach is common among education institutions.
- Internet conferencing, in which a customer and service provider can see and talk to each other — much like a videoconference only via the Internet.

Current research that has the potential to improve online interactivity includes the work being carried out to design 'virtual salespeople'. These are graphical representations of human talking heads that can interact with customers and, for instance, answer frequently asked questions. Research in this area has resulted in prototypes of this technology, in which[20]:

- users can type in natural language questions through a web page (although voice recognition technology could eliminate the need to enter questions manually by converting a user's speech into text)
- the answer to a query is determined by searching a database using keywords from the text of the question
- the textual answer is converted into speech and is verbalised by the graphical head (the mouth of the head changes shape to reflect the words being spoken).

Further research in this area is required before there will be commercially viable implementations of this approach. Successful developments in this area might, however, improve the user-friendliness of the Internet, because of the more human-like interface, while simultaneously enabling self-service forms of interaction with potential customers, which is one of the attractions of the Web for organisations.

ONLINE FEE-FOR-TRANSACTION MODEL

Travel agents, banks, stockbrokers and automotive dealers are organisations that employ the **online fee-for-transaction model** of e-commerce.[21] This approach is similar to the fee-for-service model, except that companies provide transaction-based services such as registration bookings and banking **transactions**. For example, customers can use web forms on the web sites of travel agents to fill out travel details such as dates, destinations and even seating preferences. Upon receiving these details the web server will create, complete and send the transaction(s) to the appropriate airline reservation system to finalise the booking (see chapter 3 for more details about web forms). These transactions are often exchanged, using such e-commerce technologies as EDI, between the travel agent's web server and the computer systems of the airline. Chapters 5 and 6 describe in more detail this **integration** of application systems within and between organisations using EDI.

One of the challenges for organisations using the fee-for-transaction model is the increasing complexity of the transactions being demanded by customers, who otherwise must discuss their booking or transaction requirements with a real sales consultant via phone, email or in person. For example, online travel booking forms rarely enable people to book a mixture of air flights, ocean cruises, coach tours, hotel bookings and car rentals in a coordinated fashion. These types of travel arrangements tend to be provided only in the form of travel packages, rather than enabling users to devise their own travel plans and to have the necessary bookings made in an automated manner with the different organisations concerned. The potential of this type of integrated service is discussed in more detail in this chapter when we examine **multi-organisational electronic service delivery**.

B2C VIRTUAL COMMUNITIES

One of the key challenges for companies establishing web sites is to provide customers with value-added services not provided by similar organisations, and thus increase the likelihood that these customers will return regularly to the web site. One approach being used by some companies to achieve this goal is setting up a B2C virtual community for users with a common interest in an area related to the organisation's products or services[22] (see www.ivillage.com for examples of B2C virtual communities). This 'community spirit' can be facilitated by providing customers with the opportunity to:
• exchange ideas and resources
• share experiences with the company's product or service

- engage in discussions with other people with similar interests
- provide reviews of the products or services being offered
- participate in games or contests through ongoing visits to the site
- provide their own information, which increases the value for other visitors to the site.

One of the objectives of B2C virtual communities, therefore, is to provide online methods of interaction between members of the community. Internet-based technologies that can support this interaction include[23]:

- Internet chat rooms, which can be used to support online textual communication between a small number of participants
- email lists, newsgroups, web-based conferencing and bulletin boards, which are all similar approaches to the exchange and online display of email messages that members can read, categorise and contribute.

VIRTUAL STOREFRONT MODEL (1) *merchant com.*

The **virtual storefront** model takes the form of a web site that provides customers with a full range of information, customer support and online transactional capabilities such as browsing, ordering and payment.[24] The principle behind the virtual storefront is that the web site provides customers with the opportunity to:

- browse through the 'virtual' store and see the available products
- request help from an assistant (for instance through email)
- order products and make a payment
- receive the ordered products by mail (or electronically).

The browsing of a virtual storefront is made possible using an **electronic catalogue**, which is a database containing information about the products offered by the organisation. This database can store a range of information from simple product descriptions and prices, through to detailed specifications, diagrams and customer feedback about the products. Customers can provide search terms via a web page to search the catalogue, or they can browse the products based on categories (see figure 2.5 for an example of online product browsing using an electronic catalogue).

Some virtual storefronts implement the browsing, ordering and payment process through simulating the traditional shopping experience by providing such features as '**shopping trolleys**' or 'shopping carts'. With this approach, customers can find a product they want and then add it to their trolley. The customer can view all the items in their trolley at any point and, if desired, remove items if they change their minds. Some virtual storefronts adopting this approach also allow customers to save the trolley contents so that they can return to their shopping at a later time if they wish. The shopping trolley contents are often stored in a database on the storefront web server, or in 'cookies' that are saved automatically by a web browser on the user's computer. (See chapter 3 for a definition of and discussion about cookies, chapter 4 for an outline of how web pages and databases can be linked or integrated, and chapter 3 for a description of how this integration is implemented using web programming.) Another way of preserving shopping cart information between browser sessions is by adding a temporary number to a customer's URL. This number is discarded when the customer closes the browser.

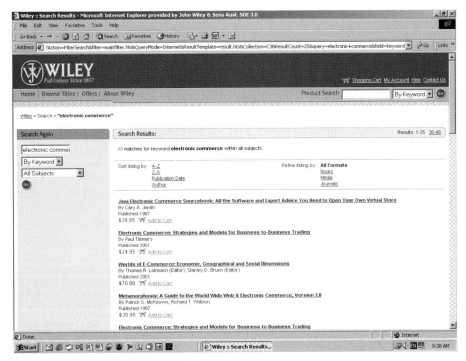

FIGURE 2.5: Browsing product catalogues (www.wiley.com)

When the customer has filled the trolley with products, he or she can then move on to the 'checkout' where the order is initiated. The order can be emailed by the system to company personnel, or input directly into the company's order processing system, after which the payment is processed and the products are delivered.

Payments to virtual storefront merchants can be made in a number of ways. The most common payment method is the credit card; the customer must provide his or her credit card details, which are then authenticated with a financial institution prior to the ordered products being delivered. Some financial institutions provide merchants with online authentication so that the credit card transaction can be approved automatically within seconds (see chapter 7 for a more detailed description of online credit card payments and the online credit card authentication process). The other e-commerce business models discussed in this chapter can also make use of this type of facility.

Some merchants also allow their customers to pay using e-cash, which is an electronic version of anonymous physical cash. Customers obtain e-cash tokens representing real cash from their bank and send these tokens to the merchant to pay for the goods. The merchant can then redeem these tokens from the issuing bank for their equivalent monetary value (see chapter 7 for a description of e-cash and how it works).

American Express has introduced a new form of **online payment** called Private Payments, by which cardholders can obtain from American Express a unique number that is linked to their card account but is valid for a period of only 30 to 67 days.[25] The unique number can be used instead of the user's card number with any merchant that accepts American Express cards. If the number is stolen, it cannot be used to make any purchases, because the number expires and is used only for a single purchase transaction. In addition, the unique number is generated only on request by the cardholder and when the cardholder's username and password are provided to an American Express web server.[26]

Another issue that must be addressed by virtual storefront merchants is order processing and the delivery of products ordered by customers. Order fulfilment requires managing inventory of products (often in warehouses), packaging orders addressed to the correct customer and delivering these products. While most virtual storefronts will outsource their deliveries to couriers and **logistics** companies, different approaches are used in warehousing and packaging. For example, Dstore[27] (www.dstore.com.au) outsources its **order fulfilment** to a warehousing company called 3PP to avoid the need for multiple distribution centres as used by online companies such as Amazon (www.amazon.com), while Wishlist (www.wishlist.com.au) handles this task internally because they believe they can ensure greater customer satisfaction.[28]

The effectiveness of virtual storefronts therefore depends significantly on the level of integration or linking between the computer systems of the web-based storefront and the organisation's internal systems, as well as between the merchant and its logistics, banking and warehousing trading partners. In the case of internal integration, the storefront web server can be linked with an inventory management system so that customers can be informed when products are out of stock. Similarly, orders created by users using the virtual storefront can be input directly into the order processing system of the organisation to be filled along with orders received via other customer channels such as fax, telephone or in person. The integration of a company's virtual storefront with the computer systems of its trading partners, in contrast to internal integration, is discussed later in this chapter when we look at **supply chain management** (or SCM). Chapters 5 and 6 explore the e-commerce technologies, such as EDI and XML, that can be used to implement this B2B integration.

A further challenge when establishing virtual storefronts is providing users with realistic or user-friendly shopping experiences — this is a challenge Internet technology is increasingly able to meet. For example:

- WinSurf (www.icominfo.com) was used until recently by Coles Online to develop an interactive graphical user interface via the Internet that does not use a web browser. WinSurf can achieve this by including animations and Windows-like application interfaces. Interestingly, however, Coles Online abandoned this interface in early 2001 and now uses a web browser interface.
- Land's End (www.landsend.com) is a clothing retailer that enables users to select from a range of physical attributes that match their physique using its virtual storefront. Outfits can then be chosen and 'worn' by a graphical model so that the user can see how the garment might look on him or her. The model can even be rotated to see front, back and side perspectives.
- Di Jones Real Estate (www.dijones.com.au) is an example of a company that uses virtual tour technology (such as QuickTime and IPIX), which provides users with a 360-degree view of real estate, and includes zoom in and out features. This Internet technology gives people a realistic online view of a property (including rooms and external views) without physically going to

the property. Baker Design (www.baker-design.com) extends this capability by showing users a floor plan of a property so that they can click on the room and then see a 360-degree view of the room (see figure 2.6).

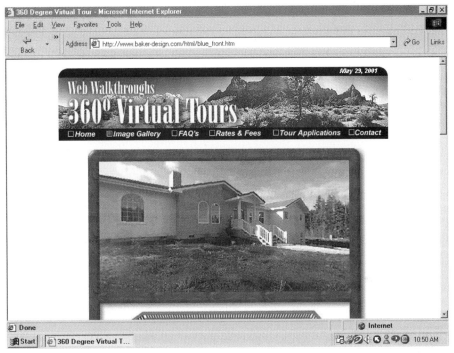

FIGURE 2.6: Interactive shopping for real estate (www.baker-design.com)

Internet consumers are increasingly demanding that virtual storefronts provide personalised services to enhance their shopping experience.[29] A consequence of this trend is that organisations must be able to learn about their customers' purchasing habits and preferences to ensure that this level of personalisation can be achieved. Online merchants can achieve this by analysing their customer order database, which contains all orders made, to determine consumer purchasing patterns or trends.

For example, analysis of the data might reveal that a particular customer tends to buy a lot of frozen dinners, so that the virtual storefront could suggest other time-saving products that might be suitable for this type of customer. The order database can also be used to determine which product lines are no longer popular, so that they can be removed or more effective promotion campaigns can be developed.

INTER-ORGANISATIONAL MODELS OF E-COMMERCE

We have seen that the company-based models of e-commerce described in this chapter are most commonly used for B2C e-commerce. B2B, B2G and G2G (or more generally inter-organisational) models of e-commerce, on the other hand, involve electronic interaction between two or more organisations. We will now examine the more common types of inter-organisational models of e-commerce.

ELECTRONIC PROCUREMENT MODEL

The **electronic procurement** model[30] is the electronic means by which an organisation purchases goods or services from its suppliers or advertises their purchasing requirements to potential suppliers. The electronic procurement model is increasingly used in G2B-type trading to reduce public administration costs — in this case, purchases by government departments. Private sector companies also use this e-commerce business model to reduce the costs associated with the purchasing of such items as stationery and office equipment.

This model can involve a number of procurement activities, such as:

- *tendering*, where organisations provide a Request for Tender (RFT) on the Web for downloading. RFTs specify in detail what product or service the client requires, so that suppliers can submit tenders based on this specification that explain what the supplier will charge, why it should be chosen over competitors and so on.
- *electronic negotiations*, where an organisation uses the Internet (such as email) to negotiate conditions, contracts and other details with potential suppliers
- *supplier sourcing*, where suppliers register on line to be added to an organisation's vendor source list so that they might be invited to bid for closed tenders
- *online procurement systems*, where an organisation's personnel can browse a web-based database of products that are offered by preferred suppliers of the organisation and make a purchase.

The Victorian Government Purchasing Board (www.vgpb.vic.gov.au) is an example of an organisation that advertises tender opportunities by providing RFTs on its web site. Most public organisations using this approach still require the bids to be delivered physically and in paper into a locked box.

The US federal government's GSA Advantage! (www.gsaadvantage.gov) is an example of a virtual storefront style of procurement system that is designed to allow federal purchasers to order small-value goods using their government credit card. The federal government negotiates prices and delivery terms with suppliers, and these product details are added to the GSA Advantage! database. Federal purchasers enter their username, password and postal code and can then browse the available products. They are able to comparison shop because the web system will display all comparable products so that the items can be compared on price and delivery lead time (see figure 2.7). Products can be added to a shopping cart and ordered, after which the corresponding suppliers will receive orders via such means as EDI or fax. The efficiencies and cost effectiveness gained from these small-value procurement systems are significant, because it is often the high-volume, low-value items such as consumables and office supplies that involve costly processes for handling their purchasing.[31]

The fact that some suppliers still have to take customer orders by fax illustrates an area in which suppliers need to become part of the web-enabled world by using the Internet.

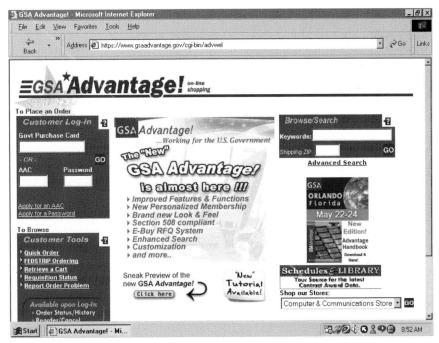

FIGURE 2.7: Electronic procurement — GSA Advantage!
(www.gsaadvantage.gov)

MULTI-ORGANISATIONAL ELECTRONIC SERVICE DELIVERY MODEL

One of the challenges of offering services via the Internet is ensuring that customers can obtain the services they require in an integrated manner. Customers are increasingly demanding that these services do not require them to deal with each of the service providers separately. This is especially difficult when negotiations and comparisons must be made between many different types of companies that are all part of the one service.

This multi-organisational electronic service delivery (MESD) model is an approach that involves the integration of related services.[32] The MESD model involves developing a single entry point, often via the Web, where customers can obtain services without having to understand the structure or relationships of the organisations providing these services and without having to deal with each organisation individually. Considerable levels of integration of computer systems between organisations are required using such e-commerce technologies as EDI, and these will be discussed briefly in the next section of this chapter. (Chapters 5 and 6 will explain in detail how e-commerce technologies are used to integrate computer systems that cross organisational boundaries.)

For example, people wanting to organise a holiday will want not only airfares, but also accommodation, car rental, tourism advice and so on. An integrated approach would involve, for instance, online questions being asked, in which people specify their flight dates and destinations, and whether they would like to book a rental car and/or accommodation at the destination. The web server can then display rental/accommodation alternatives from which to choose. Once all the arrangements are made on line, the web server can then make the bookings on the customer's behalf.

The Victorian State government applies this model to businesses and consumers via the Web in the Maxi Project (www.maxi.com.au), which involves different 'channels' of service depending on the type of customer. The web-based consumer channel, for instance, is designed around life events such as turning eighteen, getting married, changing residential address and so on. The intention is that each channel will allow consumers to complete a single online form, corresponding to their life event, which asks them for information needed by the relevant government departments. When the details are submitted, the required data can be distributed electronically to the government departments and updated in their internal systems. In this way, consumers will not be required to understand the structure of government agencies in order to interact with them, or to enter the same data multiple times. Chapters 5 and 6 discuss the B2B technologies, such as EDI, that would be required to implement this type of initiative.

SUPPLY CHAIN MANAGEMENT MODEL

The effectiveness of organisations in an e-commerce environment cannot any longer be considered purely in terms of achieving efficiencies and cost reductions internally to an organisation and between its immediate customers and suppliers. Organisations increasingly need to look at their entire supply chain, which includes their suppliers' suppliers, their customers' customers and their relationships with banks, logistics and other trading partners. The ability of an organisation to offer competitive prices in a global marketplace will necessitate, among other objectives, ensuring that its suppliers and their suppliers' suppliers (and so on along the supply chain) are also cost-effective.

Other objectives of effective supply chain management (SCM) include[33]:

- ensuring that increases and decreases in product demand by consumers can always be met within a short time period, which involves replenishing retail stock levels being depleted within hours or days (rather than weeks)
- achieving this rapid stock replenishment without maintaining high inventory levels in the supply chain, which involves products being delivered to the retailer within hours or days of an order being made, and the supplier manufacturing these products quickly once the order has been received
- providing consumers with more variety in product choice, which involves supply chains being able to alter what they are manufacturing very quickly to respond in a timely manner to rapidly changing consumer demand
- ensuring that customers' products are delivered within narrow delivery windows — perhaps as short as two hours.

Traditional approaches to achieving these objectives have involved the use of e-commerce technologies such as EDI to implement inventory management strategies such as Quick Response (QR) and Just-in-Time (JIT) manufacturing. QR is used at the retailer end of the supply chain and involves orders being filled by retail product manufacturers within days or even hours of the order being sent. Retail orders can be triggered automatically when current shelf quantities recorded in the retailer's inventory system reach predefined levels. The e-commerce technologies that make QR possible include[34]:

- point-of-sale (POS) equipment at the checkout that automatically decrements shelf quantities in the inventory database when a product is scanned and sold. This is achieved by ensuring that all products are labelled with bar codes, which are unique scannable numbers that can be read by infra-red POS scanning equipment.
- EDI exchanges of purchase orders directly between the retailer's purchasing system and the manufacturers' order processing systems to eliminate the need for data entry of order information by the manufacturers
- EDI exchanges of delivery documents directly from the manufacturer's inventory management system to the retailer's inventory management system, so that the retailer knows what products are being delivered and can take those products straight to retail shelves.

As with retailers, the cost effectiveness and efficiency of manufacturers in this scenario also depend on their ability to maintain low inventory levels while also being able to respond quickly to retail orders. JIT manufacturing is the manufacturer's version of QR, in which the manufacturer orders products from its suppliers as the items are needed in the production line and must be delivered by its suppliers within days or hours of the order being made. As with QR, JIT manufacturing is achieved using bar code scanning and EDI exchanges. (See chapter 6 for a more detailed discussion of how these e-commerce technologies are used in SCM.)

Effective SCM is not restricted to the improvement of inventory management and logistics, but should also consider a range of strategies aimed at promoting greater collaboration among members of a supply chain. For example, Efficient Consumer Response (ECR), which is the grocery industry's version of QR, has four components.[35]

- Efficient store assortment is concerned with strategies for optimising shelf space and the management of product categories.
- Efficient replenishment has the same objectives as QR and JIT.
- Efficient promotion aims to avoid inefficient, short-term promotion techniques and instead use long-term promotion strategies such as personalised promotion using the Web and databases that store consumer purchasing patterns.
- Efficient product introduction involves collaboration with suppliers to ensure that effective strategies for introducing new products are achieved based on the characteristics of the product.

The key issue with this broader view of SCM is that all supply chain members must share data so that effective planning and collaboration can achieve the ultimate objectives of SCM. For example, sales data from all retailers can be provided to a manufacturer so that this supplier is able to determine actual sales patterns, rather than relying entirely on sales forecasts, thus achieving greater market sensitivity.[36] This intelligence can be provided to the manufacturer's customers and suppliers so that production and promotions can be coordinated across the entire supply chain.

The following technical insite describes the stages of SCM integration and collaboration, in which the author's vision is that a customer will have access to data from all suppliers in a supply chain and that suppliers will be more closely linked with their customers.

E-COMMERCE REQUIRES INTELLIGENT SUPPLY CHAINS

Stage 1 — Web presence
... The web server is a standalone server, usually outside the company's firewall. It is not linked with any existing business systems. Many businesses establish this type of web presence through an Internet service provider (ISP) ...

Stage 2 — E-commerce
... Suppliers offer e-commerce services that allow their customers to place orders directly with them by linking to an internal line of business systems ...

Stage 3 — Data delivery
... Suppliers begin to deliver binary data that can be integrated into their customers' and suppliers' spreadsheets and business systems. For example, the supplier might supply a component that automatically updates the customer's spreadsheet whenever an order status changes. Having this data delivered allows the customer to proactively take steps to deal with issues like inventory shortages or missed customer delivery windows.

Data delivery improves a customer's decision support capability. One example is when a customer checks inventory to determine whether they will be able to fill a sales order on time. The ability to order data across multiple systems and suppliers means available inventory is not limited to what the customer's business system says is available in the warehouse. The available inventory is a combination of internal stock, stock in transit, and stock that could arrive (from one or more suppliers) in time to fill the sales order. Stage 3 combines information from both internal and external business systems ...

Stage 4 — Automated inter-business processes
Process integration between the decision-making systems of businesses, their suppliers, and their customers becomes bi-directional and tightly integrated. Suppliers can interact dynamically and can initiate business processes within each other's information systems by pre-defining business rules that trigger events across systems. That means that supply chains can be fully automated ...

Stage 4 is about the automation of the decision-making processes between businesses. For example, a supplier application sends a customer application a component that includes pricing information and services that let that customer automatically place orders. If the supplier's price drops to a level designated in business rules, it triggers the customer's inventory control system to start ordering stock (without human intervention) from that supplier, rather than from the competition, because that supplier in effect automated supplier selection ...

SOURCE: G. Moakley 1999, www.ascet.com/ascet/wp/Moakley.html.

EXERCISES

1. Do some web research to see whether there is any evidence of organisations at stage 3.
2. Discuss the advantages and disadvantages of each stage identified by Moakley.

THIRD PARTY MODELS OF E-COMMERCE

Third party models of e-commerce differ from those discussed previously in this chapter in that they provide electronic marketplaces in which many organisations and/or individuals can interact with one another. These online marketplaces are often established by third parties and typically provide a platform on which organisations in the same industry (or related industries) can trade with each other. One of the objectives of these marketplaces is to become the main location on the Web where organisations and/or individuals go to sell and purchase particular products or services.

ELECTRONIC MALLS

Electronic malls (or online shopping malls) are third party hosted groups of virtual storefronts[37] and act as an electronic version of physical malls or shopping centres. These malls are established to generate larger numbers of visitors by providing a variety of products and services that can be offered by multiple organisations in the one cyber-location. The virtual storefront owners can therefore benefit from the advertising and visitor traffic the electronic mall creates, in much the same way as in physical shopping malls. For this reason, they are similar to web portals but focus primarily on the retail sector.

Many electronic malls categorise the virtual storefronts based on the type of product or service being offered to assist customers in their search. Once the category has been selected, storefronts in this category are usually listed and provide a link by which the customer can 'enter' the virtual store to begin shopping. Some virtual storefronts in an electronic mall (such as the shopping mall at www.sofcom.com.au) exhibit a consistent interface and navigation style so that the customer is not required to learn a new web site design.

Third party shopping malls vary in sophistication. For example, Ozmall (www.ozmall.com.au) allows companies to add links to their web sites from Ozmall's shopping mall, and therefore offers a yellow pages model type of service. Yahoo! also provides this type of service, but the Yahoo! Store (http://store.yahoo.com.au) service also allows companies to build an entry-level virtual storefront on line using a web browser, which involves such tasks as[38]:

- entering the details of the new virtual storefront, such as the name, description, home page welcome message and email address for receiving customer orders
- viewing statistics about the use of the storefront by customers
- entering the details of products, such as product name, code, description, price and a graphic file containing a picture of the product. The product details, including inventory levels, can be uploaded to Yahoo! Store as a comma-separated text file to automate changes to the product database.
- providing payment options for customers, such as by credit card, purchase order and cash on delivery
- selecting an appropriate 'look and feel' — that is, how the products and their pictures will be displayed and what company logo graphic will be used.

An advantage organisations can gain from being a member of an electronic mall is that some third party operators offer value-added services. For example, the third parties can ensure that customer orders are received securely by implementing Internet security approaches such as Secure Sockets Layer (see chapter 8 for more detail about Internet security), and they can provide online payment services such as credit card authentication and e-cash capabilities (see chapter 7 for descriptions of these electronic payment mechanisms). This means that the virtual storefront owner can avoid the expense and complexity of setting up and handling these features, which they would otherwise need to do if they were to set up their own web site.

B2B VIRTUAL COMMUNITIES

B2B virtual communities are similar in nature to their B2C counterparts discussed earlier in this chapter except they provide an environment in which organisations can exchange information, trade and collaborate via the Web. The information and communication services provided by B2B virtual communities therefore have a strong business focus.

A typical example of a B2B virtual community is Farmwide (www.farmwide .com.au), which provides a range of online services to the Australian farming community. These include:

- web-based chatrooms for regular online chats, organised by Farmwide, with government officials, company executives and other individuals, so that their virtual community members can talk about issues with these guests
- a web-based bulletin board service to display messages posted by the Farmwide community and to permit responses to these messages
- news headlines, market price details, information about upcoming events, links to weather reports, links to agriculture suppliers and so on.

This example demonstrates that one of the key objectives of B2B virtual communities is to provide a central location where businesses with a particular focus (such as agriculture in the case of Farmwide) can obtain all the information they may require, in addition to opportunities for online discussions with similar businesses. Value-added services, such as organising regular chat sessions with people of interest to the virtual community, help increase the likelihood that users will return to the site on a regular basis.

INTERNET AUCTION MODEL

A more trade-oriented community model, when compared to virtual communities, is the Internet auction. As with electronic malls, Internet auctions also aim to bring many buyers and sellers together on a web site, but they differ in that they emulate traditional auctions by providing trading mechanisms for negotiating prices, delivery and other terms. Electronic malls, by contrast, typically offer non-negotiable retail prices.

Internet auctions typically take place over a period of time (for instance, a few days), because bidders are not necessarily all on line at the same time and can be dispersed worldwide in different time zones. Running Internet auctions for days gives all bidders an opportunity to place bids and counter-bids. The more common types of auctions found on the Internet are summarised in table 2.1 below. Chapter 1 also provided examples of Internet and reverse auctions when discussing B2C and C2C types of e-commerce.

TABLE 2.1	SIX MAJOR AUCTION TYPES
AUCTION TYPE	**KEY CHARACTERISTICS**
English auction	Starting from a low price, bidding increases until no bidder is willing to bid higher.
Dutch auction	Starting from a high price, bidding automatically decreases until bidder accepts price.
First-price sealed bid	Secret bidding process; highest bidder pays amount of highest bid.
Second-price sealed bid (Vickrey)	Secret bidding process; highest bidder pays amount of second-highest bid.
Double auction open-outcry	Buyers and sellers declare combined price-quantity bids. Auctioneer matches seller offers (lowest to highest) with buyer offers (highest to lowest). Buyers and sellers can modify bids based on knowledge gained from other bids.
Double auction sealed bid	Buyers and sellers declare combined price-quantity bids. Auctioneer (specialist) matches seller offers (lowest to highest) with buyer offers (highest to lowest). Buyers and sellers cannot modify their bids.

SOURCE: G. P. Schneider and J. T. Perry 2000, *Electronic Commerce*, Course Technology, Cambridge, MA, p. 318.

An important element of Internet auctions, and C2C auction sites in particular, is ensuring that buyers and sellers all meet their obligations. This is achieved, to an extent, by[39]:

- requiring buyers and sellers to register with the Internet auction site before they can participate. This registration process involves submitting a web form with personal details such as name, email address, postal address and credit card information. This information can help track down buyers and sellers if necessary.
- allowing buyers and sellers to provide feedback about their experiences with a particular buyer or seller. For example, sellers that develop a reputation for bad auction practices can be identified by other buyers and avoided.
- providing insurance for buyers, so that if sellers do not deliver purchased items or the products are not what was expected, then reimbursement up to a given amount will be provided to the buyer as compensation
- advising buyers and sellers of escrow services, through which the buyer pays the escrow service for the item and has the opportunity to inspect the item before the payment is passed on to the seller. This also means that buyers cannot default on their payment unless they return the item to the seller.

eBay (www.ebay.com.au) is an example of a C2C Internet auction site that implements these strategies.

Sellers can sell an item in an Internet auction by logging in using their username and password and providing the item details (such as a title, description and picture) and the auction details (including the type of auction, the reserve price and the amount by which bids should be incremented). Sellers can also update their auction item listings, and cancel or end auctions under certain conditions stipulated by the auction provider. Once the auction has ended, the seller can request the contact details of the bidder so that delivery and payment can be arranged. The seller's details are also emailed to the buyer. Contact details are sent only via email, rather than via the Web, to reduce the likelihood that this personal information will be accessed by unregistered users through the auction web site.

Buyers can start bidding first by browsing the categories of auctions available to find items for which they would like to bid. They can make a bid by specifying the maximum amount they will pay, followed by their username and password to register the bid. The maximum amount specified is used to implement *proxy bidding*; the Internet auction will automatically make bids in response to higher bids on behalf of the buyer, but only up to the maximum amount specified. This approach ensures that the bidder is not required to be on line during the entire auction.

We are also seeing the introduction of C2B Internet auctions, in which customers provide information about their purchasing needs and the third party aggregates these orders to entice suppliers. For example, LetsBuyIt (www.letsbuyit.com) negotiates with a seller (of such products as toys, computing equipment, travel and appliances) to obtain prices, which decrease depending on the number of buyers. The price, for instance, might be $10 if there are one to four buyers and $7 if there are five to 10 buyers, so that the more buyers who register to purchase the product, the more likely it is they will pay a lower price for bulk orders.

B2B Internet auctions such as Metalsite (www.metalsite.com) provide similar auction features as are found in B2C and C2C auctions, such as online registration of both buyers and sellers and various types of auction formats, including open and sealed-bid approaches. Many B2B Internet auction sites also provide additional online facilities to assist inter-organisational trade such as the ability to send and receive purchase orders, negotiate price and/or delivery terms, and display auction or purchase order histories. These auctions also provide more traditional purchasing and negotiation support, which can be communicated directly between two companies, so that they are increasingly taking the form of Internet marketplaces or exchanges, as will be seen in the following section.

Chapter 6 examines in more detail the e-commerce technology architecture that provides the platform on which Internet auctions operate.

INTERNET EXCHANGE MODEL

Internet exchanges — also referred to as electronic marketplaces or B2B portals — are more sophisticated than the more established Internet auctions, because they aim to support more business functions than just online purchasing and negotiation. Internet exchange operators intend to achieve this by merging a range of B2B e-commerce models to facilitate buyer–seller interaction,[40] such as:

- supporting entire supply chains by providing a web platform on which information sharing can be achieved and closer collaboration supported by all supply chain members[41]
- providing electronic procurement services for high-volume, low-value items such as office supplies and other consumables
- incorporating electronic catalogues, auctions and other B2B trading environments.

Commerx PlasticsNet (www.commerxplasticsnet.com), an electronic marketplace for the plastics industry, is an example of an Internet exchange that has merged many of the e-commerce models discussed in this chapter. This Internet exchange is typical of many now being established on the Web, and includes online services to support B2B trading in the plastics industry, such as:

- a marketing program including product classified advertisements, banner advertising and keyword search advertising
- an Internet auction for companies wanting to sell excess inventory quickly
- a supplier directory and a purchasing centre to find suppliers of products or services
- a customisable catalogue that allows companies to list frequently purchased items
- a facility for preparing online ordering
- the ability to send a request for quotes to which suppliers can respond
- a collaborative relationship between Commerx and Schneider Logistics, which enables companies purchasing through the exchange to track shipments and complete their freight bill payments.

The growing number of Internet exchanges worldwide is also forcing many operators (even competitors) to join their separate exchanges into one so that customers and/or suppliers are not required to use multiple exchanges. For example, General Motors, Ford and DaimlerChrysler are planning to develop a single exchange to replace the separate ones already developed.[42]

Most Internet exchanges are still under development, primarily because of the complexities involved in setting them up (see chapter 6 for a more detailed explanation of the technology underpinning Internet exchanges). As Ransdell (2000) comments:

> The technology standards needed to connect buyers and sellers, such as XML (an enhanced World Wide Web language designed to support commercial transactions), are still in development; meanwhile many software vendors are advancing their own versions of these standards.[43]

Other difficulties that must be faced by Internet exchange developers include the complexity involved in supporting many different supply chains and in providing secure, timely B2B payment systems.[44]

The following technical insite discusses a further technical hurdle for Internet exchange developers and B2B web solution developers — ensuring that the tools are provided to enable businesses to integrate their internal systems with Internet exchanges.

APPLICATION INTEGRATION WITH EXCHANGES

Electronic marketplaces may be the Next Big Thing, but companies seeking to tap this potentially lucrative channel are encountering an obstacle — the yawning gulf between their own IT systems and those of the potential suppliers and customers they meet on exchanges ...

Few business-to-business marketplaces provide integration with their participants' back-end systems. Of the 600 exchanges tracked by AMR Research, only 10 have application integration built into the exchange. That means many marketplaces fall short on their promise of huge efficiencies. 'At this point, a lot of transactions are still happening by phone and by fax and by e-mail,' says Kimberly Knickle, an AMR analyst.

To change that, integration vendors are introducing new products and seeking a prominent role as the gateways to online marketplaces. Instead of developing interfaces to as many enterprise resource planning packages as possible, application-integration vendors will start building interfaces to marketplaces, say analysts. For instance, a company could write a single interface to an integration vendor's product that would then link to several exchanges ...

Application-integration vendors are focusing on XML, which is quickly becoming the accepted method for business-to-business communication on the Web. But until entire industries create standardized XML tags for data, even E-marketplaces within the same industry are likely to use slightly different versions of XML, forcing integration vendors to support all of them. 'It's a moving target,' says Dave Power, VP of marketing at application-integration vendor Mercator Inc. ...

Application integration lets exchange participants connect directly to their partners' IT systems. Companies can evaluate product availability, for example, by linking into a supplier's inventory application, or place orders starting in their own procurement application, then follow through with a supplier's order-fulfillment package ...

The integration that takes place in marketplaces will likely be different from other kinds of application integration, because the relationships among the companies participating in marketplaces are more fleeting than conventional business relationships. Analysts say most businesses will integrate only their procurement, order-fulfillment, and inventory applications with marketplaces. And in some cases they'll provide access to these applications only through a browser ...

SOURCE: J. Sweat, 3 April 2000, 'E-Market Connections', www.informationweek.com/780/b2b.htm.

EXERCISES

1. Do some research on the Web to find examples of organisations that are developing systems that integrate Internet exchanges with the internal systems of the companies using the exchanges.

2. This technical insite suggests that B2B Internet exchange relationships will be more fleeting, while the previous technical insite argues for closer, long-term relationships between supply chain members. Argue whether both forms of B2B relationships will exist in future or whether one of these approaches will dominate.

SUMMARY

This chapter has examined a number of e-commerce models that have emerged on the Internet, and provided some insight into the evolutions some of these models are undergoing.

We described online advertising e-commerce models that provide organisations with opportunities to promote and to drive traffic to their web sites. We explained that providers of these models aim to become profitable from advertising revenue rather than from users. We also showed that the technology enabling these models is primarily databases that are accessible and searchable by users via the Web.

The company-based e-commerce models we described are intended to encourage visitors to return to the web site on a regular basis and to make purchases. The models discussed vary between industries in which, for instance, retail organisations tend to use virtual storefronts and information providers tend to use online subscriptions. All of the company-based models outlined need to support online payments and ordering, and to ensure that their web sites are integrated with (or linked to) the firm's internal systems.

Inter-organisational e-commerce models that improve the efficiency and cost-effectiveness of B2B, B2G and G2G trading were discussed. We examined models that support purchasing or procurement by organisations and enable companies to work together in tight trading relationships. We also explained the e-commerce tools, such as EDI and point-of-sale systems, that enable these models.

Finally, this chapter explored e-commerce models developed by organisations to bring buyers and sellers together in one Internet marketplace. Electronic malls that combine many virtual storefronts were discussed, as were Internet auctions and B2B virtual communities that allow businesses to interact with each other using technologies such as web bulletin boards and Internet chat rooms. Also described were Internet exchanges, which have increasingly merged many e-commerce models to provide high-quality value-added services for B2B trading.

The next chapter explores the technologies that support the B2C models of e-commerce, such as web forms and the web programming languages, which enable web forms to be linked or integrated with a company's corporate databases.

key terms

advertising-supported model
banner advertisements
click-through advertising
electronic catalogue
electronic malls
electronic procurement
integration
intellectual property
interactivity
Internet auctions
Internet exchanges

Internet search engines
logistics
multi-organisational electronic service delivery
online fee-for-service model
online fee-for-transaction model
online payment
online subscription
order fulfilment

personalisation
shopping trolleys
supply chain management
transactions
value-added services
virtual communities
virtual storefront
web portals
yellow pages model

QUESTIONS

1. How are the e-commerce models discussed in this chapter interrelated? Provide examples to illustrate your points. *Hint:* Consider the supply chain model and which of the other models the members of a supply chain can use.

2. The Web is growing rapidly, and so too are the number of virtual storefronts, electronic malls, Internet markets, Internet exchanges and web portals. Will the Web become so large that it will be unusable by businesses and individuals? Justify your answer. In your answer explain how the e-commerce models might change or evolve.

3. Many e-commerce models rely upon common technologies for them to work. Identify these common technologies and describe how they are used in the various models. As a starting point, consider what transactions are exchanged in the models and the technologies needed to support this. Also consider where web sites get their data in order to create dynamic, interactive web pages.

4. The issue of interactivity was a significant issue in many of the B2C e-commerce models. Do some research on the Web to find out what Internet technologies currently exist that improve the interactivity of the Web by providing more user-friendly features.

A GLOBAL GIANT IMPROVES ITS EFFICIENCY

By RALPH DRAYER

Procter & Gamble markets over 300 brands in 140 countries, competing in 50 different consumer product categories. In the late 1980s and early 1990s, P&G determined that swings in its product pricing were in large part responsible for massive inefficiencies in its own distribution system and throughout the entire grocery supply chain as well. These pricing swings were the result of product 'special promotion' push offers — intended to gain temporary market share rapidly — that were in vogue throughout the industry in the 1970s and 1980s.

Special promotions led wholesalers and retailers to forward-order as much as a three-months' supply of some products in order to take advantage of favorable terms. P&G estimated that one-third of existing inventory was held in the pipeline between its plants and the consumer. The company realized that the proliferation of variations in product, pricing, labeling, and packaging necessitated by extensive promotions required an explosion of SKUs (stockkeeping units) and of UPC changes, further burdening the entire order, shipping, and billing (OSB) supply-chain system — without producing value for retail customers or consumers. The bloating of the supply chain with product, together with the proliferation of product variations related to the promotional offerings, also had strong negative repercussions in manufacturing costs.

P&G responded to these clear challenges with a number of actions, some of them involving dramatic policy changes, phased over a five-year period from 1992 to 1997.

As early as 1985, P&G had begun tests using retail customers' own daily data on their warehouse shipments and retail sales to determine P&G's product shipments. These tests led to the institution of a program known as Continuous Replenishment (CRP). Using electronic data interchange (EDI) for automatic and reliable capture of customers' daily sales, P&G was increasingly able to approximate a 'just in time' supply of products through the pipeline.

P&G executives acknowledge, however, that EDI and the CRP program would not by themselves have produced the desired supply-chain efficiency. In 1992, the company instituted a comprehensive program, called Efficient Consumer Response (ECR), to drive costs that don't add value for trade customers and consumers out of the supply chain. ECR has four key areas: (1) efficient replenishment, (2) efficient promotion, (3) efficient introduction, and (4) efficient assortment.

At its simplest, Efficient Replenishment is just-in-time inventory management. Retail out of stocks are reduced while at the same time inventory turns are increased as the replenishment process is driven by consumer demand.

Efficient Assortment led to a 20 per cent reduction in the number of SKUs to be handled by P&G's product supply system as well as by retail customers, thereby cutting costs and reducing operating complexity across the supply chain. It was then found that this action also produced value for consumers. For example, cutting 26 Head & Shoulders SKUs down to 15 delivered a double-digit increase in market share on the brand.

Efficient Introduction is an extension of Efficient Assortment to new-product development. Efficient Introduction utilizes a template that tightens the criteria for introducing new product to the supply chain based on genuine customer needs.

Efficient Promotion enabled the success of all three other elements of the Efficient Consumer Response program in improving efficiency along the supply chain and building customer loyalty. In a major policy shift instituted by P&G between 1992 and 1994, P&G moved away from promotional push tactics and adopted a value pricing strategy for maximizing pull from the consumer end. Under value pricing, most promotion and pricing funds were eliminated and redirected into lower everyday list prices.

This single move dissipated the need for forward ordering by retail customers that had stuffed the pipeline full of inventory; it also eliminated the need for a complex array of SKUs linked to promotional variations in product, packaging, labeling, and price; and it ended the confusion of brand-loyal consumers as to the value of a P&G brand. P&G now estimates that incremental revenue generated by promotions did not cover the costs of those promotions. Value pricing did initially reduce sales revenues — but directly increased profitability along with its other, supply-chain, benefits ...

SOURCE: R. Drayer 1999, www.ascet.com/ascet/wp/wpDrayer.html.

Questions

1. Prepare a report for Procter & Gamble that describes and justifies which online advertising models it could utilise. In the report provide examples of real, suitable online advertising venues for each of the models proposed.

2. Prepare a report for Procter & Gamble that:
   - identifies company-based and/or inter-organisational e-commerce models that can be used in their entire supply chain (from consumers to their suppliers' suppliers)
   - describes how each e-commerce model will be used by the supply chain members and why they will benefit from using the model.

3. Prepare a report for Procter & Gamble that proposes the development of an Internet exchange. In the report, consider what value-added services will need to be provided for the buyers and sellers in Procter & Gamble's industry.

4. Identify the technologies that will be required by Procter & Gamble to implement each e-commerce business model proposed in questions 1, 2 and 3. In addition, describe briefly the role of each technology.

SUGGESTED READING

Kalakota, R. and Robinson, M. 2001, *E-business 2.0: Roadmap for Success*, 2nd Edition, Addison-Wesley Longman, Reading, MA.

Lawrence et al. 2000, *Internet Commerce: Digital Models for Business*, 2nd Edition, John Wiley & Sons, Brisbane.

Schneider, G. P. and Perry, J. T. 2000, *Electronic Commerce*, Course Technology, Cambridge, MA.

Strauss, J. and Frost, R. 2001, *E-Marketing*, 2nd Edition, Prentice Hall, New Jersey.

Turban, E., Lee, J., King, D. and Chung, H. M. 2000, *Electronic Commerce: A Managerial Perspective*, Prentice Hall, New Jersey.

Whiteley, D. 2000, *e-Commerce: Strategy, Technologies and Applications*, McGraw-Hill, London.

END NOTES

1. See, for example, Strauss, J. and Frost, R. 2001, *E-Marketing*, 2nd Edition, Prentice Hall, New Jersey.

2. AltaVista 2000, AltaVista Advanced Search Tutorial — How AltaVista Works, http://doc.altavista.com/adv_search/ast_haw_index.html.

3. Google 2000, Google Search Technology: Why Use Google, www.google.com/technology/index.html.

4. Berst, J. 2000, Why All Software May Be Shareware Soon, 2 February, http://zdnet.com/anchordesk/story/story_4412.html.

5. Schneider and Perry 2000.

6. Schneider and Perry 2000.

7. See Nielsen 1997 (end note 8) for an argument concerning the active nature of Internet users when compared with television viewers and the implications of this view for Internet advertising.

8. See, for example, Strauss and Frost 2001; Nielsen, J. 1997, 'Why Advertising Doesn't Work on the Web', 1 September, www.zdnet.com/devhead/alertbox/9709a.html.

9. Meskauskas, J. 2000, 'Are Click-Through Rates Really Declining?', http://clickz.com/cgi-bin/gt/article.html?article=3179.

10. Sterne, J. 1999, *World Wide Web Marketing: Integrating the Web into Your Marketing Strategy*, John Wiley & Sons, New York; Preston, P. 2000, 'Web Marketing Is Promising to Revolutionise the Banner Ad', *New Media Age*, 3.

11. Lawrence et al. 2000.

12. See, for example, http://shopping.altavista.com, which allows users to search for products and then see a list of companies that provide the product and their prices.

13. Schneider and Perry 2000.

14. ProQuest 2000, 'IP Address-Based Access to ProQuest', www.proquest.com/hp/Support/PQD/IP.html.

15. King, S. 2000, Stephen's Comments, 25 August, www.stephenking.com/sk1_082500.html.

16. ZDNet 2000, 'Stephen King Puts *The Plant* on Ice', 29 November, http://uk.news.yahoo.com/001129/15/aqf4f.html.

17. Sayer, P. 2000, 'Stephen King's Online Novel *The Plant* Dries Up', 29 November, www.nwfusion.com/news/2000/1129plant.html.

18. ZDNet 2000.

19. Schneider and Perry 2000.

20. Marriott, A., Pockaj, R. and Parker, C. 2001, 'A Virtual Salesperson', in Rahman, S. M. and Bignall, R. J. (Eds), *Internet Commerce and Software Agents: Cases, Technologies and Opportunities*, Idea Group Publishing, Hershey, PA.

21. Schneider and Perry 2000.

22. Timmers, P. 1999, *Electronic Commerce: Strategies and Models for Business-to-Business Trading*, John Wiley & Sons, Chichester, UK.

23. Whitaker, V. M. and Parker, C. M. 2000, 'The Factors Enabling and Inhibiting the Development of Agricultural Internet Virtual Communities: An Australian Case Study', 8th European Conference on Information Systems, 3–5 July, Vienna, Austria.

24. Lawrence et al. 2000.

25. American Express 2000, Private Payments, www26.americanexpress.com/privatepayments/info_page.jsp.

26. American Express 2000, FAQ, www26.americanexpress.com/privatepayments/faq.jsp.

27. Dstore was acquired by Harris Scarfe Holdings.

28. Howarth, B. 2000, 'Dstore struggles to deliver', *Business Review Weekly*, 14 July, pp. 72–5.

29. Howarth 2000.

30. Timmers 1999.

31. Sutherland, G. 2000, 'Business Hubs, BOSS', *Australian Financial Review*, August, pp. 56–7.

32. Clarke, R. 1999, 'Electronic Services Delivery: From Brochure-Ware to Entry Points', www.anu.edu.au/people/Roger.Clarke/EC/ESD.html.

33. Christopher, M. 1999, 'Creating the Agile Supply Chain', www.ascet.com/ascet/wp/wpChristopher.html.

34. AAPN 1999, 'Quick Response — How It Works', www.usawear.com/qr.htm.

35. Bhulai, S. 1997, 'Efficient Consumer Response', www.cs.vu.nl/~sbhulai/ecr/index.html.

36. Christopher 1999.

37. Timmers 1999.

38. Sofcom 2000, Sofcom Store Builder, www.sofcom.com.au/mall/builder.

39. eBay 2000, http://pages.ebay.com.au/help/basics/n-is-ebay-safe.html.

40. Seybold 2000. 'Setting Your B-to-B E-Market Strategy', Patricia Seybold Group, 16 March; Wilson 2000, 'B-To-B Traders Turn Up Heat on Vendors', www.internetwk.com/lead/lead051900-1.htm.

41. Sutherland, G. 2000, 'Business Hubs, BOSS', *Australian Financial Review*, August, pp. 56–7.

42. Foley, J., Bacheldor, B. and Wallace, B. 2000, 'E-Markets Are Expanding', 28 February, www.informationweek.com/775/marketplace.htm.

43. Ramsdell, G. 2000, 'The Real Business of B2B', *Business Review Weekly*, 14 July, pp. 74–83.

44. Ramsdell 2000.

CHAPTER 3

THE TECHNOLOGY OF BUSINESS TO CONSUMER ELECTRONIC COMMERCE

Learning objectives

You will have mastered the material in this chapter when you can:

- describe the basic web computing model and how it supports passive B2C tasks such as marketing
- understand how the basic web computing model can be extended to perform business transactions
- explain the significance of state information in web B2C transactions
- describe different programming approaches that can be used to implement B2C applications
- discuss the security aspects of web B2C transactions.

'In a market economy, anybody can trade with anybody, and they don't have to go to a market square to do it. What they do need, however, are a few practices everyone has to agree to, such as the currency used for trade, and the rules of fair trading. The equivalent of rules for trading, on the Web, are the rules about what a URL means as an address, and the language the computers use — HTTP — whose rules define things like which one speaks first, and how they speak in turn.'

Tim Berners-Lee 1999, *Weaving the Web: The Past, Present and Future of the World Wide Web by Its Inventor*, Orion Business Books, London, p. 39.

INTRODUCTION

B2C commerce relies on having a common, readily available and agreed-upon method of communication between the business and the consumer. To date, the telephone has fulfilled this role; however, it is restricted in this capacity. Although the telephone is a practically ubiquitous form of communication, it has a very poor user interface, which limits its usefulness for B2C commerce applications. While many businesses use the telephone to facilitate the automation of client-oriented tasks such as inquiries and bill payments, the telephone is limited to voice input and numeric input via the keypad. Numeric input via the keypad severely restricts the range of data entry options available, and voice input requires human intervention at some stage, thus negating the advantages of automating the B2C connection.

In contrast to the telephone, the World Wide Web offers a very rich set of interface options that include not only complete alphanumeric data options but also multimedia and mouse-operated hypertext to tailor the appearance of the interface. While the Web is not yet a ubiquitous means of communication like the telephone, it is well on the way to achieving this status. Internet penetration into Australian households is increasing rapidly: as of May 2000, 33 per cent of Australian homes had Internet access, compared with 22 per cent in May 1999 and 14 per cent in May 1998.[1]

Owing to factors such as ease of use, platform independence and its non-proprietary nature, the Web has become a widely used communication channel for B2C commerce. While other systems such as Wireless Application Protocol (WAP) capable mobile phones are also enabling technologies for B2C commerce, such systems largely derive from or in some way resemble the web model. So we will examine the web model in detail as a channel for B2C transactions.

THE BASIC WEB COMPUTING MODEL

The World Wide Web computing model is a form of **client/server computing**. Web browsers are clients that make use of facilities provided by a web server. With this approach, the processing required to perform a function is effectively divided in two and distributed between the client and the server. A client computer requests services from a server, which performs some processing as a result of the request and then provides a response. Upon receiving the response, the client also does some processing. In the web model, the browser is mainly responsible for providing the user interface to processes that are performed on the web server. The standard components of the web client/server model are **Hypertext Markup Language (HTML)**, **Hypertext Transfer Protocol (HTTP)** and Transmission Control Protocol/Internet Protocol (IP). HTML provides the user interface detail, HTTP provides a set of commands for requesting services and receiving responses, and TCP/IP provides a means of communication between the browser and the server. The basic web client/server model is shown in diagrammatic form in figure 3.1.

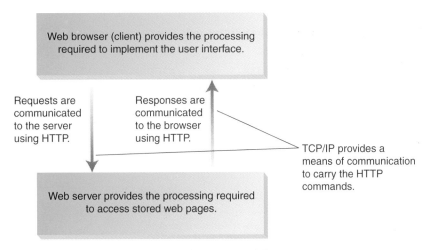

FIGURE 3.1: The basic web client/server model

HTML

HTML is, to use the words of the World Wide Web Consortium (W3C), the *lingua franca* for publishing hypertext on the World Wide Web.[2] The requisite skills for writing HTML are well documented and beyond the scope of a single chapter, so we will resist the urge to squeeze an HTML tutorial into this chapter. It is more important that we consider the essential design aspects of HTML and its limitations. Put very simply, HTML is the language that defines how documents appear on the Web. As with anything that is put simply, that is an oversimplification, as one of the hallmarks of HTML is that the appearance of any document can (and will) vary from browser to browser owing to factors such as browser version, configuration and screen resolution.

HTML is a scheme for marking up a document by using tags to specify four main elements. These are:

- key formatting aspects of the document
- the source and placement of images and other multimedia enhancements such as videos
- the placement and destination address of hypertext links
- meta information that describes the document without affecting its contents.

Tags are simple commands written in plain text and contained between less than (<) and greater than (>) symbols. Because they are written in plain text, HTML documents can be readily produced with any plain text editor, although most people prefer to use HTML-specific editors.

HTML documents consist of a head section and a body. The head section contains information about the document, such as its title. Normally, the contents of the head section are not displayed, but they are often used for indexing purposes by search engines. Metatags are often used in the head section to define details such as author, keywords and date of creation, details that may be used to assist in describing and therefore searching for the document. The body contains the visible portion of the document. It holds the content and defines how it should appear.

Unlike using a word processor (where you explicitly declare how a document should appear), HTML specifies *abstract* styles for formatting. The browser converts abstract format information into an actual presentation. Thus, a document written in HTML may appear differently on two different browsers owing to varying interpretations of the abstract formatting concepts. For instance, a section of text declared to be a heading can be specified as level 1 (most important) down to level 7 (least important). HTML does not define how a level 1 heading should be displayed; the browser does. As an example of how this logical definition can manifest itself as differing physical styles, one browser may be configured to display a level 1 heading as 24-point bold text using a Times New Roman font, whereas another may be configured to display the same heading as 32-point italic text using an Arial font.

HTML was first developed by Tim Berners-Lee while working at the CERN research centre in Switzerland as part of his original World Wide Web proposal. Since Tim Berners-Lee's first draft of HTML in 1992 there have been four standard versions of HTML released by the W3C. The HTML 2.0 standard, which was also published as RFC 1866, was finalised in early 1996 and defined the core HTML features that were widely agreed upon in 1994. HTML 3.2 added tables, **applets**, text-flow around images, superscripts and subscripts, while maintaining backwards compatibility with HTML 2.0. Unfortunately, it takes time to formalise standards, yet development does not slow down. While the standards were being developed, organisations such as Netscape had begun to add new features to HTML that were not included within the existing or proposed specifications. For example, frames were already in widespread use before the release of HTML 3.2, yet were not covered by the standard. Proprietary extension began to threaten the universal nature of the Web. Interoperability is only possible when standards are adhered to, so HTML 4.0 was released in December 1997. HTML 4.0 attempted to rein in the proprietary extensions that had been proliferating by adding support for style sheets, scripting, frames and embedded objects as well as improving accessibility for people with disabilities and support for multicultural usage. HTML 4.01, which was released in December 1999, fixed a number of bugs in the HTML 4.0 specification.

The evolution of HTML demonstrates an important point. The Web was never designed with e-commerce in mind. HTML was designed as a simple, platform-independent way of formatting reports for display on screen. With that goal in mind, HTML needed to support only a reasonable number of levels of headings, bold and italic text, lists, and fixed and variable width fonts. The aim was always that when the HTML document was rendered, it would be via translation of a logical concept of appearance to a physical appearance. Unfortunately, when many people design web pages they ignore this fact and expect that how a page appears on their own browser defines how it will appear on everyone else's browser. Such assumptions coupled with poor design skills result in pages that can be awkward or unpleasant to view for some users. Some developers choose to justify this by stating that their site is best viewed with a particular browser and/or at a particular screen resolution.

This practice disenfranchises potential clients by expecting them to alter their choice of viewing conditions to match the developer's requirements. By way of analogy, how would you feel if you arrived at the drive-through of a fast food restaurant only to be told that the driveway was optimised for a make and model of car that was different from yours and that therefore you could not be served!

The addition of non-standard frames by Netscape (now a part of the standard) and tables in version 3.2 of HTML have both resulted in an extension of this travesty of the original HTML design concepts. Tables are often used to implement columnar page layouts, a purpose for which they were never designed and a role in which their use is a compromise at best. Frames have two nasty habits. First, they use up the already limited screen real estate that is available on a web browser. Poor design often results in the important contents of a web site being squeezed into a subset of the screen, thus requiring the user to manually operate the scroll bar in order to read the page. Second, some users are again disenfranchised by an inability to view with frames. With older browsers that do not support frames, the user is often presented with a message telling them that the site is inaccessible to them. Visually impaired users who make use of screen readers that convert text into speech also struggle with frames.

An important addition to HTML introduced in version 4.0 is the Cascading Style Sheet (CSS). Style sheets assist in separating the formatting details from the content of the document by externally defining such details as font style, colour and size. One style sheet can then be applied to a number of documents to maintain a common look and feel. A further benefit is that end users can override a supplied style sheet with their own. This means that not only the web page authors but also the end users can alter the presentation and formatting of documents without sacrificing device independence or adding new HTML tags.[3]

As well as being a strength of HTML, simplicity is also a major weakness. SGML (Standard Generalized Markup Language), the parent language, is much more powerful but also much more complex. Extensible Markup Language (XML) was conceived as a means of bridging the gap to regain the power and flexibility of SGML without adding too much complexity. The W3C is developing XHTML as the next step in the standardisation of HTML. The approach used in XHTML is to reformulate the current HTML definition into an XML application. This has the advantages of making the XHTML standard easier to process and maintain while maintaining a high degree of backward compatibility with existing browsers. As well as bringing the rigour of XML to web pages, XHTML recognises the need to port web-style interfaces to other platforms such as mobile phones, information kiosks, personal digital assistants and pocket computers.[4]

JAVASCRIPT

JavaScript is a scripting language that is embedded within HTML and interpreted by a web browser to allow processing to be done by the browser. JavaScript was developed by Netscape and released as part of the Netscape 2.0

browser. It was originally called LiveScript, but the name was changed in order to align it more closely with **Java**. Note, though, that Java and JavaScript are not the same. JavaScript is an object-based language, whereas Java is a true object-oriented language. JavaScript is designed as a scripting language, which means that it is used to create small programs within another application, in this case a web browser. Java, on the other hand, is intended for developing more complex systems and can be used independently of a web browser. The syntax of the JavaScript language is similar in some ways to Java, which in turn is similar to C++.

Microsoft's Internet Explorer features another scripting language called VBScript, which features syntax and expressions based on Visual Basic. In an attempt to ensure compatibility with Netscape browsers, Microsoft reverse engineered JavaScript and released their own version called JScript as part of Internet Explorer 3.0. The first release of Microsoft's JScript was largely compatible with JavaScript, but there were minor differences that resulted in compatibility problems.

Netscape encouraged other manufacturers of web browsers to incorporate JavaScript and, in an attempt to standardise its use, also submitted the JavaScript language specification to the standards body ECMA (European Computer Manufacturer's Association). The result is the ECMA-262 standard for ECMAscript, which attempts to combine the best of JavaScript and Jscript.

There are now a number of versions of JavaScript, JScript and ECMAscript in use. Because of slight differences, programs written for any one particular version may not work successfully on all of the other available versions. Table 3.1 shows the versions of JavaScript and JScript incorporated in various browsers.

TABLE 3.1	BROWSER AND JAVASCRIPT VERSIONS
BROWSER	**JAVASCRIPT VERSION**
Netscape 2.0x	JavaScript 1.0
Netscape 3.0	JavaScript 1.1
Netscape 4.0	JavaScript 1.2
Netscape 4.5	JavaScript 1.3
Netscape 5.0	JavaScript 1.4
Internet Explorer 3.0	JScript v1 (can be upgraded to 2)
Internet Explorer 4.0	JScript v3 (ECMAscript compliant)
Internet Explorer 5.0	JScript v5 (ECMAscript compliant and roughly equivalent to JavaScript 1.4)

JavaScript is basically intended for client-side processing, although Netscape produce web servers that support a server-side form of JavaScript. Examples of client-side processing tasks include:

- verification of entered data, such as checking the validity of dates or ensuring that essential fields are not left blank
- performing calculations such as extended price and total price.

JavaScript is an interpreted language. The source code is passed to the run-time interpreter (which is inside the web browser). The interpreter reads one line of program code at a time, checks it for syntax errors and converts the line of code to specific instructions for the computer, which then executes them.

JavaScript code is embedded in HTML between special SCRIPT tags, as follows:

```
<SCRIPT attributes>
 JavaScript source code
</SCRIPT>
```

A typical example is:

```
<HTML>
<HEAD>
<TITLE>Example</TITLE>
<SCRIPT LANGUAGE="JavaScript">
<!-- HIDE FROM OLD BROWSERS

    code goes here

// --> STOP HIDING
</SCRIPT>
</HEAD>
<BODY>

    HTML goes here

</BODY> </HTML>
```

In general, the best place to put the <SCRIPT> and </SCRIPT> tags and Java-Script code is within the <HEAD> section of an HTML document. Not only does it keep the code in an obvious place but it also ensures that the JavaScript is loaded into the browser's memory first. If the code is located elsewhere within an HTML document, then the code might not be loaded if the user happens to activate a link or stops the download before the page has finished loading. Such a situation would result in the JavaScript code being inoperable.

It is also possible to save JavaScript as a separate file and call it from within a page, as follows:

```
<SCRIPT SRC="URL to script file"> ... </SCRIPT>
```

The filename for the JavaScript source must have the extension .JS.

```
<SCRIPT SRC="example.js"> ... </SCRIPT>
```

HTTP

In the computer world a protocol refers to a set of rules for the exchange of data between computers. HTTP is a high-level protocol that works in conjunction with TCP/IP, the group of protocols that govern data transfer over the Internet. HTTP performs four main functions.
1. It enables a web browser to request a file from a web server.
2. It enables a web server to send a file to a web browser.
3. It carries information for the web browser on how to interpret the contents of the file. For example, is it a web page, an image in GIF format or a Portable Document Format (PDF) file?
4. If a requested file cannot be sent from the web server for some reason, it carries information about the error condition.

To understand how HTTP works, let us examine what takes place when a user requests a web page by clicking on a link that points to the URL http://www.aserver.com/index.html. First, the browser looks at the URL. From this it knows:
• the protocol to be used to request the file from the server (http://)
• the host address (www.aserver.com)
• the path and file to be retrieved (/index.html).

Next, the browser contacts the server and requests the file by sending an HTTP command. The HTTP command sent to the server is GET followed by the file and the version of HTTP. This is usually followed by one or more ACCEPT statements, which tell the server which MIME types the browser can accept. Each line ends in a carriage return and the HTTP command is completed by sending a blank line. The HTTP command can also include a range of other statements to convey such information as the host address and the browser type. For example, below is a copy of the HTTP header contents for an actual request from a browser using a GET.

```
GET /index.htm HTTP/1.0
Connection: Keep-Alive
User-Agent: Mozilla/4.72 [en] (WinNT; I)
Host: 139.132.83.143
Accept: image/gif, image/jpeg, */*
```

The server's reply begins with an HTTP response header containing version information, the status of the connection and the document MIME type as well as other relevant information. Once again, this is followed by a blank line that marks the end of the HTTP component of the reply. The content of the requested file then begins immediately after the blank line. Here is an example of a typical reply.

```
HTTP/1.0 200 OK
Server: Microsoft-IIS/3.0
Date: Wed, 27 Sep 2000 07:14:34 GMT
Content-Type: text/html
Accept-Ranges: bytes
Last-Modified: Sun, 27 Aug 2000 23:30:01 GMT
Content-Length: 7117

<HTML>
<HEAD>
<TITLE> ... etc.
```

HTTP is a fairly simple protocol. Basically, the browser sends a REQUEST and the server sends a RESPONSE. There is no handshaking or acknowledgement of receipt of message from either end of the connection. Unlike in a telephone connection, neither the browser at one end nor the server at the other keep the link open after the server has responded to the browser's request. Once the server has finished sending the requested file it closes the connection and waits for the next request, so each individual web page requested, image included on a page or file downloaded requires a new and unique connection to be established over the Internet to the appropriate server. A web page that includes nine different embedded images would therefore require 10 concurrent connections to be made to the server. One consequence of this is that if the server is busy or Internet traffic is heavy, then some images may load on a page faster than others.

The two basic request types are **GET** and **POST**. In a GET request the browser is asking the server to return the contents of the specified file; the browser is 'getting' the file from the server. This type of request is associated with clicking on links and retrieving new pages.

A POST request is a request for the server to accept the presented data, and is used to send information to the server. The information sent is usually associated with a form on a web page in which the user fills out details that have to be sent to the server for processing. **Forms** will be discussed later in this chapter. It is the ability to return information that allows us to develop interactive applications over the Web. A request to 'get' a file can also include a limited amount of other information that is passed on to the server, so a GET can also be used for interactive applications.

The first line of the response from the server always contains the protocol version number followed by a message that tells the browser whether its request was successful or not. The result of the request is given as a three-digit status code followed by a short message. The usual response for a successful request is '200 OK'. The remainder of the HTTP response consists of a response header containing information, especially about content type (or MIME-type) and size, followed by a blank line and then the body of the request. The body is typically the HTML code for a requested web page, or the binary data for an image or other type of requested file. (HTTP/1.0 specifications can be found at www.ietf.org/rfc/rfc1945.txt. HTTP/1.1 specifications are at ftp://ftp.isi.edu/in-notes/rfc2616.txt.)

A HANDS-ON INTRODUCTION TO HTTP

By following a few simple steps you can communicate with a web server and pretend to be a web browser by sending your own HTTP commands. This will enable you to observe first hand the interaction that takes place between browser and server when a page is requested. Simply start up *telnet* on your computer and follow the instructions. The instructions have been written for Microsoft's telnet, which comes with Windows, but the same technique can be used with any telnet program on any computer.

1. From the menu select *Terminal...Preferences* and then make sure the tick is selected in the checkbox for *Local Echo*. This step is necessary so that you can see what you are typing.
2. From the menu select *Terminal...Start Logging*, enter a suitable name for a log file and click on *Open*. This will capture all the text that is received into a file for later viewing.
3. From the menu select *Connect...Remote System*.
4. Enter the address of the server as the *Host Name*. Do not include http:// as part of the address.
5. Enter 80 as the *Port* value and click on *Connect*. The terminal type does not matter.
6. Whatever you type now will be sent to the web server. Type in the following HTTP command exactly as shown and then press the [Enter] key twice.

   ```
   GET / HTTP/1.0
   ```

7. You will now see the result of the request displayed on the screen followed by a prompt that says 'Connection to host lost'.
8. From the menu select *Terminal...Stop Logging*. You can now open the captured file with Notepad or another word processor to examine the response, which will begin with lines of HTTP.

TCP/IP

TCP/IP is a suite of protocols that was originally developed by the Advanced Research Project Agency (ARPA) of the US Department of Defense for connecting different computer platforms. Since its original development it has evolved to the point where it is now a de facto standard that forms the basis of communication over the Internet. The two main protocols involved in TCP/IP are Transmission Control Protocol (TCP) and the Internet Protocol (IP), hence the name.

With web communication, HTTP makes use of TCP in order to establish a communication session with a remote computer (either a browser or a server). While HTTP is responsible specifically for managing the interaction and communication between web servers and browsers, TCP is responsible for the error-free delivery of an entire message from a source computer to an addressed computer, irrespective of what data are contained in the message. The contents of HTTP requests and responses are passed to TCP, which concerns itself only with the addresses. Each message is broken up into small packets of data known as datagrams, which are then passed to IP, which is responsible for the transport of each individual datagram.

IP is the basic transport mechanism of the Internet. IP datagrams are individual entities that on their own do not represent a transmitted message. By analogy, breaking a message into datagrams is like breaking a book down into pages and sending each separately in its own envelope. The message is not received until all datagrams have been received and assembled in the correct order; the act of transmission does not involve a dedicated communication session. The end-to-end communication that takes place via TCP is referred to as a virtual connection; at the IP level, datagrams provide connectionless communication.

The conversion between the binary and the decimal form is shown in table 3.2 and is based on the fact that each binary digit (normally referred to as a bit) represents the absence or presence of a number from a power series based on the number 2. By analogy, our normal numbering system is base 10, and each decimal digit represents a value from a power series based on the number 10. With binary numbers, instead of having units, tens, hundreds and thousands columns as we do with decimal numbers, we have columns representing 1s, 2s, 4s, 8s and so on. As we move to the left through a binary number, each bit is worth twice the previous bit.

TABLE 3.2		CONVERSION OF A BINARY IP ADDRESS TO ITS DECIMAL FORM						
128	64	32	16	8	4	2	1	← Decimal value of each bit
1	1	0	0	1	0	0	1	128 + 64 + 8 + 1 = 201
0	0	1	0	1	1	1	0	32 + 8 + 4 +2 = 46
1	1	1	0	0	1	1	0	128 + 64 + 32 + 4 + 2 = 230
1	1	0	1	1	0	1	0	128 + 64 + 16 + 8 + 2 = 218

Each IP datagram includes a source address, destination address, the raw data encapsulated for transmission and some error detection information to help guard against transmission errors. The source and destination addresses are unique 32-bit binary numbers, which are normally represented in dotted quad form to make them readable. A dotted quad address consists of four numbers in the range of 0 to 255 separated by full stops. Each number, then, represents 8 out of the 32 bits of the IP address. For example, the IP address of www.microsoft.com as a 32-bit binary number is:

11001001 00101110 11100110 11011010

However, this is better represented for human consumption as 201.46.230.218.

IP is both the strength and the weakness of the Internet. It is IP that enables each computer on the Internet to exist as a unique entity and communicate with any other computer with an IP address. The TCP/IP protocol suite has existed for more than 20 years and the current version of IP is version 4 (IPv4). Rapid growth of the Internet has stretched TCP/IP close to its limit, since many of our modern requirements were never considered in the original design. One significant issue involves the addressing scheme. IP version 4 is limited to 32-bit addresses, which gives a theoretical maximum of $4\,294\,967\,296$ addresses, although in practice fewer addresses than this are actually available. It has been predicted that with the current rate of growth of usage of the Internet we will run out of IP addresses by 2010 or even earlier. IP version 6 (IPv6) will feature a 128-bit addressing scheme, which will provide around 3.4×10^{38} addresses — which should meet all foreseeable needs, even allowing, for example, for dedicated IP addresses for appliances and telephones in order to permit Internet control.

EXTENDING THE WEB COMPUTING MODEL TO PERFORM TRANSACTIONS

The web model that we have looked at so far is suitable for providing a basic web presence for marketing purposes but does not allow for transactions to be performed. In order to perform business transactions, such as purchases on line, we need a model that is capable of both interactivity and centralised storage of the transaction data. The interactivity is made possible through the use of HTML forms and the centralised storage is made available via the web server. The question then is where does the processing take place?

If we consider a standard database application such as Microsoft Access, we can view it as consisting of three main functional components. These are:
- *presentation services:* the user interface and display
- *functional logic:* routines associated with querying the database, processing the data and formatting the information
- *data management:* storage and retrieval from database files.

In a typical stand-alone database application (for example one based on Microsoft Access), all three functions are performed within the one computer. Client/server computing divides these functions into processes that are performed over two or more computers. For example, a web browser is a process running on a computer at the user end (a client computer), whereas a web server is a process running on a computer at the remote end (a server computer). With client/server architecture, client processes request services and data from server processes. Clients and servers are typically separate computers and exchange messages and data over a network.

In two-tiered client/server computing, the client talks directly to the server with no other intervening processes. Two-tiered client/server architectures, as shown in figure 3.2, are often characterised as 'fat client/thin server' or '**thin client**/fat server'. A third possibility, known as a 'distributed function' model, is to share the processing required for the logic layer.

In general, clients manage the user interface, validate data entered by the user, dispatch requests to server programs and execute some business logic. Servers accept requests from clients, execute database retrieval and updates, manage data integrity, control transactions, execute business logic and send data back to clients.

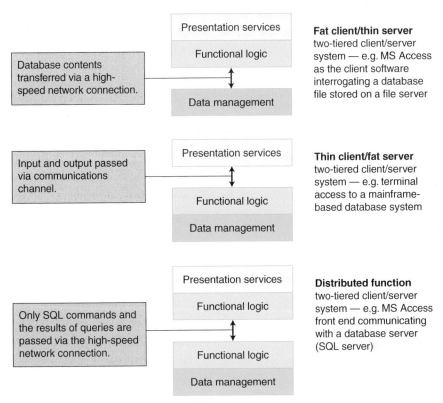

Fat client/thin server
two-tiered client/server system — e.g. MS Access as the client software interrogating a database file stored on a file server

Thin client/fat server
two-tiered client/server system — e.g. terminal access to a mainframe-based database system

Distributed function
two-tiered client/server system — e.g. MS Access front end communicating with a database server (SQL server)

Presentation services

Functional logic

Database contents transferred via a high-speed network connection.

Data management

Presentation services

Input and output passed via communications channel.

Functional logic

Data management

Presentation services

Functional logic

Only SQL commands and the results of queries are passed via the high-speed network connection.

Functional logic

Data management

FIGURE 3.2: Client/server models

Three-tiered client/server computing introduces a third layer of processing between the client and the server. It shifts some processing away from both the client and the server to allow for 'thin client' and/or 'thin server'. The middle layer can potentially handle such diverse tasks as transaction tracking, business logic, resource control, security, authentication, report generation and translation from legacy applications.

Separation of presentation, functional logic and data means that the presentation tier can be tailored to meet the needs of the user without affecting the logic tier or the data tier. It also means that different languages and technologies can be used for each tier of the system, allowing for greater choice of system components. Software designed to act as the middle tier of a three-tier system is referred to as 'middleware'.

Web-based B2C systems are typically three-tiered applications, although thin client and distributed function models are also possible. With three-tiered systems, the middleware component is usually associated with the web server, and communication with the data management layer may be facilitated by such technologies as **Open Database Connectivity (ODBC)**, **Java Database Connectivity (JDBC)**, **Distributed Component Object Model (DCOM)** and **Common Object Request Broker Architecture (CORBA)**.

ODBC is an Application Program Interface (API) developed by Microsoft that standardises the interface to a range of database servers. ODBC provides a layer of abstraction between an application and a database so that the application does not need to know proprietary details. You can think of the abstraction layer as being like a translator that converts database requests from the web server into commands that the database server understands. Each database server has its own ODBC driver that converts Structure Query Language (SQL) commands to native commands and translates the output to a compatible form. SQL is a programming language that is used by nearly all contemporary database engines. JDBC, which was developed by Sun Microsystems, is modelled on ODBC and allows Java applications to access a wide range of databases. Because it is written in Java it is able to function on operating systems other than Microsoft's Windows.

DCOM and CORBA are two competing standards for creating distributed systems by integrating objects that are distributed over a network. For example, DCOM can be used to create a complex system by linking together existing applications such as Microsoft Access and Excel using Object Linking and Embedding (OLE) and **ActiveX** components. DCOM is a Microsoft standard that applies only to the Windows operating system, whereas CORBA is also available for other operating systems.

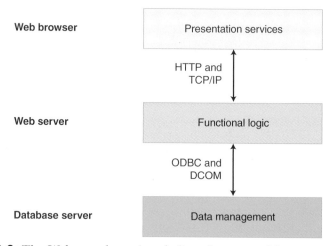

FIGURE 3.3: The Web as a three-tiered client/server architecture

Figure 3.3 shows generically how the web model operates as a three-tiered client/server architecture, although variations on this do exist. For example, it is not uncommon for some of the functional logic to be carried out on the browser as well as on the web server. It is also technically feasible for the one physical computer to act as both web server and database server.

FORMS

A form is a section of HTML code that defines a user interface on a web page to allow the user to enter data that can then be sent to the server for processing. For example, in the case of an online purchase, the user would be prompted to enter a name, address, product number, purchase quantity and credit card number. The entered data would be sent to the server when the user clicks on the form's *Submit* button. Forms are defined by declaring a block between <FORM> and </FORM> tags and then defining the required elements within the block. When defining a form for input, two important attributes must be set: ACTION and METHOD. ACTION specifies the URL that will be contacted when the form is submitted by clicking on the submit button. This URL normally points to a server-based process such as a CGI script that will accept the values entered into the form. METHOD specifies whether a GET or a POST is used by the browser in order to send the data to the server. These two methods will be discussed later. Table 3.3 lists the standard form elements and how they are used.

TABLE 3.3	FORM ELEMENTS AND THEIR APPLICATION
FORM ELEMENT	**HOW IT IS USED**
Text box	Provides a single-line field to allow entry of text. The basic input element for most field-oriented data entries
Multi-line text box	Similar to a text box but allows for multiple lines of text. Often used for tasks such as feedback forms and web-based email systems
Password box	Similar to a text box but entered text is displayed as an asterisk to maintain confidentiality
Checkbox	Provides a 'tick the box'–type field for data entry requiring a Yes/No reply
Radio button	Provides a way of selecting one and only one from a number of options.
Hidden field	Provides a way of holding data without displaying it. The contents will be passed to the server as for other fields but the user cannot change them. Useful for storing temporary information such as a **Session ID**. The contents of the hidden field are usually set when the page is first loaded.
Image	Provides a way of creating an input control with a custom appearance that operates like a button
Select box	Provides a way of selecting one or more items from a presented list. Operates similarly to a drop-down menu
Submit button	Sends the contents of all elements defined within the form to the URL specified by the ACTION attribute using the specified method
Reset button	Resets the contents of all elements back to their initial values

Most form elements are specified using the <INPUT> tag along with the details of the required control, as follows:

```
<INPUT
   TYPE="control type"
   NAME="control name"
   VALUE="default value">
```

where TYPE may be set to text, password, radio, checkbox, hidden, image, submit or reset.

The NAME attribute is especially important. Its value must be unique (that is, no two controls can share the same name), since NAME is used by the script to access the VALUE currently set for that control. For example, with a `text` type control, the value made available to the script corresponds to what the user has typed in.

Form elements can also act as both inputs and outputs for JavaScript. When used in conjunction with JavaScript, each element is treated as an object within the JavaScript language and each object has a number of events associated with it that can initiate a JavaScript function. For example, a text box could use an `onChange` event to initiate a function that checks whether the entered data comprise a valid email address.

SENDING DATA VIA HTTP

Data are sent as NAME=VALUE pairs, where NAME is the name of a control on the form and VALUE represents the current contents of that control. If there is more than one NAME=VALUE pair, then each pair is separated from the others by an ampersand character (&). How the NAME=VALUE pairs are sent depends on whether the method specified on the form is a GET or a POST.

If the method used for communicating with the web server is GET, then when the submit button is pressed, the contents of the form are appended to the URL and sent to the server as if it was requesting a page. The URL and form data sent together as part of the GET request appear as follows:

```
action?name=value&name=value&name=value
```

where 'action' represents the URL specified by the ACTION attribute of the FORM tag. The action ends with a question mark. For example:

```
/cgi-bin/test.pl?Surname=Jones&Firstname=Tom
```

The resulting HTTP header contents would then be:

```
GET /cgi-bin/test.pl?Surname=Jones&Firstname=Tom
  HTTP/1.0
Connection: Keep-Alive
User-Agent: Mozilla/4.72 [en] (WinNT; I)
Host: 139.132.83.143
Accept: image/gif, image/jpeg, */*
```

If the method used for communicating with the web server is POST, then the contents of the form are encoded exactly as with the GET method, but rather than appending them to the URL, the contents are sent in a data block as part of the POST operation. For example, the HTTP header contents for the same data sent using a POST would be as follows.

```
POST /cgi-bin/test.exe HTTP/1.0
Connection: Keep-Alive
User-Agent: Mozilla/4.72 [en] (WinNT; I)
Host: 139.132.83.143
Accept: image/gif, image/jpeg, */*
Content-Length: 27

Surname=Jones&Firstname=Tom
```

In general, POST is preferred to GET, since there are no limits on the amount of data that can be sent. With GET, long lines may cause problems. However, before specifying the method in the <FORM> tag, you should consult with the web server administrator and check what the CGI script is expecting to receive.

THE COMMON GATEWAY INTERFACE

The term **Common Gateway Interface (CGI)** refers to the defined standard method for the web server to communicate with a script. It defines how the user data (which have been sent from a form on a web page) are passed from the web server to the script and how the script passes its output back to the server. CGI defines two main sources of input data available to scripts. These are:

- **environment variables**
- **standard input** (stdin).

Input data from a form that the browser has sent during a POST request are received by the web server via HTTP. Before the server invokes a script, it fills out the environment variables defined by the CGI with the data that are to be passed into the CGI script. Figure 3.4 shows the main elements of the interaction and identifies seven steps in this interaction, which we will expand upon with a simple example. Please note that this example is intentionally trivial in terms of the processing and what is achieved so that the details of the steps are not masked by unnecessary complexity.

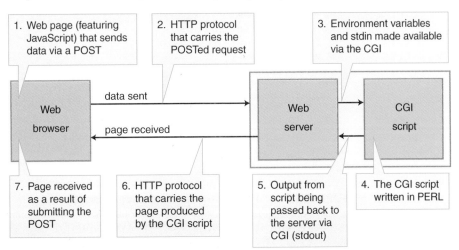

FIGURE 3.4: Seven steps in the interaction between a web browser and a CGI script

STEP 1. THE WEB PAGE THAT POSTS THE DATA

The web page currently being viewed by the browser has already been retrieved via a GET request. The HTML code for this page follows and the actual output that is displayed on the browser is shown in figure 3.5. Points that are important to our example are:

- the form defined within the HTML
- the form ACTION that points to a CGI script called 'demo.pl'
- the form METHOD is a POST
- the JavaScript embedded in the page that will perform some processing (data validation in this case) before invoking the CGI script.

```
<HTML> <HEAD>
<TITLE>Demonstration</TITLE>
<SCRIPT>
<!--
function validateForm(form) {
if (!checkFilled(document.demoform.textstring))
   return false;
else
   return true;
}

function checkFilled(textfield) {
   if (textfield.value.length == 0) {
      alert("A value is required!");
      textfield.focus();
      return false;
   } else
      return true;
}
//-->
</SCRIPT> </HEAD>
<BODY>
<H1>Enter some Text</H1>
<FORM NAME="demoform"
   ACTION=/cgi-bin/demo.pl"
   METHOD="POST"
   OnSubmit="return validateForm(this)">
<INPUT TYPE="text" NAME="textstring">
<INPUT TYPE="submit" VALUE="Submit">
</FORM>
</BODY> </HTML>
```

FIGURE 3.5:

The browser display for step 1 of the browser–CGI script interaction example

STEP 2. THE HTTP PROTOCOL THAT CARRIES THE REQUEST

The contents of the HTTP protocol that carries the request and the form data from the browser to the web server are as follows:

```
POST / HTTP/1.0
Referer: http://www.demo.com/frontend.html
Connection: Keep-Alive
User-Agent: Mozilla/4.72 [en] (WinNT; I)
Host: 139.132.83.143
Accept: image/gif, image/jpeg, */*
Content-type: application/x-www-form-urlencoded
Content-length: 15


textstring=FRED
```

Important points to note here are:
- the POST command as the first line
- the attached data for the POST request (textstring=FRED), which tells the server that the user has typed 'FRED' into an object called 'textstring'
- the content length of the posted data (15), which describes the number of characters in 'textstring=FRED'.

If the form had used a GET instead of a POST, then the first line of the HTTP would have been:

```
GET /cgi-bin/demo.pl?textstring=FRED HTTP/1.0
```

STEP 3. THE ENVIRONMENT VARIABLES AND STANDARD INPUT

The environment variables that would be set are as follows:

```
GATEWAY_INTERFACE=CGI/1.1
CONTENT_TYPE=x-www-form-urlencoded
CONTENT_LENGTH=15
HTTP_ACCEPT= image/gif, image/jpeg, */*
HTTP_USER_AGENT= Mozilla/4.72 [en] (WinNT; I)
REMOTE_ADDR=139.132.83.143
SERVER_SOFTWARE=Apache/1.1
QUERY_STRING=
REQUEST_METHOD=POST
```

The significant points to note about the environment variables and standard input are:
- the CONTENT_LENGTH of 15, which derives from the HTTP contents
- the REQUEST_METHOD of POST, which also derives from the HTTP contents.

Standard input would pass across the body of the POSTed document as follows:

```
textstring=FRED
```

If the form had used a GET, then there would be no standard input and the last two environment variables would be:

```
QUERY_STRING=textstring=FRED
REQUEST_METHOD=GET
```

STEP 4. THE PERL SCRIPT THAT PROCESSES THE REQUEST

The **Perl** script that receives the form data is as follows:

```perl
#!/usr/local/bin/perl
require "cgi-lib.pl";

MAIN:
{
# Read in all the variables set by the form
  &ReadParse(*input);

# Print the header
  print &PrintHeader;
  print "<html><head>\n";
  print "<title>Demo form output</title>\n";
  print "</head>\n<body>\n";

print <<ENDOFTEXT;

<H1>This is the output of our demo</H1>

You entered $input{'textstring'}
<P>

ENDOFTEXT

# Close the document cleanly.
  print "</body></html>\n";
}
```

The important points to note about the script are that it:
- retrieves the typed information from the form
- creates a new web page and 'prints' it to the web server.

STEP 5. THE OUTPUT FROM THE SCRIPT

The result of running the script is that the following lines are effectively 'printed' to **standard output**, which then becomes an input to the web server.

```
Content-type: text/html

<html><head>
<title>Demo form output</title>
</head>
<body>
<H1>This is the output of our demo</H1>

You entered FRED
<P>
</body></html>
```

In this example the HTTP component consists of only two lines: the `Content-type` followed by a blank line. The remainder consists of the data that are sent by the HTTP protocol — in other words, the HTML for the web page.

STEP 6. THE HTTP PROTOCOL

The HTTP contents that transfer the resultant web page from the web server to the browser are as follows:

```
HTTP/1.0 200 OK
Content-type: text/html

<html><head>
<title>Demo form output</title>
</head>
<body>
<H1>This is the output of our demo</H1>

You entered FRED
<P>
</body></html>
```

The output from the script is passed through the server; hence, this is the same as for the previous step with one significant addition: the first line that specifies the protocol version and result of the request.

HTTP-based interaction between a client and a server includes a header that contains information about either the request (from the client to the server) or the response (from the server to the client).

STEP 7. THE WEB PAGE RECEIVED

Figure 3.6 shows the HTML produced by the script as it would be displayed on a browser.

FIGURE 3.6: The displayed web page. Step 7 of the browser–CGI script interaction example

STATE INFORMATION

Every time a person accesses a web page or invokes a CGI script, the server responds as if it were the first time. There is no record of a person contacting the server before because the protocol used to facilitate web communication, HTTP, is **stateless** in nature. This means that when a browser contacts a web server, the server has no knowledge of previous requests made by the browser, neither does it maintain an ongoing communication session with the browser once the required page has been served. Each request for a web page is therefore a new communication with no carry-over of status or 'state' information from a previous communication. This can be a problem when you consider that a transaction may run over a long period of time. For example, when a person is selecting items to place in an online shopping trolley, each page that is viewed is treated as a separate entity, yet the server needs some way of letting the person gradually build up a list of required items that does not disappear each time the person links to a new page. How do we get around this? There are three basic techniques to choose from. We can use:

• cookies
• embedded session information in a URL
• hidden fields in a form.

COOKIES

Cookies were designed to overcome the stateless nature of the Web by providing a way of maintaining state information between client requests. Cookies are useful for having the browser remember specific information, such as the location within a site of a user's last visit, time spent or user preferences.

A cookie is just a small packet of data that is sent by a web server to a browser as part of the HTTP header. The cookie is stored by the browser on the client computer and, once set, can be read by a server on a subsequent visit only if it is the same web server that sent the cookie initially. The data stored in the cookie can be used, among other things, to uniquely identify a client over multi-page accesses, thus creating the essential link between multiple pages to establish a session for a transaction. Cookies are used for such tasks as:

• storing passwords and user IDs for specific web sites. Many subscription-based online databases use this scheme.

- storing preferences for start pages (site personalisation). Microsoft and Netscape use cookies in order to implement personalised starting pages on their web sites.
- passing data between forms for applications such as online ordering systems and shopping trolleys. When used with online ordering systems, the cookie holds a list of the items to be purchased before the transaction is committed.
- web site tracking.

In essence, a cookie can contain a number of items of information. Each item of information has a name and a value. For example, a cookie may contain a data item called `userID` and its associated value. Cookies can also contain information such as when the cookie is to expire. Cookies are stored for a predetermined period of time. When the cookie is created, it can be given an expiry time and date if required. Cookies that have a definite expiry time and date are stored in the cookies.txt file on the client machine until the expiration time and date are reached. Cookies that do not have an expiry time set are valid for the current session only and are stored only in memory.

Although cookies are an excellent way of maintaining state information between web pages, they are not without their problems. Cookies are not a part of an official standard for HTML or HTTP; they were created by Netscape and later adopted by other browser manufacturers such as Microsoft. Despite their widespread acceptance, there are often annoying differences between the way they are handled by different browsers. There is no guarantee that a web-based system that relies on cookies will always work correctly, and users have the option of telling the browser not to accept them. Also, caches and proxy servers can interrupt the passing of cookies, resulting in some strange interactions between browsers and servers.

Some people regard the use of cookies as an invasion of privacy, as they enable Webmasters to track where you travel over their particular web site. Privacy and the ethics associated with using cookies are discussed in chapter 10.

EMBEDDING SESSION INFORMATION IN A URL

A **session ID** provides a unique identifier for a user so that multi-page accesses can be linked. By keeping track of session ID, the server is able to relate a user to a previous connection and thus create a virtual session. That way, data sent from one page can be matched up with data sent from another in order to complete a transaction that occurs over multiple pages. Session IDs can be implemented by appending state information onto the *additional path information* at the end of the URL. This information becomes input data for a CGI script, which is then responsible for the task of collating and processing the inputs from multiple individual sessions in order to create the virtual session.

HIDDEN FIELDS

Hidden fields can be used to store state information but are also useful for passing data back from the server to a JavaScript program. When used to store state information, the server produces a form that contains the required information as values stored in hidden fields. When the form is submitted to the server, the values in the hidden fields are also sent back to the server; thus, the state information is maintained.

Server-side processing can occur in a number of ways. Three basic approaches commonly used to support the custom development of programs for server-side processing are:

- the CGI model
- the Application Program Interface model
- the embedded script model.

With the CGI model, prompted by the result of a request from a browser, small programs called CGI scripts are run on the web server. If a requested URL points to a script instead of a file (such as a web page or graphic file) the web server loads and executes the script. CGI scripts are executed in real time, producing HTML as their output, the content produced dynamically by the script in response to the user's request. Web pages can be generated with unique contents that are determined while the script is running, typically as the result of interrogating a file or database on the server. A common example of this is when a search engine provides the user with the results of a query.

When looking at requests and URLs, CGI scripts can be differentiated from normal web pages in two ways. First, CGI scripts can usually be identified by the filename extension, which can be CGI or PL for scripts written in Perl, or EXE for scripts written in C++ and similar compiled languages. Second, CGI scripts are usually stored in a specific directory of the server to keep them separate from normal web pages. Typically, the directory for scripts is called /cgi-bin, hence this often occurs as part of the URL. Any requested file that is located in the /cgi-bin directory is treated as a script to be executed rather than served directly as a web page. It is therefore not possible to view the contents of a script from a browser.

Unlike most computer programs, there is no user interaction or graphical interface possible when CGI scripts are called, as they operate as a batch process. That means that when a CGI script is run, it takes the input data given by the Common Gateway Interface, processes these data, passes the output back to the server via the Common Gateway Interface, and then stops. Since CGI scripts typically receive input from forms on web pages, which they use as the basis for processing, and pass their output back as HTML, the web browser not only is the client but also provides the user interface.

The Application Program Interface (API) model provides a more efficient, if slightly less standardised, alternative to CGI. In theory, an API is a way of extending the functionality of a web server by adding extra program code to it via a predefined software interface that is in some ways analogous to the way that a plug-in can extend the functionality of a web browser. For example, a custom-developed dynamic link library (DLL) file can be added to a server running on a Windows NT computer to enable it to provide custom features. This approach is more efficient as the DLL code effectively becomes a permanent part of the server's code, thus eliminating the need for loading program code on demand and passing data back and forth across an interface, as occurs with CGI scripts. Unfortunately, there are two different API standards commonly used with web servers. Netscape produced a standard for its web servers known as NSAPI, and Microsoft produced a similar but incompatible standard for its Internet Information Server (IIS) and personal web server known as ISAPI. In order to be as versatile as possible, some web servers support both NSAPI and ISAPI as well as CGI.

PERL

In theory, any programming language can be used for creating CGI scripts. Common languages in use include Perl, Visual Basic, C++ and Pascal. Perl is commonly used for creating CGI scripts for a number of reasons. First, it is available for almost any computer platform. It is mostly used with Unix-based web servers but Windows and Apple versions of Perl are available, which means that Perl scripts can generally be used on any web server. Second, Perl is an excellent language for text processing tasks such as finding documents that contain keywords (web searches). Third, there are many freely available Perl scripts to implement common tasks such as search engines, site guest books, emailing of web form data, and online shopping trolleys.

PHP, ACTIVE SERVER PAGES AND COLDFUSION

With a CGI script written in a language such as Perl, the script itself is responsible for the creation of the HTML and the content required to produce each web page. In effect, the essential elements of the web page are embedded within the script. While this approach would seem straightforward to a person with a strong background in programming, it does tend to make the web page layout difficult to update.

An alternative approach is to embed lines of script within HTML files. Instead of having a script on a server that contains or reads in HTML, we have an HTML document that contains a script in much the same way as we embed JavaScript, except that in this case the script will be executed by the server instead. This approach is exemplified by three commonly used products: **Active Server Pages (ASP)**, **ColdFusion** and **PHP**. Figure 3.7 shows how the server processes the embedded script in order to produce a web document that contains only HTML (that is, no embedded script).

FIGURE 3.7: Processing the embedded script to produce a web page

Such scripting languages for server-side processing may take the form of extra HTML tags that are processed by the server extension (e.g. ColdFusion) or languages that resemble JavaScript or VBScript (Active Server Pages) and exist between <SCRIPT> and </SCRIPT> tags.

COLDFUSION

ColdFusion is a middleware product that was designed to make it easy to link web pages to standard databases. The user interface consists of ColdFusion Markup Language (CFML) tags embedded inside the HTML of web pages' *templates*. CFML tags allow SQL database commands to be built directly into the web page templates. The server processing consists of either an API link or a small CGI executable program (depending on the server being used) that links to the ColdFusion middleware, which in turn interacts with the database. No extra client-side software is required.

ColdFusion is available for a range of Windows NT, Windows 95 and Solaris-based servers. On Windows NT servers, the ColdFusion middleware component operates as a Windows NT system service program, which means that it is always running as a background process — hence, there is no delay while it loads.

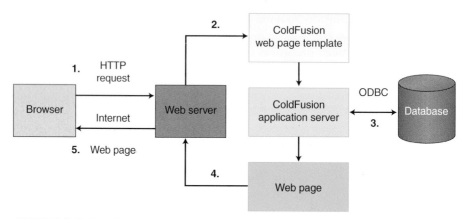

FIGURE 3.8: Producing a web document from a ColdFusion template

Figure 3.8 shows the steps involved in producing a web document from a ColdFusion template. These steps can be described as follows.
1. The user activates a link to a ColdFusion web page template (with a CFM or CFML extension) and sends an HTTP request to the server.
2. The web server retrieves the CFML file and passes it into the ColdFusion Application Server (effectively an extension of the server).
3. The ColdFusion Application Server processes the ColdFusion Markup Language (CFML) tags in the template. This typically involves interrogating a database via ODBC.
4. The results of processing the CFML are substituted into the file and HTML is not changed. The result is a web page with information that has been created dynamically.
5. The produced web page is sent to the browser.

Here is an example of a form on a web page template incorporating the CFML tags that calls a ColdFusion page and passes a value back to ColdFusion for processing. Note that the form's action attribute (shown in bold) and the text box name (also shown in bold) are structured in the same way as CGI scripts.

```
<HTML>
<HEAD>
<TITLE>ColdFusion Demo Page 1</TITLE>
</HEAD>
<BODY>
<H2>Enter a Message</H2>
<FORM
    ACTION="/cfdocs/demopage2.cfm"
    METHOD="post">
<INPUT
    TYPE="text"
    NAME="Message">
<INPUT
    TYPE="submit"
    VALUE="Submit">
</FORM>
</BODY>
</HTML>
```

The following code shows the template incorporating the ColdFusion commands (shown in bold). In this example, the field named 'message' from the form is returned.

```
<HTML>
<HEAD>
<TITLE>ColdFusion Demo Page 2</TITLE>
</HEAD>
<BODY>
<CFOUTPUT>
<H2>#Form.Message#</H2>
</CFOUTPUT>
</BODY>
</HTML>
```

On the following page we present an example of a more complex ColdFusion web page template that performs a database query. The first line of the query component establishes the source of the data. NAME="CourseList" specifies the name of the table of data that is being examined. The second line contains the SQL query that will be passed to the database. SELECT*FROM CourseList means pull out information from all the columns in the table and display them.The output component lists the fields to be displayed along with the required HTML tags for formatting. From the Output section we see the results placed under the relevant column headings, CourseNumber and CourseName.

```
<!--- Start of Database Query --->
<CFQUERY
    NAME="CourseList"
    DATASOURCE="cfsnippets">
SELECT * FROM CourseList
</CFQUERY>
<!--- End of Query -- ->

<HTML>
<HEAD>
<TITLE>Department List</TITLE>
</HEAD>
<BODY>
<H2>Course List</H2>

<!--- Start of Output Block -- ->
<CFOUTPUT QUERY="CourseList">
(#CourseNumber#)</B> #CourseName#<BR>
</CFOUTPUT>
<!--- End of Output Block --->

</BODY>
</HTML>
```

ACTIVE SERVER PAGES

Active Server Pages (usually referred to by the acronym of ASP) are a form of server-side scripting technology developed by Microsoft and based on their Visual Basic language. Basically, Active Server Pages are a server-side equivalent of VBScript.

As for Perl scripts and ColdFusion, Active Server Pages can produce web pages dynamically and can be integrated (or connected) with server-side databases.

ASP embeds the scripting language in HTML documents. As with Cold-Fusion templates, ASP files contain both HTML and scripting commands. There are, however, differences between ColdFusion and Active Server Pages. Single lines of Active Server script or small blocks of code are contained between <% and %>. Script commands embedded this way are processed by the server and the results of processing are included in the output. Anything outside of these delimiters is assumed to be HTML and passed straight on to the browser by the server.

Procedures can be defined between <SCRIPT> and </SCRIPT> tags in a similar fashion to JavaScript. Note, however, that the script must specify that the language is VBScript and that the code is to be run at the server. The following line of code demonstrates the syntax for achieving this:

```
<SCRIPT LANGUAGE=VBScript RunAt=server>
```

In addition to being able to receive data from the browser via POST and GET, Active Server Pages can also communicate with each other using a facility called 'session variables'. This is effectively a built-in, predefined use of cookies that is designed to help overcome the stateless nature of HTTP. Session variables can be created and manipulated by ASP documents to maintain state information between web pages. For example, in the first page presented to a user, the user can log into the web system. A *LoggedIn* session variable can be initialised as follows:

```
Session("LoggedIn") = "yes"
```

Here is a simple example of an ASP document, which uses a session variable to determine if the client is logged into the web application. (A common error made by programmers is to omit one or other part of the delimiter <%, %>. Always check that if you have opened a delimiter, you have also remembered to close it.)

```
<HTML>
<HEAD>
<TITLE>ASP Test 1</TITLE>
</HEAD>
<BODY>
<%   If Session("LoggedIn") = "" Then %>
        You are not currently logged in.
<%   Else %>
        You are currently logged in.
<%   End If %>
</BODY>
</HTML>
```

In this example, if the session variable has been initialised, the web browser will receive the following web document.

```
<HTML>
<HEAD>
<TITLE>ASP Test 1</TITLE>
</HEAD>
<BODY>
        You are currently logged in.
</BODY>
</HTML>
```

If, however, the session variable has not been initialised, then the web browser will receive the following web document.

```
<HTML>
<HEAD>
<TITLE>ASP Test 1</TITLE>
</HEAD>
<BODY>
          You are not currently logged in.
</BODY>
</HTML>
```

In addition to session variables, ASP documents can access the object data from the calling document (through the POST/GET method) using the *Request* object. For example, consider the following web document that calls an ASP document.

```
<HTML>
<HEAD>
<TITLE>ASP Test 2a</TITLE>
</HEAD>
<BODY>
<FORM
      NAME="Test"
      METHOD="POST"
      ACTION="test1.asp">
<INPUT
      TYPE="TEXT"
      NAME="Message">
<INPUT
      TYPE="SUBMIT"
      NAME="Submit"
      VALUE="GO">
</FORM>
</BODY>
</HTML>
```

The ASP script, test2a.asp, can then use the *Request* object to obtain the value of the text box called *Text1*, as shown in the following code.

```
<HTML>
<HEAD>
<TITLE>ASP Test 2b</TITLE>
</HEAD>
<BODY>
<%   If Request.Form("Message") <> "" Then %>
        You typed in <%=Request.Form("Message")%>
<%   Else %>
        You did not type anything in the text box
<%   End If %>
</BODY>
</HTML>
```

Compare this with the earlier ColdFusion example, which achieves basically the same result. Note, however, that for simplicity, the ColdFusion example did not feature an IF test to check whether or not the text box held any data. Both ASP and ColdFusion include standard programming constructs such as IF tests and loops.

PHP

Unlike both ColdFusion and Active Server Pages, which are proprietary products, PHP is a freely available open-source, cross-platform product (as is the Linux operating system). PHP support can be added to most web servers through API-style interfaces to readily available DLL files or precompiled object libraries.

The PHP language borrows many elements from Perl, but was designed specifically to be embedded inside HTML in a similar manner to Active Server Pages. Lines of PHP are enclosed between <? and ?>, and the resulting HTML files are saved with the extension PHP.

JAVA

The Java programming language was originally developed by Sun Microsystems for use in embedded systems to control appliances and machinery. The developers recognised that because it is both powerful and multi-platform in nature, Java is also well suited as a language for developing applications to extend the functionality of web browsers. Thus, it has been adapted for web use as a 'network-centric computing platform' that lets developers create applications that can run on virtually any combination of computer hardware and operating system.

In the web environment we normally work with Java applets, small Java applications that are invoked from web pages. When invoked, Java applets are downloaded from a web server (via an <APPLET> tag), then run by the browser. Complete stand-alone Java applications are also now possible. For example, Sun Microsystems created a web browser called HotJava that was written exclusively in Java.

The **Java Virtual Machine** is the basis of the multi-platform nature of Java. The virtual machine is a program running on the client computer that pretends to be another computer designed specifically to run Java *bytecode*. Executing bytecode on the virtual machine can be likened to running Intel *machine code* on a Windows computer with a Pentium processor. When bytecode executes on the virtual machine it is slower than real machine code (because of the overhead of running the virtual machine) but still much faster than interpreted systems such as JavaScript. The Java Virtual Machine can be (and has been) adapted for almost all available computers.

CREATING AND USING JAVA APPLETS

Java applets consist of compiled code. Unlike JavaScript, no source code is sent to the client; only bytecode is sent. The bytecode is produced using a development environment such as the 'Java Development Kit', Symantec Visual Café, Borland Jbuilder or Microsoft J++ (JDK), which incorporate tools to allow Java source code to be debugged and compiled.

Java applets are embedded into HTML in a similar manner to images. Generically, the required tags and attributes are as follows.

```
<APPLET
    CODE= name of applet   (.class extension is optional)
    WIDTH= width in pixels
    HEIGHT= height in pixels
    CODEBASE= URL of applet
    ALT= alternate text
    NAME= applet's name
    ALIGN= alignment
    VSPACE= whitespace above & below applet
    HSPACE= whitespace either side of applet>

<PARAM
    NAME="parameter name"
    VALUE="value">
```

The <APPLET> tag specifies the required information for the browser to download a copy of the required bytecode. The compiled Java applets that are downloaded have a filename extension of class. The <PARAM> tags allow specific run-time parameters to be passed to the applet. The browser then starts the applet, which may run in the browser windows or in its own windows and have its own user interface. Here is an example of HTML code that uses the <APPLET> and <PARAM> tags.

```
<HTML>
<HEAD>
<TITLE>Demonstrate a Java Applet</TITLE>
</HEAD>
<BODY>
<APPLET
    CODE="Lake.class"
    WIDTH=320 HEIGHT=400>
<PARAM
    NAME=image
    VALUE="boat.gif">
<PARAM
    NAME=overlay
    VALUE="">
<PARAM
    NAME=href
    VALUE="">
<IMG
    SRC="boat.gif">
<BR>Your browser doesn't support Java applets
</APPLET>
</BODY>
</HTML>
```

In this example, a line of text between the <APPLET> and </APPLET> tags is displayed only if the browser does not support (and therefore doesn't understand) these two tags.

JAVA AND SECURITY

Java is not only faster than JavaScript but is also more powerful. It is possible to perform certain system operations in Java (for example to create, execute or delete files on the client computer, or establish Internet connections to remote computers); hence, Java can present a potential security risk. In general, applets loaded over the Net are prevented from reading and writing files on the *client* file system, making network connections except to the *originating host*, and starting other programs on the client. This form of in-built system security is referred to as the 'Java Sandbox'. In other words, Java programs that are downloaded to a computer from another source (e.g. the Web) cannot play around outside their own sandbox.

ACTIVEX

ActiveX is Microsoft's name for a family of components and technologies based on their Component Object Model (COM). ActiveX controls, which are one part of the ActiveX family, are a system that enables pre-compiled objects to be downloaded to a browser and executed. In this respect, ActiveX controls compete with Java, with the notable exceptions that:

- Java is multi-platform. This makes it a better choice for cross-platform development, but Java applets tend to run slower on Windows computers than ActiveX controls.
- ActiveX controls run on Windows computers only. Because ActiveX controls are developed exclusively for Windows computers as native code (not Bytecode) executables, they should run more efficiently in the Windows environment.

While Java is a programming language, ActiveX is actually an architecture for creating and using objects with a wide variety of languages. Strictly speaking, the actual Java-based technology that competes with ActiveX controls is really JavaBeans, a Java-based component architecture!

CREATING AND USING ACTIVEX CONTROLS

ActiveX controls can be created with a range of tools including Visual Basic, Delphi and C++, or even Java. The browser acts as a container for the control, just as forms in Visual Basic (but not HTML forms) are a container for visual controls. ActiveX controls can be called by scripts within the browser to extend the functionality of JavaScript or VBScript. Also, ActiveX controls can potentially be used by other Windows applications. If you look within the System directory of a Windows computer you may notice files with an OCX extension. These are ActiveX controls that have been installed on your system, possibly either by Windows applications that you have installed or by your web browser.

Controls are embedded in a web page using the <OBJECT> tag to download as required. Once downloaded, they are registered with the Windows registry and remain on the system. Unlike Java applets, they do not need to be downloaded each time they are used. The following example illustrates how ActiveX controls are integrated into an HTML file.

```
<OBJECT
   ALIGN=CENTER
   CLASSID="clsid:99B42120-6EC7-11CF-A6C7-
      00AA00A47DD2"

   WIDTH=200
   HEIGHT=200
   ID=MyObject
   CODEBASE= "http://foo/bar/
      myoc.ocx#ver=4,70,0,1062">

<PARAM
   NAME="ScrollStyleX"
   VALUE="Circular">

</OBJECT>
```

ID is the name by which the control is known. In this example, the control is known as 'MyObject'. CLASSID is a unique identifier for the ActiveX control. This identifier is effectively a serial number by which it can be traced. The CODEBASE parameter is where the URL of the control is specified. If the control has not previously been downloaded and registered with the computer, then it will be downloaded from this URL.

ACTIVEX AND SECURITY

As with Java, ActiveX can present a potential security risk because it has full access to the host computer's system. It can potentially create, read and delete files or establish communication sessions over the Internet. ActiveX takes a very different approach to security from the 'Java Sandbox'. Code signing is used to prevent the spread of malicious ActiveX components. Code signing doesn't prevent malicious code from being run. Instead, it places the onus for the software being safe to use on the software's creator. Code signing clearly identifies the publisher (creator) of an ActiveX control, and also allows you to validate the integrity of code (that is, determine if it has been altered in any way by anyone other than the original author). It doesn't absolutely prevent problems but it does provide a mechanism for trust and legal action if necessary.

The code signing technology used is called Authenticode. Software authors that develop ActiveX objects pay the certificate authority to register the code and issue a certificate. The certificate uses a digital signature system based on a public key and private key. When a control is downloaded the unique ID can be used to check its authenticity with an independent certificate authority.

The problem is that once the user has accepted the ActiveX control, it is placed on the user's hard disk. If the control turns out to be malicious, the user will be able to identify the author — but by this time, of course, the damage will have been done.

B2C TECHNOLOGY IN ACTION

The Coles-Myer Group operates a web portal that provides links to around 14 different online shopping services. Despite being a part of the one retail group, these services demonstrate a variety of approaches that can be taken in establishing B2C web sites.

'MyerDirect', 'Gifts To Go', 'Officeworks', 'Travelshop@NOW' and 'AFL Footy Store' use Active Server Pages to provide the required processing and database links for their online shopping baskets. Most of these sites also use JavaScript to enhance the interactivity of the web pages with cosmetic features such as mouse rollovers and pop-down menus. In some cases, the JavaScript is also an integral element of the ordering process. For example, when a user visits the 'Officeworks' site, the system runs a small Java applet that does a quick check on the browser configuration. If the configuration does not match what is required, the user is then given instruction on reconfiguring the browser.

'MyerDirect' also makes use of a commercial product called 'RedMeasure' to monitor each user's page accesses as they travel through the web site. 'Red Sheriff', the developers of 'RedMeasure', claim that it is more accurate than traditional measurement systems such as cookies, counters and server logs, which tend to underestimate by 20 per cent or more owing to the influence of proxy servers.

'Kmart Online', 'Target Online' and 'Music@Now' operate in a similar fashion to 'MyerDirect' but use ColdFusion, rather than Active Server pages, as the database access and server scripting tool of choice.

'Harris Technology' and 'Vintage Cellars' use a commercial product called Xworks to implement their shopping baskets. Xworks is a compiled, executable file that is run in a similar manner to a CGI script. It is written in Microsoft Visual FoxPro and designed to link into a corporate database system called 'Quids' (an acronym for Quotations, Inventory, Distribution and Sales), which handles all aspects of the respective company's sales in real time. Many online shopping systems operate as batch processes. Stock levels and prices are updated once a day, and orders are also gathered into batches to be processed. In contrast to this, with Xworks and the Quids database, the web pages that are produced reflect livestock levels and prices. As purchases are made on line, stock levels are adjusted automatically. Technical details of the Harris Technology web site are available at www.ht.com.au/thissite.htm.

'Coles Online' differs markedly from all of the above approaches in that it abandons the standard web browser altogether as the user interface. Instead, the user has to download and install a specific application which, when launched, communicates over the Internet to allow the customer to place orders. Although it still appears to the user as a graphical interface that strongly resembles a web browser, it is in fact a PC-to-mainframe connectivity program called WinSurf from a company called 'ICOM Informatics'. Customers using the WinSurf program are interacting directly with a program on a mainframe computer rather than communicating with a web server.

(continued)

Maintrame connectivity via the Internet is normally based on terminal emulation programs that give a text-only solution; however, WinSurf provides a web-style interface. By using this approach, 'Coles Online' are not only providing an effective, easy-to-use interface but are also maintaining their investment in mainframe technology as well as integrating their online sales with existing systems (especially their supply chain management systems). While the WinSurf program is designed specifically for communication with mainframe computers, it does make significant use of web browser technology including HTML for formatting, HTTPS and SSL for security, and ActiveX and Java for client-side processing.

EXERCISES

1. Visit the Coles-Myer portal at www.colesmyer.com.au and familiarise yourself with the available online services. Can you identify the different technologies discussed?

2. Find out more about WinSurf by visiting the manufacturer's web site at www.icominfo.com. What other web-related products are available from the manufacturers of WinSurf, and how could they be used in e-commerce?

SECURITY OF B2C TRANSACTIONS

So far, we have considered mechanisms for communication, processing and user interface but we have not yet considered the need for security. Any electronic communication can potentially be intercepted, and since both HTML and HTTP are based on plain text, it is a simple matter to intercept web-based transactions and either alter the information or record it for later nefarious use. In order to provide for security of transmitted data some form of encryption of data is essential. Unfortunately, the current version of IP was designed well before e-commerce had been thought of and thus does not include any in-built encryption mechanism to ensure the security of transmitted data. IP version 6 will incorporate security directly into the protocol to overcome these limitations in the current version of IP, but in the meantime, most current security schemes are add-ons to IP.

The two major schemes currently used are **Secure Sockets Layer (SSL)** and **Secure HTTP (S-HTTP)**. SSL secures all data sent across a connection between two computers that are communicating using TCP. It effectively sits between HTTP (or another high-level protocol such as FTP) and TCP. If a URL begins with https:// instead of http:// then it is an indication to the browser that it should use SSL to establish a secure connection with the web server in question.

Rather than operating on the TCP level, S-HTTP secures the contents of the entire HTTP request and response message. It is effectively a replacement for HTTP in the communication process between browser and server. It operates in much the same way as HTTP except all messages are packaged into a secure envelope that encapsulates the encrypted requests and responses.

SUMMARY

The Web provides a readily available standard interface for B2C applications. The basic web computing model is a simple form of client/server computing that uses HTML and JavaScript to provide the formatting for the user interface. The link between browser and server is via HTTP requests and responses, which are communicated using TCP/IP. Because the basic web computing model is suited only to passive B2C activities such as marketing, we need to extend it by factoring in the ability to process transactions on the server. By extending the client/server model to three tiers, the web server can also take on the role of middleware by initiating further processing to perform business functions and link into databases to store transaction details.

When this three-tiered client/server model is applied, form elements such as text boxes provide the inputs to processes running on the server via the Common Gateway Interface. The CGI is responsible for initiating the process, passing across the input data and returning the results of processing to the web server in the form of a web page that can be served to the client. A major problem of client/server computing via the Web is that it does not use dedicated connections between the client and the server, therefore no state information is maintained between web pages. This necessitates the use of cookies, hidden fields or session IDs appended to URLs in order to maintain state information between pages and thus to establish a virtual session.

When developing programs for use with web-based client/server applications, programming languages such as Perl can be used to create scripts that produce HTML as their output. Alternatively, scripting languages such as ASP, ColdFusion and PHP are designed to be embedded inside HTML and interpreted by the server before the HTML is sent to the client.

Java and ActiveX provide ways of developing self-contained components of a web-based system that can coexist with HTML and be launched via a web page. Components developed using Java are known as applets and can be used on any computer that has the Java Virtual Machine installed. ActiveX components are one part of a comprehensive Microsoft architecture and can be used only on computers that use a version of Microsoft Windows as their operating system. Because both Java and ActiveX applications have the potential to access system resources and therefore cause damage and loss of data, appropriate security measures need to be taken to prevent them from being misused.

Neither the web computing model nor TCP/IP were developed with e-commerce in mind, so there is no in-built method for protecting the integrity and privacy of transaction data. Security of B2C transactions is therefore achieved via additional systems such as SSL and Secure HTTP, which enable transactions to be encrypted.

The next chapter will cover ways of developing and maintaining electronic trading systems. It will further examine client/server computing and the importance of networks to information systems, and will look at development methodologies for e-commerce.

key terms

Active Server Pages (ASP)	environment variables	Perl
ActiveX	forms	PHP
applet	GET	POST
client/server computing	hidden fields	Secure HTTP (S-HTTP)
ColdFusion	Hypertext Markup Language (HTML)	Secure Sockets Layer (SSL)
Common Gateway Interface (CGI)	Hypertext Transfer Protocol (HTTP)	session ID
Common Object Request Broker Architecture (CORBA)	Java	standard input
	Java Database Connectivity (JDBC)	standard output
cookie	JavaScript	stateless
Distributed Component Object Model (DCOM)	Java Virtual Machine	thin client
	Open Database Connectivity (ODBC)	

QUESTIONS

1. Do a web search on 'web servers' and find out which web servers support CGI, NSAPI and ISAPI.

2. How effective is the Web as a ubiquitous communication medium for B2C applications? What limitations does it have?

3. What is meant when we describe the Web as 'stateless' in nature? Why is this a problem?

4. Describe the techniques used to maintain state information on the Web.

5. List as many alternatives for the development of server-side processing as you can and discuss the relative advantages and disadvantages of each.

6. What is meant by 'platform independence' and how does a client/server architecture help to achieve this?

7. As part of a B2C application you have just designed a web page that includes forms for input and JavaScript. What issues need to be considered to ensure that the application functions correctly for all clients?

8. Throughout this chapter we have presented various examples of code. Try out each of the code sequences and attempt to troubleshoot any problems you encounter.

9. Prepare a report on 'malicious' code in Java and ActiveX.

IMPULSE AIRLINES AND VIRGIN BLUE

During 2000 two new airlines entered the domestic aviation market in Australia. Impulse Airlines and Virgin Blue began operations as domestic carriers in competition with Ansett and Qantas. Part of the strategy of both Impulse and Virgin Blue was to make their cut-price fares very accessible by allowing flight bookings to be made over the Internet. By June 2000 Impulse Airlines was reported in the media as making 20 per cent of its bookings via its web site, and Virgin Blue began accepting bookings via its web site soon after. Both airlines used an 'off the shelf' airline reservation system called 'Open Skies' that is distributed by Hewlett Packard. (Qantas acquired Impulse Airlines in May 2001.) 'Open Skies' is a multi-tiered distributed reservation system designed for small to medium-sized airlines that includes 'Take Flight' and the newer 'SkyLights E-Suite' online Internet booking systems. As of February 2001, more than 20 airlines around the world are using 'Open Skies'. 'Open Skies' is a significant product for the global airline industry, as discussed in the following press release from their web site.[5]

Open Skies History

Open Skies was organized in 1994 to provide innovative and efficient automation products and services to the airline industry. Today, Open Skies is recognized as one of the fastest growing providers of hosted airline reservation solutions. Open Skies' wide array of complementary products including advanced revenue management systems and integrated e-ticket/e-commerce solutions is providing airlines throughout the world an opportunity to move into the future, while still maintaining low costs.

Open Skies' original chairman [was] David Neeleman, whose extremely successful airline, Morris Air, was the first innovator of the ticketless transaction. On July 1, 1993, Morris Air became the first airline in the United States (and, to the best of our knowledge, in the world) to offer ticketless travel to its passengers booking reservations directly with the airline. It has been stated that a 'major untold factor' in Southwest Airlines' acquisition of Morris Air was Morris Air's automation resources and expertise. Morris Air enjoyed outstanding profitability and steady growth, eventually operating 22 Boeing 737-300 aircraft. On December 31, 1993, Southwest Airlines acquired Morris Air.

Dave Evans, Chief Architect at Open Skies, developed Morris Air's innovative and low-cost technology solutions that provided the early roots of Open Skies systems today. These products were developed for use on Hewlett-Packard's ultra-reliable, scalable 3000 computer line with its highly optimized MPE/ix operating system as well as the TURBO IMAGE/SQL database management system. Following the acquisition of Morris Air, Dave Evans performed consulting services for Southwest Airlines on their use of an application of the Morris Air technology. Southwest Airlines used those solutions to provide handling of their own e-ticket transactions previously not possible on their existing legacy host. Mr Evans founded Open Skies, Inc. in June 1994 to pursue the emerging and fast growing opportunities in providing similar solutions for the world's airlines.

Hewlett Packard acquired Open Skies in October 1998 as part of the HP e-services strategy.

In November 2000, Navitaire, formerly PRA Solutions, one of the airline industry's leading application service providers, acquired Open Skies, Inc., to broaden its revenue enhancement offerings for the airline industry. Navitaire is majority-owned by Accenture, the venture capital unit of Andersen Consulting.

Open Skies' Internet booking system, Skylights, provides many airline customers such as jetBlue, Go Fly Airlines and others with advanced, yet very effective Internet booking capabilities. Other products such as an airport check-in kiosk, an automated airline customer support database, and an extensive reporting package have been added in order to provide airline customers with a wide array of one-stop, integrated solutions.

Open Skies and its hosted reservation solution is innovative technology, providing solutions to the world's leading low-cost and efficient airlines. Today, these vital products are designed to increase airline profits and optimize airline asset utilization in a manner unobtainable from any other system.

Questions

Before answering these questions, visit the web site of either Virgin Blue (www.virginblue.com.au) or another airline that uses Open Skies to facilitate Internet bookings (consult the Open Skies customer list located at www.openskies.hp.com/customer.htm).

1. What are the five steps involved in making an online booking with the Open Skies system?

2. For what purposes is JavaScript used in the Open Skies system? You may need to look through the source code of the web pages used for online bookings.

3. What methods are used by the Open Skies system to overcome the stateless nature of the Web?

4. Which client/server model is used by 'Take Flight' and 'Skylights E-Suite' online Internet booking systems?

5. What processing is carried out and where is the processing performed?

SUGGESTED READING

Bates, C. 2000, *Web Programming: Building Internet Applications*, John Wiley & Sons, Chichester, UK.

Castro, E. 1999, *Perl and CGI for the World Wide Web: Visual Quickstart Guide*, Peachpit Press, Berkeley, CA.

Comer, D. E. 1997, *The Internet Book: Everything You Need to Know about Computer Networking and How the Internet Works*, Prentice Hall, New Jersey.

McComb, G. 1997, *Web Programming Languages Sourcebook*, John Wiley & Sons, New York.

Negrino, T. and Smith, D. 1999, *JavaScript for the World Wide Web: Visual Quickstart Guide*, Peachpit Press, Berkeley, CA.

Schneider, G. P. and Perry, J. T. 2000, *Electronic Commerce*, Course Technology, Cambridge, MA.

Stein, L. D. 1997, *How to Set Up and Maintain a Web Site*, Addison-Wesley Longman, Reading, MA.

Winfield Treese, G. and Stewart, L. C. 1998, *Designing Systems for Internet Commerce*, Addison-Wesley Longman, Reading, MA.

END NOTES

1. Australian Bureau of Statistics 2000 (May), 8147.0 'Use of the Internet by Householders, Australia', www.abs.gov.au/Ausstats.

2. W3C, HTML Home Page, www.w3.org/MarkUp.

3. W3C, Web Style Sheets, www.w3.org/Style.

4. W3C, 'XHTML 1.0 — The Extensible HyperText Markup Language', www.w3.org/TR/xhtml1.

5. Reproduced from 'Navitaire, Open Skies History', www.openskies.com/html/history.htm. The web site has since been changed to www.navitaire.com.

CHAPTER 4

DEVELOPING AND IMPLEMENTING ELECTRONIC TRADING SYSTEMS

Learning objectives

You will have mastered the material in this chapter when you can:

- appreciate the structural changes that are occurring as business becomes electronic
- recognise the importance of network effects
- understand the various systems development methodologies that are being used to develop electronic commerce systems
- define rapid application development, joint application development and prototyping
- appreciate the operation of client/server models and distributed systems
- define legacy systems
- understand integration issues in e-business
- appreciate web management issues
- understand the importance of project management in e-business development
- appreciate the importance of risk management in e-business.

'The Internet and technology related to it will radically transform human resources management and the future shape of organisations. Speed, rather than size, will determine success, and connectivity, rather than internal efficiency, will be what managers measure themselves by.'

Sir Gil Simpson, Chief Executive of New Zealand information technology company Aoraki Corporation, quoted in 'Technology forces a new view from the top', by David James, *Business Review Weekly*, 28 July 2000, p. 63.

INTRODUCTION

In the networked economy, consumers are connecting to online businesses, businesses are connecting to suppliers, and governments are connecting to citizens, businesses and other governments, and vice versa. Kevin Kelly (1998), in his book *New Rules for the New Economy*, states that:

> The dynamic of our society, and particularly our new economy, will increasingly obey the logic of networks. Understanding how networks work will be the key to understanding how the economy works.[1]

A world governed by networks is rewriting the rules on how to build companies, market products and create value. This **network effect** is the basis for a new approach to marketing business to global markets, using different business models, strategies and rapidly evolving new technologies. Table 4.1 illustrates the rise of the networked economy and how it is changing the way in which we live and do business.

TABLE 4.1	THE NETWORKED ECONOMY
NETWORKING PRINCIPLES	**EXAMPLES**
Number of computing chips increasing	Number of chips in objects other than computers is rising faster.
Connecting everything to everything	Windows Millennium Edition (ME) is designed to turn the home computer into a hub for connecting appliances to the Internet.
Transmission of small amounts of data and receipt of input from neighbour make inert objects animated nodes.	A PC, like a single brain neuron in a plastic box, when linked by telcos into a neural network, becomes part of the World Wide Web.
Dumb parts, properly connected, yield smart results.	The chips connected are the hardware. The software that runs through it is the networked economy.

SOURCE: Adapted from Kevin Kelly 1998, *New Rules for the New Economy*, Viking, New York, pp. 9–17.

Many companies have found that just having a web presence is not enough in the new economy — each part of the organisation may have to change to support this new way of doing business. E-commerce is multidisciplinary and should involve personnel from all parts of the organisation such as sales, information technology, marketing, accounts, customer relations, manufacturing, product development and distribution. As well, academic institutions the world over are having a difficult time trying to develop e-commerce degrees: should they be part of a business degree — for example a master's in Business with an E-commerce strand, a master's in E-commerce as a stand-alone degree or a master's in Science with an E-commerce strand? The authors of this book and its companion, *Internet Commerce: Digital Models for Business*, believe degrees should also reflect this multidisciplinary nature — thus, our authors are from Computing Sciences, Information Systems and Business faculties, computing consulting firms and the law, and have consulting and practical experience.

E-commerce applications are set to become mission-critical, so organisations need to consider investing in entire replications of their systems. Availability on a 24-hour/7-day basis means that duplicate systems running mirrored software and data in different geographical areas will be necessary.[2]

In this chapter we examine various systems development methodologies that are used in developing e-commerce sites. Each methodology must deliver the ability to develop top-quality e-commerce sites at *Internet speed*; for this reason **Rapid Application Development** and prototyping are important. A **prototype** is a working model of the proposed system that allows end users to interact with the system before it is completed to make sure it meets their needs. The use of **Joint Application Development** is also important in light of the multidisciplinary nature of e-commerce. Extensible Markup Language (XML) is rapidly becoming the *lingua franca* of inter-organisational communications on the Internet, and many systems developers and software engineers are using **Unified Modelling Language (UML)** as a standard object-oriented design language. Almost every maker of software development products endorses UML, including IBM and Microsoft (for its Visual Basic environment).

SYSTEM DEVELOPMENT METHODOLOGIES — BACKGROUND

The development of computer and information systems should follow a methodical approach to planning, analysis, design, construction and evolution, but, as mentioned above, the pace of change is now at Internet speed, so developers have to put systems in place a lot faster than was the case up to the early 1990s.

In the 1960s and 1970s systems were developed from a **process-oriented** perspective — that is, systems analysts examined the business processes, such as payroll and invoices, that were to be computerised and developed systems in third-generation computer languages, such as COBOL, that carried out these processes. Later methodologies, in which the emphasis was on data and relationships between data, evolved from database technology, and were referred to as **data-oriented systems**. This mirrored the rise of relational database software systems such as Oracle. However, it became apparent to analysts that there was also a time-dependent aspect of systems that was not given enough emphasis in the process-oriented or data-oriented methodologies, hence a **behaviour-oriented** perspective was developed.[3] This focuses on the dynamic nature of the data and the need to understand how real-world events impact on the data recorded in the system. Many methodologies emphasise one perspective or another, mirroring the technological developments that have taken place. In reality, analysts have found that systems development needs to take all the perspectives into account, as illustrated in figure 4.1.

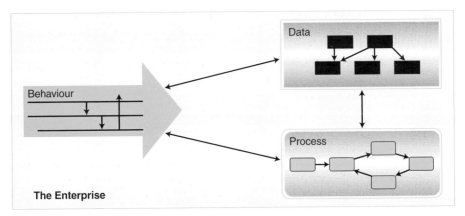

FIGURE 4.1: Systems development perspectives
SOURCE: Adapted from T. Olle et al. 1991, *Information Systems Methodologies: A Framework for Understanding*, 2nd Edition, Addison-Wesley, London, p. 13.

OBJECTS AND COMPONENTS

Object-oriented and component-based approaches to software development mean that a software component 'can provide the physical packaging and distribution of object-oriented abstractions in a manner that is largely language-neutral'.[4] Three competing component specifications are Common Object Request Broker Architecture (CORBA), Enterprise JavaBeans and Microsoft's COM family.

WEB DEVELOPMENT METHODOLOGIES

In the past, the information technology industry has been criticised for failing to deliver systems on time and on budget. Analysts and developers have been working to try to improve systems development and implementation timelines and to bring systems in on budget. Development of e-commerce systems often requires integration with **legacy systems**, which often hold critical corporate data. These legacy systems are existing company databases — for example, those developed in third-generation languages, such as COBOL, or back-end systems, such as electronic data interchange (EDI). The rapid deployment of the new economy has meant that there has been an explosion of methodologies to cope with developing e-commerce sites that have fast time-to-market, meet budget parameters and satisfy low risk thresholds. Some well-known methodologies include Dynamic Systems Development Method (DSDM), Microsoft: Solutions Framework (MSF) and Microsoft's .NET, Foundation by Andersen Consulting, Rational Unified Process, PricewaterhouseCoopers' SUMMIT D and IBM's E-BUSINESS.

Whatever the method, they all share some aspects in common — namely, establishing requirements, planning and setting up strategies, analysis and design, prototyping, implementation, testing and evaluation. Iteration of the various phases is emphasised in most methods, as is breaking the project into smaller-sized projects that can be delivered on time and on budget. Figure 4.2 illustrates a generalised approach to systems development. Prototyping and iteration help to keep to shorter time frames and to ensure usability issues are kept in front of the design team. In short, the principles of Rapid Application Development and Best Practice Quality Control need to observed. Many methodologies also emphasise the use of expert user panels to ensure that the system is satisfactory. Each iteration cycle needs to begin with a plan for what is to be accomplished and end with an evaluation of whether the objectives have been met.

The following sections will outline selected methodologies and provide examples of how they have been used.

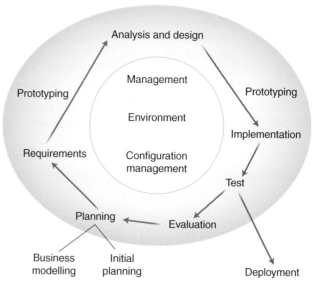

FIGURE 4.2: Project iteration cycle

SOURCE: Adapted from www.rational.com.

JOINT APPLICATION DEVELOPMENT

As has been stated previously, getting a large project on line requires the skills of many personnel. A useful development approach is called Joint Application Development (JAD), which relies on a mix of skills from various individuals.[5] Table 4.2 illustrates the roles and duties of members of a JAD team.

JAD has the following advantages.

- It improves motivation and performance of team members as it focuses on analysing tasks and providing solutions. The team benefits from being involved in detailed planning, group dynamics, obtaining results and solving problems for other people.
- It allows for simultaneous gathering and consolidating of large amounts of information.

- Discrepancies are resolved immediately with the help of the facilitator.
- It provides useful information for Work Process Improvement efforts.[6]

TABLE 4.2	JOINT APPLICATION DEVELOPMENT PERSONNEL	
TITLE	**ROLE**	**DUTIES**
Facilitator	Key person in the team, able to liaise with management and get the best out of the team	Responsible for planning, executing and managing a project
Management sponsor	Person who provides the backing of management	Attends first and final JAD session to review the results and make comments
Information specialists	Assist end users and develop a design according to end users' needs	Create prototypes, advise on new technology or hardware. Must be good listeners
Scribe	Captures the important decisions made, who made them and why	Documents the JAD sessions
End users	Assist in designing and agreeing systems	Work with computer personnel in a structured environment

SOURCE: Adapted from Joint Application Development, www.netmation.com/docs/bb12.htm.

GOING ON LINE

The following list of issues should be considered when taking your business on line.[7]
- Develop an online strategy document.
- Ensure there are enough funds to go on line and stay on line. Many dot.com companies have suffered from fast cash burn and have closed — for example thespot.com.au.
- Investigate current and future infrastructure needs.
- Study best practice web site design and hosting. It is often useful to visit web sites that set out best practice guidelines, such as www.treasury.gov.au.
- Factor in testing and maintenance of the web site.
- Make sure customer relationship management is carried out on line.
- Ensure trust and security issues are taken seriously — policies should be posted on line.
- Realise that marketing and branding have to be carried out both on and off line.
- Take into account legal matters such as copyright and contracts — get legal advice before putting up your web site. (Legal issues are discussed in greater detail in chapter 10.)
- Maintain competitive advantage by value-adding on line.

DYNAMIC SYSTEMS DEVELOPMENT METHOD

The Dynamic Systems Development Method (DSDM) is a framework of controls for the development of IT systems to tight time scales. It is independent of any particular set of tools and techniques, and can be used with object-oriented and structured analysis and design approaches in environments ranging from the individual PC to global distributed systems.[8] This methodology is based on collaboration — it encourages all the stakeholders to work together to ensure that the system developed is an amalgam of the right mix of skills and knowledge. It relies on a system of prioritising activities but is flexible enough to allow for changes in priorities. Table 4.3 outlines the system development features of DSDM.

TABLE 4.3	DSDM SYSTEMS DEVELOPMENT FRAMEWORK
PRINCIPLES	**COMMENTS**
Ensure there is active user involvement.	DSDM is a user-centred approach. If users are not closely involved throughout the development life cycle, delays will occur as decisions are made and users may feel that the final solution is imposed by the developers and/or their own management. Users are not outside the development team, acting as suppliers of information and reviewers of results, but are active participants in the development process.
Empower DSDM teams to make decisions.	DSDM teams consist of both developers and users. They must be able to make decisions as requirements are refined and possibly changed. They must be able to agree that certain levels of functionality, usability etc. are acceptable without frequent recourse to higher level management.
Focus on frequent delivery of products.	A product-based approach is more flexible than an activity-based one. The work of a DSDM team is concentrated on products that can be delivered in an agreed period of time. This enables the team to select the best approach to achieving the products required in the time available. By keeping each period of time short, the team can easily decide which activities are necessary and sufficient to achieve the right products. *Note:* Products include interim development products, not just delivered systems.
Make fitness for business purpose an essential criterion for acceptance of deliverables.	The focus of DSDM is on delivering the necessary functionality at the required time. The computer system can be more rigorously engineered later if such an approach is acceptable. Traditionally, the focus has been on satisfying the contents of a requirements document and conforming to previous deliverables, even though the requirements are often inaccurate, the previous deliverables may be flawed and the business needs may have changed since the start of the project.
Ensure iterative and incremental development converge for an accurate business solution.	DSDM allows systems to grow incrementally. Therefore, the developers can make full use of feedback from the users. Moreover, partial solutions can be delivered to satisfy immediate business needs. Iteration is inherent in all software development. DSDM recognises this and, by making it explicit, uses iteration to continuously improve the system being developed. When rework is not explicitly recognised in a development life cycle, the return to previously 'completed' work is surrounded by controlling procedures that slow development down. Since rework is built into the DSDM process, the development can proceed more quickly during iteration.
Realise that all changes during development are reversible.	To control the evolution of all products (documents, software, test products etc.), everything must be in a known state at all times. This means that configuration management must be all-pervasive.

SOURCE: dsdm.software.plc.uk.

The following technical insite outlines the methodology used by a software firm in Sydney that specialises in developing commercial web sites. Superior Software for Windows develops database applications using Microsoft SQL Server, ASP.Net, Access, Visual Basic, XML and Exchange Server.

technical
INSITE

THE SUPERIOR SOFTWARE FOR WINDOWS (SSW) SYSTEM DEVELOPMENT METHODOLOGY

BY ADAM COGAN

The SSW System Development Methodology involves dividing a project into separate phases, each designed to emphasize customer interaction and satisfaction. On completion of each phase, we walk-through the outcomes with the customer to ensure that a clear, shared understanding of the project exists between all parties. The customer has the opportunity to confirm work to date and accept the work before we proceed to the next phase of the project.

Generally, a separate quotation is provided for each phase at the commencement of the phase, though an estimate for the full project is provided at the beginning of the project.

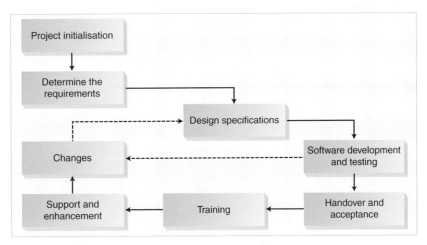

FIGURE 4.3: Systems development methodology

SOURCE: www.ssw.com.au

The phases are:

Phase I — Project initialisation
A project is initialized through a Superior Software for Windows visit to the client. This meeting is free of charge. The purpose of the meeting is to:
- introduce the Superior Software for Windows team
- explain our development methodology
- demonstrate a sample specification and products
- discuss our Terms and Conditions
- assess the overall scope of the client project.

(continued)

Phase II — Determine the requirements

The next step in the development process is to identify the client's needs and opportunities more closely. The purpose of this stage is to gain a solid understanding of the business requirements. We do this by meeting with the client project manager and users alike. From this meeting we will produce a **User Requirements Document** which outlines the business needs and the best software solutions.

Prior to this meeting it is beneficial for the client to prepare an outline of requirements, the members involved in this project and the main users.

Note: If this project involves converting an existing system, for example from Access to ASP, and no functionality changes are necessary, this phase may not be required.

Phase III — Design specifications

The **design specifications** of the systems are identified from the User Requirements document. Design specifications include all the necessary steps for design, delivery and implementation of the project. Superior Software for Windows ensures that solid foundations are prepared for the project. We walk through this document with the client for acceptance and signoff. At this stage we also like to get users to have a look at some of our past databases to get ideas and see our standard look and feel.

Phase IV — Software development and testing

Construction of the software is carried out during this phase, along with alpha testing and verification by our team. Any changes required in the design are made using the Superior Software for Windows Change Request System. There are two methods for reporting changes:
1. electronic submission (preferred)
2. manual submission.

In each case SSW requires client approval for nominated changes.

SSW follows 13 different rules for developing better code. See SSW's 13 Rules to Better Code for more information at their web site, www.ssw.com.au.

Phase V — Handover and acceptance

The software is installed at the customer's site for beta testing and acceptance by the customer. Once accepted, the software is ready to be installed into the production environment for 'live' use.

Phase VI — Training

Training can be carried out during this phase. A User Guide and On-line Help can also be provided if required.

Phase VII — Support and enhancements

One of the most important aspects of software development is the post-implementation support.

Support is defined as ensuring the database maintains its current functionality. The support cost is 15 per cent of the total project cost. Otherwise it will be charged on an hourly basis. It does not include data corruption. Onsite visits will be charged on an hourly basis, unless otherwise agreed upon.

Enhancements are defined as changes to the delivered software package. There are two methods for reporting changes:
1. electronic submission (preferred)
2. manual submission.

In each case SSW requires client approval for nominated changes.

SOURCE: www.ssw.com.au.

EXERCISES

1. What is meant by beta testing?
2. What is meant by data corruption and why does SSW preclude it from their maintenance section?
3. Research the 13 rules for better code on the SSW site and debate each rule with your fellow students.

RATIONAL UNIFIED PROCESS

Rational Software has developed **Rational Unified Process (RUP)** as a software development approach that:

- emphasises quality through best practice
- minimises risk
- reduces time-to-market through an iterative approach
- provides standard templates
- employs rapid development methodology.

Strategic planning sessions are held to define project goals and objectives. RUP utilises **Use Case modelling** to describe a system from a user's viewpoint. Use cases are scenarios for system use and can be used to specify system requirements, as well as to test functionality of the resulting system.[9] RUP also provides checkpoints for all activities that are part of the planning, analysis, design, implementation and testing of the new system.

The following technical insite shows how Deloitte and Rational successfully implemented an e-business solution to improve an enrolment process for California's Medi-Cal and Healthy Families Enrolment On-line. This case study illustrates the e-software paradox — namely, that for a company to compete, it must not only develop high-quality software but also develop it at Internet speed. Figure 4.4 illustrates this e-software paradox.

technical INSITE

E-SOFTWARE DEVELOPMENT

E-business development using RUP: an e-software paradox example

In an attempt to ensure that Californians, especially children, were enrolled in a national health insurance program, parents were asked to fill out a complex 28-page booklet of forms and worksheets. The complexity of the task meant that many people were deterred from joining California's Medi-Cal and Healthy Families Program. The California HealthCare Foundation (www.chcf.org) and its Medi-Cal Policy Institute (www.medical.org) decided that an e-business solution would improve the enrolment process.

Planning issues

In the early stages of planning, it became clear that the task was more complex than simply creating web-enabled versions of the existing paper forms. The objectives were to develop an e-business solution that would be:

- an interactive, interview-style application
- highly accurate

(continued)

- easy to use
- quick to develop, test and implement on line.

After examining a competitive bid process, CHCF selected Deloitte as its e-business solution provider and the Deloitte Solution Centre used Rational Unified Process (RUP) as the software development process.

Challenges

The challenges that faced the design team are outlined below.

1. The paper forms were complex, difficult to use and did not accurately capture some key information.
2. There were two distinct user groups — professional users who would help enrol people on a regular basis and self-enrolling users, so usability would be a key factor in the success of the enrolment web site.
3. The e-business application would need to seamlessly integrate with the California State legacy mainframe system.

Requirements

The requirements were therefore to:

1. develop a highly user-friendly online system that would capture a wide spectrum of complex data
2. ensure robust error checking processes would increase the quality and validity of the data
3. ensure the security and confidentiality of the data that are collected, stored and transmitted
4. work with the existing mainframe system
5. develop a system quickly (within a three- to four-month development window) without compromising on quality.

Solutions

RUP emphasised use case modelling to ensure that all team members worked towards a common goal — to develop the system that users needed. Checkpoints ensured that the developers were able to control and manage risk and move the project to completion on time and on budget. Furthermore, these checkpoints allowed the developers to overcome the risk and concern the client had about going on the Internet and using new technologies. RUP has been developed by internationally recognised experts (namely, Grady Booch, Ivar Jacobson and James Rumbaugh of Rational Software) in Unified Modelling, use case modelling, software architecture and iterative development.

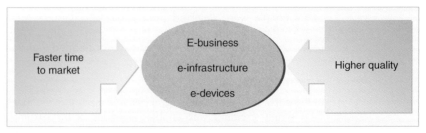

FIGURE 4.4: The e-software paradox: Today software development organisations face shorter development cycles, yet must produce a higher quality in Internet time.

EXERCISES

1. Visit the Rational site (www.rational.com) and study some of their success stories. Write up a short report on one of them.
2. Research the Rational Unified Process on the Web and prepare a report outlining its strengths. If you can identify any weaknesses, write them down and suggest ways to overcome them.
3. Prepare a report on the importance of usability studies and Human Computer Interaction research in Internet commerce applications. A useful site to start with is www.hcibib.org.
4. Compare and contrast RUP and DSDM.

NEW BUSINESS MODELS

As we saw in chapter 2, new business models are necessary if businesses are to be competitive in the new Internet economy.[10] Such businesses need to take note of:

- business information storage
- customer service
- time to market.

As well, they must reconcile various supply chain management and enterprise resource planning projects by combining business objectives, organisational relationships and technical requirements within a business strategy. The principles of e-commerce offer the business world innovative and compelling techniques to enhance competitive advantage through strategic use of information. In particular, e-commerce provides a new means of creating, sustaining and escalating competitive advantage by:

- driving down the cost of transacting business
- deepening customer relationships
- creating new markets in the MarketSpace through virtualisation.[11]

As can be seen in figure 4.5, the new marketspace provides links among suppliers, customers and partners.

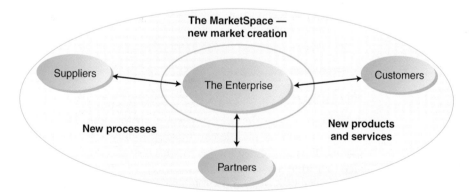

FIGURE 4.5: The MarketSpace
SOURCE: Andersen Consulting, www.itcontracting.com.au/articlenewton1.htm.

MOBILE COMMERCE MODELS

M-commerce has the potential to be worth $13 billion by the year 2003, representing 7 per cent of all e-commerce transactions.[12] The construction industry in the United Kingdom is the biggest single user of the mobile phone. The following short scenarios show how mobile e-commerce could be utilised.

FUTURE MOBILE E-BUSINESS SCENARIOS

Business trip to Hong Kong

An employee of a large firm is getting ready for a business trip to Hong Kong. Details of the flight, travel time and the destination are available on the employee's mobile phone. Upon arrival at the destination a message flashes up on the phone providing a map of the city together with the details of a local car rental firm, a taxi service and a nearby hotel. As the employee explores the city he or she is able to use the built-in GPS system to track progress and request online information about places of interest.

Real estate scenario

The Ericsson R380 is a WAP-enabled mobile phone with a built-in personal digital assistant — the keypad flips up to show a large touch-sensitive screen. Imagine the following scenario. A real estate agent visits a property he is currently managing as a rental premises. He sees a problem with a broken window. The agent can immediately pull out the PDA or mobile phone, log the disorder and by the time he or she arrives back at the office there is an email on the PDA or desktop that the problem has been, is being or will be resolved.

Civil engineer scenario

A civil engineer is making a site visit to inspect a water detention tank. The engineer dictates the report straight into a smart phone, which converts the report into text that it stores on the database back at the office. If the voice technology is not sufficiently developed, the office assistant would have the report typed up ready for final editing by the time the engineer arrived back at the office. There is no need for paper, pen or even a briefcase, only a smart phone or PDA.

SOURCE: Based on R. Gupta and R. Randall 2000, m-Commerce — September 2000, Real estate, www.ey.com/global/gcr.nsf/UK/Real_Estate_-_ebusiness_-_mcommerce.

EXERCISES

1. Devise scenarios in which such mobile devices could be used to save money and time in a commercial environment.
2. Prepare a report on the latest offering in mobile devices.

INTERACTIVE TELEVISION MODELS

Television is considered a one-way transmission. The challenge is to make it interactive so that people can make purchases, send email and play interactive games. This requires a means by which users can return information to the service provider. This avenue, or pathway, is called a **back channel**, which can be:
- part of a bi-directional cable
- a telephone line so the set-top box is able to use a modem to call the service provider and transmit the data.[13]

COLLABORATIVE E-BUSINESS MODELS

An outstanding example of collaborative e-business at work is provided in the technical insite below.

LIVELINK: A worldwide collaborative web model

The International Organization for Standardization (ISO) is using a worldwide extranet. The ISO, which manages the development, maintenance and distribution of more than 11 000 ISO standards in English, French and Russian, is a federation of national standards bodies from more than 120 countries. At any one time, there are about 7000 projects and 200 000 people contributing to ISO standards development.[14]

The ISO Central Secretariat's Livelink-based extranet will probably be the largest extranet in the world. The extranet allows for delegation of administration over the Web because it is not feasible to administer working documents for 7000 projects centrally.[15] Advantages include:

- helping virtual teams collaborate across organisational, geographic and technical boundaries
- providing an online focal point
- helping groups meet deadlines
- a robust document management base
- open, seamless integration of all the collaborative working tools to build a web-based intra/extranet business solution
- affording employees and external collaborators complete, but controlled, access to Livelink's integrated services
- a web browser allowing full access so the system can be deployed without requiring any work on the client side
- speedy deployment of collaborative and knowledge management services
- expected streamlining of the entire process of standard development
- improved document handling — such as working documents for meetings, meeting minutes, statistics and reports — with more than 200 000 people working on developing, revising and producing standards documents and documents produced for the 40-plus international meetings yearly
- expected provision of valuable tools for building consensus and tracking overall progress
- publishing standards on line in a secure environment.

SOURCE: Based on 'ISO builds worldwide Extranet with Livelink', www.open_text.com/customers/case_studies/livelink_case_study_iso.pdf.

EXERCISES

1. Prepare a report on other examples of such collaborative models.
2. Investigate the difficulties of dealing with multiple languages in such an extranet. Prepare a report of what problems could arise and what technical solutions could be employed to help solve multilingual extranets.

CLIENT/SERVER MODEL

'Client/server' describes the relationship between two computer programs in which one program, the client, makes a service request to another program, the server, which fulfils the request. This model has become one of the main ideas of network and Internet computing. For example, the web browser acts as a client requesting services (such as web pages and files) from a web server. Client and server programs are often part of a larger program or application.[16] As another example, computers using Transmission Control Protocol/Internet Protocol (TCP/IP), which underpins the Internet, may make client requests for files from File Transfer Protocol (FTP) servers on other computers on the Internet.

INTERNET BUSINESS TECHNOLOGIES AND STANDARDS

We will now examine the major trends in technology and how these will affect e-business.

MANAGING SECURITY AND STANDARDS

Security of payment systems and electronic transactions rate as a high concern with e-commerce. Transactions between trading partners, customers and suppliers must be secure and non-refutable. E-business demands standards between trading partners, and a common language that enables exact and efficient processing of transactions.[17]

ENTERPRISE INTEGRATION

The effective use of information entails integrating the technology within an organisation. The e-business must provide a sound foundation from which to build its financial and operational systems. E-commerce applications must be aligned with the back-end enterprise resource planning (ERP) systems to provide total integration for e-business and for the customer. ERP vendors J. D. Edwards and PeopleSoft are teaming with companies such as IBM and SynQuest to create e-commerce software bundles that completely integrate back-end ERP systems with front-end EC systems.[18]

TECHNOLOGY CONVERGENCE

Widespread use of the Internet Protocol (IP) sees the convergence of voice, data and video media. As bandwidth across the globe increases and broadband media become popular (Excite@Home for example), e-business will utilise all types of communication transport as an integrated service. Efficiencies are found in user convenience — for example, data networks can be used to handle voice communications.[19]

The following core capabilities for enterprise-wide application have been identified[20] and are further developed in table 4.4:
- infrastructure to support **synchronous** and **asynchronous** communications. For example, in program-to-program communication, synchronous communication requires that each end of an exchange of communication

responds in turn without initiating a new communication. An example of asynchronous communication is found in the client/server model. A server handles many asynchronous requests from its many clients. The client is able to proceed with other work or must wait on the service requested from the server.[21]

- data transformation between applications
- supporting services such as security and directories
- higher level business processes and workflow automation
- mechanisms that provide gateways to other technologies.

TABLE 4.4	MIDDLEWARE INFRASTRUCTURE COMPONENTS	
COMPONENTS	**EXAMPLES**	**COMMENTS**
Services	Security, system management, directory services, events	Security services such as access control, digital rights management
Distributed middleware	Common Object Request Broker Architecture (CORBA), Distributed Component Object Model (DCOM), Java 2 Enterprise Edition J2EE	Middleware allows different types of systems, applications and databases to connect together.
Operating systems	Unix, NT, AS400, Linux, Windows Millenium Edition	Interoperability is the key.
Platforms	Mainframe, Workstation, PC, Laptops, hand-held devices	The growing use of wireless devices is noted.

SOURCE: Commonwealth of Australia 2000, 'The Integration of Business E-Commerce Systems: Scoping Study for the National Electronic Authentication Council (NEAC)', August, p. 12, www.dcita.gov.au or www.noie.gov.au.

As well, it is vital to recognise that architectures and standards apply at many levels, including the business, application and technical levels. Figure 4.6 illustrates the interaction of the three architectures. Organisations store information in many different data formats, so in order to communicate with other organisations these data must be transformed or translated — for example ASCII to EBCDIC format. Common data standards include Extensible Markup Language (see www.w3.org/XML), Electronic Data Interchange (EDI) and Open Buying on the Internet (see www.openbuy.org). XML allows any sort of data to be delivered in a structured way over the Internet; it combines data format, structure and semantic information. XML/EDI is EDI implemented in XML.[22]

The issue of content management is a vital one, since businesses must be able to reuse data and information about a variety of products in a global market in which customers might have widely differing requirements.

Global

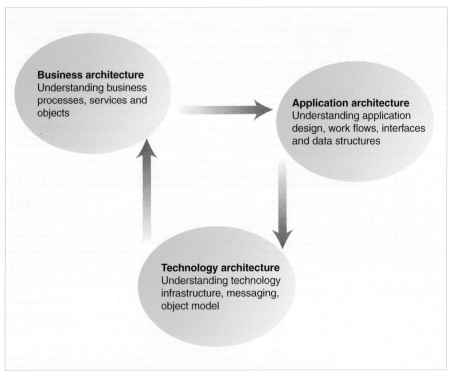

FIGURE 4.6: Business, application and technology architectures

SOURCE: E-Commerce Security: The Integration of Business E-commerce Systems.
Commonwealth of Australia copyright 2000, p. 15.
Reproduced by permission.

INTERNET INTER-ORB PROTOCOL

Internet Inter-ORB Protocol (IIOP) is an object-oriented programming protocol that allows distributed programs written in different programming languages to communicate over the Internet.[23] It is a critical part of the **Common Object Request Broker Architecture (CORBA)** industry standard. Companies will be able to write programs that communicate with their own or other companies' existing or future programs, no matter where they are stored, just by knowing the service and a name — it is not necessary to understand how the program works. Microsoft has developed a similar strategy called **Distributed Component Object Model (DCOM)**, which will be able to communicate with programs designed for CORBA via software bridges. Sun Microsystems developed a protocol called the Remote Method Invocation (RMI) to serve its cross-platform framework for the Java programming language. Programs that use RMI can be mapped to IIOP. JavaBeans is Sun's component object model for Java, which means it can work with other component approaches such as Microsoft's COM family. Enterprise JavaBeans focus on business application logic that encapsulates common business services such as credit rating and address checking. Figure 4.7 illustrates the evolution of web-object architectures.

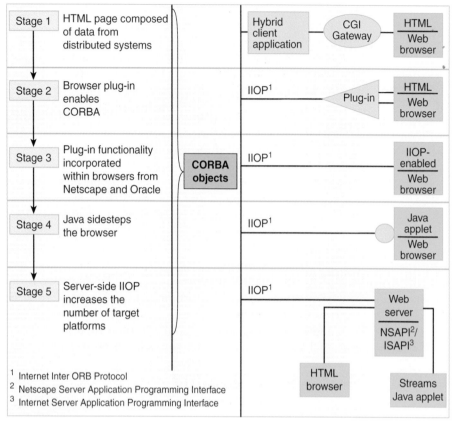

FIGURE 4.7: Evolution of web-object architectures
SOURCE: Based on P. May 2000, *The Business of Ecommerce: From Corporate Strategy to Technology*, Cambridge University Press, Cambridge, UK, p. 204.

 # DATABASE MANAGEMENT SYSTEMS

Many e-commerce sites use dynamic rather than static web pages — that is, content for the web pages is taken from internal databases.[24] Database technology allows large amounts of data to be stored in an efficient way. The database server, or set of database servers in a data centre, are usually separate boxes. Clients can make requests for data from dedicated data servers that respond with the requested data. Thus, clients are able to work in a client/server or distributed environment, making the data independent of the owner or a special computer. Advantages include that:

- any device, with proper authorisation and with a database connector, is able to add, modify and delete information in the database
- client computers do not have to perform the database queries, thereby reducing traffic going over the Internet

- databases use stored procedures (stored as database objects), triggers and rules for better integration with applications
- running applications on the database management systems helps to balance the processing load in a typical three-tier (database server/web application server/client browser) Internet application[25] (see the case study at the end of this chapter).

DATA WAREHOUSING

The huge explosion of information and transaction data being generated by the Internet has meant that companies have to rethink their analysis of business data. A **data warehouse** is a copy of the business transaction data specifically structured for query and analysis.[26] Data are copied, organised around time, transformed and analysed. Orders or production data are completed before going into the data warehouse, thus freeing up resources on the operational system and creating an archive. Data warehousing therefore provides the following advantages.

- It allows for analysis of data over time — by the week, month or year.
- It allows users to understand the correlation between activities of different groups within a company.
- It allows for cheap storage of data in their final state.
- It enables a company to compare snapshots of data.

DATABASE INTEGRATION

In traditional inter-business online commerce, databases are shared in structured formats. Electronic data interchange (EDI) is an example of how databases can be linked. On the Web it is difficult to maintain the capture and sharing of data derived from existing databases. The protocols that drive the Web exchange data in semi-structured forms. This has the effect of making the transmission of transactional type data very difficult using traditional databases. The data include items as diverse as invoicing, payroll systems and employee personal details. The Web operates systems that are designed to distribute more complex material such as software and operational manuals that are more correctly designated as semi-structured.

On the Web, the interaction of databases can be facilitated with **middleware**. This form of software acts as a middle operations gateway between the client and the servers operating the web sites. Middleware operates as the translator of structured data, the structured data to be reprocessed and then transmitted in a semi-structured format via the Web. There are a number of software/middleware packages that permit small-scale exchange of structured data, such as inventory systems, between databases. These include Oracle and mSQL (Dbperl).[27] One of the most effective middleware packages is Sybase, which accepts **Structured Query Language (SQL)** commands embedded within HTML forms. SQL is a standard fourth-generation language for relational database systems. This enables structured data to be exchanged through a CGI system and then displayed in HTML form at the client end. The way these processes occur is shown in figure 4.8.

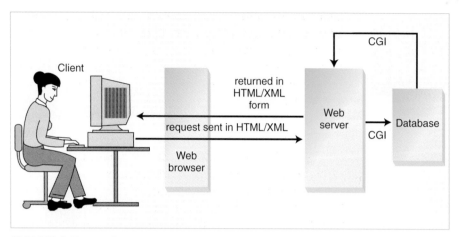

FIGURE 4.8: Database integration

Further developments in database integration and use on the Internet include object request brokering (ORB), which has already been discussed. This software acts as a broker that finds, retrieves and delivers information and data. Further details can be found at www.corba.org.

ORACLE'S SOLUTION

Naturally, then, many companies are faced with the challenge of ensuring that all their software is able to communicate — for example customer-facing applications with enterprise applications and supplier applications. Oracle (www.oracle.com) recommends having one data centre connected to the Internet where all applications and data are consolidated.[28] Amazon.com sells its products in 168 countries worldwide but has a presence in only three — the United States, England and Germany.

Such integration brings to e-business the following benefits:
- global efficiency, as illustrated above
- administrative efficiency — that is, customers, employees and business partners do the work using self-service applications on the Web
- demand-based manufacturing, as illustrated by Dell.com
- simplification of business applications — for example, order entry applications for sales personnel, web store applications for customers and reseller management applications should all be the same.

JAVABEANS

JavaBeans is a portable, platform-independent component model written in the Java programming language. It enables web developers to write reuseable components of web pages of Internet software once and run them anywhere. JavaBeans-based products include Corel, IBM, Lotus, Rogue Wave and Stingray software among many others.

In the following technical insite, examine figure 4.9 then read how an e-commerce business model works.

BUILDING A VIRTUAL STORE

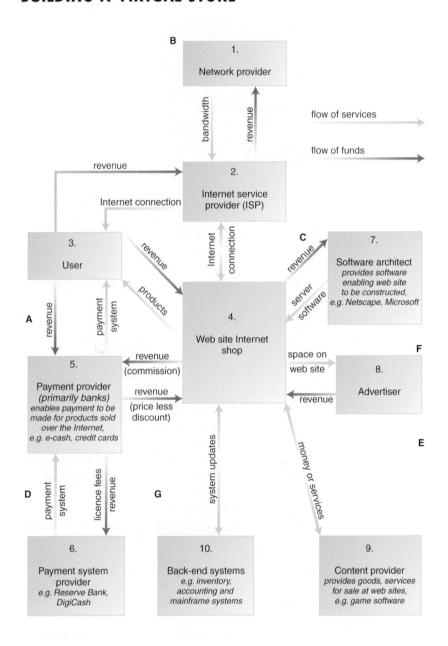

FIGURE 4.9: An Internet business model for taxation purposes

SOURCE: Australian Taxation Office 1997, 'Tax and the Internet',
Discussion Report of the ATO Electronic Commerce Project,
Australian Government Publishing Service, Canberra, p. 13.

Examine the illustration opposite to understand the e-commerce business model.

• Transaction Group A

The User, or potential 'Internet Shop' customer, pays a fee to the Internet Service Provider (ISP) who supplies an Internet connection. This gives the user access to various Internet services such as the World Wide Web, email, file transfer protocol, telnet etc. The User visits a web site or 'Internet Shop'. An Internet Shop may vary greatly in size, from a large retail/wholesale organisation to a single-person operation. Thus, they may visit a virtual shopping mall, such as a Cybermall site (www.cybermall.com) or an individual shop, such as Harris Technology (www.ht.com.au). ('Shop' has been used for convenience only.) The User decides to purchase goods and/or services. To pay for these items, the User obtains a payment system from a financial institution — the Payment Provider. Payment Providers also provide various services related to the system (settlement, authorisation etc.). The web surfer is able to buy goods or services from the web site, and in most cases uses a credit card to complete the purchase, although some sites accept special digital payments such as digicash, which is obtained from banks such as St George (www.stgeorge.com.au).

The Internet Shop purchases a permanent Internet connection or space on the ISP's computers from the ISP. A web hosting site (e.g. www.uunet.com) allows individuals or companies to use the host's server to store web pages.

• Transaction Group B

To provide the User with access to the Internet, the ISP purchases a set amount of bandwidth from a Network Provider. In Australia this could be Telstra or Optus. Some ISPs are bypassing these Network Providers and setting up their own overseas links. For example, Ozemail installed its own high-speed satellite connection to the United States.

• Transaction Group C

Software architects supply the Internet Shop with the software required to enable connection to an ISP and to allow customers to browse the shop. These could be browser software packages such as Netscape Communicator with Navigator or Internet Explorer from Microsoft. Many e-commerce software packages are available, such as IBM Net.Commerce or iCat Electronic Commerce Suite.

• Transaction Group D

Payment systems providers supply the underlying technology and expertise required to run the payment providers computer systems. Payment providers pay licence fees for this service. Some of the payment systems might be via credit card, electronic wallets or electronic cash.

• Transaction Group E

The Internet Shop purchases goods and services from a content provider. The Internet Shop may purchase the rights to a product or may be one of many shops offering a product.

• Transaction Group F

Advertisers purchase space on web sites through the Internet Shop. Advertising fees are negotiated on a fixed or 'fee per click' basis, depending on the site's popularity.

• Transaction Group G

The Internet Shop maintains its back-end systems through system updates. This automates the process of updating inventory, accounting and mainframe systems.

SOURCES: Based on G. Shelly, T. Cashman and M. Vermaat 2000, *Discovering Computers 2001: Concepts for a Connected World*, Course Technology, Cambridge, MA, pp. 7.55–57; E. Lawrence 1998, 'Setting Up a Shopfront', in *Hands On Solutions: E-commerce*, CCH Australia, pp. 10–13.

(continued)

EXERCISES

1. Experiment with setting up your own storefront by going to www.store.yahoo.com and following the instructions.
2. After you have set up your shopping site, prepare a report outlining the advantages and disadvantages of using such a methodology.

PROJECT MANAGEMENT: METHODS AND ISSUES

Project management is a fundamental skill required to succeed in e-business because Internet technologies are relatively new to the information technology (IT) industry, and e-business strategies have a significant impact on enterprises, and also because of the potential financial scale of future e-business developments.[29] As e-business, and its implementation using information technology, have such a significant impact on an enterprise, the management of resources and risks associated with e-business development requires a mix of both business and IT project management skills. Organisations are seeking project managers with broader experience across IT and business, yet the global IT skills shortage is predicted to continue for the next several years (see the IT&T Industry Skills Task Force web site, www.aiia.com.au/skillstaskforce.htm, for further details). Therefore, enterprises face the risk of not being able to acquire the appropriate level of project management skills needed to meet e-business development demands.[30]

Perhaps the most well-known and -utilised project management method, even today, is the waterfall method.[31] This approach uses the analogy of a waterfall to illustrate the life cycle of development activities towards a solution. The waterfall is traditionally applied, Lowell Authur explains, by performing the waterfall steps — namely, *requirements analysis, design, build, test* and *implement* — in sequence, then checking the requirements, design and coding in the system test phase. Some project management methods seriously short-change the requirements analysis phase. These are typically based on IEEE standards, have a heavy 'software engineering' flavour and substitute a '**functional design specification**' for the system requirements statement. These approaches often fail to appreciate the significance of user needs, and in effect replace the 'what'-oriented, user-focused requirements analysis phase with a 'how'-oriented, technical/synthetic/constructive conceptual design phase.[32]

The common problem experienced even today with this approach is that the time between requirements and testing is usually so significant that major problems have been overlooked until it is too late to go to the expense of major redevelopment. The originator of the waterfall project management method, W. Royce, claims that the model has been oversimplified and misinterpreted. 'The original model supported the engineering processes of prototyping and incremental refinements to arrive at the final product.'[33]

The Evolutionary Development Model attempted to address the shortcomings that the waterfall method began to experience through the eighties. Arthur's version of the evolutionary development model draws inspiration from Dr Shewart's 1983 Plan, Do, Check, Act (PDCA) Life Cycle (see figure 4.10) and then applies iterative prototyping to each of the major phases identified in the waterfall model.

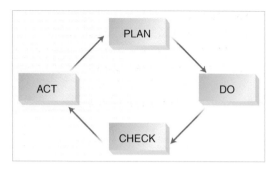

FIGURE 4.10: Dr Shewart's PDCA Life Cycle

SOURCE: Based on Lowell J. Authur 1992, *Rapid Evolutionary Development*, John Wiley & Sons, New York.

Perhaps the most significant modern project management methodology milestone is Barry Boehm's Spiral Model (see figure 4.11). Boehm's model is a risk-driven approach to evolving the fundamental IT project phases of requirements, design and implementation (where implementation is code, test and install) identified by previous IT development models. High risks are identified early in Boehm's model and immediately addressed through prototypes, simulations, models or benchmarks. Each cycle starts by determining its objectives, alternatives and constraints. The model then evaluates each alternative relative to the objectives and constraints of that cycle.

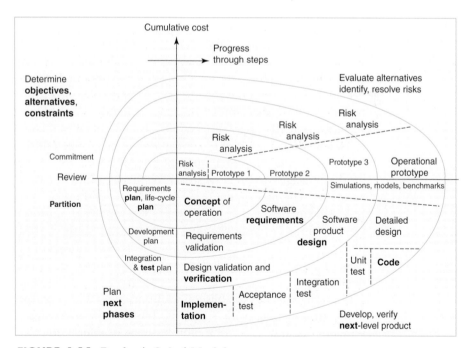

FIGURE 4.11: Boehm's Spiral Model

SOURCE: Barry W. Boehm 1988, 'A Spiral Model of Software Development and Enhancement', *IEEE Computer* 21(2), May, pp. 61–72. © 1988 IEEE.

Boehm's model addresses a constantly changing environment through regular reviews with key project stakeholders, who direct the objectives, alternatives and constraints. Risks in staying within these project parameters are then primarily addressed through prototyping.

RAPID APPLICATION DEVELOPMENT (RAD)

Acceptance of an iterative life cycle approach to IT development, however, initially grew with an increase in the number of IT development tools. James Martin coined the term Rapid Application Development (RAD) in his 1991 publication of the same name. Martin identified four key elements, which he called the four pillars of RAD.[34] These were:

- tools
- methodology
- people
- management.

The four phases in Martin's RAD life cycle[35] are:

- *requirements planning:* High-level managers, executives and knowledgeable end users determine the system requirements.
- *user design:* End users and IT staff participate in JAD workshops, where a group of users and/or team members interact, learn from one another and discuss problems for resolution. A structured workshop can be used to define requirements and design system externals.[36]
- *construction:* The same IT staff who created the design now generate the code using CASE tools code generators. Those involved use integrated CASE tools to support the rapid prototyping of system design, employing an integrated toolset that supports modelling, prototyping and code reusability. Prototyping tools that have maintained strength in the market have been those that are not tied to particular process or data modelling tools such as Microsoft's Visual Basic. Rational and other vendors are now releasing RAD support tools that can be applied in a component fashion.[37]

  Timeboxing, a method of controlling scope, applied during analysis or construction, imposes an immovable deadline on the completion of a task, activity, stage or system by strictly controlling functionality.[38]
- *cut-over:* The new system is delivered to the end users.

A working example of a RAD development approach is the DSDM Consortium's Dynamic Systems Development Method (DSDM). Figure 4.12 illustrates the DSDM processes and flows. The consortium emphasises that how the three phases overlap and merge is left to a particular project to decide.[39]

Cisco Systems has established an Internet-enabled enterprise that conducts online transactions with suppliers, business partners and customers. Cisco developed a strategy to solve most business problems quickly (in 30 to 90 days) using common, scalable infrastructure. The company was quick to recognise the importance of business culture in their technology solutions, and they have successfully put their ideas into practice.

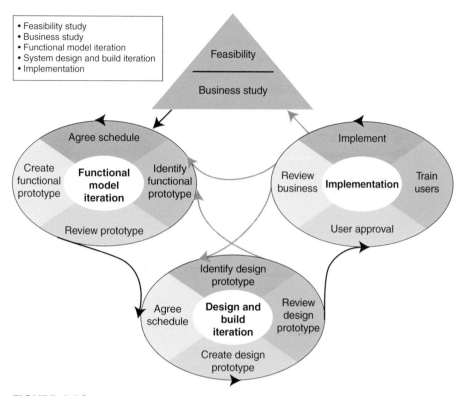

- Feasibility study
- Business study
- Functional model iteration
- System design and build iteration
- Implementation

Feasibility

Business study

Agree schedule

Create functional prototype | **Functional model iteration** | Identify functional prototype

Review prototype

Implement

Review business | **Implementation** | Train users

User approval

Identify design prototype

Agree schedule | **Design and build iteration** | Review design prototype

Create design prototype

FIGURE 4.12: DSDM process diagram

SOURCE: F. Cross 2000, 'Towards a RAD Approach to Electronic Business Project Management', MDP Project A, UTS, June, p. 35.

DEFINITIONAL FRAMEWORK FOR RAD

Collating the foundations of RAD from Boehm's Spiral and Martin's RAD principles with what contemporary literature and references considered to be RAD characteristics, RAD is therefore *a risk-driven evolutionary IT development methodology that employs disciplined iterative planning and control, and leverages prototyping and development process automation tools and techniques to regularly deliver functionality that avoids specifications becoming obsolete.* This definition emphasises that evolutions, or iterations of development, have a controlled scope and scheduling. The definition also brings risk back into focus as a key element that drives the scope of each development cycle.

E-business is a growing phenomenon, so demand for effective implementation is inevitable. Organisations must embrace change and react to it quickly. E-business development must be a joint effort throughout. Organisations require vision, design, culture change, corporate commitment, compatible management processes and external relationships. E-business demands standards and systems integration.[40]

Given these issues, the following synergies exist between e-commerce IT development and a RAD project management approach.

- RAD is designed to manage the changing requirements inherent in e-commerce development.

- RAD uses Joint Application Development (JAD) workshops and relies on constant user involvement, as does e-commerce development.
- RAD promotes prototyping and component reuse, both of which are appropriate to the ability to deliver quick responses to the changing demands of the e-commerce environment.
- RAD requires a high level of commitment to avoid excessive bureaucracy and promote a changing mindset, as does e-commerce.
- RAD requires a disciplined focus on principal objectives to meet project goals and targets.[41]

EXTREME PROGRAMMING

Extreme programming (XP) aims to:
- develop better quality software
- introduce shorter cycle times
- lower costs with a revised development cycle.

XP assumes that the four project variables of cost, time, scope and quality can be controlled. Further information on this topic may be found at www.xprogramming.com and www.extremeprogramming.org.

AUDITING E-COMMERCE

An e-commerce audit begins with a process of information gathering and risk assessment. Some of the risks associated with e-commerce are set out in table 4.5 below and must be addressed both during systems development and after implementation.[42]

TABLE 4.5	ADDRESSING RISKS IN E-COMMERCE
RISK	**COMMENTS**
Strategic	A competitor could use the Internet to gain competitive advantage. Barnes and Noble lost competitive edge to upstart Amazon.
Economic	To ensure sufficient Return on Investment (ROI), try pilot projects, take a long-term view on ROI and use strong project management skills.
Security	Ensure network architecture is designed for security — use encryption, authentication technologies, intrusion detection systems.
Reliability	Automate business rules and controls, use intelligent filtering technologies and test new e-commerce systems comprehensively.
Disruption	Build redundancy into e-commerce networks, use mirroring on different servers in different geographical areas.
Image	Hackers can vandalise web sites and embarrass organisations — e.g. hack attacks on government sites such as the CIA.
Moral	Have appropriate usage policies in place for staff.
Legal	Obtain legal advice during system design, authenticate users and apply appropriate legal rules to different locations. Do not assume the Internet is not policed.

SOURCE: D. Powell 2000, *Consuming E-commerce*, CP Australia, September, p. 43.

SUMMARY

In the networked economy, businesses are realising that to succeed they must improve their access to markets and increase their inter-organisational and intra-organisational efficiency. System development methodologies that are proving useful include Rapid Application Development and Joint Application Development. Because of the multidisciplinary nature of e-commerce, multidisciplinary teams are essential to the success of the projects. Many large organisations' web development methodologies include Dynamic Systems Development Methodology (DSDM), Rational Unified Process and IBM's e-business methodology. The evolution of web object architectures illustrates the convergence of the Web, CORBA and Java. Project management techniques must also be put in place and risk management cannot be ignored.

key terms

asynchronous	enhancements	Rational Unified Process (RUP)
back channel	functional design specification	Structured Query Language (SQL)
behaviour oriented	Joint Application Development	support
Common Object Request Broker Architecture (CORBA)	legacy systems	synchronous
data-oriented systems	middleware	timeboxing
data warehouse	network effect	Unified Modelling Language (UML)
design specifications	process oriented	Use Case modelling
Distributed Component Object Model (DCOM)	project management	user requirements document
	prototype	
	rapid application development	

DISCUSSION QUESTIONS

1. Write a report on 'The Networked Economy', outlining its advantages and disadvantages.

2. Prepare a research paper on one of the following methodologies:
   • The Booch Method Reference
   • Application Development Method (ADM)
   • Process Engineering Methodology.

3. Debate the following statement:

   The Internet is a collection of nodes and these nodes need to speak to one another. (Microsoft's) .NET aims to provide that flexibility.[43]

4. Research current project management practices for developing e-business sites.

VIRTUAL VINEYARDS TAPS INTO REAL-TIME, ONLINE WINE SALES

case study

For Virtual Vineyards, selling wine not just when it's time but in real time is an online business that's growing 20 per cent a month.

Combining a knowledge of spirits and high technology, the company's founders took their business online four years ago with a shopping-cart model that lets customers see what's actually in stock when they place an order.

'This is not just a catalog on the Web; we allocate wine to an order,' said Cyrus Khoshnevisan, director of engineering for Virtual Vineyards in Palo Alto, California. 'Once you sell out of a vintage of wine, it is gone, so we have to have a real-time inventory.'

This use of real-time inventory at an e-commerce site is fairly unique, according to International Data Corp. 'It's more indicative of companies who are on the cutting edge,' said Juliana Nelson, a senior analyst with IDC in Mountain View, California. A recent IDC report on the top 100 e-commerce vendors revealed that only two-thirds of these market leaders operate back-end systems that are integrated with a Web front end, allowing such features as real-time inventory tracking.

In January 1995, Virtual Vineyards started its e-commerce site with the purchase of a Sun Solaris–based Web server to host its Web pages internally. The firm developed an ordering system based on Oracle Corp's Oracle8 database software and outsourced credit-card verification to Cybercash Inc.

Legal issues involved in selling alcohol, including which states it can be shipped to, encouraged Virtual Vineyards to keep distribution in-house. 'We facilitate the sale through legal channels so people can purchase wine,' Khoshnevisan said. To ensure that the purchaser is of the legal age to buy alcohol, the company requires an adult signature when the wine is delivered by UPS, FedEx or other service.

Toasting the host

In time, however, the popularity of the Web site made outsourcing it more appealing. In December, the Virtual Vineyards site handled 223 000 unique visitors, according to Media Metrix Inc. As those Christmas season sales taxed the single T-1 line coming into on-site Web servers, Virtual Vineyards opted to have Frontier GlobalCenter of Sunnyvale, California, host its Web site.

'Originally, we were on a single T-1 with a single point of sale, but that was not enough bandwidth,' said Khoshnevisan. From a cost perspective, outsourcing Web hosting bought additional reliability, performance and security at the same price as purchasing the additional bandwidth would have.

Virtual Vineyards now spends between US$5000 and US$10 000 a month to host its Web services with Frontier GlobalCenter. 'If we had bought a fractional T-3 for the bandwidth, it would cost the same amount, but bring the headache of maintaining the network infrastructure,' said Khoshnevisan.

Instead, Frontier GlobalCenter provides the 24-by-7 network management and operations. 'We have a number of facilities around the country ... that are high-spec, hardened facilities with on-site network operations and on-site

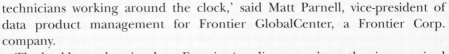

technicians working around the clock,' said Matt Parnell, vice-president of data product management for Frontier GlobalCenter, a Frontier Corp. company.

The backbone that ties these Frontier 'media centers' together is comprised of two OC-48 connections with a bandwidth capacity of 5G bps. This backbone services some of the largest Web sites in the world, including Yahoo! and The Washington Post. Multiple points of presence make it possible for Frontier to mirror its customers' sites and connect Internet users to the geographically closest server. Although Virtual Vineyards hasn't opted to mirror its sites yet, the company still benefits from Frontier's well-established infrastructure.

'Virtual Vineyards is sitting in these same buildings and getting the same advantages as other customers,' said Parnell. 'Since this is our business, we build networks to a much higher level than an individual company could,' he said.

Monthly hosting charges can range from US$3000 to tens of thousands of dollars, depending on the amount of bandwidth and space required.

As it grew in size, Virtual Vineyards also changed its credit authorization service supplier from CyberCash to Signio Inc. (formerly PaymentNet Inc.). Virtual Vineyards decided to make the switch because it viewed Signio as an up-and-coming company with good customer service.

'They have software on our servers and [after customers establish] SSL-based connections across the Internet, we can do credit-card captures and authorizations,' Khoshnevisan said.

E-commerce sites pay for authorized transactions according to the number that come through each month. After a one-time setup fee of US$250, monthly charges range from US$49 for 250 transactions to US$229 for 2000 transactions.

Distilling the network infrastructure

The setup involves Sun Microsystems Inc.'s Solaris-based Sparc 5 and Sparc 10 servers that run Netscape Communications Corp's Enterprise Server to deliver both the external Web site and an internal intranet. Both are connected to a Sun Solaris–based E3000 database server running Oracle's Oracle8i database server software and Signio's credit-card authorization server. All of this is hosted at Frontier's Sunnyvale Media Center. To keep traffic evenly balanced between the Sparc 5 and 10, Frontier uses Radware Ltd's WSD-Pro load balancer.

The network fabric that underlies Virtual Vineyards' Napa and Palo Alto offices along with Frontier's Sunnyvale Media Center is stitched together via a Pacific Bell T-1 by Cisco Systems Inc.'s 2500, 2600 and 1605 routers, respectively, two of which connect locally to a LAN via a Cisco 2916M XL Fast Ethernet Switch; the third connects via a basic 10BaseT Ethernet hub.

Although Frontier's high-bandwidth connection to the Internet could service all of Virtual Vineyards' internal Internet traffic through the Cisco 1605, the company has chosen to route most of that traffic through a Cisco 2500 router in Palo Alto that connects to the Internet via T-1 to PSINet Inc., the company's ISP. Eventually, Virtually Vineyards intends to push its internal Internet traffic through the 1605 in Sunnyvale once its Cisco IOS Firewall software is updated.

To monitor performance on its Web site, Virtual Vineyards subscribes to Keynote Systems Inc.'s Web site response service, Keynote Perspective. 'We use Keynote to make sure we are competitive and as fast as we can be,' said Khoshnevisan. Keynote Systems, of San Mateo, California, provides its customers with daily reports on how well their Web sites are performing.

As a customer places an order on the Virtual Vineyards Web site, the order is recorded in a transaction table. The payment server detects transactions as they occur and handles credit-card authorization through a secure connection to Signio. The order is then verified and processed by Virtual Vineyards' customer-service department via the company intranet. At that point, the order is sent to the company's warehouse for packing and shipping. Orders placed by 10 a.m. are sent that day. Virtual Vineyards maintains an extranet with Limestone International, its Napa, California–based distribution subsidiary. Through SSL and passwords, data are securely exchanged and orders are filled.

Shipments are automatically monitored using the tracking ID assigned by UPS or FedEx. Upon verification of delivery, the system notifies customers via e-mail.

Spicing up the design

A combination of consultants and in-house HTML writers designed the Virtual Vineyards Web site, now in its third generation. The result was a template-driven site that is routinely updated using text editors. 'One thing about Web design is that it is never-ending,' Khoshnevisan said.

For the fourth iteration of its Web pages, Virtual Vineyards is considering using an outside agency for design. 'Writing with JavaScript and new HTML takes a certain amount of knowledge that you can't have in just a few people,' he said. The new designs will include Java-based pages for the first time and debut before the Christmas holiday, he said.

To gain additional exposure on the Web, Virtual Vineyards uses an affiliate promotion program. Partners that place an icon for virtualvin.com on their site gain 8 per cent referral commissions on all sales from that location. The company has also purchased keywords and placed advertisements with the search engine sites Yahoo! and Excite.

'We did take a look at people who say, "We promise on searches that you will show up first," but we did not find one that was reliable to our satisfaction,' said Khoshnevisan.

SOURCE: K. Sullivan 1999, www.zdnet.com/solutions/stories/0,5918,2315043,00.html.

Questions

1. Outline the advantages and disadvantages of outsourcing the hosting of an e-commerce site.

2. Visit the web sites of Sun, Oracle and Cisco; investigate their e-business strategies and prepare a short report on the advice they offer e-commerce companies.

3. Do a search for ZDNet's Internet X-Ray, which is mentioned in this article. Write a short report on its usefulness as an interactive web tool.

SUGGESTED READING

Amor, D. 1999, *The e-business ®evolution: Living and Working in an Interconnected World*, Prentice Hall, New Jersey.

Commonwealth of Australia 2000, 'The Integration of Business E-Commerce Systems: Scoping Study for the National Electronic Authentication Council (NEAC)', August, p. 11, www.dcita.gov.au or www.noie.gov.au.

Kelly, Kevin 1998, *New Rules for the New Economy*, Viking, New York.

Lawrence et al. 2000, *Internet Commerce: Digital Models for Business*, 2nd Edition, John Wiley & Sons, Brisbane.

May, P. 2000, *The Business of Ecommerce: From Corporate Strategy to Technology*, Cambridge University Press, Cambridge, UK.

END NOTES

1. Kelly 1998, p. 9.
2. May 2000, p. 199.
3. Olle, T. et al. 1991, *Information Systems Methodologies: A Framework for Understanding*, 2nd Edition, Addison-Wesley, London, pp. 52–6.
4. Grady Booch, quoted in May 2000, p. 200.
5. Joint Application Development, www.netmation.com/docs/bb12.htm.
6. Joint Application Development, www.netmation.com/docs/bb12.htm.
7. Williams, G. and Behrendorff, G. 2000, *To Web or Not to Web?*, Australian CPA, August 2000, p. 51.
8. 'What is in DSDM?', http://dsdmtest.software.plc.uk/gs_02_01_overview_02.asp#What.
9. May 2000, p. 244.
10. Commonwealth of Australia 2000.
11. Newton, S, 1999, 'Electronic Business: Critical Success Factors for Implementation — A Case Study of a Manufacturer of Electronic Parts', Collecter99 Conference Student Proceedings, Wellington, New Zealand, November.
12. Gupta, R. and Randall, R. 2000, m-Commerce – September 2000, Real estate, http://www.ey.com/global/gcr.nsf/UK/Real_Estate_-_ebusiness_-_mcommerce.
13. Manktelow, N. 2001, 'Interactive TV waits for prime time', IT section, *Sydney Morning Herald*, 20 February, p. 3.
14. 'ISO builds worldwide Extranet with Livelink', www.opentext.com/customers/case_studies/livelink_case_study_iso.pdf.
15. 'ISO builds worldwide Extranet with Livelink', www.opentext.com/customers/case_studies/livelink_case_study_iso.pdf.
16. Definition from www.whatis.com.
17. Newton 1999.
18. Newton 1999.
19. Newton 1999.

20. www.whatis.com.

21. Definitions from www.whatis.com.

22. Middleware Infrastructure Components. Commonwealth of Australia 2000, p. 18.

23. Definitions from www.whatis.com.

24. Amor 1999, p. 87.

25. Amor 1999, p. 88.

26. Amor 1999, p. 101.

27. Lawrence et al. 2000, pp. 67–9.

28. www.oracle.com.

29. Gomolski, Barbara 2000, Gartner Institute Director of Research, www.gatnerinstitute.com/resource/re_ebizart.htm.

30. This section on project management is taken from F. Cross and E. Lawrence 2001, 'E-Project Management: A RADical Approach to E-Business', unpublished paper.

31. Authur, Lowell J. 1992, *Rapid Evolutionary Development*, John Wiley & Sons, New York.

32. Clarke, R. January 2000, 'The Conventional System Life Cycle'. This document is at www.anu.edu.au/people/Roger.Clarke/SOS/SLC.html.

33. Authur 1992, p. 19.

34. University of Dallas, Graduate School of Management, June 2000, MGT 7378: Advanced Systems Analysis and Design, http://gsmweb.udallas.edu/mraising/mgt7378/chap_13/sld002.html.

35. University of Dallas, Graduate School of Management, June 2000, MGT 7378: Advanced Systems Analysis and Design, http://gsmweb.udallas.edu/mraising/mgt7378/chap_13/sld004.html.

36. Viasoft Inc. web site. Global Topics Knowledge Base. June 2000, http://vpweb.viasoft.com/demo15/segments/lds00001/method/meth/mm900/mm900nd2.htm.

37. Rational web site, www.rational.com/media/news/factsheet.pdf.

38. Viasoft Inc. web site. Global Topics Knowledge Base. June 2000, http://vpweb.viasoft.com/demo15/segments/lds00001/method/meth/mm900/mm900nd2.htm.

39. Stapleton, Jennifer 1997, *DSDM Dynamic Systems Development Method*, Addison-Wesley, Cambridge, MA, p. 4.

40. Cross, F. 2000, 'Towards a RAD Approach to Electronic Business Project Management', MDP Project A, UTS, June, p. 35.

41. Cross 2000.

42. Powell, D. 2000, *Consuming E-commerce*, CP Australia, September, p. 43.

43. Anonymous 2000, 'Building the Business Internet: Tech-Ed 2000', *Communiqué*, September, p. 18.

CHAPTER 5

BUSINESS TO BUSINESS INFRASTRUCTURE

Learning objectives

You will have mastered the material in this chapter when you can:

- understand and define the terms XML, XSL, DTD and XML/EDI
- define and understand the term extranet
- define and understand the term VPN (Virtual Private Network).

'The prediction I can make with the highest confidence is that the most amazing discoveries will be the ones we are today not wise enough to foresee.'

Carl Sagan and Ann Druyan 1998, *Billions and Billions: Thoughts on Life and Death at the Brink of the Millennium*, Ballantine Books, New York.

While every business across the globe differs in some respect, each striving to meet unique objectives in sales, profit growth, market share, customer satisfaction or service, there are certain core objectives that apply universally. Key objectives[1] (see figure 5.1) continually challenge businesses to make the most of available infrastructure and, in particular, information technology.

Businesses need to accelerate their knowledge of trading partners, customers and end users. The flow of routine business transactions and goods must be efficient and visible. Optimal time to market for products and services is paramount. Errors in routine transactions, costs of inventory, and manufacturing and accounting cycles should be constantly monitored and reduced where possible.

Businesses must also eliminate non-value tasks and transactions; duplication of processes between partners; the costs of paper transactions; and operational barriers between trading partners. Competitive advantage should constantly be improved by providing better customer service; streamlining critical business information flows and, most important, maximising positive return on investment.

THE B2B TRANSFORMATION

In an effort to reduce cost and improve efficiency, electronic commerce emerged in the 1980s with the use of electronic messaging technologies and, in particular, electronic data interchange (EDI). EDI technology enables the exchange of information and electronic documents (invoices, for example) between business partners. Organisations found that they could communicate both internally and between partners in a more efficient and standardised manner. EDI was quickly recognised as an effective vehicle for reducing costs incurred in processing, handling and storage of product, and thus improving the overall profitability of the business.

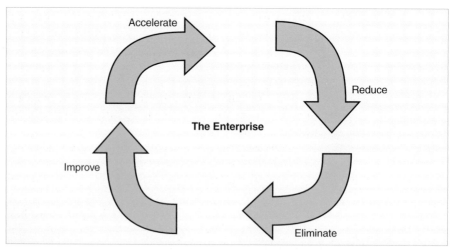

FIGURE 5.1: The Accelerate–Reduce–Eliminate–Improve cycle

SOURCE: TradeGate ECA and PIEC 1998, 'Pharmaceutical Industry Electronic Commerce Directions and Guidelines', TradeGate Australia, Sydney (www.tradegate.org.au).

The widespread adoption of the Internet in the early 1990s presented a milestone for e-commerce. The Internet has emerged as a low-cost, easy-to-use medium that encourages social interaction and knowledge exchange on a global scale. For businesses, this technology presents a new and highly effective avenue for conducting business. The router manufacturer Cisco is a prime example[2] of how a company has transformed its business using Internet technology.

The Internet allows business to transform itself from the closed 'one-to-one' EDI market model to that of the networked enterprise — it has provided the infrastructure for buyers and sellers to communicate, collaborate, and procure goods and services. **Extensible Markup Language (XML)** plays a vital role in this business to business infrastructure.

This collaborative infrastructure has manifested itself in various models of cooperative B2B e-commerce. One example is the **extranet**, usually a private marketplace offering communication and collaboration among trading partners. The **Virtual Private Network** is one derivation of the extranet model.

XML

Extensible Markup Language was created by the World Wide Web Consortium (W3C) to compensate for the restrictions of Hypertext Markup Language (HTML). HTML, a derivative of **Standard Generalised Markup Language (SGML)**, employs a rigid yet simple structure that optimises the client's browser document viewing. HTML is outstanding for describing to a computer (or browser) the appearance of displayed information. HTML specifies, for example, whether a line of text should be bolded, a larger font or a different colour.

SGML is a highly complex, general-purpose metalanguage used to define rules for the management of differing document types.[3] As a universal standard, SGML not only describes the way document data are represented but also the data themselves. Paradoxically, because SGML is such a complex language, it permits many alternatives for the presentation of data (thus minimising its effectiveness as a standard) and has limited application in the Internet environment. For these reasons, its mainstream implementation as an Internet technology has been limited.

Unfortunately, HTML has several limitations.[4]

- HTML does not allow individual elements on a page to be 'marked up' semantically. It is not possible in HTML to reproduce specifications or schema of database structures.
- HTML describes only the appearance of documents and cannot cater for content aspects — it is unsuitable for querying.
- HTML is not extensible — it is not possible to define new tags for particular requirements.

XML (derived from SGML) retains SGML's power while reducing its complexity. Where HTML describes the *layout* of information, XML describes what *kind of information* is being displayed.

XML is a **metalanguage**, which allows the user to define new tags describing particular data, and (as we will see) optionally create a set of rules called **Document Type Definitions (DTDs)**. Users may define their own new tags to suit their purpose and the types of data — for example purchase order number, supplier ID or delivery address.

XML provides a framework for describing documents, as in

```
<identifier> content </identifier>
```

where the user or developer defines the identifier and content, so that

```
<PONumber>999-1234</PONumber>
```

would essentially describe the purchase order identifier and actual content.

Any standard XML parser can read, decode and validate this text-based, self-describing document, extracting the data elements in a platform-independent way. Although the W3C developed the XML standard with the 'next generation' of web development in mind, application developers recognise the simplicity and power of this self-describing format and its ability to be deployed in application integration projects involving disparate platforms and applications. This paradigm works well between two entities that understand the defined tags and their meanings; however, developers may go beyond this to develop their own DTD and schema alternatives. To assist further, applications may access the data objects through another standard called the **Document Object Model (DOM)**.

DOM

The document object model is an Application Programming Interface (API) specification for HTML and XML documents.[5] DOM allows application programs to analyse document structures and add, modify and interpret document attributes. DOM is designed to be used with any programming language and is supported by major software vendors such as Microsoft.

DTDS AND XML SCHEMAS

XML provides a framework for the creation of tags and explicit document specification. However, it is very important that those who use these XML documents understand application-specific tags that may be created in the course of B2B e-commerce. When groups of users agree on certain document types they may do so using document type definitions (DTDs). DTDs are schemas that specify the valid tags and document classes within an XML document — they define the document type.

DTDs are developed at the time of XML application development and are normally used only to control XML tools and verify the validity of XML documents.

A DTD might be as follows.

```
<!ELEMENT purchaseorder (PONumber, POName, PODescription)>
<!ELEMENT PONumber (#PCDATA)*>
<!ELEMENT POName (#PCDATA)*>
<!ELEMENT PODescription (#PCDATA)*>
```

In addition to element names, the special symbol `#PCDATA` is reserved to indicate character data. `PCDATA` stands for Parseable Character data. For more information, refer to www.w3.org/xml.

XML schemas define and describe a class of XML documents by defining, constraining and documenting the meaning, usage and relationships of the parts of a document.[6] These parts include data types (e.g. character and date), elements (e.g. POName, as opposite), and their content and attributes with their corresponding values[7] (e.g. 'Warehouse Purchase Order 1', bold).

In particular, XML schemas address one of the major flaws in XML — the absence of data types. Although DTDs allow tags and structures of a document class to be defined, the content of the document elements and the values of attributes are always text strings.

XML schemas introduce other types, such as number and time, into XML and also permit user-defined types. The XML schema also supports modularisation, making reuse possible. For further information, refer to www.w3.org/TR/NOTE-xml-schema-req.

XSL

The layout of an XML document is not defined in the XML document itself or the DTD.[8] As a fundamental principle of XML, content should be separated from layout or presentation information. The layout or presentation of the XML document may be defined by the **Extensible Style Language (XSL)**, or by Cascading Style Sheets (CSS). A document may also have more than one XSL style sheet, resulting in more than one presentation for the document.

XSL supports a variety of outputs, including screen display, and may also be used to display XML documents as HTML. This has the advantage that XML documents are correctly interpreted by HTML-only browsers. The code below illustrates an XML document interpreted by XSL and presented as HTML.

An XSL style sheet document might read as follows.

```
<?xml version='1.0'?>
<xsl:stylesheet xmlns:xsl="XSLdoc" version="1.0">

<xsl:template match="PObold">
<strong><xsl:apply-templates/></strong>
</xsl:template>

<xsl:template match="POitalic">
  <i><xsl:apply-templates/></i>
</xsl:template>

</xsl:stylesheet>
```

With this style sheet, the following XML document:

```
<?xml version='1.0'?>
<PObold>Purchase Order <POitalic>999-1234</
POitalic></PObold>
```

would be transformed into:

```
<?xml version="1.0" encoding="utf-8"?>
<strong>Purchase Order <i>999-1234</i></strong>
```

XLINK AND XPOINTER

To enable elements to be inserted into XML documents in order to create and describe links between resources, the **XLINK** and **XPOINTER** standards have been defined.[9] These standards use XML syntax to create structures that can describe simple hyperlinks of HTML, as well as more sophisticated links, such as links to applications and other external objects. For further information, refer to www.w3.org/TR/xlink.

XPATH

XPATH is another W3C recommendation that has been created to provide a common syntax for querying and addressing the contents of XML documents.[10] It also provides basic facilities for manipulation of strings, numbers and boolean values. As SQL operates with relational databases, XPATH uses a compact, non-XML syntax to facilitate the retrieval of XML documents (or subsets of documents) from XML sources, such as a database. XPATH is also used by the XSL Transformation language (XSLT), XLINK and XPOINTER. For further information, refer to www.w3.org/TR/xpath.

BENEFITS OF XML

The XML standard promises an open interface for secure B2B Internet commerce that will be sure to entice small to medium enterprises (SMEs). For I-commerce software vendors and industry groups, XML's universal data interchange format offers a standards-based language to use with other protocols, such as HTTP and TCP/IP. Vendor support has been forthcoming with database vendors Oracle and IBM supporting XML natively; version 5.0 of the Microsoft and Netscape web browsers interpret XML; and Sun Microsystems considers the standard to be the portable data language for Java.

IBM have created a complete suite of tools that will enable developers to create XML applications. They include Bean Markup Language, XML Editor Maker, DataCraft, Dynamic XML with Java, PatML, TeXML, XML Bean Maker, XML TreeDiff and XML Productivity Kit for Java.[11]

The immediate benefits of XML-based e-commerce with its promise of simple implementation, wide availability, and lower costs are sure to entice both large and small organisations. With these benefits and the backing of the major e-commerce players, XML is sure to become a recognised standard.

The benefits of XML are outlined below.

- XML is based on open standards — data and presentation tags are separate; the language is extensible; stylesheets can be self-controlled; and XML is flexible enough to be used in both business to business e-commerce and application integration.

- XML has industry support. W3C adopted XML in 1998; other major industry groups such as OASIS, OBI, CommerceNet and BizTalk have all endorsed the use of XML in B2B exchange.
- XML documents can be transmitted using HTTP. XML is supported by the infrastructure of the Internet.

XML/EDI

One interesting consequence of the XML movement is the collaboration of XML standards technology with the EDI environment. The **XML/EDI** framework, created by the XML/EDI Group,[12] is striving to streamline the interaction of the Internet and EDI in today's business environment. In 1997 the XML/EDI Group was formed as a group of professionals from around the world who would together focus on the creation of a B2B framework. The framework is an international effort involving individuals from small and medium enterprises as well as major technological companies.

Essentially, three core models are required to be supported by XML/EDI. These are:
- online real-time or 'Interactive'
- forms-based
- batch transactions (a set of XML/EDI data to be processed in a single computer transaction).

XML/EDI business transactions will take place via servers, desktops and laptops using:
- a general-purpose document browser as the user interface
- a common language for the description of templates and associated conversion rules
- distributed processing to support centralised functions.

In essence, XML/EDI is the fusion of five technologies (see figure 5.2). These five technologies are[13]:
- *XML*
- *EDI*
- *templates:* rules for the expression of XML (often DTDs are used for this purpose)
- *agents:* applications that interpret templates to perform the desired functions. Agents also interact with the XML transaction and the user to create new templates for each new specific task. They are often written in the Java or ActiveX language.
- *repository:* the component that provides the semantic foundation, or dictionary, for business transactions. The repository allows users and software agents to 'look up' or 'cross-reference' EDI elements or entities.

Each component adds unique tools that leverage the other components. In the past, EDI has been quite static; today the XML/EDI framework provides an exciting, dynamic process that can be infinitely extended.

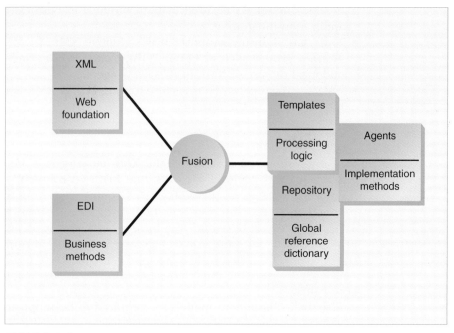

FIGURE 5.2: XML/EDI e-business framework

SOURCE: XML/EDI Group.[14]

Currently, XML is not able to replace EDI as a messaging and transmission standard. EDI bodies such as EDIFACT have spent years developing standards that associate tags with particular values. These tags and values in an XML schema do not currently exist in a commonly agreed data dictionary — thus, XML is not expected to replace EDI but to complement it. Table 5.1 compares XML and EDI solutions, after which EDI and XML coding examples are presented.

TABLE 5.1	XML AND EDI SOLUTIONS COMPARED
XML-BASED SOLUTION	**EDI-BASED SOLUTION**
Optimised for easy programming	Optimised for compressed messages
Uses existing Internet connection	Frequently uses value-added networks (VANs), charging between $1 and $20 per message
XML message format learned in hours	EDI message format takes months to master
Requires only JavaScript, Visual Basic, Python or Perl script writers	Requires highly trained programmers

SOURCE: www.xmls.com/resources/whitepapers/
XMLSolutions_Peaceful_Co-Existence.pdf.

EDI PURCHASE ORDER

```
ISA*00* *00* *08*61112500TST *01*DEMO WU000003
*970911*1039*U00302000009561*0*P?
GS*PO*6111250011*WU000003*970911*1039*9784*X*003020
ST*850*397822
BEG*00*RE*1234**980208
REF*AH*M109
REF*DP*641
REF*IA*000100685
DTM*010*970918
N1*BY*92*1287
N1*ST*92*87447
N1*ZZ*992*1287
PO1*1*1*EA*13.33**CB*80211*IZ*364*UP*718379271641
PO1*1*2*EA*13.33**CB*80211*IZ*382*UP*718379271573
PO1*1*3*EA*13.33**CB*80213*IZ*320*UP*718379271497
PO1*1*4*EA*13.33**CB*80215*IZ*360*UP*718379271848
PO1*1*5*EA*13.33**CB*80215*IZ*364*UP*718379271005
CTT*25
SE*36*397822
GE*1*9784
IEA*1*000009561
```

XML PURCHASE ORDER

```xml
<?xml version="1.0" ?>
<?xml:stylesheet?>
<purchase-order
    <header>
    <po-number>1234</po-number>
    <date>2000-08-08</date><time>12:05</time>
    </header>

    <billing>
    <company>XYZ Supply Store</company>
    <address>
    <street>601 Pennsylvania Ave. NW</street>
    <street>Suite 900</street>
    <city>Washington</city><st>DC</st><post-
      code>20004</postcode>
    </address>
    </billing>

    <order items="1" >
    <item>
    <reference>097251</reference>
    <description>Widgets</description>
    <quantity>4</quantity>
    <unit-price>11.99</unit-price>
    <price>47.96</price>
    </item>

    <tax type="sales" >
    <tax-unit>VA</tax-unit>
    <calculation>0.045</calculation>
    <amount>2.16</amount>
    </tax>
.. etc. ...
```

XML/EDI TRADING SYSTEM

With beginnings in the age of the VAN, when bandwidth was relatively expensive, EDI has been based upon compressed, cryptic message formats. These formats (such as EDIFACT and ANSI X12) save on message size but are inherently complex and are difficult to program and interpret by humans. XML overcomes these complexities by storing metadata within the message itself, thus making programming easier and more efficient. XML also uses the HTTP protocol as the transport mechanism, making transmission across the Internet inexpensive and convenient.[15]

The high costs associated with EDI have in the past meant that large enterprises have generally implemented EDI with the top tiers of their supply chain. Often this has meant that EDI systems operate between large-scale operators and neglect the small to medium-sized operators in the supply chain.

With an XML/EDI trading model (see figure 5.3), it is possible for large companies to extend their electronic supply chain beyond the large operators. By installing an XML/EDI translator on the enterprise web server, large-scale operators can effectively leverage their existing high-cost EDI implementations and open their doors to smaller trading partners. By utilising this XML/EDI translation engine, large companies can transmit XML documents (such as purchase orders and invoices) to *all* their trading partners across the Internet. Using this model, trading partners still using traditional EDI are not restricted by the new technology.

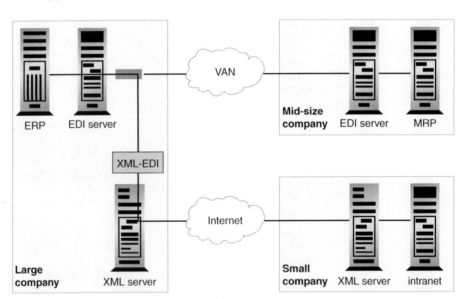

FIGURE 5.3: XML/EDI trading system

SOURCE: www.xmls.com/resources/whitepapers/
XMLSolutions_Peaceful_Co-Existence.pdf.

Small to medium-sized enterprises have traditionally not realised high gains from electronic data interchange. Since EDI is expensive, these firms have not gained the economies of scale afforded large companies — dealing with an electronic document can be just as expensive as dealing with a paper one.

Costs associated with computer power, skilled programming staff and VAN transmission costs have curbed implementation in the small enterprise.

However, with XML/EDI technology, these small to medium-sized enterprises may now participate in the trading partner network. By its very nature, XML/EDI utilises the HTTP protocol, thus enabling smaller enterprises to use web server and browser technology to access, print and transmit documents. With the simple implementation and low-cost entry, XML/EDI allows small and large trading partners alike to leverage new technology and import XML data directly into their corporate trading systems.

EBXML

In November 1999 the United Nations body CEFACT and OASIS partnered to implement a new standard named electronic business Extensible Markup Language (**ebXML**). EbXML focuses on creating a set of consistent components with which to conduct global B2B e-commerce, including modelling tools, XML and other Internet technologies.

Currently, there are more than 500 standards for XML schemas around the globe, depending on the application required. OAGI, RosettaNet, cXML and fpML are examples of the differing implementations. EbXML is a relatively new member in the common call for XML standardisation and XML-based e-business; however, it promises to be much more than 'just another standard'.

In contrast to vertically focused standards such as RosettaNet (www.rosettanet.org) or broad horizontal standards such as OAGI, ebXML represents a horizontal standard that has been designed to be used in depth with any vertical industry. EbXML is focusing on small to medium-sized enterprises (SMEs) in the global sphere as the target audience for the standard. Klaus-Dieter Naujok, ebXML's chairman, explains.

> Aside from the messaging specification, which allows you to move information back and forth, we include a 'discovery process'. This allows you to create a file of your e-business and business process capabilities and store it in our repository. When you do business using ebXML, you get the capability to discover the trading capabilities of your partner, so you know what you're going to have to have in order to do business with them. We're not just saying, 'Here's a purchase order.' We're tying it to a business process.[16]

The following insite is based upon the industry body BizTalk.org and discusses XML and B2B infrastructure.[17]

technical INSITE

XML AND B2B INFRASTRUCTURE

BizTalk™ is an organisation of businesses that support the adoption of XML for e-commerce and B2B integration. In particular, BizTalk.org is working towards establishing a framework that enables industries to create e-commerce standards for their unique sets of goods and services. Its goal is to provide an XML schema repository on the Internet where people can store and reference various types of data exchange schema.

(continued)

The BizTalk™ framework (see table 5.2) aims to achieve friction-free integration and provide the foundation for a glue-less world. The framework consists of:
- a technical specification that defines how to use XML in a consistent way
- a code set that defines a small number of mandatory and optional XML tags
- the www.biztalk.org web portal.

TABLE 5.2	THE BIZTALK™ FRAMEWORK	
NAME	**WHAT IT MEANS**	**ADVANTAGES**
Transport independence	A heterogeneous mix of applications will invariably require more than a single technical mechanism for exchanging data. Every approach to the application 'glue' will yield discovery of a hard-coded approach to data transport. The BizTalk™ framework is designed to be transport agnostic (independent).	Removes the transport decision from the glue layer
Location technology independence	Distributed computing platforms like COM™ and CORBA depend on several key assumptions, including: • sharing of a security domain context • sharing of a calling convention standard • sharing data types at the binary level • having a way to locate and activate the other application. In these distributed environments, a major assumption (and flaw) is that these applications are designed with each other in mind — an assumption that is invalid in a best-of-breed scenario. To adapt, solution implementers end up implementing glue layers. In these glue layers, the differences between applications are handled by a number of approaches that include: • hand coding around differences • using technology bridges • manually tracking differences in type, meaning, content and security. The BizTalk™ framework allows uncoupling of applications and setting up an infrastructure that will manage the flows of information being integrated. It does this by providing the mechanisms that abstract the location and technology dependencies — Location Technology Independence.	Reduces or eliminates complexity that lives between applications Reduces the costs associated with implementation, testing and maintenance of code Eliminates the need to share security contexts yet remain secure Eliminates code that manages location

Flexible data and transformation	Two applications rarely share exactly the same information and business event model. Invariably, transformation capabilities must be utilised to ensure alignment. The code involved in satisfying this alignment requirement may include function or method location, ordering parameters and coding around return conventions. The flexible nature of XML and the existence of XML Style Sheets (XSL) simplify the programming tasks associated with data transformation to a degree that makes the need to manage transformation within an adapter or glue layer unnecessary. Through publication of these XML documents, customers and software developers can access information and XSL maps that have been published to assist with transformation — and in cases where customers have common combinations of applications.	Removes the need for the adapter layer to share the same schema or data format with the partner application, or use an intermediate form of data.
XML tags	The term 'tags' is used to describe the special markup required by the W3C XML standard — technically referred to as 'Elements and Attributes'. The standard itself only describes how to create these markup tags and outlines the benefits of using them to describe data; it does not provide the tag names, their description or format (collectively known as schema). The BizTalk framework specification solves these key problems by defining three types of XML tags. Applications that use these tags can automatically determine these essential facts.	The special XML tags, or codes, defined by the BizTalk framework address schema issues and simplify application integration.

SOURCE: www.biztalk.org/library/about_XML.asp.

EXERCISES

1. What is meant by a glue-less world and the glue layer?
2. Visit the BizTalk site and outline any changes to the framework as discussed above.
3. How does the BizTalk framework tie in with the .NET program?

THE EXTRANET

WHAT IS AN EXTRANET?

Today the technology is available to extend information exchange beyond the company boundaries to reach a much larger audience, allowing businesses to reap great benefits from their existing Internet-based networks — more specifically, to adopt a new form of business communication enabling the company to simplify and enhance its communications with business partners, suppliers and customers both internationally and domestically.

This concept is known as the extranet. It uses Internet technology, including standard web servers, email clients and web browsers. This makes extranet development far more economical than the creation and maintenance of proprietary networks and applications. It enables trading partners, suppliers and customers with common interests to form a tight business relationship and a strong communication bond.

THE EXTRANET AND B2B E-BUSINESS

Technical and cost advantages are, of course, very important. But the real significance of the extranet is that it is the first non-proprietary technical tool that can support the rapid evolution of e-commerce and e-business. Extranets have emerged as a system for effective two-way communication and controlled information exchange, and as a global mechanism for the procurement of goods and services at the wholesale level.

The extranet can provide an ideal medium for collaboration between business partners and as a vehicle for improving customer relationships. Streamlining communication between trading partners can aid the organisation in many trade-related activities, including:

- product planning and design
- efficient distribution of product fact sheets and legal documentation
- scheduling by using interactive calendars
- competitive information acquisition
- enhancing customer relationships via product visibility and cross-selling.

Avnet Electronics Marketing, a business unit of Avnet, Inc.,[18] offers one illustration. The company sells electronic components to more than 100 000 trading partners worldwide. With companies like IBM and Toshiba as customers, Avnet decided that the extranet was the best way to offer the best customer service and hence outdo the competition.

Three groups of people access the extranet — suppliers, Avnet Electronics Marketing employees and customers. The suppliers tap the extranet to view information on sales volume, sales opportunities and quotation responses. Customers use the site to access information on products, pricing and inventory. Avnet's employees can find personal information, including medical insurance options and employee directories.

The result is that everyone in the supply chain, from suppliers to customers, uses the system and can work seamlessly from anywhere in the world at any time. The goal is to make the customer satisfied — to push forward the customer experience and increase the value of the product and service. Figure 5.4 illustrates the Avnet Electronics Marketing extranet architecture.

FIGURE 5.4: Part selection screen, Avnet Electronics Marketing extranet

SOURCE: www.avnet.com. Reproduced courtesy of Avnet, Inc.

THE KNOWLEDGE FACTORY

Extranets are also likely to redefine the business evolution of the enterprise into 'the knowledge factory'. To survive and prosper in the new digital economy, businesses must position themselves as high-tech enterprises, as aggressively evolving 'knowledge factories' that are internationally competitive. Hence, an extranet must be capable of:

- gathering relevant data from suppliers, customers and other key sources (such as universities, the business community or the government)
- adding value by creating information (new knowledge), often jointly with strategic partners
- disseminating (selling) the added-value product to the customers.

Through the extranet, a business is adding value for the customer and thus creating competitive advantage. By empowering the customer — treating the customer as a business partner — the extranet involves the customer in the business process, becoming part of the decision-making process.

Order tracking at FedEx is a prime example of how the customer has become a trusted partner in the business. FedEx have enabled the customer to 'see' into the business while providing a value-added service. By entering a parcel code, the customer can find the exact location of the parcel, with information on pick-up time and expected delivery time available for perusal. While the customer is at the site, clever cross-promotional advertisements and offers of free software downloads entice the customer to stay, further enhancing the experience and the customer value.

A study from Visa International has found that the extranet architecture will be increasingly utilised in the expected B2B e-commerce market boom of the next four years.[19] Conducted by consulting firm Wharton Econometric

Forecasting Associates Group, the study estimates that the worldwide market for commercial e-commerce is expected to exceed US$1 trillion by 2003. The study, which Visa claims is the 'most comprehensive evaluation of the commercial electronic marketplace to date', predicts a trend towards the use of extranets, rather than the Internet, as the preferred medium for e-commerce. Currently, the Internet accounts for more than 95 per cent of e-commerce activity. By 2003, 27 per cent will be generated over extranets linking organisations to particular suppliers or supplier networks. Visa says the results suggest 'significant opportunities' for banks to meet the needs of their commercial customers for a 'fully automated order-to-payment-to-reporting process'.

BENEFITS OF THE EXTRANET

The extranet is a key business initiative in B2B e-commerce (see table 5.3). It provides a mechanism for improving efficiencies through trading partner collaboration and digital information exchange. Furthermore, the extranet provides a meeting place for trading partners with a vested interest in their supply chain, its success and its future. The extranet is a simple yet effective means of attaining and sustaining critical mass among e-commerce trading partners.

The extranet offers the customer a unique view of the company. It allows the customer to participate in the decision-making processes within the company by invoking a sense of visibility in the business. The customer experiences a closer relationship with the company and therefore creates a stronger bond with the company and the brand. The extranet offers the organisation one avenue for enhancing the customer relationship and thus improving competitive advantage.

TABLE 5.3 EXTRANET BENEFITS[20]
BUSINESS BENEFITS
Cost-effective • Reduces need for distribution of physical documentation • Based on Internet infrastructure, not proprietary VAN
Secure, auditable architecture
Scalable architecture
Moderate setup cost
Low user training costs
Technology agnostic (based on universal HTTP protocol)
Increases customer and partner loyalty and commitment
Ideal environment for project collaboration
CUSTOMER BENEFITS
Personalised content
Immediate access to information, rich in format
Ease of use
Increased sense of community

SOURCE: R. H. Baker 1997, *Extranets: The Complete Sourcebook*, McGraw-Hill, New York.

EXTRANET ARCHITECTURE

The technology of the extranet is based on the infrastructure and protocols of the Internet — in particular, TCP/IP for networking and HTML, SMTP and XML for presentation and interpretation of information. Regardless of access technology or back-end database systems, extranets typically require the following components (see figure 5.5)[21]:

- *TCP/IP deployment:* Extranets are built upon the infrastructure of the Internet, which in turn has been structured around the TCP/IP protocol. The corporate network must also ensure an IP application is installed across machines on the network and the network itself.
- *browser:* The web browser interprets markup languages such as HTML and XML. The browser runs on top of the IP stack and, through protocols such as the Point-to-Point Protocol (PPP), communicates with the network and web server.
- *web server:* A web server application typically runs on the NT, Unix or Linux operating system, although other platforms such as Macintosh can run such applications. The software can range in complexity from a simple web server that supplies static HTML pages to customers through to a sophisticated e-commerce transaction server utilising the Secure Sockets Layer (SSL) (discussed in chapter 7) and digital certificates.
- *remote access server:* A multi-protocol remote access server links remote users to corporate resources, applications and Internet access via a telephone line. A remote access server should support all protocols that are to be run on the corporate network.
- *Client dial-in software:* Remote dial-in software should be installed on the remote user's computer and should be available across operating systems (Macintosh and PC) to ensure a full range of access. This software initiates the call, negotiates the connection and also terminates the connection upon ending the session.
- *Internet connection device:* A router connects the extranet to a third-party Internet service provider (ISP). The device generally supports the Internet Protocol (IP) and IPX (Novell's Internetwork Packet eXchange) protocols and IP packet filtering. Typically, a leased line or modem is used to connect to the ISP.
- *firewall:* When extending network access to external partners — beyond the boundaries of the enterprise — it is essential to utilise a firewall (typically Unix or NT based). The firewall screens all inbound traffic (including IP addresses and applications) for unwanted material and potential intruders into the network.

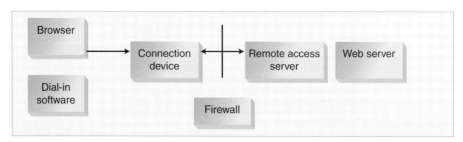

FIGURE 5.5: Extranet architecture[22]

SOURCE: Based on R. H. Baker (1997).

EXTRANET SECURITY

An extranet is used to aid collaboration among interested communities. The open nature of the extranet means that internal company information, such as databases, product information, accounting records, even email, may be open to misuse by intruders, so security measures must be put in place to regulate access.

Securing the extranet is similar to securing other types of networks; since it is based on Internet infrastructure, the basic principles of computer and network security apply. Security principles will be dealt with in detail in chapter 9.

According to GE Information Services, there are four major steps involved in initiating a security plan.[23]

1. Make security a priority in the early planning stages of the extranet.
2. Analyse the security risks as well as the value of the information being published. Will the extranet be visible on the Internet? How much of the data are sensitive? Are there connections to back-end database systems?
3. Apply the correct level of authentication and encryption technology.
4. Limit access from inside and outside the system.

SECURING THE EXTRANET TRANSACTION — THE ROLE OF ENCRYPTION AND AUTHENTICATION

Transaction security is of the utmost importance in an extranet environment. The protection of passwords, account numbers, credit card details and other such information is paramount. Trading partners and consumers alike must have sufficient confidence in the system to buy and sell goods and services electronically. To minimise concern,[24] and protect the data being exchanged by trading partners, the e-commerce system must address four security areas, as described below.

EXTRANET CONFIDENTIALITY AND PRIVACY

There is little doubt that as a business grows, communication with trading partners and the use of online private information will increase in the course of daily operation. As the community becomes more dependent on the business to act as a carrier of vital and sensitive information, so too will the community members demand that these transactions be kept confidential and the privacy of members' information ensured.

The threat of unauthorised monitoring of this information (packet sniffing), with unauthorised people 'hacking' into systems to monitor and interpret traffic, presents a real danger to the Internet community today. With the right equipment and 'know-how', hackers can gain access to entire networks and even compromise systems of trading partners connected to the business.

The Privacy Rights Clearinghouse (PRC), in conjunction with the principles laid out by the OECD in 1980, have released guidelines for implementing privacy in the organisation.[25]

GENERAL PRINCIPLES OF EXTRANET SECURITY

- *Openness.* There should be a general practice of openness about practices and policies with respect to personal information published in extranet systems. Means should be available to establish the existence and nature of personal information and the main purposes of its use.

- *Purpose specification.* The purpose for collecting personal information on the extranet should be specified at the time of collection. Further uses should be limited to those purposes.
- *Collection limitation.* The collection of personal information on the extranet should be undertaken by lawful and fair means and with the knowledge and consent of the subject. Only that information necessary for the stated purpose should be collected — nothing more.
- *Use limitation.* Personal information should not be disclosed on extranet systems for secondary purposes without the consent of the subject or by authority of law.
- *Individual participation.* Individuals should be allowed to inspect and correct their personal information — an extranet is directly suited to this purpose. Whenever possible, personal information should be collected directly from the individual.
- *Quality.* Personal information should be accurate, complete and timely, and be relevant to the purposes for which it is to be used. Extranet architecture supports this principle.
- *Security safeguards.* Personal information should be protected (by reasonable security safeguards) against such risks as loss, unauthorised access, destruction, use, modification or disclosure. Access to personal information should be limited to those within the organisation with a specific need to see it. Extranet security models support this principle.
- *Accountability.* Someone within the organisation, such as the chief information officer or an information manager, should be held accountable for complying with its privacy policy. Privacy audits to monitor organisational compliance should be conducted on a regular basis, as should employee training programs. Extranets are an auditable technology.

EXTRANET DATA AND NETWORK SECURITY

The following technical insite describes several guidelines from the OECD[26] for general privacy of data in the workplace.

technical INSITE

A QUESTION OF SECURITY

Here are a series of questions to take into account when considering the security of data, in particular in the extranet environment.
- Do you have staff specifically assigned to data security? Do staff members participate in regular training programs in order to keep abreast of technical and legal issues?
- Is physical access restricted to computer operations and paper/micrographic files that contain personally identifiable information? Do you have procedures to prevent former employees from gaining access to computers and paper files?
- Are sensitive files segregated in secure areas or computer systems and available only to qualified persons?
- Do you have audit procedures and strict penalties in place to discourage telephone fraud and theft of equipment and information?
- Do all employees follow strict password and virus protection procedures? Are employees required to change passwords often, using 'foolproof' methods?

(continued)

- Is encryption used to protect extremely sensitive information (a particularly important measure when transmitting personally identifiable information over public networks such as the Internet)?
- Do you regularly conduct 'systems penetration tests' to determine if your systems are 'hacker' proof?
- If your organisation is potentially susceptible to 'industrial espionage', have you taken extra precautions to guard against leakage of information?

EXERCISES

1. Prepare a report on changing passwords using 'fool-proof' methods.
2. Prepare a report on systems penetration testing.

ELECTRONIC MONITORING

Employers are now using a variety of monitoring practices, including telephone systems that allow supervisors to listen in to calls; computer keystroke monitoring systems; video monitoring systems; and Internet usage tracking systems.

The guidelines[27] for such systems are outlined below.

- Does the organisation have a policy that states the types of monitoring being conducted and the uses made of monitoring data? Does the policy include procedures to safeguard sensitive personal information encountered in the process of monitoring? Is this policy communicated to all employees at time of hiring?
- If telephone monitoring is being conducted, does the organisation provide telephones that are not monitored and can be used for personal calls?

Further details on security and privacy issues are in chapters 9 and 10.

EXTRANET DATA INTEGRITY

For e-commerce to succeed, the contents of the electronic transaction must remain unmodified during transmission from sender to recipient[28] — the data cannot be altered, defaced or lost during transmission whether by accidental means or otherwise.[29] Transmissions must be tamper-proof so that the unauthorised addition, deletion or modification of messages cannot occur between parties.

In contrast to transaction confidentiality, whereby the focus is on the monitoring of data, transaction integrity is concerned with modification of data during transmission.

The process of ensuring transactional integrity must include an auditing process that records the data trail of electronic transactions and in itself must be secure.[30]

By its nature, transmission of data occurs between machines and across networks. Therefore, controls are required to ensure integrity and validity of data. This electronic checking system is described as one in which key data are electronically matched; under constant review; and subject to continuous scrutiny to maintain appropriate levels of data integrity (see figure 5.6). If users lose confidence in the integrity of the data, they are likely to stop using the system.

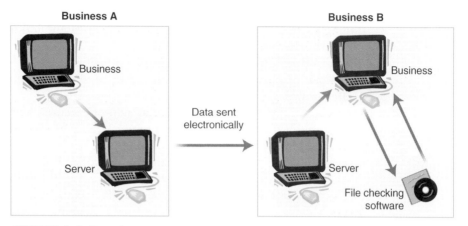

FIGURE 5.6: Data integrity system in an electronic environment

THE VIRTUAL PRIVATE NETWORK (VPN) EXTRANET

WHAT IS A VPN?

A Virtual Private Network (VPN) utilises a public network, such as the Internet, to transmit private data. Extranet VPNs offer cost and security benefits for an organisation. VPNs allow managers to use the Internet to connect trading partners rather than using a private network. VPNs also allow administrators to selectively encrypt data depending on their requirements — see figure 5.7 for a VPN model architecture.

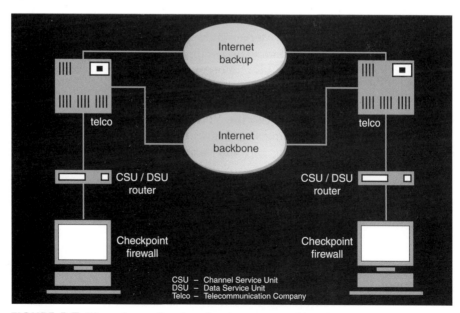

FIGURE 5.7: Flow chart of a virtual private network
SOURCE: FishNet Security, www.fishnetsecurity.com.

For B2B extranets, VPNs are useful when a company needs control over trading partner interaction. VPNs allow authentication and access control to specific host computers and applications.

From VPNet[31] technologies, VPN extranets allow:

- network managers to increase the span of the corporate network cost-effectively
- remote users to access their corporate network securely and easily
- corporations to communicate with business partners securely
- enterprises to outsource hosting of servers and applications
- service providers to increase business by providing value-added services.

With a VPN extranet, trading partners are free to choose their own ISP. All that is required is for each member of the community to have Internet access.

VPN software is configured with the IP address of the VPN equipment on the main extranet site. This way, member traffic can be carried over multiple ISP networks. Members are provided with VPN software and an installation program.

Extranet VPNs may also be used as an alternative security model to that of the Secure Sockets Layer (SSL). In situations where a trading partner is known and visits many times, the extranet VPN can become an effective mechanism for allowing controlled access by community members.

A share-trading scenario illustrates how extranet VPNs can be leveraged. A stockbroking firm has valued customers who wish to share trade on a daily basis. Each valued customer is issued with VPN software that they load on to their home or office computer. The software includes a digital certificate and dialling program that connects the user to a pre-arranged ISP.

When the customer connects to the ISP and logs on to the system, the digital certificate is validated. The ISP then establishes a secure '**VPN tunnel**' back to the VPN server in the stockbroking office. The customer can then execute normal trading across this completely secure virtual private network. SSL technology can also accommodate the above scenario. However, the extranet VPN has further advantages.

Where extranet VPNs excel is in the security management of the user when connected to the VPN. By connecting customers to the extranet VPN, the stockbroking firm knows the individual characteristics of each customer on the system and can assign these customers to groups with differing privileges.

Further, a valued customer can be given additional privileges in return for a high level of patronage to the stockbroking firm. A valued customer could be given unlimited web surfing or access to valuable research material, for example.

The principle is that once a customer is verified, he or she may be allowed access to as little or as much information as is deemed appropriate by the stockbroking firm (or host). Such functionality is not available with implementation of the 'vanilla' SSL protocol. With the addition of digital certificates, extranet VPNs can utilise server access control lists to grant and deny access to resources on the virtual network.

VPN EXTRANET TECHNOLOGY

Popular among emerging VPN standards are the **PPTP** (Point-to-Point Tunnelling Protocol), **L2TP** (Layer 2 Tunnelling Protocol) and **IPSec** (IP Security).[32] These specifications describe the protocols to be used for tunnelling. All are proposed for inclusion in the release of IP version 6; IPSec is presently included in IP version 4. PPTP was an initiative from Microsoft and the company Ascend to support packet tunnelling in their remote access hardware and software. The founders of PPTP combined with Cisco and its L2F protocol to produce the hybrid L2TP protocol.

IPSec is generally preferred within the IP environment because of its in-built security. PPTP and L2TP are most appropriate for multi-protocol environments but require the data privacy, integrity and authentication of IPSec. Without IPSec, PPTP and L2TP cannot support an extranet model.

TABLE 5.4	VPN TECHNOLOGY STANDARDS COMPARED		
	PPTP	**L2TP**	**IPSec**
Mode	Client/server	Client/server	Host-to-host
Purpose	Remote access via tunnelling	Remote access via tunnelling	Intranets, extranets, remote access via tunnelling
OSI Layer	Layer-2	Layer-2	Layer-3
Protocols encapsulated	IP, IPX, AppleTalk etc.	Ip, IPX, AppleTalk etc.	IP
Security: User authentication	None (use PAP,[4] CHAP,[5] Kerberos, Token ID etc.)	None (use PAP, CHAP, Kerberos, Token ID etc.)	None (use PAP, CHAP, Kerberos, Token ID etc.)
Packet authentication	None[1]	None[3]	Authentication header
Packet encryption	None[2]	None[3]	ESP[6] header
Key management	None[1]	None[3]	ISAKMP[7]/Oakley, SKIP[8]
Tunnel services	Single point-to-point tunnel, no simultaneous Internet access	Single point-to-point tunnel, no simultaneous Internet access	Multipoint tunnel; simultaneous VPN and public access

Notes:
1. Not in standard, not offered
2. Vendor-specific implementation only
3. Refers to IPSec for implementation
4. Password Authentication Protocol
5. Challenge Handshake Authentication Protocol
6. Encapsulating Security Payload
7. Internet Security Association and Key Management Protocol
8. Simple Key Management for Internet Protocol

SOURCE: Infonetics Research (1997).[33]

SUMMARY

XML promises to be a recognised standard in the world of B2B e-commerce. Its open, simple interface, wide availability and low implementation cost make it the ideal platform for small and large enterprises alike to implement B2B e-commerce efficiently and effectively. EbXML, a recent derivation of XML, provides a set of consistent components with which to conduct B2B e-commerce on a global scale. XML/EDI technology builds upon the framework of traditional EDI. By reducing cost of entry, XML/EDI allows smaller trading partners to participate in industry supply chains once restricted to large corporations.

Extranets provide a mechanism for improving supply chain efficiencies and enhancing trading partner collaboration. Extranets allow users to participate in online communities and exchange information — they are a key business initiative in B2B e-commerce. The extranet VPN is an invaluable addition to the extranet model that allows authentication and access control of customers to network resources including computers and documents.

key terms

Document Object Model (DOM)	extranet	Virtual Private Network
Document Type Definitions (DTDs)	IPSec	VPN tunnel
	L2TP	XLINK
ebXML	metalanguage	XML/EDI
Extensible Markup Language (XML)	PPTP	XML schemas
	Standardised General Markup Language (SGML)	XPATH
Extensible Style Language (XSL)		XPOINTER

QUESTIONS

1. Investigate the latest progress in the XML standards 'race'. Write a report on new developments and state your opinion on whether ebXML will emerge as the recognised standard or whether a new standard is likely to emerge.

2. Write a report on XML/EDI outlining the advantages and disadvantages of the technology.

3. Do some research and prepare a report on the types of software packages that handle the taxation issues in a global economy.

4. Debate the pros and cons of collaboration between traditional business competitors commonly known as 'co-opertition'.

5. Prepare a report on PAP and CHAP methods of user authentication.

THE AUTOMOTIVE NETWORK EXCHANGE

In this chapter we have seen how extranets assist organisations and trading communities to improve supply-chain processes and assist with communication and collaboration. In contrast to traditional EDI, extranets allow small and large corporations to participate in the trading supply chain at relatively low cost. Extranets allow for efficient exchange of mission-critical data between organisations, including transmission of trading and computer-aided design (CAD) documents and online design collaboration to assist product design and manufacture.

What is the ANX?

The Automotive Network Exchange (ANX) is a Virtual Private Network service allowing for efficient and secure B2B communications among automotive suppliers and vehicle manufacturers. The Automotive Industry Action Group (AIAG) and its task force, comprising automotive industry partners including Chrysler Corp., General Motors Corp. and Ford Motor Co., began work on the ANX in 1994. The ANX (potentially the world's largest business VPN) is designed to meet the highest quality standards in security, performance and privacy, and offers trading partners a common set of business practices; value-added services; a high level of security, and superior accessibility via the Internet. An automotive industry action group study has predicted that cost savings to trading partners from using the ANX will be significant, with telecommunications charges being reduced by US$1 billion per year — equating to US$71 per vehicle.[34]

How does it work?

The ANX enables automotive trading partners to communicate across the supply chain by leveraging the power of Internet technologies, including email, cost-effective EDI ordering, high-speed data transfer of documents (e.g. CAD files), and robust security through the Internet protocol IPSec and a VPN model.

By moving to a VPN structure, based on the IPSec protocol, the ANX eliminates the need for expensive leased lines traditionally used in value-added networks (VANs).[35] In addition, the ANX uses digital certificate technology from the company Verisign. These digital certificates act as electronic credentials between trading partners and allow secure communications and transactions to occur across the entire ANX.

The ANX, however, is not a typical VPN. Instead of utilising one ISP for communications, the ANX has several ISPs (called certified service providers or CSPs), all competing for the business of the trading partners who participate in the network. In this model, these CSPs do not become complacent about pricing models and service while remaining technologically innovative.

The CSPs must also comply with a strict service level agreement with the ANX overseer, Telcordia. When a car-maker assembly line shuts down, it costs approximately US$1 million per hour. To avoid shutdowns, the CSPs must meet more than 120 performance metrics including downtime, throughput, packet loss and latency. CSPs are also rated on their disaster/recovery plans and help desk service performance.

The ANX streamlines communications across the supply chain by allowing trading partners to connect via CSPs. High-volume trading partners may connect directly to ANX via special exchange points. These exchange points utilise high-speed hardware and software to allow CSPs to interoperate on the ANX.

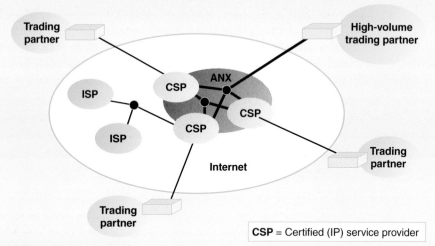

High-performance, reliable extranet for automotive industry

CSP = Certified (IP) service provider

FIGURE 5.8: The ANX
SOURCE: Based on AIAG, www.idsystems.com/reader/1999_06/engi0699_sb.htm.

Latest developments

In December 1999 the AIAG agreed to sell all interest in the ANX to Science Applications International Corporation (SAIC). With this transition, AIAG can now focus on setting and managing future standards for the ANX service.

SAIC plans to add new features to the existing ANX infrastructure, including videoconferencing, telephony, online communities and application service provider (ASP) functionality servicing engineering and back-office requirements.[36] The network will provide the necessary bandwidth to support these initiatives and, in the near future, the ability to support three-dimensional virtual reality design sessions. This infrastructure promises to radically alter the traditional five-year design cycle and improve the automobile design cycle to less than three years.[37]

Questions

1. Car companies are extremely competitive these days. Discuss how the ANX allows these competitors to coexist and to share in the cost savings from using one extranet facility.

2. Investigate digital certificate technology by identifying three major certificate vendors and discuss their technology implementations.

3. Establish 10 performance criteria of your own. Discuss these criteria and why service level agreements are so important to this size of infrastructure.

4. Investigate how you would construct an 'online car parts design centre'. Discuss how you would connect designers together on the extranet, how they would communicate and schedule meetings, and how the designs could be communicated to the car manufacturer.

SUGGESTED READING

Adams, M., Hardy, J., Bray, D., Cavill, M. and Swatman, P. 1999, *Driving Forces on the New Silk Road: The Use of Electronic Commerce by Australian Businesses*, Australian Department of Foreign Affairs and Trade.

Baker, R. H. 1997, *Extranets: The Complete Sourcebook*, McGraw-Hill, New York.

Bayles, D. 1998, *Extranets: Building the Business to Business Web*, Prentice Hall, New Jersey.

Hagel III, J. and Armstrong A. G. 1997, *Net Gain: Expanding markets through virtual communities*, Harvard Business School Press, Boston, MA.

Kalakota, R. and Robinson, M. 1999, *E-business: Roadmap for Success*, Addison-Wesley Longman, Reading, MA.

Lawrence, E., Corbitt, B., Tidwell, A., Fisher, J. and Lawrence, J. R. 1998, *Internet Commerce: Digital Models for Business*, 1st Edition, John Wiley & Sons, Brisbane.

Means, Grady, and Schneider, David 2000, *Meta-Capitalism*, John Wiley & Sons, New York.

Pfaffenberger, B. 1998, *Building a Strategic Extranet*, IDG Books, Foster City, CA.

Siebel, Thomas M. and House, Pat 1999, *Cyber Rules: Strategies for Excelling at E-Business*, Currency/Doubleday, New York.

END NOTES

1. TradeGate ECA and PIEC 1998, 'Pharmaceutical Industry Electronic Commerce Directions and Guidelines', TradeGate Australia, Sydney.
2. www.cisco.com.
3. 'XML Backgrounder', www.softwareag.com/xml/about/ e-XML_Backgrounder_WP03E0700.pdf.
4. 'XML Backgrounder'.
5. 'XML Backgrounder'.
6. 'The Technology Report', Volume 1, No. 3, September 1999, CommerceNet, www.commercenet.com/research/technology-applications/1999/EC1.3-03XMLSchemas.html.
7. XML Schema Part I: Structures, W3C Working Draft, 6 May 1999, http://w3.org/TR/xmlschema-1.
8. 'The Technology Report', September 1999.
9. www.w3.org/TR/xlink.
10. www.w3.org/TR/xpath.
11. Walsh, Jeff 1999, 'IBM unveils series of XML tools', *InfoWorld* 20 (47), p. 41.
12. Peat, Bruce, and Webber, David 1997, 'The E-Business Framework', XML/EDI Group, www.xmledigroup.org/xmledigroup/start.htm.
13. Peat and Webber 1997.
14. Peat and Webber 1997.

15. www.xml.com/resources/whitepapers/
    XMLSolutions_Peaceful_Co_Existence.pdf.

16. www.commercenet.com/research/standards-frameworks/1999/EC1.4-
    03ebXML.html.

17. www.biztalk.org/library/about_XML.asp.

18. www.avnet.com.

19. O'Shea, Peter 1999, 'Worldwide study predicts trend towards extranet
    use', *E-Commerce Today*, Issue 31, February, www.ecommercetoday.com.au/
    ecom/au_art/a3125_03.htm.

20. Baker, R. H. 1997, *Extranets: The Complete Sourcebook*, McGraw-Hill, New
    York.

21. Baker 1997.

22. Baker 1997.

23. GE Information Services 1999, 'Entering the Extranet Era',
    www.geis.com/geiscom/downloads/extranet.v3.pdf.

24. Kalakota, R. and Whinston, A. B. 1997, *Electronic Commerce: A Manager's
    Guide*, Addison-Wesley Longman, Reading, MA, p. 136.

25. Merkow, Mark 1999, 'Information Privacy: The Other Side of the
    E-commerce Coin', *The E-Commerce Guide*, Internet.com, http://
    ecommerce.internet.com/outlook/article/0,,7761_207511,00.html.

26. Merkow 1999, p. 3.

27. Merkow 1999, p. 3.

28. Kalakota and Whinston 1997.

29. Lawrence et al. 1998, p. 122.

30. Lawrence et al. 1998, p. 122.

31. 'A virtual private networking primer', www.vpnet.com, p. 1.

32. Infonetics Research Inc. 1997, 'Virtual Private Networks — a partnership
    between Service Providers and Network Managers', www.infonetics.com.

33. Infonetics Research Inc. 1997.

34. 'Car Talk', CIO Web Business Magazine, http://www2.cio.com/archive/
    printer.cfm?URL=webbusiness/080199_anx_print.cfm.

35. 'AIAG taps Verisign, Inc. to secure automotive industry's EC service',
    www.wpc-edi.com/Insider/Articles/V3/III-7d.html.

36. 'AIAG Spins off ANX network: SAIC to accelerate development', AIAG,
    8 December 1999, http://209.186.190.204/press/anx/9128%2D99.html.

37. 'Extraordinary Extranets', webreference.com, 27 August 1997,
    www.webreference.com/content/extranet/examples.html.

Learning objectives

You will have mastered the material in this chapter when you can:

- define enterprise application integration (EAI) on an intra- and inter-enterprise level
- describe the technologies behind EAI
- outline the EAI architecture
- illustrate the technology components behind B2B integration
- describe cataloguing, order processing, payment systems, work flow management and content management
- appreciate the human factors behind EAI
- understand the applicability of ROI in B2B integration.

'Technology is reshaping this economy and transforming businesses and consumers. This is about more than e-commerce or e-mail, or e-trades, or e-files. It is about the 'e' in economic opportunity.'

US Secretary of Commerce William M. Daley, 15 April 1998, 'The Emerging Digital Economy', www.doc.gov/OPA/SPEECHES/Ecom.htm.

INTRODUCTION

We have seen how, more than ever, enterprises now depend on strategic relationships with partners and suppliers to create efficient, productive supply chains. In this chapter we will concentrate on studying enterprise application integration from an intra-company and inter-company perspective. The efficient management of information and systems has become paramount. Indeed, the management of information in the business is so critical that it may be the single determinant in the success or failure of the business.[1] This chapter will show how XML and middleware products are helping enterprises in their bid to become e-businesses and will outline the importance of ROI (Return on Investment) metrics to these enterprises.

If management of this information is so essential, how is it achieved? The answer lies in the careful and strategic management of B2B applications — enterprise applications. These may include all manner of ERP (enterprise resource planning), **CRM (customer relationship management)**, HR (Human Resources) and SCM (supply chain management) applications, which form the backbone of the B2B infrastructure. As companies enter the race of the digital age, the successful participants will be those who effectively integrate their applications and automate processes spanning the extended enterprise.

Successful integration relies on efficient, seamless communication of information across a diverse range of business applications and systems, from 'out of the box' solutions to large, back-end legacy systems. Using eMarketplace models and technology such as XML, businesses can reach any customer, supplier or trading partner in the supply chain.

ENTERPRISE APPLICATION INTEGRATION (EAI)

Enterprise application integration (EAI)[2] is a business term for the plans, methods and tools aimed at modernising, consolidating and coordinating the computer applications in an enterprise. Driven by an ever-increasing rate of change and degree of complexity in technology and business, companies must ask the following questions[3]:

- What are the trends that will drive application integration and investment?
- How will technical advances affect the organisation and its deployment of such applications?
- What is the optimal e-business architecture?
- What integrated architecture will work effectively?

WHY EAI?

There are compelling reasons for enterprise-wide integration of applications.

- Emerging technologies (such as intranets and extranets) encourage organisations to adopt and integrate new applications that exploit these technologies.

- Applications must often operate in real time, communicate with each other and serve an unknown number of users at any one time.
- Organisations wish to leverage legacy databases and ensure connectivity with new applications.
- The coming of the digital age has meant that customers, the organisation and its applications must be able to interact seamlessly and electronically, regardless of platform, data format or physical location.

Technologies used in EAI[4] include:

- object-oriented programming
- distributed architecture models using message brokers with Common Object Request Broker Architecture and COM+ (as discussed in chapter 4, page 132)
- the integration of **enterprise resource planning (ERP)** with new business processes and incorporation of new data standards via Extensible Markup Language (XML), middleware and **message queueing**.

Information technology has the inherent ability to shrink the effects of time and space and provide humans with added reach through information support. The use of electronic tools such as the PC helps the person (particularly the customer) to accomplish tasks faster. By using the vast information resources available today, the time to search, compare and purchase a particular product in the market is drastically reduced. This shortening of work has the effect of radically changing the dynamics of the customer–vendor relationship. The success of **just-in-time (JIT)** systems has shown how organisations must adapt to the increasing demands of the customer base, following the customer-centric model.

Company managers have always had to effectively manage the coordination of markets, products and geographic locations that constitute the organisation. However, within the enterprise, buffers in assets, or global time lag, no longer afford the company any latitude. Management must face these new threats and begin embracing e-business at the organisational level, adapting a culture of continuous innovation and interdependence.[5]

EAI TECHNOLOGIES

Since there is a need for real-time integrity and process integration within the enterprise, a scalable, robust application framework is necessary. The increased technical complexity of systems and the accelerated change cycle times in business process mean that[6]:

- enterprises need new capabilities quickly and at a lower cost — they must integrate with existing and developing systems, both internally and externally
- deployment of large-scale distributed systems is changing the way applications are designed, developed and used
- heterogeneous e-applications must communicate and interact among themselves
- there is a shortage of skilled software developers
- **plug and play** software components are needed for the e-enterprise environment.

Figure 6.1 illustrates the integration architecture framework.

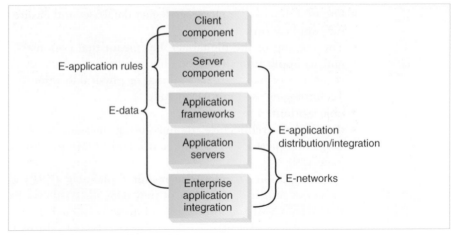

FIGURE 6.1: Integration architecture

SOURCE: F. Hoque 2000. *E-enterprise: Business models, architectures and components*, Cambridge University Press, Cambridge, UK, p. 234. Reprinted with permission.

INTEGRATION ARCHITECTURE EXPLAINED

Table 6.1 provides the information necessary to interpret figure 6.1.

TABLE 6.1	INTEGRATION ARCHITECTURE EXPLAINED	
TITLE	**WHAT THEY DO**	**EXAMPLES**
Client components	Manage user interface and some application logic	Determine how a user navigates the system — e.g. JavaBeans, ActiveX
Server components	Implement server-side business logic — e.g. facilitate how a purchase order is created	May facilitate what kind of data about a user need to be extracted — e.g. CORBA, Enterprise JavaBeans, Distributed Component Object Model (DCOM)
Application frameworks	Provide a framework for the whole system	Collection of large objects or applications — e.g. IBM San Francisco Project and ecWorks suite
Application servers	Often physically host and manage client and server components as well as application frameworks	Perform load-balancing tasks to ensure optimum system performance — e.g. WebSphere (IBM)
Enterprise application integration	Set of integrated systems that combine legacy systems, custom applications and packaged applications with web functionality	Uses middleware frameworks and object technology — e.g. CrossWorld, Extricity

SOURCE: Hoque (2000, pp. 231–50).

MIDDLEWARE TECHNOLOGY

As we learned in chapter 4, middleware is software that operates between an application — for example a database — and the transport layer that performs the services and hides the details of that layer. There are many EAI middleware technologies available; however, individually these technologies are very often not the 'total solution' for the enterprise. The following table outlines the major technologies employed in EAI and how these relate to the integration process.

TABLE 6.2   MIDDLEWARE TECHNOLOGIES BEHIND EAI

SOFTWARE	HOW IT WORKS	FURTHER INFORMATION
CORBA	Provides software interoperability between platform services (or objects) written in languages such as C++ and Smalltalk. Allows for a distributed, heterogeneous environment and operates transparently to the programmer	www.corba.org
EJB (Enterprise JavaBeans)	Provides software portability and adhere to the 'write once, run anywhere' philosophy of the software language Java. EJBs can run on any operating system, and the application programming interfaces (APIs) provide access to underlying enterprise, standards-based services.	http://java.sun.com/products/ejb
XML	Provides an easily used mechanism for developing enterprise or supply chain–specific integration languages. XML is simple to understand, separates content and presentation layers, and is a common, open standard.	www.w3.org/xml
SOAP (Simple Object Access Protocol)	SOAP is a platform-, language- and model-independent mechanism to pass commands and parameters between HTTP clients and servers. It is an XML-based protocol that consists of three parts: • an envelope framework for describing what is in a message and how to process it • a set of encoding rules for defining datatypes • a convention for representing remote procedure calls and responses.	www.w3.org/TR/SOAP
Distributed Component Object Model (DCOM)	DCOM is an extension of the Component Object Model (COM) and is a protocol that enables distributed software components to communicate over a network in a reliable and secure manner.	www.microsoft.com/com/tech/DCOM.asp

The following technical insite describes just some of the 'out-of-the-box' integration solutions currently on offer in the marketplace.

EAI SOFTWARE

iPlanet™ ECXpert is an example of messaging software that eases integration challenges and uses robust digital certificate, encryption and authentication technology.[7] ECXpert is an Internet commerce exchange application that enables encrypted transmission of documents and messages among heterogeneous trading partner systems, and can convert information from one format to another. It combines the wide availability, speed and low cost of the Internet with powerful security features and data transformation capabilities, enabling an organisation — directly or through a service provider — to expand trade with a broader range of companies, while lowering the overall cost of transactions across the supply chain.

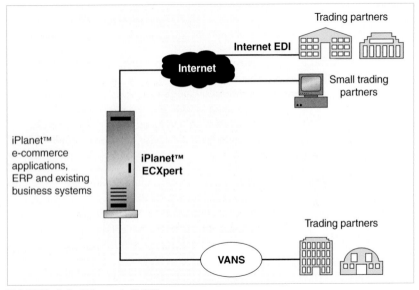

FIGURE 6.2: iPlanet's ECXpert

SOURCE: www.iplanet.com/products/iplanet_ecxpert_ds.pdf. Sun, Sun Microsystems, the Sun logo, Java, JavaScript, iPlanet, and all Sun, Java and iPlanet based trademarks are trademarks or registered trademarks of Sun Microsystems, Inc. in the United States and other countries. Courtesy of iPlanet.

WebMethods's *B2B Integration Server* solves many enterprise application integration issues by using XML and an XML-based Web Definition Language (WDL) to automate data exchange in the supply chain.[8] The use of XML instead of higher-overhead environments such as CORBA or DCOM makes implementation simpler and more cost-effective.

Although the server uses XML to communicate between applications and differing data types, it is not necessary for applications on either side of the server to be written in XML. The WDL (as described above) provides a method of defining access to applications — these may include databases such as Microsoft SQL Server and ERP applications such as SAP and PeopleSoft. The Integration server runs on all platforms supporting Java, including IBM AIX, Microsoft NT, Sun Solaris and Linux.

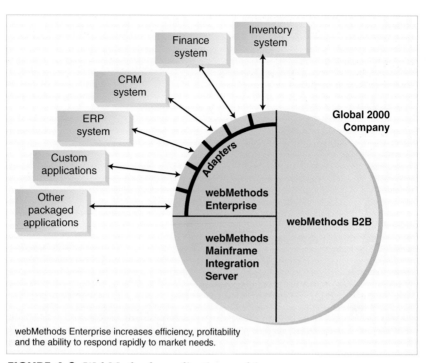

webMethods Enterprise increases efficiency, profitability
and the ability to respond rapidly to market needs.

FIGURE 6.3: WebMethods application architecture

SOURCE: www.webmethods.com/content/1,1107,wMEnterprise,FF.html.

EXERCISES

1. Visit Netscape's web site and prepare a report on the product ECXpert or its latest equivalent.

2. Compare and contrast two integration packages that you have researched. What are the key differences?

APPLICATION TECHNOLOGY

In this section, we will examine the following application technology components:

- cataloguing
- order processing
- payment systems
- work flow management
- content management
- personalisation.

CATALOGUING

Similar in concept to the printed mail-order catalogue, the web catalogue may contain products, pictures, video and product pricing. Collecting and maintaining product information for hundreds (or thousands) of catalogue products and developing the application to support these products is both a major organisational effort and a complex job for the e-commerce developer.

The right software, however, can make this task easier. Sterling Commerce's 'Synchronize' is suited to integrating and maintaining catalogues.[9] Most e-commerce storefront products on the market can organise the catalogue into groups of products (sorted, perhaps, by departments or sections), and may be combined with a search utility to make products easy to locate. Oracle's Internet Commerce Server and Microsoft's Site Server Commerce Edition have powerful indexing and shopping cart capabilities. IBM's Net.Commerce goes one step further with Product Advisor, which helps customers develop a profile of what they want and shows them how to find it.

Many e-commerce products also come with catalogue page templates that may be used repeatedly to reduce development time. Connecting to or importing data such as prices and product descriptions can also be a major issue. Products such as Catalogue International's Cat@log[10] may easily link information from many different databases.

ORDER PROCESSING

To aid the consumer with the online experience, catalogue selections are usually placed into a 'shopping cart' or 'trolley'. Selections are then stored in a database so the customer may review what has been selected before going to the 'checkout'.

There may be many details involved with shipping and taxes, so it is important to choose software with multiple currency and tax support. Microsoft's Commerce Server utilises a shopping cart facility.[11]

Many other kinds of calculations are associated with orders, discounts, coupons and volume breaks that should be considered. Most e-commerce software can do *some* of these calculations.

There are also many possible connections to accounting systems. Some software products such as INEX's Dynamic NT[12] come with complete accounting and inventory software. More commonly, programs provide connections to legacy data and accounting systems. As might be anticipated, companies like IBM[13] and Oracle[14] are particularly careful to honour their legacy and back-end systems.

PAYMENT SYSTEM

The payment system is perhaps the most critical piece of software in the e-commerce suite — electronic payment systems are discussed further in chapter 7. The organisation needs to establish a sense of safety and security without being overbearing. Consumers must be able to select a mode of payment and the software must verify their ability to pay. This can involve credit cards, electronic cash or purchase orders.

Specialised software such as CyberCash,[15] CommercePOINT eTill[16] and Microsoft Wallet[17] can verify the purchaser and the purchase. E-commerce software packages should also work with Secure Sockets Layer (SSL) or Secure Electronic Transfer (SET) technologies for encryption of data transmissions. Most e-payment solution providers will require that your company establish a special bank account to handle the online transactions.

Overall, there are no perfect solutions. There are advantages to differing products — some are robust, and others may scale well. None, however, can be installed, configured, run and updated without some degree of adjustment. E-commerce products are built on top of other complex software (operating systems and other servers). The relationships between components are critical, which leads to problematic architecture.

WORK FLOW MANAGEMENT

In general terms, **work flow management** (or work flow automation) software allows an enterprise to manage the quality of work produced. Work flow management software allows an organisation to create work flow models and components to effectively manage internal processes (or objects) and ensure quality, consistent output.

For example, a company could use a work flow management system to manage the flow of product documentation to a web site or into a catalogue system. The work flow model in this example could be established to force all content and product information to progress through a series of 'checking' steps to ensure quality control. The series of steps could possibly include product verification by product owners, legal vetting by the legal department, and 'web readiness' by the web development team. In a similar fashion, work flow management can also be applied to handling customer enquiries and regulating the flow of products from manufacturer to retail outlet across the supply chain.

Typically, a work flow management system utilises a *work flow engine*. The work flow engine stores and interprets all the business rules required to verify an object or process as it passes along the work flow. Through each step in the work flow, the work flow engine applies the business rules to the process. If the process passes the 'test', it moves on to the next step in the work flow until finally, reaching the end of the work flow, it is released to the environment.

CONTENT MANAGEMENT

Content management systems provide an infrastructure for creating and maintaining the common pool of assets that comprise a web site. These assets may include content, imagery, sound files, graphics and application components such as Java applets.

For small web sites, content management poses little problem, since HTML pages may be created, modified and posted to the production environment with relative ease. Often, these pages may be written, coded and placed in production by the same person. However, on large web sites and in large organisations, the coordination of web site assets and the management of skill-sets and enterprise-wide approval processes complicate matters considerably. For these reasons, content management systems are invariably used to automate processes and streamline web development.

To eradicate the problems mentioned above, content management systems generally separate content from HTML code. This is done primarily to allow business-focused workers to create and refine actual content while technical workers may create and maintain HTML and JavaScript/Java applet code. The content management system will allow these two distinct working streams to coexist and, when required, assimilates the content and code to produce the final HTML page as viewed by the user. This infrastructure also integrates well with work flow management systems, mentioned in the previous section. Work flows may be established for content and for source code, thus creating an environment of quality control.

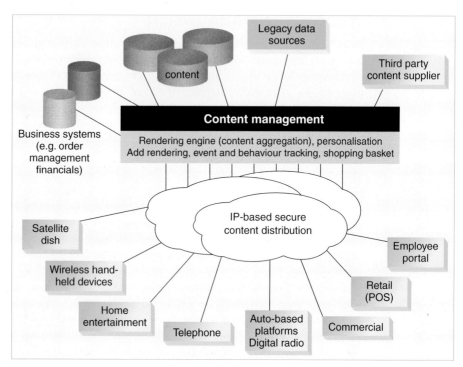

FIGURE 6.4: Content management systems
SOURCE: PriceWaterhouseCoopers 2000, 'Content Management and Personalization: The eBusiness Imperative'. Slide.

Table 6.3 describes various processes involved in content management.

TABLE 6.3	CONTENT MANAGEMENT
WORK TASK	**DESCRIPTION**
Web authoring	Creating the content
Metatag tagging	Describing the content through the use of metatag descriptions and keywords
Editing	Updating/maintaining the content
Collaborating with other people	Allowing a team (or several business units) to edit pages together
Work flow organising	Ensuring the right people are doing the right things to the site and ensuring that only approved content is posted to the site

Securing the site	Keeping out unwanted intruders in sensitive or secure site areas
Versioning the site	Managing the changes to the site through version control
Scheduling	Managing the release of the site and its updates
Templating	Displaying content in a consistent and correct format
Syndicating	Allowing content to be displayed by other organisations
Personalising	Allowing content to be tailored to an individual's needs

PERSONALISATION

The key to a successful web site is return visitation by customers. Keeping a web site interesting and compelling presents a major challenge to companies in the B2C and B2B space. Providing a **personalisation** engine is just one mechanism for improving content relevance for customers.

Personalisation is the act of recognising a customer, subscriber or visitor as an individual and modifying actions based upon information known about the customer. Thus, personalisation improves the interaction for the customer through relevance of information and service, and for the company through higher margin selling and higher revenue.

Several types of personalisation may be used. These include:

- *implicit personalisation:* the recording and assessment of day-to-day customer actions. Examples include purchase and transaction history, click-streams and session-specific data such as browser type, access speed and site of origin. This is often referred to as *inference tracking.*
- *explicit personalisation:* information explicitly entered by the customer into the database system. Examples include date of birth, email address and postcode.
- *profiling:* involves collecting customer information on a systematic basis so that this information can be used to enable one-to-one marketing efforts
- *collaborative filtering:* recommends products and services to the customer based on purchases made by customers with similar tastes. Examples include Amazon.com and winepros.com.au.

 # EAI CHECKLIST

In general, there are several areas of focus when considering integration. Table 6.4 illustrates the implications for suppliers and for buyers when considering EAI integration.

TABLE 6.4	QUESTIONS TO ASK ABOUT INTEGRATION	
QUESTION	IMPLICATIONS FOR SUPPLIERS	IMPLICATIONS FOR BUYERS
What level of integration is required?	Most offer some document exchange, but only some offer full integration with back-end catalogue and transactional systems.	Some exchanges provide access only to raw data; others can integrate data directly into ERP or procurement applications.
What integration platform will be used?	Popular integration tools do not necessarily provide mapping between back-end applications and exchanges.	Off-the-shelf applications such as Ariba, SAP and webMethods are easier to integrate than legacy or custom-built programs.
How long will integration take?	Links to customised or legacy applications could take months for each marketplace.	Many buyers are holding off on integration until they develop a standard interface that works with multiple exchanges.
Will the integration method work for my business?	Some e-Marketplaces use inflexible catalogues that do not account for subtle differences between industries.	Some e-Marketplace integration strategies are designed to fit the buying needs of just a few large players.
Does the integration methodology work for my back-end applications?	Some e-Marketplaces have difficulty integrating with customised and industry-specific catalogues and applications.	Some e-Marketplaces handle integration for only the most popular back-end applications.

SOURCE: Based on www.internetweek.com/lead/lead102300-1.htm.

In the following technical insite, we look at an Australian B2B procurement marketplace.

technical INSITE

CORPROCURE — B2B E-PROCUREMENT

corProcure is an independent, Internet-based business to business procurement marketplace that aims to deliver value to trading partners through the application of Internet-enabled procurement techniques and technologies.[18] Conceptualised in July 2000, corProcure (www.corprocure.com.au) is a joint venture between 14 Australian companies including AMP, BHP, Coles-Myer and ANZ.

FIGURE 6.5: corProcure home page

SOURCE: Reproduced courtesy of corProcure.

The vision of the corProcure Marketplace is to be accessible and valuable for all businesses, no matter what their size or type. The benefit of being a horizontal marketplace (meaning that it is not industry specific) selling indirect goods (goods that are not strategic to core business) is that it is relevant to all businesses. corProcure has both an on- and off-line role in the procurement process of its customers. Off line, corProcure's strategic sourcing experts arrange pre-contract negotiations for buyers and suppliers. On line, corProcure's auction experts expedite procurement processes by electronic reverse auction, reducing a three- to four-month tendering process to four weeks. Once a contract has been arranged, it is fulfilled in the corProcure Marketplace. By transacting electronically rather than using paper-based requisitioning and invoicing, the procurement process is dramatically simplified, saving time and money.

corProcure technology

corProcure's technology platform allows organisations 'one to one' transactional efficiency with 'one to many capability'. This means that the marketplace is able to translate many languages, so one participant can speak to others without necessarily having the same system. corProcure utilises an architecture that blends product offerings from Commerce One, TIBCO and other third party software vendors on a Microsoft Windows/Intel-based hardware platform. Access to the environment is via the Internet, through both Microsoft IIS-based and custom Commerce One and TIBCO access portals. Data are stored in a combination of Microsoft SQL Server and Sun's iPlanet Lightweight Directory Access Protocol (LDAP) databases. corProcure provides a hosted interface

(continued)

for buyers and suppliers via a Commerce One product suite. The exchange platform provides the value-added service of supplier document hosting, while the hosted buyer interface is provided in a 'bolt-on' eProcurement package specifically deployed to host multiple buying organisations within the one physical hosting location/server facility.

The future

corProcure is actively pursuing its objective of providing an open marketplace by building several adaptors to connect 'non-Commerce One' eProcurement systems to the corProcure Marketplace. In addition, the company has several key buyers perusing the eProcurement solution hosted by corProcure. The hosted solution allows buyers to enjoy the process and cost benefits associated with adopting an eProcurement system within a shorter time frame than required for a full eProcurement implementation.

With respect to the supplier community, corProcure has developed several new incentive packages designed to enable suppliers in the corProcure Marketplace at minimal cost to the supplier. The packages are specifically designed to allow suppliers to become familiar with trading via the corProcure Marketplace with minimal risk, the objective being to 'ramp-up' supplier volume once the supplier is comfortable with managing its corProcure Marketplace account. These incentive packages should provide many suppliers with quick and easy access to the B2B world.

EXERCISES

1. Explain the term 'compression of the procure-to-pay cycle time'.
2. Prepare a report on:
   - Commerce One technology
   - TIBCO technology
   - iPlanet technology.

SUPPLY CHAIN INTEGRATION (INTER-ENTERPRISE)

What is a **supply chain**? As we saw in chapter 2, it is the network of relationships that an enterprise maintains with its trading partners to enable the manufacture and delivery of its product to the marketplace.[19] Ideally, the chain consists of many companies that interact in an efficient, effective and unified manner to provide the customer with the best quality product, delivered within the shortest possible time frame.

Since integration is of prime importance, the process focus shifts from within the enterprise walls to outside the business. The focus shifts to the supply chain and the collaboration between trading partners. The challenge for the company of tomorrow will be to integrate the processes of its supply chain while allowing the flexibility to change in response to customer demand.

TRADITIONAL SUPPLY CHAIN INEFFICIENCIES

Traditional inefficiencies within the supply chain have been attributable to several key factors.[20] These include:

- lack of adequate information across the supply chain — for example, does the organisation have adequate fulfilment mechanisms in place?
- inconsistent data. The lack of up-to-date and coherent information makes decisions difficult. For example, the organisation must be aware of current stock levels.
- no integration. Organisations experience information 'brick walls' or barriers where they are unable to access critical information across enterprise boundaries.

SUPPLY CHAIN MANAGEMENT TECHNIQUES

Supply chain management techniques provide:

- efficient, timely access to the market
- cost-reduction possibilities
- new techniques such as Vendor Managed Inventory and streamlining distribution channels.

New technology has increased the ability to integrate processes through collaborative information sharing. The Internet, data warehousing or mining, and ERP applications form the basis of this technology. In the digital age, information replaces physical inventory. As part of this trend, **supply chain management (SCM)** shifts the focus from inventory management to information management.

SCM is setting the scene to change the traditional supply chain because it is based on inter-enterprise collaboration and demands the seamless integration of processes and technology. Companies like Woolworths and Coles-Myer have taken steps down the path by evolving from traditional enterprise-centred models to the information-centred model.

THREE MODELS FOR SUPPLY CHAIN INTEGRATION

B2B integration dictates a change in the way the company participates and interacts with the supply chain. A collaborative approach to the trading partner relationship and the sharing of information across company boundaries is critical. This collaboration by businesses, especially if it involves Internet technology, may be thought of as an extranet. Large Internet companies such as Netscape, Oracle and Sun Microsystems are cooperating to ensure that their extranet products can work together by standardising on JavaScript and Common Object Request Broker Architecture (CORBA). Point-to-Point Tunnelling Protocol (PPTP) is supported by Microsoft, which is collaborating with American Express and other companies on an Open Buying on the Internet (OBI) standard. The groupware product Notes, from Lotus, is promoted as being well suited for extranet use. Following in table 6.5 are three business models for the management of the supply chain and B2B integration.

TABLE 6.5	THREE MODELS FOR SCM AND INTEGRATION	
MODEL NAME	TRADITIONAL MODEL	NEW MODEL
Integrated make-to-stock	Quantities and schedules for production are provided independently of actual customer requirements.[21] Disadvantages: • inefficient purchasing methods • product overdesign • lengthy inventory pipelines	Quantities and schedules for production are provided according to actual customer requirements.[22] Advantages: • product configuration according to channel destination • altering the product characteristics to suit end market (postponement) • reduced overhead • improved quality • complete control of material flow
Vendor Managed Inventory (VMI)	In a traditional model, the retailer was required to contact the wholesaler when goods needed replenishment. Disadvantages: • stock levels often depleted before new stock arrives on the shelves • requires the retailer to be 'operationalised' and to constantly monitor stock levels and undertake menial administration tasks	The Vendor (Wholesaler) Managed Inventory[23] model creates a customer (retailer) demand system. This model (used predominantly in the packaged goods and retail areas) ensures that retail inventory levels are replenished automatically. Advantages: • frees retailers to focus on what they do best — e.g., on-selling goods to the general public or further marketing and advertising
Build-to-order (just-in-time manufacturing)	Traditionally, the wholesaler manufactured products according to its requirements. Disadvantages: • customer needs are ignored • stockpiling of unwanted products	Build-to-order systems match the demand and supply requirements in real time[24] as we move from mass production to mass customisation. This type of manufacturing and delivery model is also known as 'just-in-time' manufacturing.[25] Geared directly to the customer, this system is used predominantly by the leaders in B2B e-business. Customers are demanding build-to-spec product that is: • affordable • available • delivered instantly. Dell Computers[26] supports this model in its business. This model is more efficient since it is inherently a 'pull' system. When the customer signifies the intention to purchase, the system responds by interrogating information sources across company boundaries to indicate availability, customisation levels and expected delivery times.

The following technical insite shows how the company Fruit of the Loom has begun to utilise the Vendor Managed Inventory model to improve supply chain efficiencies.

USING THE VMI MODEL

Back in 1995 the company Fruit of the Loom[27] set up a Vendor Management Inventory system to help in the exchange of order and forecasting data between the organisation and its distributors. The company is a leading international basic clothing company producing such items as underwear, casualwear and activewear for the screenprint T-shirt and fleece market. It sells its products to more than 10 000 accounts, including major discount chains and mass merchandisers, wholesale clubs and screenprinters.

By 1998 more than 95 per cent of its sewing operations had been moved to Mexico, the Caribbean and Central America. The company uses contract manufacturers in order to:
• balance internal capacity requirements
• manufacture low-volume specialty garments
• accommodate seasonal or one-time programs
• bridge capacity in the move from domestic to offshore sewing.

Fruit of the Loom believes in continually enhancing its information systems capabilities. For example, it has developed an order entry system to help activewear retailers order from wholesalers through the Internet and via the implementation of Electronic Data Interchange (EDI) with its major retail customers.

It has also developed a Vendor Managed Inventory (VMI) program to enable the company to partner with its customers while allowing these customers to maintain optimal inventory levels. Fruit of the Loom believes that its VMI program and other information systems enhancements have helped it to improve utilisation of its own inventories by matching production more closely with customer point-of-sale information.

Snickelways Interactive, working with the ConText Group, managed to seize a Fruit of the Loom consulting opportunity at the end of 1995. Working for its new client, Snickelways broke new electronic ground by building the first commercially successful extranet, which grew into other business to business and business to consumer solutions. Table 6.6 illustrates some of the ways in which this was set up.

TABLE 6.6	SETTING UP A SUCCESSFUL EXTRANET	
STAGE	**DETAILS**	**ADVANTAGES**
Project Web Pilot	Helped distributors set up their own web sites to collect sales orders and offer products from Fruit of the Loom (www.fruit.com)	Small businesses could check distributors' inventories and the status of their orders. The system would suggest alternatives for out-of-stock items, and search alternative warehouses.
Implementation	Used Broder Bros (www.broderbros.com) as single distributor	With no firewall, the Broder Bros system manager had to periodically transfer inventory data file from corporate system to web-based catalogue.

(continued)

STAGE	DETAILS	ADVANTAGES
Creating the prototype web site	Six full-time staff members worked for 12 weeks. The pilot site cost more than $500 000. The prototype ran on a Windows NT platform with O'Reilly's web site server software.	Information was extracted from the distributor's database to ensure the dynamically generated results of an online product search were up to date.
Expansion	To reduce costs, off-the-shelf software was used, and the web server was maintained at a single point. Thirty of its 50 distributors signed on to the Fruit of the Loom's project called Activewear Online (www.fruitactivewear.com/awonline). Uses Sun Enterprise servers and an Oracle database.	Fruit of the Loom's sponsorship paid for installation and maintenance of the web server.
Divide and conquer	Snickleways Interactive developed web page design and programs for generating page templates. It saved money, provided consistency and still allowed for distributor customisation. Fruit of the Loom Systems – with Compuware – took over installation and maintenance of distributor sites (www.compuware.com).	Important work included greater scalability and ability to handle greater number of transactions.

Useful information on the Vendor Managed Inventory model can be found at www.vendormanagedinventory.com.

Australian pharmaceutical wholesalers Australian Pharmaceutical Industries Ltd, Faulding Healthcare, HAS Trading Company and WH Soul Pattinson have also implemented e-commerce to achieve supply chain management efficiency.[28] The five wholesalers supply 95 per cent of the Australian retail market. A study by the Pharmaceutical Electronic Commerce and Communication project (PECC), a federal government, Multimedia Victoria and Telstra funded project, estimates e-commerce will save the wholesalers 24 per cent in supply chain management costs.

SOURCES: www.fruit.com/static/company/index.cfm; D. Kosiur 1997, *Understanding Electronic Commerce: How online transactions can grow your business*, Microsoft Press, Redmond, WA, pp. 151–69.

EXERCISES

1. Explain what is meant by 'optimal inventory levels'.
2. Describe how using the VMI model would assist small suppliers wishing to collaborate with major manufacturers.
3. Write a report on PECC describing how e-commerce has assisted the participating companies and their respective supply chains.

MANAGING THE HUMAN FACTOR

The transition to e-business means creating an environment of reinvention — of continuous innovation — by aligning business strategies, processes and applications quickly and continually. Peter Schumpeter, the Harvard economist, talked of creative destruction — by destroying old ways of doing business, breaking free from tradition to reinvent oneself for new times and opportunities.[29] In the same way, with e-business traditional management processes need to be revisited. Meeting the ever-changing demands of the customer means creating a new mindset of innovation and entrepreneurial spirit. This chapter investigates key organisational factors that are considered instrumental in establishing and sustaining a successful e-business.

THE VIRTUAL ORGANISATION

As an increasing number of staff do more and more work through networked workstations, the e-business moves towards the concept of the *virtual organisation*, a structure in which members of the organisation are virtually and instantaneously linked with all personnel and information, both horizontally and vertically. This permits company-wide communication and enables 'ad-hoc' teams to aggregate to accomplish customer-driven tasks for which individuals are chosen based upon knowledge and aptitude and not formal title. When combined with the speed of information flow, these interdependent, linked formations present real challenges to management. Becoming an e-business means accepting these challenges, forming a virtual organisation — one with the right skills, attitudes and systems in place to exploit their potential in the market effectively.

LEVERAGING INTERNET TECHNOLOGY

The use of Internet technology permits the enterprise to manage organisational interdependence more effectively. The innovation of the networked organisation has arisen from two concepts.
• Networked firms foster communicative environments.
• Networked organisations are seen to allow firms to retain small company responsiveness while allowing for expansion, both in size and complexity.
The advantages of a shared, networked approach are illustrated in figure 6.6 on the following page.

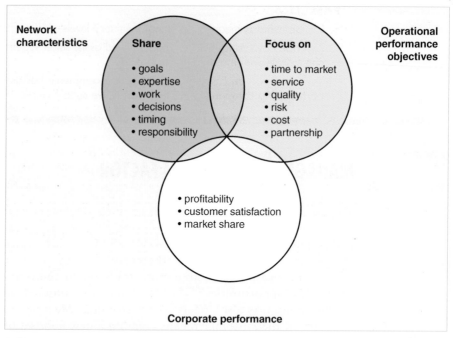

Network characteristics

Share
- goals
- expertise
- work
- decisions
- timing
- responsibility

Focus on
- time to market
- service
- quality
- risk
- cost
- partnership

Operational performance objectives

- profitability
- customer satisfaction
- market share

Corporate performance

FIGURE 6.6: Performance emphasis within the firm

SOURCE: M. S. S. Morton 1991, *The Corporation of the 1990s*, Oxford University Press, Oxford, UK, p. 201.

LEVERAGING KNOWLEDGE MANAGEMENT

The creation of the virtual organisation is also driven by other important trends, as described by Skyrme.[30]

- Organisations today need a balance of the highly innovative and the tightly coordinated.
- More and more work will be knowledge work — processing information, not physical product.
- Knowledge does not exist in isolated compartments. Its capacity to grow is enhanced if expertise can be tapped from as wide an 'expert' base as possible — people with different perspectives, experiences, age, gender, knowledge and cultural traits.
- Tasks and the interrelationships among various tasks are becoming more complex.
- The role of managers is changing from 'director' to 'facilitator', 'coach', 'mentor', 'advisor' and indeed 'peer' in the exchange of knowledge and experience.
- Project teams need to come and go as needs dictate. It is vital to assemble the best team to do the best job in any time or space.

The virtual organisation, the e-business, must be in a continuous state of innovation to survive. Byrne, in his article 'The Virtual Corporation',[31] defines it as a new corporate model, 'a temporary network of independent companies, suppliers, customers, even erstwhile rivals, linked by information technology to share skills, costs and access to one another's markets'.

THE E-BUSINESS LEADER

The appointment of a competent, enthusiastic e-business leader — a champion — is essential to a successful e-business venture. Studies indicate that the most significant factor in successful implementation is a vocal and talented e-business advocate within the organisation.[32] This leader, or facilitator, must be business oriented and be capable of embracing the direction and mission of the organisation. The person must possess a high level of communication skill, be marketing savvy and be capable of selling the e-business initiative to all levels of management. The person must report directly to the managing director, CEO or board of directors. It is imperative that the role be senior so as to sustain the e-business momentum.

The champion must also be a communications facilitator capable of creating and maintaining a sense of cohesion and consistency within the e-business. The person must encourage and advocate the e-business at all times and hence facilitate communication between members of teams, teams and virtual organisations.

THE E-BUSINESS TEAM

While engaging the skills of a competent leader is critical, as is management support, the formation of a balanced, multidisciplinary e-business team with best-of-class competencies is vital.[33] The e-business project team will be the group that creates, maintains and sustains the e-business initiative. The team will have total responsibility for the e-business transition.

TradeGate[34] suggests that the team should include representatives from the following areas:
- operations, purchasing and finance
- legal and human resources
- information systems
- sales and marketing.

The team must have its own vision, mission and goals that are fully aligned with the e-business in general. Cross-departmental participation provides a feeling of collaboration and ownership across the organisation.

VIRTUAL TEAMS

The Ford Motor Company participated in a virtual organisation model by adopting videoconferencing and CAD/CAM technology to develop its *global car*. By moving product development to the virtual environment, Ford established a web-based development shop with a virtual team of developers. Ford intended to create a car that would incorporate the best in world engineering and design while adopting the task of single design, worldwide market acceptance.

By moving product design and development to the virtual world, Ford found that virtual teams could:
- perform tasks in the information-based environment that mirrored those in the physical world
- transcend time and geographic limitations that characterise information management in the physical world
- build and test in a simulated environment 24 hours a day, seven days a week from anywhere in the world

- develop common global specifications and components
- contract external suppliers as required
- see the project and the product ensuring global market and global appeal
- sleep in one time zone while others work on the project — and all in the same team.

CROSS-FUNCTIONAL APPLICATIONS

Managing the transformation to a process-centred organisation will be critical to businesses attempting to integrate. It will apply to all processes through the supply chain — from manufacturing through to sales and customer service. Companies will be driven by their process capabilities, which in turn are driven by the applications and their successful integration. By focusing on end-to-end processes, the companies will be able to achieve satisfactory performance from their applications.

To reap the rewards of increases in profitability and competitive advantage through differentiation, companies must learn to be innovative and evolutionary in their approach to application integration. The five stages of evolution for the organisation in the journey toward application integration are set out in table 6.7.

TABLE 6.7	APPLICATION INTEGRATION
STAGES	**OBJECTIVES**
Stage 1: Cross-functional business unit	The goal here is to produce a dependable, consistent, quality product or service. Companies must focus on automating existing functions and tasks (see chapter 4 on JAD teams).
Stage 2: Strategic business unit	The organisation begins to concentrate on serving the customer end-to-end from initial contact through to fulfilment. Companies in this stage of development consolidate the supply chain by combining distribution and transportation, and manufacturing and purchasing, into operations. See Dell Computing at www.dell.com.
Stage 3: Integrated enterprise	The objective is to focus on cost reduction and internal efficiencies. The goal is high customer focus, leveraging the ability to quickly deliver high-quality products at low cost. Investment is in operational flexibility and supply chain integration, implementation of decreased cost strategies by using the principles of 'best of breed' or 'preferred partner' schemes. Compaq have released the product BusinessBus 2.0, an application that integrates messaging, CRM, ERP and legacy system communication into one centralised management system. Chemical manufacturer Solutia has saved 'tens of millions of dollars in implementation costs', says Ray Mooney, Solutia's integration manager.[35]

Stage 4: Extended enterprise	Creation of market value becomes of prime importance. 'Extended enterprise' describes a multi-enterprise supply chain with shared information structures. Extended enterprises means supply chain management, outsourcing and self-service for customers and employees alike. The goal is profitable growth through customer-centric products and services. EDS formed its EDS Business Intelligence Services unit in partnership with A.T. Kearney and NCR Corp. to provide 'extended enterprise' services to clients. The group creates information arsenals by bundling management and solutions consulting with technical delivery to enterprise accounts.
Stage 5: Inter-enterprise community	Focuses on market leadership. Companies consolidate into true inter-enterprise communities in which members share goals and objectives using multiple media including the Internet. Cross-enterprise business transactions are streamlined. See chapter 4, Livelink and www.opentext.com, and WebEx at www.webex.com/home/default.htm.

SOURCE: R. Kalakota and M. Robinson 1999, *E-business: Roadmap for Success*, Addison-Wesley Longman, Reading, MA, p. 105.

EAI RETURN ON INVESTMENT

At the centre of every successful business is the simplest of strategies — profitability. **Return on investment (ROI)** measurement in any venture will always be of the highest priority to an organisation, and the e-business solutions present no exception.

The formula for traditional ROI measurement may be given by:

$$\frac{(\text{Total Benefits} - \text{Total Costs})}{\text{Total Costs}}$$

equating to a percentage value representing the benefit returned to the enterprise. A positive ROI figure (e.g. 0.35), indicates that the quantifiable benefits of the solution exceed the cost of its implementation, while a negative value (e.g. −0.25) indicates that the costs outweighed the benefits for the project.

EAI: A SIGNIFICANT INVESTMENT

A recent survey by the GartnerGroup[37] involving 20 enterprise e-commerce sites has shown that despite vendor and internal staff claims of 'low-cost' entry, the average cost to develop and launch an e-commerce site is $1 million for hardware, software and labour. 'Contrary to market hype, developing a competitive E-Commerce site takes about 5 months, requires the help of outside companies and costs more than $1 million.'[38] AMR Research in association with Jupiter and Sterling Commerce (October 2000) estimate that the approximate cost to integrate back-end purchasing applications with their first e-Marketplace is US$300 000 and the second e-Marketplace integration is US$50 000.

Naturally, these costs are associated only with high-end, high-transactional sites and do not include the risks and costs associated with business model and organisational change. Logically, for the smaller trading partner in a supply chain the cost would not be as great; however, the risks involved in becoming an e-business remain the same.

Other findings from the survey are outlined below.
- Costs will increase 25 per cent annually during the next few years.
- On average, the labour component was 79 per cent of the cost, the hardware 11 per cent and the software 10 per cent.
- Most enterprises used more than one professional service company.
- Deploying an e-commerce platform or an e-commerce application suite yielded no material cost advantage either way.
- No enterprise claimed to be 'on budget' for the project.

FIGURE 6.7: Electronic commerce site costs
  SOURCE: R. Satterthwaite 1999, 'CEO and CIO update: An E-commerce Web site can cost more than $1 million', GartnerGroup. Gartner Inc. press release, May 1999.

It is important to understand that being an e-business involves cost and risk. To achieve maximum strategic advantage through e-business, the organisation must make changes to internal and external processes and incur substantial capital outlay. It may risk destabilising the current business process. Therefore a cautious, managed approach is vital.

The rapid growth environment of e-business is largely due to several key factors. The key factors for ROI identification are:
- increased revenue
- capital cost reduction
- process simplification
- inventory reduction.

INCREASED REVENUE

Internet-based technology is not restricted by traditional sales channel constraints such as distribution network limitations, international timelines, and cultural and language barriers. Access to online information is 24 hours a day,

7 days a week. Potential consumers may view online catalogues, read about products, and be assured that products ordered over the Internet are received easily and inexpensively.

CAPITAL COST REDUCTION

Companies lower procurement costs by consolidating purchasing and developing relationships with suppliers to benefit from volume discounts and closer integration into the manufacturing process. Using the Internet, companies can instantly and effectively communicate with a wide range of suppliers and utilise EDI over an extranet framework to reduce order processing, labour, printing and mailing overheads.

Placing the service in the hands of the trading partner reduces company personnel overhead. An individual salesperson can realistically handle only as many customer accounts as he or she can physically visit or contact by telephone. By contrast, an organisation can add new trading partners or consumers at little or no extra cost. Since the sales force has been encapsulated by Internet technology and is not restricted by physical store size or personnel numbers, its reach is bound only by the capacity of the infrastructure.

The real value of Internet-based service, then, is not direct sales or revenue; it is the reduced costs of serving the consumer combined with the improved service that keeps the consumer coming back. Companies will be able to implement cost-cutting strategies that include automation of wholesale purchasing to trading partners.

PROCESS SIMPLIFICATION

Internet technology may further reduce procurement costs by automating or streamlining purchasing and ordering processes. Using server-based transaction software and the Internet as the medium, order acceptance, processing and requisitioning may use built-in approval and routing processes. By providing product catalogue information, shopping baskets and reorder facilities, cost savings come from increases in procurement efficiency, usage control and process quality improvement. St George Bank has found major efficiencies in simplifying and digitising the payment cycle.[40] By reducing paper to electronic record transcriptions, Internet data are directly integrated with the bank's internal systems, thus reducing cycle time and labour costs.

INVENTORY MANAGEMENT

Accurate transaction records lead to more intuitive forecasts on items that move well and those that do not. Improved forecasting allows the manufacturer to finetune the inventory and cut losses incurred by stock over-capitalisation. By utilising an extranet architecture and sharing information with potential trading partners, the organisation may begin to stock based on the historical needs of the partner. With the potential to reach all trading partners instantaneously at low cost, Internet technology plays a key role in reducing inventory overhead.

Lowes Menswear has managed to stock 25 per cent more stock on the same floor space by reducing the number of unwanted or slower moving items from the floor.[41] This has led to an increase in sales of 20 per cent by providing customers with what they want, and reducing warehouse space and distribution costs.

WHY IS BUSINESS TO BUSINESS ROI DIFFERENT?

Traditional ROI, when applied to the B2B enterprise, tends not to truly represent an accurate metric and must be complemented by factors including 'measurable tangibles', such as increased revenue and cost savings, and 'non-measurable intangibles', such as client satisfaction and market timing.

In fact, ROI in B2B is a difficult item to measure — if it can be measured at all. A recent survey from *InformationWeek* showed that only 17 per cent of IT managers were formally required to demonstrate potential payback of e-business initiatives.[42] In the survey it was highlighted how the Internet had increased the speed of business — so much so that ROI was not considered a high priority. The creation and maintenance of competitive advantage was cited as the main impetus for e-business deployment.

ROI has manifested itself as a shift from the tactical use of technology to the strategic use of technology.[43] This shift credits technology with the potential to:
- enhance the customer relationship and increase retention
- strengthen the trading partner relationship.

The strategic-based technology proposition looks beyond the tactical (bookings, financial transactions, information requests) to enterprise-enabling technologies that can pinpoint where companies can make money by identifying the properties and desires of the customer. Strategic technologies such as data warehousing and data mining allow the organisation access to critical customer information and the ability to enhance relationships and ensure expectations are met. Maintaining and expanding strategic relationships will require companies to deliver superior marketing, operational, financial and distribution services in a cost-effective manner.

The following technical insite provides a snapshot of how some companies approach ROI.

technical INSITE

NEW AGE ROI

In January 1999, Milacron Inc., a $1.7 billion machinery manufacturer and producer of tools, tooling and industrial products in Cincinnati, launched www.milpro.com. This site uses Open Market's Transact commerce server and LiveCommerce catalogue software. Speaking of ROI for the project, Alan Shaffer, VP Industrial products, observes: 'Return on investment? We never even discussed it ... This isn't an IT project, it's another market channel. Very few people do ROI on expanding their market channels.'[44]

Milacron sees its e-business efforts as a way to boost customer service. It has provided free services to encourage customers and new customers to use the site. The Milpro wizard offers advice on tools and industrial products. The Job Shop mall allows customers to post classified ads and talk to other customers about products. Milacron's tracking of site usage relates directly to three of the top five ROI criteria from the *InformationWeek* survey:
- improving customer satisfaction (87 per cent of IT executives)
- lowering the cost of product promotion (70 per cent)
- increasing direct access to customers (68 per cent).

The other two measures were lowering operational costs (85 per cent) and adding new customers (72 per cent). To compound the difficulty in ROI measurement, the enterprise must also take into account another key aspect of nearly all e-business initiatives — they are cross-functional. United Parcel Service is attempting to develop new metrics for its customers to help measure the payoff from e-commerce initiatives. Alan Amling, e-commerce director, says, 'E-Commerce cuts across the entire organisation, and if we just continue to focus on the person who runs the shipping dock, that's not going to cut it'.[45]

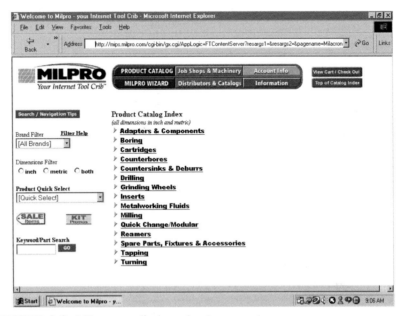

FIGURE 6.8: Milpro catalogue selection

SOURCE: http://mips.milpro.com.

One point is certain: in the emerging era of e-business, traditional planning models that base ROI payback on a five- to ten-year cycle cannot be used. Companies aiming to successfully compete in the e-business arena must calculate ROI figures in terms of a rapid one- to two-year cycle, and these metrics must be flexible enough to adapt as the company's strategy evolves.

EXERCISES

1. Do you agree with the statement 'Traditional ROI planning models that base ROI calculations on five- to ten-year cycles cannot be used in e-business'? Why/why not?

2. Prepare a report on:
   • Open Market commerce server
   • LiveCommerce Internet catalogue software.

3. What other metrics could be used by B2B exchanges to justify the large investment required?

E-BUSINESS ROI GUIDELINES

Table 6.8 provides seven suggestions that may be used by the enterprise to manage and measure ROI.

TABLE 6.8	E-BUSINESS ROI GUIDELINES
GUIDELINE	**EXPLANATION**
Conduct internal measurement first.	Focus on internal processes and measure the 'before' and 'after' of the same process in the same context. While it is easy to use metrics gained from other enterprises incorporating e-business, it is essential that the enterprise develop its own, internal metrics.
Segment process.	Enterprise-wide analysis is practically impossible for the majority of organisations. It is better to examine a process that involves intersystem and interpersonal transactions in discrete form and measure the timing and costing for each information flow.
Adapt existing re-engineering studies.	Benchmark and re-engineering studies developed before e-business implementation may prove useful in terms of data and process definition. The key to this approach is to re-measure the process in the same way before and after the e-business implementation.
Develop industry-specific supply-chain metrics.	While e-business strategies include cross-functional tools and processes, the enterprise should ensure that the organisation's success metrics are the same as those used to measure the current effectiveness of business units.
Link e-business metrics to the bottom line.	The enterprise vision should be directly linked to the specific business performance objectives. E-business initiatives should be quantified and prioritised against the high-level strategic vision and objectives. The value of the e-business should be identified, both in terms of direct benefits (cost reduction) and esoteric benefits (enhanced customer service).
Measure e-business value to trading partners.	Many suppliers to e-commerce drivers have experienced increased costs as they respond to incompatible demands from customers. The enterprise should ask specific questions about how the implementation has resulted in process change, or change in the cost of production for their trading partners. A study into how the e-business solution 'fits' with the trading partners is also important.
Measure competitive advantage.	Extended solutions will give the enterprise competitive advantage through the customers' perceived value of information and reduced costs. This advantage should be measured where possible.

SOURCE: J. Young 1999, 'Critical Factors for Short-term E-Commerce Success: Managed Care Applications and Vendors', GartnerGroup research paper.

SUMMARY

In this chapter we have seen how integration of applications, systems and processes across the supply chain has become of critical importance to B2B companies. The complexities associated with application integration are considerable, and involve many technologies and the collaboration of trading partners across the network.

Middleware architectures, which use technologies such as CORBA and Enterprise JavaBeans, present possible solutions that enable companies to communicate and collaborate across the supply chain. An open and extensible structure that can accommodate the numerous and often varied platforms of trading partners in the supply chain is essential.

Calculating return on investment is challenging for e-business. ROI metrics can often be intangible and thus extremely difficult to measure. Traditional methods for improving ROI, such as gaining process efficiency and increasing revenue, have been augmented in the B2B space by metrics such as customer satisfaction and customer retention.

key terms

content management systems	enterprise resource planning (ERP)	return on investment (ROI)
customer relationship management (CRM)	just-in-time (JIT)	supply chain
enterprise application integration (EAI)	message queuing	supply chain management (SCM)
	personalisation	
	plug and play	

QUESTIONS

1. Find examples of B2B marketplaces. How do these differ from B2C marketplaces?

2. Find press releases on positive B2B ROI and write a report outlining the key ROI drivers in each case.

3. Prepare a report on content management issues.

4. What is meant by personalisation and why is it important?

5. It is often still difficult to convince business managers to fund electronic commerce ventures. Outline how you would go about convincing a CEO to invest in an e-commerce enterprise. Examine issues such as the financial impact, strategic fit, impact on customers, priorities and culture changes.

Orica Chemicals

One of Australia's largest chemical companies, Orica, has recently established a B2B marketplace. Believing that many current industry portals and exchange hubs do not add real value to customer–supplier relationships, Orica needed to make a definitive choice either to join these industry marketplaces or to build their own presence. In September 2000, Orica Chemicals (a division of Orica Limited) established a B2B marketplace. The marketplace was initially piloted with 12 customers in Australia and New Zealand, its principal aim to establish how a traditional manufacturer could improve the customer relationship and provide added value to the supply chain.

The web-based shopfront (www.orica-chemicals.com) currently has a customer base of approximately 100 registered clients. Andrew Crawshaw, e-business manager for Orica Chemicals, planned to have all customers linked and actively using the new technology by December 2000. However, he notes that the task was made difficult by the industry's reluctance to adopt new technology.

FIGURE 6.9: The Orica Chemicals home page

The site was expected to contribute to overall sales by 10 per cent, or just under $3 million in the month of November 2001. In two years, Crawshaw hopes that the site will generate 30 per cent of all sales for the company.

Orica Chemicals offers the customer several advantages. These include:

- an integrated process model that means that customers can order across many product lines, with guaranteed delivery
- online search and retrieve facilities that enable customers to find chemical products quickly and efficiently based on search by product name, acronym or brand name
- search results that enable the customer to view details on product specifications, establish a regular product list and add products to orders
- modification of the regular product list and quantities on each product
- the ability to view delivery status of existing orders
- the ability to manage account reports and view outstanding invoice status and invoice detail.

BROWSE CATALOGUE

Orica Chemicals provides the facility for customers to browse the Orica product database. Search criteria can include product name, the product acronym, brand name, product industry (e.g. automotive), or its application (e.g. adhesive, vitamins). Results are returned as shown in figure 6.10. Products returned in this list may be added to the customer's regular product list by clicking on the check box to the right of each product on the screen.

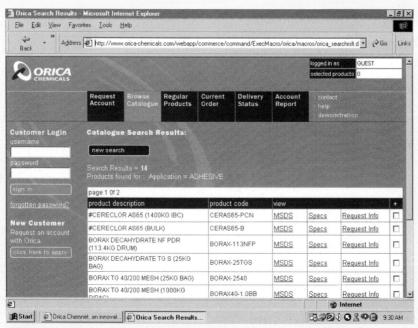

FIGURE 6.10: Orica Chemicals search results

      SOURCE: www.orica-chemicals.com/webapp/commerce/command/
ExecMacro/orica/macros/orica_searchrslt.dzw/report.

CURRENT ORDER STATUS

Customers may view order status for all outstanding current orders. The customer may modify the order to add or delete products and modify product quantities. Reordering of current orders (see figure 6.11) may also be achieved, saving customers time in the order process.

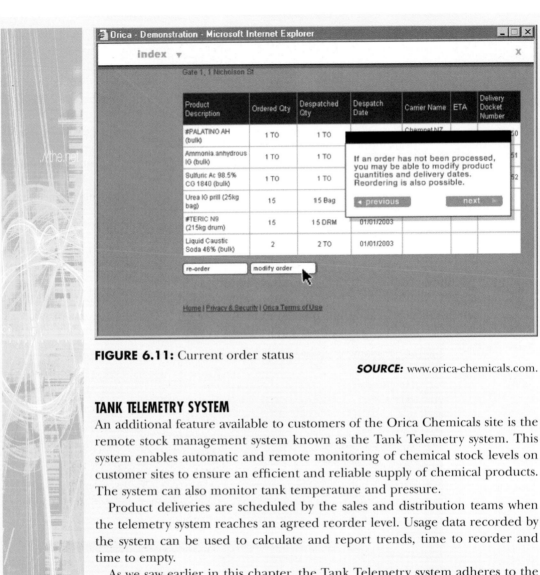

FIGURE 6.11: Current order status

SOURCE: www.orica-chemicals.com.

TANK TELEMETRY SYSTEM

An additional feature available to customers of the Orica Chemicals site is the remote stock management system known as the Tank Telemetry system. This system enables automatic and remote monitoring of chemical stock levels on customer sites to ensure an efficient and reliable supply of chemical products. The system can also monitor tank temperature and pressure.

Product deliveries are scheduled by the sales and distribution teams when the telemetry system reaches an agreed reorder level. Usage data recorded by the system can be used to calculate and report trends, time to reorder and time to empty.

As we saw earlier in this chapter, the Tank Telemetry system adheres to the principles of the Vendor Managed Inventory model, whereby usage data are shared between trading partners to ensure efficiency in the supply chain.

Benefits of the Tank Telemetry system include that it:
- enables customers to focus on growing business and not operations
- enables remote visual assessment of requirements for both customer and Orica Chemicals personnel
- monitors plant consumption and provides trends analysis
- reduces risk of stock-outs
- reduces the cost of unnecessary or ill-timed deliveries
- frees up time and resources
- builds culture of trust, commitment and cooperation.

It is simple to request an online account by visiting www.orica-chemicals.com, where there is also a demonstration site.

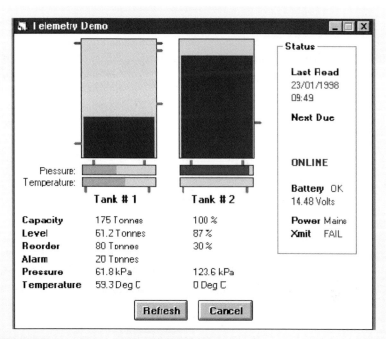

FIGURE 6.12: Tank Telemetry system

> **SOURCE:** www.orica-chemnet.com/Business/CHE/
> CHEMNET/WCHE0003.nsf/webnav2/services.

Questions

1. Identify the technology you have seen used in Orica Chemicals to service customers. Debate whether you would build your own service or purchase 'out-of-the-box' software to establish the web presence.

2. Find other examples of Vendor Managed Inventory and discuss how these systems assist trading partners in the supply chain.

3. Explain why building a culture of trust and commitment is so important to Orica Chemicals.

SUGGESTED READING

Alston, R. 1999, 'Australia's E-commerce Report Card', Australian Department of Communications Information Technology and the Arts paper.

Ariba Business-to-Business eCommerce Solutions 1999, 'Business-to-Business eCommerce: How Businesses Can Reduce Costs and Cash in on the Net Economy', Ariba advertising material.

Gregson, W., Creyke, P. and Webster, B. 1998, 'Pharmaceutical Electronic Commerce and Communication (PECC) — The Way Forward', Australian Department of Industry, Science and Tourism paper.

Linthicum, David 2001, *B2B Application Integration: e-Business-Enable Your Enterprise*, Addison-Wesley, New York.

Morton, M.S.S. 1991, *The Corporation of the 1990s*, Oxford University Press, Oxford, UK.

Peppers, Don, and Rogers, Martha 2001, *One to One B2B: Customer Relationship Management Strategies for the Real Economy*, Doubleday, New York.

END NOTES

1. Kalakota, R. and Robinson, M. 1999, *E-business: Roadmap for Success*, Addison-Wesley Longman, Reading, MA, p. 82.

2. Definition at www.whatis.com.

3. Kalakota and Robinson 1999, p. 83.

4. See www.whatis.com.

5. Morton 1991, p. 189.

6. Hoque, F. 2000, *E-enterprise: Business models, architectures and components*, Cambridge University Press, Cambridge, UK, p. 234.

7. Merkow, Mark 1999, 'Braving the Challenges of Web-to-Legacy Integration', E-Commerce Outlook, Internet.Com, http://ecommerce.internet.com/outlook/print/0,1282,7761_179101,00.html, p. 3.

8. Karpinski, R. 1998, 'webMethods XML Server Integrates Commerce Apps', www.internetwk.com/news/news0324-10.htm.

9. www.sterlingcommerce.com/solutions/market_solutions/sterlingsync.html.

10. http://ecommerce.internet.com/reviews/article/0,1281,3691_119831,00.html.

11. www.microsoft.com/commerceserver/default.htm.

12. www.inex.com.

13. www.ibm.com.

14. www.oracle.com.

15. www.cybercash.com.

16. http://ecommerce.internet.com/outlook/article/0,1281,7761_125731__3,00.html.

17. www.microsoft.com.

18. www.corprocure.com.au/companyinfo.

19. Kalakota and Robinson 1999, p. 197.

20. Kalakota and Robinson 1999, p. 217.

21. Kalakota and Robinson 1999, p. 211.

22. Kalakota and Robinson 1999, p. 217.

23. Kalakota and Robinson 1999, p. 218.

24. Hibbard, Justin 1999, 'Assembly online', *InformationWeek* 729, p. 84.

25. Hill, Suzette, 'Supply Chain Management in the age of e-commerce', *Apparel Industry Magazine*, 60 (3), p. 61.

26. www.dell.com.

27. www.fruit.com.

28. Gregson, Creyke and Webster 1998.

29. McKeown, P. and Watson, R. 1996, *Metamorphosis — A Guide to the World Wide Web and Electronic Commerce*, John Wiley & Sons, New York, p. 6.

30. Skyrme, D. 1997, 'The Virtual Corporation', Management Insight No. 2, www.skyrme.com/insights/2virtorg.htm.

31. Byrne, J. A. 1993, 'The Virtual Corporation', *Business Week*, February 8, p. 36.

32. TradeGate ECA and PIEC 1998, 'Pharmaceutical Industry Electronic Commerce Directions and Guidelines', TradeGate Australia, Sydney, p. 22.

33. Zimmerman, F. 1997, 'Structural and Managerial Aspects of Virtual Enterprises', Conference Proceedings of the European Conference on Virtual Enterprises and Networked Solutions — New Perspectives on Management, Communication and Information Technology, PaderBorn, Germany.

34. TradeGate ECA and PIEC 1998, p. 22.

35. Connor, Deni 1999, 'Compaq aims to simplify application integration process', *Network World* 16 (28), p. 22.

36. Markowitz, Elliot, and Scannell, Tim 1999, 'Integrator partnerships hold key to enterprise success', *Computer Reseller News* 18, p. 58.

37. Satterthwaite, R. 1999, 'CEO and CIO update: An E-Commerce Web site can cost more than $1 million', June, GartnerGroup.

38. Satterthwaite 1999.

39. Wilson, T. 2000, 'Integration — Key to Survival', internetweekonline, www.internetweek.com/lead/lead102300.htm.

40. Adams, M., Hardy, J., Bray, D., Cavill, M. and Swatman, P. 1999, 'Driving Forces on the New Silk Road: The Use of Electronic Commerce by Australian Businesses', Australian Department of Foreign Affairs and Trade, Annex 4 (c).

41. Adams et al. 1999, Annex 4 (a).

42. Dalton, Gregory 1999, 'E-Business Evolution', *InformationWeek* 737, pp. 50–66.

43. Berchiolli, Diann M. 1999, 'Leveraging technology for ROI', *Lodging Hospitality* 55 (6), p. R4–R5.

44. Wilder, Clinton 1999, 'ROI: E-business strategic investment', *InformationWeek* 735, p. 50.

45. Wilder 1999, p. 53.

CHAPTER
7

ELECTRONIC PAYMENT SYSTEMS

Learning objectives

You will have mastered the material in this chapter when you can:

- describe various types of electronic payment systems and explain how they operate in a B2B and B2C context
- identify the security needs of online electronic purchasing systems
- define EDI and demonstrate how invoicing and payments can be made
- explain the advantages and disadvantages of EDI relative to other forms of electronic payment systems
- describe and explain the value of various forms of e-cash systems
- evaluate the utility of stored value cards and smart cards as part of an electronic purchasing system.

'And money is like muck — not good except it be spread'

Francis Bacon, 'Of Seditions and Troubles', 1625 (quoted in *The Times Book of Quotations* 2000, Bath Press, p. 480).

INTRODUCTION

In the 1990s the emergence of electronic payment systems revolutionised the way we buy and sell goods and services. The transfer of funds electronically is a major component of any e-business venture, whether B2C, B2B or B2G. In this chapter we will explore the various types of electronic payment systems currently in use and some that are now being mooted. An **electronic payment system (EPS)** is a process that describes how value (usually **money**) is exchanged for goods, services or information. In some areas the EPS will be part of a value-adding process while in others it can be a direct payment, with no value being added to the good or service. We will look first at electronic payment systems and the technology behind them in a B2C environment before providing an overview of the technology behind B2B transactions.

B2C ELECTRONIC PAYMENT SYSTEMS

There are many ways to pay for goods electronically, such as by using credit cards, e-cash, e-cheques (e-checks) and stored value cards. The most popular form of payment over the Internet is via credit card. Banks all over the world have invested in magnetic strip card technology to ensure that processing credit cards and cheques is done efficiently, securely and quickly.

CREDIT CARDS ON THE INTERNET

A credit card transaction is an instruction by a customer for funds to be transferred into a business's account and charged against the customer's account. The customer gives the instruction to the seller directly, by handing over the card or by telephoning, emailing or faxing details such as card number, name on the card, expiry date and type of card (e.g. Visa or MasterCard). Normally, once a month customers are expected to make a payment to their bank either to settle all recent transactions or to pay a minimum amount. The primary steps involved are shown in figure 7.1.

Credit card numbers can be sent over the Internet encrypted or unencrypted. Encryption is the process of enabling information/data/knowledge to be coded in such a way that it cannot be read without a decoding system or key. All Internet browsers provide some level of data security. A 40-bit Secure Sockets Layer (SSL) (see chapter 8 for further details) is typical for most browsers available worldwide and is adequate for most common data transfer situations. A 128-bit SSL is used by financial institutions and Internet-capable software suppliers. Roughly speaking, 128-bit encryption (the number refers to the size of the encryption key) is 309 485 009 821 345 068 724 781 056 times stronger than 40-bit encryption.[2]

Web sites should inform buyers that their credit card is protected by encryption. Unencrypted dealings with credit cards are analogous to giving your credit card number over the phone. Customers can check if their browser supports session encryption by looking for a small closed lock in Internet Explorer or a small unbroken key in the Netscape browser family.

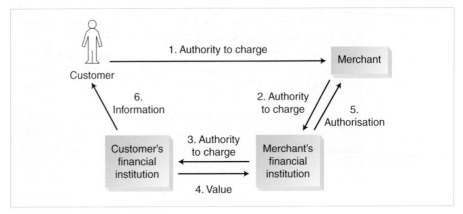

FIGURE 7.1: Steps in a credit card transaction
SOURCE: Australian Information Industry Association Ltd 1999, 'Getting Paid on the Internet: What you need to know to receive credit-card payments'.[1]

Prodigy Internet® and MasterCard® have been specially developed for online and offline purchases. The Prodigy card guarantees online fraud protection and offers a points-based reward program that allows credit card holders to redeem points for free Prodigy Internet Access.[3]

HOW CREDIT CARDS WORK ON THE INTERNET

Table 7.1 sets out the way in which credit card payments are processed.

TABLE 7.1	CREDIT CARD OPTIONS
TYPES OF MERCHANTS	**HOW THEY DEAL**
Offline merchants	Open a merchant account with a bank Accept only point-of-sale transactions or those that occur when you present credit card at the store
Special Internet merchant account	Processed by banks or third party services — e.g. www.cybercash.com, www.icat.com or www.camtech.com.au
Specialised software	Trintech offers online credit card transaction capabilities (for e-business and mobile e-business) — see www.trintech.com.

SOURCE: H. M. Deitel, P. J. Deitel and P. R. Nieto 2000, *E-business and E-commerce: How to Program*, Prentice Hall, New Jersey, pp. 136–7.

As mentioned in table 4.1, Trintech is a specialist software company offering online credit card transactions for both e-business and mobile e-business.

FIGURE 7.2: The Trintech web site

Remember also, in chapter 2 you learned about American Express online payment called Private Payments, which provides the user with a unique number that can be used to authenticate a single purchase transaction.

ANSI Standard X4.13-1983 is the system used by most US national credit card systems. Here are what some of your credit card numbers mean.[4]

- The first digit in your credit card number signifies the system — 3 = travel/entertainment cards (such as American Express and Diners Club), 4 = Visa, 5 = MasterCard and 6 = Discover Card.
- The structure of the card number varies according to the system. For example, American Express card numbers start with 37, Carte Blanche and Diners Club with 38.
- For American Express, digits 3 and 4 are type and currency, digits 5–11 are the account number, digits 12–14 are the card number within the account, and digit 15 is a check digit.
- For Visa, digits 2–6 are the bank number, digits 7–12 or 7–15 are the account number, and digit 13 or 16 is a check digit.
- For MasterCard, digits 2–3, 2–4, 2–5 or 2–6 are the bank number (depending on whether digit 2 is a 1, 2, 3 or other). The digits after the bank number up through digit 15 give the account number, and digit 16 is a check digit.

There is a wealth of information on how credit cards work at www.howstuff-works.com, and more on the workings of credit cards on the Internet can be found in Alex Toussaint's 'Processing Credit Cards for Online Payment' at http://msdn.microsoft.com/workshop/server/commerce/creditcard.asp.

The following technical insite describes a new way of using credit cards on the Internet.

TRIPLE C: CYBERSPACE CREDIT CARDS

The Discover desksh•p[SM] 2.0 virtual credit card is able to generate a single-use card number — a unique credit card number used for purchases at a single web site — so that a Cardmember's actual account number never travels to online stores. Because each single-use card number becomes exclusive to the online store where purchases are made, recurring charges such as Internet service provider fees or back-ordered items can be billed to that same number.

If a Cardmember is surfing the Net and decides to purchase something, the Discover desksh•p virtual credit card will automatically pop up when the Cardmember lands on the merchant's checkout page. The Cardmember can simply click on the Discover desksh•p icon and choose to fill the checkout form automatically with the single-use card number and shipping information so that the transaction is completed with ease. The Discover® Cardmember never has to leave the merchant's site to enjoy the benefits of this virtual credit card.

Advantages of the virtual credit card are:
- the capability to store all user names and passwords for any web site so they are readily available
- access to real-time account information via the Discovercard.com account centre
- the ability to check statement summaries, transfer balances and pay Discover Card bills
- access to Discover Card's Internet ShopCenter[SM].

The Discover Card is partnered with Brodia (www.brodia.com/platform), which provides platforms and core applications to enable personal commerce, payments and identity management on any mobile or other network-connected device. It is also partnered with Orbiscom (www.orbiscom.com), which is a software technology service provider deploying controlled, protected online payments.

SOURCE: Adapted from 'Discover® Card introduces Discover deskSh•p[SM] 2.0: the first real solution for safer, easier online shopping', Discover financial Services press release, 2001.

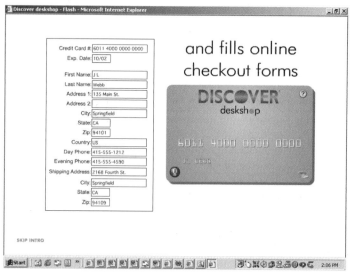

FIGURE 7.3: Discover desksh•p's automatic online checkout form
SOURCE: https://discoverdeskshop.card2.novusnet.com/ discover/service/app_Home.htm.

EXERCISES

1. Visit the web sites mentioned here and prepare a report on the advantages and disadvantages of such a system.
2. Investigate what type of technology is behind this system. For example, what type of encryption and security protocols protect the card?
3. Discover Card generates a single-use card number for each purchase. Prepare a report on the advantages of such a system.
4. Check out what other merchants are using this system.
5. Prepare a report on the Electronic Commerce Modelling Language.

EFTPOS

Electronic funds transfer at point of sale (EFTPOS) refers to when the purchaser is physically at the point of sale, such as the checkout in a supermarket or in a petrol station. EFTPOS operates on either credit or debit cards, immediately debiting the value of the exchange against an existing bank account. On credit cards, EFTPOS systems check the validity of the card status and then credit the value of the exchange against the credit card account for future payment by the cardholder (see figure 7.4). This method of payment has proved popular with virtual shoppers too, as several online shops (e.g. www.woolworths.com.au) use mobile EFTPOS machines when they deliver goods to clients.

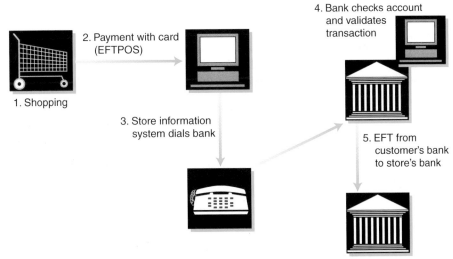

FIGURE 7.4: EFTPOS, payments and shopping

ELECTRONIC CHEQUES

Electronic cheques (spelt *checks* in the United States) operate as though you were being issued a set of numbers from the bank: each number represents a cheque. This is a virtual chequebook without the physical cheques. You use each set of numbers only once — like a cheque. Figure 7.5 illustrates an eCheck™ from www.echeck.com.

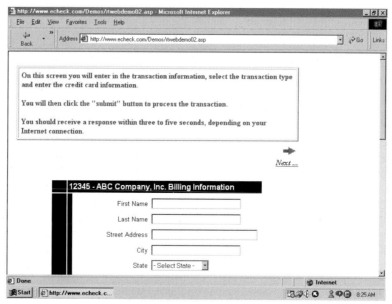

FIGURE 7.5: An electronic cheque, or eCheck™

SOURCE: www.echeck.com/Demos/rtwebdemo02.asp.

With eCheck™, the payer writes the cheque on a computer, signs it and emails it over the Internet. The payee receives it, verifies signatures, endorses it, writes a deposit slip and signs it. The endorsed cheque is then sent by email to the payee's bank for deposit. Bank personnel verify signatures, credit the deposit, and then clear and settle the endorsed eCheck™ by sending it on to the payer's bank, where signatures are once again verified and the amount of the eCheck™ is debited from the payer's account.[5] For more information on eChecks visit www.echeck.org, which contains tutorials on how these cheques work, such as www.echeck.org/demos/meeting92299/EcheckTutorialMMA.pdf.

E-WALLETS

Electronic wallets have been designed to make it easier to shop on line. If customers sign up for e-wallet, later when they shop on line they need to enter their billing and shipping information only once. The e-wallet software will then instantly fill out online order forms with a click of a mouse. To make gift giving easier, the wallet can also store the shipping addresses of friends and family. Electronic Commerce Modelling Language (ECML) a universal format for online checkout form data fields, was launched in June 1999. ECML provides a simple set of guidelines for web merchants that enables digital wallets from multiple vendors to automate the exchange of information between consumers and merchants. ECML works with any web-security software and enables electronic wallets to feed customer information automatically into the payment forms of participating merchants.[6] For further details, see the web site www.ecml.org.

DIGITAL CASH AND PREPAID CARDS

At a more experimental level, increasing use of the Internet and the Web for commercial transactions is creating a need for another type of EPS — digital cash. Digital cash has the advantage of being weightless, since it is really just a series of zeros and ones that can be transported at high speed across the Internet. CyberCash is a company that offers a secure means to conduct credit-card transactions on the Internet. It is designed specifically for use by Cyber-Cash's operators. However, digital cash has had a difficult time: its issuers either went bankrupt (DigiCash), dropped the product (CyberCash) or moved into another business. First Virtual Holdings' product is now being sold by MessageMedia. Several demonstrations on **e-cash** are found at www.ecash.net/Demo, as shown in figure 7.6. eCash™ markets a system by which financial institutions can allow for real-time direct debit from bank accounts.

Digital money is represented by a small string of encrypted digits, or electronic tokens, that can be used as a substitute for money to purchase various goods and services in an electronic environment, usually the Internet. For example, token or exchange value certificates can be used on the Internet or on private networks. SITA (Société Internationale Transportation Aéronautiques), for example, provides a private network that supports the booking processes and traffic planning of most of the world's airlines. Digital cash replaces money in the transaction but depends on an institution, such as a bank, to provide the monetary value for the digital transaction.

Figure 7.6 shows the eCash™ Demos page.

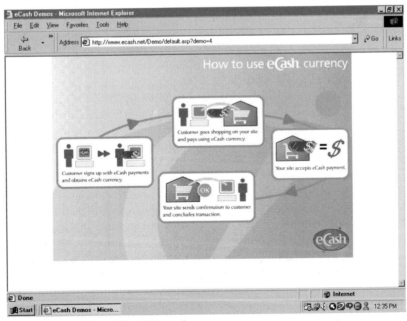

FIGURE 7.6: How eCash™ works

SOURCE: 'How to use eCash', www.ecash.net/Demo. Reproduced with permission of eCash Technologies, Inc.

Yahoo offers PayDirect at its web site at www.paydirect.yahoo.com. This system allows consumers to:

- send money to anyone in the United States with an email address
- pay for an auction item they have won
- create custom links on their web page to expedite direct payment by creditors
- send a group bill to collect money for a party.

Another area that looks promising is prepaid cards. Research is being undertaken by CommerceNet — see the CommerceNet Security and Internet Payments Research Group at www.commerce.net. Prepaid cards that are used for online payments are typically distributed as simple scratch-off, embossed plastic or magnetic stripe cards. The cards are available in different denominations and can be purchased from a retailer with any payment mechanism, but most typically using anonymous cash. When distributed to retailers the cards are inactive; they must be activated prior to use as a payment instrument.[7] Prepaid cards offer an attractive alternative to credit cards, especially for young people who are not eligible for a credit card.

The prepaid cards are easy to source, brand and distribute. The required Internet technologies can be readily assembled using commodity building blocks such as the generic browser, SSL, any SQL database, any server technology and the appropriate scripting language, given the technical ability to set it up. The only real area of technical differentiation is in passing purchase authorisation back to online merchants. Research is continuing, but already some well-know credit card companies have been moving into the area. American Express has signed a distribution agreement with 7-Eleven to create and distribute the 7-Eleven® Internet Shopping Card. Visa has recently started to offer prepaid cards, called Visa Buxx, through some of its member banks.

One of the problems with using digital-cash systems is the need to ensure the security of the payment being made. Three major protocols have been developed to try to ensure that all electronic payments made over the Internet are secure. These protocols are:

- *STT.* Developed by Microsoft and Visa, STT uses a two-keyed authentication and encryption system that enables purchases to be completed using credit cards in a method similar to offline credit card usage. Each user is authenticated by an electronic certificate or credential that is unique to them. Any transaction must be verified by this credential.
- *SEPP.* This protocol was developed by IBM, MasterCard, Netscape, Verisign, RSA, Terisa Systems, SAIC, GTE and CyberCash using existing credit card procedures. However, SEPP differs from STT in that SEPP uses other forms of communication and other existing and private networks, as well as the Internet, to process the exchange of value involved in the transaction. In effect, it uses existing EFT infrastructure to operate.
- *SET.* This protocol was developed by both of the major credit card providers Visa and MasterCard to establish a uniform, secure communication standard for Internet commerce and is designed to become the standard for e-commerce. SET trials began in 1997. **SET** uses the Internet rather than existing EFT infrastructure. On 4 June 1998 SET Co. awarded the right to use the SET trademark to the first four vendors of SET-compliant software,

GlobeSet Inc., Spyrus/Terisa Systems, Trintech and Verifone. These companies' wallet applications were determined to be compliant with the SET 1.0 protocol. Check www.setco.org for SET protocols.

The following points illustrate the advantages of SET.[8] Primarily a secure communications standard, SET:

- enables bankcard payment on the WWW
- provides for special security needs
- ensures privacy of financial data
- features strong authentication policies for participants
- offers special purpose certificates
- provides message integrity
- offers non-repudiation for dispute resolution
- hides bankcard number from most merchants
- sustains existing relationships — cardholders with their banks, merchants with their banks
- provides interoperability
- supports end-user choice of payment card
- provides links to existing systems

IBM's superSet project is to extend SET to other payment instruments such as micropayments and cheques.

However, the uptake of SET has been slow, and it appears that SSL has become the de facto standard.

One global organisation that has an interest in EPS is CommerceNet (www.commerce.net). CommerceNet has put in place portfolios that deal with five initial areas:

- infrastructure (EDI, robustness, network management and related infrastructure services)
- financial service (payments, Rosetta Net, eCheck™)
- trust and security (public key infrastructure (PKI), security showcase and encryption)
- information access (catalogues, directories, agencies and search interoperability)
- architecture and markets (eCo framework, iMarkets, vertical markets).

CommerceNet issues an email newsletter on electronic commerce matters. To receive it, send an email to buzz-request@lists.commerce.net. In both the subject line and the body of the message, type the word 'subscribe'.

OTHER DIGITAL CURRENCY PRODUCTS

New digital cash products are entering the market. These products are being marketed for a variety of reasons.

- People like the anonymity of digital cash as opposed to credit cards.
- Many people do not have access to credit cards: young people do not qualify for a credit card, and some cultures do not feel comfortable with credit cards.
- Auctions and C2C e-commerce have also created a need for online payment systems between individuals other than via a credit card.

- Merchants might find digital cash more convenient since credit card costs cut into merchants' revenue. Therefore, sites selling small items, such as a single song, need to be able to accept micropayments ranging from a tenth of a cent to $10. Millicent (see figure 7.7) is an account-based micropayment scheme originally developed at DEC's System Research Center in 1995 (see www.millicent.digital.com).

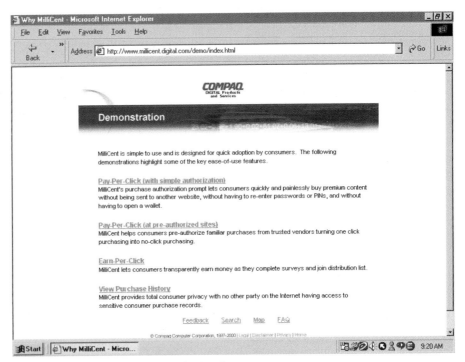

FIGURE 7.7: The Millicent web site demo page

Some of the new digital cash techniques are itemised below.
- Consumers can now store value in an online account and deduct from it the price of small purchases. This technique was pioneered by iClickCharge. IBM and Compaq use a similar technique, as does Fairfax for its archived articles.
- Qpass makes no initial charge but accumulates payments and deducts the final amount from a credit card.
- Trivnet and Ipin use ISPs to track customers' online spending and add it to their bill.
- Flooz issues gift certificates. The giver uses a credit card to pay money into an account. The recipient of the gift certificate can then spend the money in the account at a participating online merchant. At the beginning of 2000, there were US$5 million worth of flooz certificates.
- Consumers are being paid in 'beenz' to visit web sites, fill in forms or go shopping on line. They can then spend the 'beenz' at participating sites.
- CyberGold allows consumers to convert 'cyberdollars' into real money.
- PayPal has been developed by Confinity to enable people to open an account at the web site and then email dollars to other people (money can be transferred via Palm Pilots).

- E-Gold allows clients to fund their accounts by purchasing gold or other metals and then transferring units of those metals (measured by weight) by entering a recipient's account and a password.
- Various online bartering schemes exist such as BarterTrust, BigVine and LassoBucks.
- A British firm called Oakington has developed software that allows for the automatic payment of taxes and 'time escrow' so that a transaction does not clear until the goods arrive.

Another digital cash product is the wallet, a small software program that is used for online purchase transactions. It allows for several methods of payment to be defined within the wallet. It may take several different kinds of credit card. Microsoft offers its Passport wallet to store credit card details and shipping addresses. This information is sent over a secure connection to online merchants.

Research on digital cash has concentrated on trying to resolve the technical and social difficulties that exist. As a result, a number of new alternatives are being developed. For example, in 1995 at the University of Newcastle, the Monetary Systems Engineering Group developed Millicent, an account-based transaction protocol for low-value transactions that allows a vendor to verify a transaction without contacting a central authority and without expensive encryption. Millicent uses brokers and scrip. Brokers look after account management, billing and establishing accounts with merchants. Scrip is electronic cash that is valid only for a specific vendor.

A more detailed discussion of digital cash systems is to be found in Furche and Wrightson (1996) (see suggested reading list at the end of this chapter). Developments in the design and use of digital cash in Australia can be viewed at www.cs.newcastle.edu.au/Research/pabloins/mseg.html.

SMART CARDS (STORED VALUE CARDS)

Smart cards are a form of EPS that use a plastic card with a microchip that stores information, usually about value. Value stored on the card acts as a substitute for cash. Smart cards, or, more correctly, **stored value cards (SVCs)** can store more information and perform more functions than the magnetic stripe cards that are more commonly in use internationally. It is estimated that there are more than 600 million smart cards in operation throughout the world either as magnetic stripe cards or as SVCs with microchips. They are used to store information about people's health, as identity cards and security cards, and as electronic signatures for digital mobile phones. Australian and European trials of smart cards as substitutes for cash by companies like Visa and Mondex suggest that smart cards will eventually replace the common magnetic stripe cards now used in EFTPOS and banking transactions using ATMs.

Visa has introduced smart Visa cards in the United States. Further details may be found at www.visa.com/pd/smart/smartlz.html.

FIGURE 7.8: A magnetic stripe card

FIGURE 7.9: An SVC — the front and back of one of Telstra's phone cards

Smart cards are really microcomputers that rely on another medium or reader to supply the power source to make them work. Smart cards have a small chip embedded, usually in a plastic card. This chip acts like a micro-computer with a typical input/output device, a microprocessor, and ROM and RAM memory (see figure 7.10).

Smart cards or SVCs can store everything found in a wallet or purse. They operate mostly by transfer of data or value from the card to a business system, usually without verification, which makes them different from online payment systems. The protocols used in this process are:

- programming cards, assigning serial numbers and loading keys to increase and decrease the value of cards. This is called personalisation.
- the allocation of transaction reload capability, which enables the stored value on the card to be added to when desired
- a debit transaction process facility that enables a business system to download value and debit the loading system for the value of a transaction.

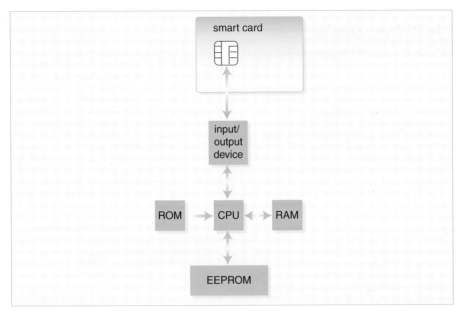

FIGURE 7.10: Components of a smart card and internal communication flow
SOURCE: A. Furche and G. Wrightson 1996, *Computer Money: A Systematic Overview of Electronic Payment Systems*, dpunkt, verlag für digitale Technologie GmbH, Heidelberg, Germany, p. 65. Reproduced by permission.

Smart cards can also store university transcripts, personal records, medical information, hospital files, social security information, employment records — in fact, any personal or organisational information that needs to be stored and portable. One day in Australia an SVC could be developed that would be our driver's licence, Medicare card, Bankcard and bank debit card as well as containing our medical records and personal CV. The limitations to this development relate to privacy and other legal, social and political issues, which are discussed in the next chapter and can be more fully explored in Tyree (1997) (see suggested reading at the end of this chapter).

In Thailand, Lenso has developed an SVC for international telephone calls that operates at Lenso telephone points. In this case, the consumer buys a card for either 250 or 500 baht ($A10 or $A20) and then uses the value stored on the card to make international phone calls. The value stored on the card is downloaded at the conclusion of the telephone call. This is a closed system. The cards are manufactured by Lenso, who receive payment when they are purchased. The business system, the international telephone point, downloads the value, capturing the payment just as a coin-operated telephone captures coins. This SVC is non-reusable and discarded after the value is used up. A similar smart card system is used in the car park under Melbourne Central. On entering the car park, the customer is given a smart card that can then be used to store/record the value of purchases made throughout this very large shopping complex. The system is designed to give the exiting customer a 50 per cent discount on car-parking charges for every $10 spent in the shopping complex. The system also recognises each additional $10 unit of purchases as a credit for further discount for future use of the car park.

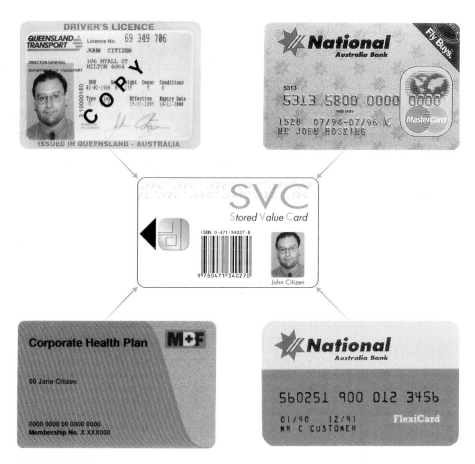

FIGURE 7.11: In the future, it is possible that an SVC could contain all of these elements.

The Microbus public transport system in Bangkok, Thailand, has recently introduced an SVC that is purchased from the bus driver and then given value by the consumer passing bank notes into a machine either on the bus or at a number of offices throughout metropolitan Bangkok. Each trip is then debited against the card when it is put into the card reader in the bus. In this case, the SVC is reusable and can be 'topped up' at any time.

In China reusable SVCs are employed to activate electricity meters, and in Singapore a tourist card (SVC) is being developed to eliminate the need for money changers. Already there are banks in Asia that have electronic reader machines that convert currency by reading the currency electronically, eliminating the human interface in the transaction. These are true EPSs, since each eliminates the intermediary process of human handling. Stored value is transferred from a card to another organisation's account. This is then adjusted through an electronic banking system.

For those interested in pursuing this subject further, there is a Smart Card Technical Issues Starter Kit at www.anu.edu.au/people/Roger.Clarke/DV/SCTISK.html.

TYPES OF SVCs

Closed-system SVCs are smart cards on which the intrinsic value of the card is fixed. Such cards include fixed-priced, pre-paid telephone cards or pre-paid transport tickets. In this case, the owner of the card and the provider of the service are the same. Open-system SVCs are smart cards on which the intrinsic value of the card can be changed. These cards can be recharged in value. They can be described as an electronic wallet, where the value on the card can be increased each day or at any regular interval. Most commonly, the owner/ issuer of such open-system SVCs is not the service provider. For example, a bank can issue an open-system SVC (e.g. Thai Danu Bank's SMART Cash card), and this card can then be used in any store or for any purchase or transaction where there is a card reader.

Both closed- and open-system SVCs will have an impact on the transaction process and the accounting of money throughout the economic systems they engage. In effect, they complicate the value exchange process (see figure 7.12).

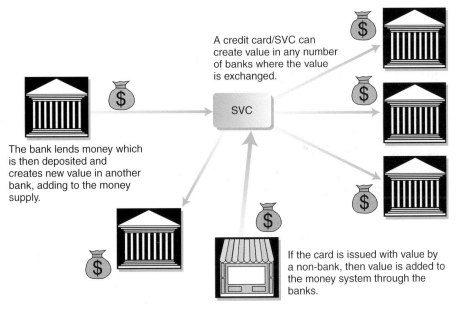

A credit card/SVC can create value in any number of banks where the value is exchanged.

The bank lends money which is then deposited and creates new value in another bank, adding to the money supply.

SVC

If the card is issued with value by a non-bank, then value is added to the money system through the banks.

FIGURE 7.12: SVCs in the exchange process

ADVANTAGES AND RISKS OF SVCs IN BUSINESS

In a very detailed evaluation of smart cards in Australia, the Centre for Electronic Commerce at Monash University has come to the following conclusions.

- Smart cards will have a significant impact on the banking system and the way it operates.
- Smart cards will affect the way money is exchanged.
- Smart cards may erode the traditional role of banks in the payment systems used in society, although the Australian banks and others, such as those in Thailand, are in the forefront of the development and issue of SVCs and other smart cards to maintain their traditional roles.

- Smart cards have the potential to allow institutions other than banks to issue value and thus create money, which has been the traditional role of banks. For example, a company could issue smart cards for transactions in its own stores or enterprises that could be issued on credit and thus create money. This could impact on the supply of money and the level of inflation in an economy.
- Smart cards and SVCs are expensive to establish, and the potential profitability of the new value and service created by the cards will be lessened at least in the short run.
- SVCs should improve the efficiency of electronically transferring funds for low-value, high-volume transactions.
- SVCs should offer consumers a great range of choice in payment methods and should improve convenience.
- SVCs and smart cards will probably increase costs to consumers by the need for suppliers to cover costs.
- SVCs may not be affordable to all consumers, thus raising equity issues in society.
- The existing protections for consumers when using current payment systems and cards do not always apply with SVCs.
- Smart cards are more secure than magnetic stripe cards.
- SVCs could be more secure than cash, depending on the card design and the method of recording stored value.
- The trials on SVCs currently in operation in Australia (Visa, Transcard, MasterCard, Quicklink and Mondex) are technically incompatible!

B2B ELECTRONIC PAYMENT SYSTEMS

The idea of electronic commerce was suggested in the 1960s by financial institutions who began investigating ways to automate their back-end banking systems. Initially, these systems were capable of basic electronic processing of cheques; however, soon they managed to process credit card and wire-transfer transactions electronically.

ELECTRONIC FUNDS TRANSFER AND EFTPOS

The 1970s saw the introduction of **electronic funds transfer (EFT)** between banks and financial institutions and the gradual emergence of the customer-focused automatic teller machine (ATM), which has since proven to be immensely popular with the general public.

EFT and electronic funds transfer at point of sale (EFTPOS) are electronic tools currently in use effectively to transfer the value of exchange process for goods or services or information. EFT is any transfer of funds initiated through an electronic terminal, telephone, modem, computer or magnetic tape so as to order, instruct or authorise a financial institution to debit or credit an account.[9] EFT utilises computer and telecommunication components both to supply and to transfer money or financial assets.

ELECTRONIC DATA INTERCHANGE

During the late 1970s and early 1980s another component of e-commerce emerged as a result of businesses striving to reduce the 'paper trail' and improve efficiency. Electronic messaging technologies and in particular **Electronic Data Interchange (EDI)** lead the way in the automation of the business process and, intrinsically, business process re-engineering. EDI is the automated exchange of structured business documents (such as purchase orders and invoices) between an organisation and its customers, suppliers or other trading partners.

Traditional (non-Internet) EDI is actually a set of specifications for formatting documents designed specifically to automate business flow — within a business and between businesses — by replacing paper documents with electronic ones.

Using EDI, a business document (such as a purchase order) may be transmitted by a communications application across the trading network and automatically processed by a receiving application residing with the trading partner. Subsequently, the trading partner communications application can generate and send back to the original party a reply EDI document (such as an invoice), which can be automatically interpreted at the receiver end. This entire process is paperless, highly efficient and requires little or no human intervention.

The strength of EDI lies in its ability to enable organisations with different business and computer systems to link those systems cost-effectively. By structuring the transfer process and standardising the format of these electronic documents, EDI enables purchasers and suppliers to communicate and transact in a faster, more efficient manner. Thus, EDI represents an effective technology for reducing the overheads associated with paper processing, product verification, handling and storage.

EDI processes must have the following characteristics.
- The exchange of information must be in a structured format so that the data are placed and found in predetermined places in the electronic message.
- The format or structure of the information must be agreed upon by both the receiver and the sender.
- The data must be machine readable. EDI does not involve the sending of data by fax from one organisation and then the rekeying of those data in the new place of operation.

TRADITIONAL EDI

Traditional EDI systems require communication between two or more trading partners. Hence, the network infrastructure must contain two major components — a communications channel that delivers the EDI documents across the trading network, and conformance to EDI standards.

COMMUNICATIONS CHANNELS

The communications channel of a trading network is dictated by the complexity of the trading network and the type of communication link. There are three major communications channels available to EDI users.

DIRECT LINK EDI

Direct link networks (ISDN leased lines and high-speed modem dial-up) represent the simplest EDI communications method. Direct link EDI allows a business to communicate with trading partners by 'dialling-up' the trading partner's network and transmitting EDI documents as required.

Typically, trading partners install and maintain their own direct link lines. Issues with speed, protocols and reliability across the trading partner network make direct link EDI prohibitive to smaller businesses. Hence, direct link EDI is suited primarily to large organisations transmitting large volumes of data on a regular basis.

PRIVATE NETWORKS

A private (proprietary) network is a closed network available to a selected group of trading partners. Typically, a 'hub' company manages document handling overheads and protocol conversion facilities for 'spoke' trading partners. These 'spoke' companies can dial up the private network using a standard modem and perform their EDI transfers for the cost of a telephone call.

VALUE-ADDED NETWORKS

A **value-added network (VAN)** is a third party network or intermediary capable of providing reliable, secure transmission of documents between trading partners. Typically, VANs are analogous to a post office or clearing house, providing not only transmission services, but also EDI support services such as protocol conversion, speed conversion, mailbox services and value-added services such as technical support, consulting, training and EDI-to-fax services.

Initially, VANs provided mailbox services to trading partners on the network. Incoming EDI documents from trading partners were stored in electronic 'mailboxes', from which they could be retrieved at a later time by the intended recipient. VANs now also support administrative facilities such as document auditing, message tracking, usage reporting and billing services.

VANs can also convert EDI documents between formats for trading partners. Using in-house EDI translation software, a VAN offers translation services that convert documents between standards such as X12 and EDIFACT, between standard and proprietary formats and to other media types such as email and fax.

TABLE 7.2	ADVANTAGES AND DISADVANTAGES OF A VAN
ADVANTAGES	**DISADVANTAGES**
• 24 × 7 operation, accessible globally • Typically toll-free or local telephone number • Multi-speed, multi-protocol support across trading partners	• Interruption of VAN services • VAN processing delays • Data alteration and lack of data integrity

VANs store and send on information and data in forms that are acceptable by the businesses receiving the data. VANs function as intermediaries for large numbers of businesses, acting as a focal point for multi-transactional, multi-nodal businesses. VANs act as a router of data, and a consultancy point for new business.

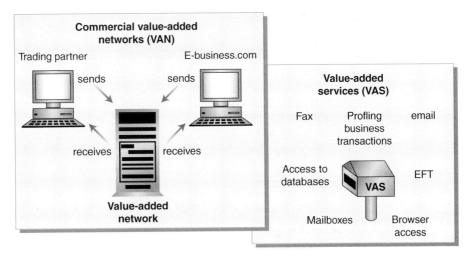

FIGURE 7.13: VAN architecture

The most important VANs in Australia include Tradelink and T-Net, which are run by Telstra, and EXIT, which is run by OTC, Australia. The network processes used in an EDI transaction are shown in figure 7.14.

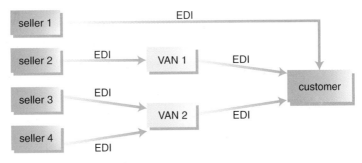

FIGURE 7.14: How EDI works

EDI STANDARDS

The EDI communication process illustrated in figure 7.14 depends on the existence and acceptance of specific EDI standards and protocols that have to be adopted by each user in both simple and complex EDI relationships. Linking a customer with a supplier in an EDI relationship involves a hierarchy of communication levels, each of which has different accepted standards and protocols.

Most standards and protocols used in EDI communications are derived from the International Consultative Committee for Telephony. EDI standards for messages usually involve the data being broken down into smaller packages for transmission and sent to a receiver, where they are reassembled into a coherent message (see figure 7.15).

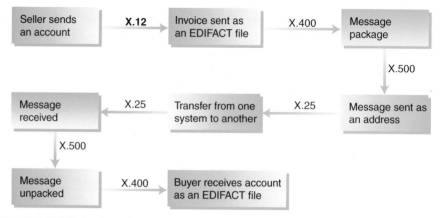

FIGURE 7.15: EDI process protocols

The exchange protocols used in the EDI process above perform different functions. The X.25 standard allows electronic messages to be broken up into specific packages of information (packets), which are sent to the receiving PC and enable reassembling of the original information sent. The **X.25 protocol** controls the EDI process at the communications level. At another level, the **X.400** and **X.500 protocols** enable the message to be handled by the sending and receiving PCs. They are not concerned with content but, in the case of the X.400, with how the data can be broken up and packaged and, in the case of the X.500, with addresses and directories used in the EDI process.

As a result of the need for specific standards for successful EDI processes, a number of standards have been established throughout the world, including **TRADACOMS** in Great Britain. In Australia, **EDIFACT** is the standard used in EDI. EDIFACT (electronic data interchange for administration, commerce and transport) is the United Nations–agreed standard for EDI transmission. This protocol is recommended within the framework of the United Nations. The rules of EDIFACT are approved and published by UN/ECE in the United Nations Trade Data Interchange Directory (UNTDID), and are maintained under agreed procedures. The details of EDIFACT syntax, message structures and specific protocols can be found at www.unece.org/trade/untdid/texts/d422_d.htm.

BENEFITS OF TRADITIONAL EDI

Firms worldwide have benefited from productivity gains through using traditional EDI by this leveraging of computer-to-computer transaction exchange. Traditionally, only large firms have employed EDI technology because it is an expensive, proprietary technology. Nonetheless, EDI is found to be a standard part of nearly all large and medium-sized firms because it can typically save 5 to 10 per cent of procurement costs. Two notable examples[10] are set out below.

- General Electric in the United States uses EDI with its trading partner network to reduce inventory levels. Safety stock has been reduced from 35 to 10 days' worth. This has occurred because GE can purchase material and have it delivered more often and more efficiently using EDI. The average cost of purchase orders has fallen from US$52 to US$12.

- Astra Pharmaceuticals in Australia receives orders from customers using EDI technology. Since the types of orders are complex (often 90 lines in length), the chances of error and incorrect ordering are high in a manual system. With EDI and the use of standard electronic documents, order errors are dramatically reduced. Order fulfilment once took 24 hours — it now takes 20 minutes. Advantages of traditional EDI also include:
- the ability to maintain control over the movement of materials
- a reduction in labour costs
- a reduction in routine tasks that can often cause errors
- a reduction in stockholding and accounts receivable
- an increase in cash flow due to the effective management of trade creditors
- an increase in customer service
- a move to one-time entry and elimination of superfluous administration.

SHORTCOMINGS OF TRADITIONAL EDI

Although EDI has provided such firms with many benefits in terms of cost reduction and general efficiency improvement, EDI is an expensive means of doing business. Small and medium-sized firms tended not to be EDI capable because of the inherent costs in proprietary software purchase, hardware installation and ongoing maintenance.

Typical costs of implementing translation software may range from $5000 (for a PC-based system) through to $250 000 (for a mainframe application). Transaction and subscription fees may also apply. In general, typical monthly fees are $50 and transaction fees of 50 to 70 cents per transaction apply.[11]

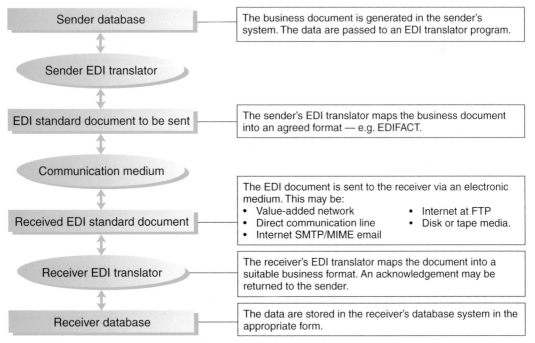

FIGURE 7.16: The EDI process

SOURCE: PIEC and TradeGate, www.tradegate.org.au/ec-projects/ ec-for-industry/pharmaceutical/Directions2.pdf.

INTERNET EDI

The traditional e-commerce landscape has seen EDI as an effective means for transmission of business documents between organisations. However, economies of scale have proven to favour the large organisations who perform large volumes of transactions. Although EDI has been standardised through ANSI and EDIFACT, high operational costs, extensive customisation requirements and the need for value-added network providers (VANS) have hindered widespread adoption.

The ubiquitous and open nature of the Internet brings a new dimension to EDI — Internet EDI. The Internet's inherent low-cost transport mechanism and standardised protocols offer organisations the opportunity to participate in B2B e-commerce at low cost. Moreover, the Internet offers a deeper interaction for trading partners.

Internet EDI offers the trading partner community not only basic transactional capability, but also online catalogues, pricing information, scheduling and delivery information, and even new ways of actioning procurement such as online auctions.

Internet EDI also offers broad connectivity through worldwide connections, allowing buyers and sellers to transact on a global scale. It offers a simple, platform-independent vehicle for information exchange through the TCP/IP protocol and the emerging common standard Open Buying on the Internet (OBI).

OBI provides trading partners with a simple standards-based solution through a flexible platform-independent architecture. The OBI standard focuses on the Internet transaction and the components of which this is comprised — namely, EDI, digital certification and supporting back-end database systems.

The Bank Internet Payment Systems (BIPS) project developed by the Financial Services Technology Consortium (FSTC) will enable better B2B e-commerce. BIPS is a project to develop an open specification for bank customers to securely negotiate and communicate payment instructions to bank systems over the Internet.

This project, which began in 1996, is supported by a number of large banks, including Citibank, and is closely linked with existing EFTPOS payments systems like SWIFT, which is used across Australia.

The following technical insite shows IBM's model for hub and spoke.

technical INSITE

HUB AND SPOKE MODEL
A PRACTICAL APPROACH TO WEB-BASED INTERNET EDI

BY SHIWA FU, JEN-YAO CHUNG, WALTER DIETRICH, VIBBY GOTTEMUKKALA, MITCHELL COHEN AND SHYHKWEI CHEN

Internet EDI offers the advantages of traditional EDI with low-cost entry for trading participants. Through the use of the Internet infrastructure and Java technology, the hub–spoke architecture as described above may be used effectively.

The two major components to the Internet EDI configuration are the server site (hub) and trading partner PC (spoke). By using Java-based EDI software within a standard browser environment and the infrastructure of the Internet, EDI may be performed. This alleviates the need for expensive EDI software to be pre-installed, VAN infrastructure and traditional EDI translation software.

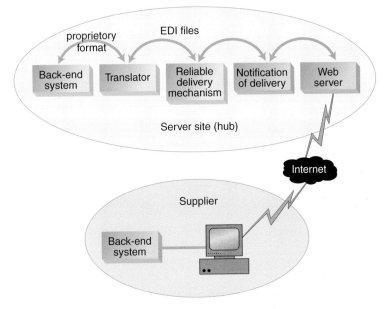

FIGURE 7.17: Hub and spoke

SOURCE: © 1999 IEEE.

The hub back-end system generates a purchase order, which will fulfil the order to the trading partner. The purchase order in proprietary format is converted to EDI format by the translator. The EDI file is placed in the mail repository system via a reliable transaction delivery mechanism (such as IBM MQ-Series). The mail repository sends a notification (email or text message) to the desired supplier. On receiving the notification, the supplier uses a web browser to log on to the web server. At this point, the browser detects the Java applets and downloads both the Java applets and the EDI file. The Java applets translate the EDI file into form-based content that is viewable within the browser. In addition to the display of the EDI file, the Java applets will also transfer data that can be exchanged with the supplier's back-end accounting or ERP system.

The supplier can prepare a reply document (e.g. an invoice) using two methods:
1. by manually entering data within the browser using the Java applets. These data would include product details, units of measure, delivery costs and GST if required
2. by using a back-end system to generate the reply document, which is transferred to the browser by the adapter.

(continued)

The Java applets then send the prepared document back to the web server. On the web server side, a stand-alone operating program (Daemon) detects the document and deposits it into the mail repository. From the repository, the invoice is sent via the delivery mechanism in the hub's back-end accounting or ERP system.

Once the invoice is in the hub's back-end system, standard EDI business processes are followed in order to match the invoice with the purchase order, and payment follows.

SOURCE: www.research.ibm.com/iac/papers/icdcsws99.pdf.

EXERCISES

1. Explain why it is called the hub and spoke model.
2. Do some research to find other examples of the hub and spoke model.

INTERNET EDI COMPONENTS

Internet EDI is generally comprised of the components outlined below.[12]

BACK-END DATABASE SYSTEM

Fundamental is an application system with a database for information storage. Generally, it will have its own proprietary format (SAP or Siebel). A translator is required to take proprietary format back and forth from EDI format. XML Solutions have developed an application called XEDI to help automate the process of converting between EDI and XML. XEDI can tag additional XML data along with the document that enables full recovery of the original EDI document on the other end. XML Solutions is also working with the XML/ EDI group's standardisation effort to create industry standards for these translations.

TRANSLATOR

A translator converts proprietary format to EDI standard format. New Era of Networks Inc. (NEON) recently released its PaperFree EDI adapter, which provides connections between XML dialects such as Biztalk and RosettaNet, and widely used EDI formats such as X12 and EDIFACT.

MAIL REPOSITORY

A database is utilised for the mailbox system, a web server to list and serve documents and applets. The hub creates and maintains mailboxes for each spoke. Mail is stored in inboxes and outboxes. The mail repository also provides email, audit and control, tracking, querying and reporting. Unread EDI documents can be monitored and suppliers contacted.

WEB SERVER

The web server provides authentication of suppliers through user ID. Suppliers access their own mailbox and have read access to the incoming documents. Web servers use SSL encryption for security.

ADAPTER

An adapter converts hub documents for the supplier from EDI into a proprietary format.

 ## OPEN BUYING ON THE INTERNET (OBI)

The OBI Roundtable is a standard for B2B Internet commerce. It is an open, flexible design intended for the high-volume, low-dollar transactions that account for 80 per cent of most organisations' purchasing activities. Version 1.0 of the standards document contains an architecture as well as technical specifications and guidelines. For more information on OBI, visit www.openbuy.org.

OBI is not a product or service — it is a freely available standard that adheres to the following guiding principles:
• common business vision
• vendor neutrality
• interoperability
• value-added services
• cost-effectiveness
• robust infrastructure
• flexibility.

OBI architecture can be viewed as the interaction of four entities:
1. purchasing officer
2. buying organisation
3. selling organisation
4. payment authority.

OBI contains an architecture, detailed technical specifications and guidelines, together with compliance and implementation information. The OBI standard provides buying and selling organisations with an easy-to-use, standards-based solution that achieves interoperability through a flexible, technology product–neutral architecture. The OBI standard is for Internet business requisitions that combine web technologies, such as digital certificates using **X.509 protocol**, with legacy or back-end systems such as EDI.

Using open standards for trading and open financial exchanges like the BIPS Project 10, developed by the Financial Services Technology Consortium (FSTC), will enable better B2B e-commerce. The FSTC sponsors project-oriented, collaborative research and development on interbank technical projects affecting the whole financial services industry. Further details may be found at www.fstc.org.

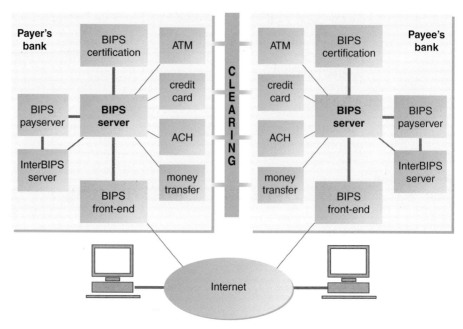

FIGURE 7.18: The Bank Internet Payments System (BIPS) project

SUMMARY

Electronic payment systems are becoming an increasingly important part of B2B and B2C payment transactions and the exchange of value. The Internet has enabled consumers to access many products and services that can be selected, ordered and paid for electronically. Electronic catalogues are being developed that will allow businesses and consumers to order anything from automobile components to pizzas and wine. EPSs using smart cards, online EFTPOS-type systems and digital-money systems enable businesses and consumers to pay electronically.

EPSs can vary from simple transactions using magnetic-stripe cards, in which customers' details are exchanged for goods or services and an account is sent, to more complex systems where an online purchasing system can debit existing bank accounts of the purchaser and credit bank accounts of the seller. This new form of purchasing has reduced the importance of cash or money as the only form of transaction or exchange of value. Traditional forms of exchange such as money are being replaced by these new methods of exchange, which are effectively diversifying the nature and complexity of B2B dealing and consumer-to-seller transactions in terms of both cost and convenience. In a more complex way, B2B transactions of data and exchange of value have been used increasingly in many industries, especially in the retailing and automobile industries. EDI transactions enable more efficient allocation of resources for production and servicing, and permit better planning and inventory control in businesses. Financial uses of EDI through VANs enable more efficient transactions and monitoring of manufacturing or service provision.

Electronic purchasing enables more cost-effective and time-effective transactions to occur. However, in the process there are security demands that have to be recognised and addressed by both businesses and consumers. The nature of these security issues as they affect e-commerce and electronic payment systems is discussed in detail in the next chapter.

key terms

e-cash	electronic payment system (EPS)	TRADACOMS
EDIFACT	electronic purchasing	value-added network (VAN)
Electronic Data Interchange (EDI)	money	X.25 protocol
electronic funds transfer (EFT)	SET	X.400 protocol
electronic funds transfer at point of sale (EFTPOS)	smart card	X.500 protocol
	stored value card (SVC)	X.509 protocol

QUESTIONS

1. Find out as much as you can about the following EDI standards and protocols: WINS, IDI, CCITTX25, CCITX.400, CCITX.500, ANSI X.a2, EDIFACT, TRADACOMS, EANCOM, Financial EDI, Hybrid EDI.

2. (a) Visit the DigiCash web site (http://digicash.com), collect detailed information about how it works and make an evaluation of its potential.
   (b) Now investigate another digital cash system called CyberCash, which was developed in the United States, at www.cybercash.com. Prepare a report on its status now.

3. Examine these sites on SET:
   (a) www.mastercard.com/set
   (b) www.setco.org.
   Suggest some apparent advantages and disadvantages of SET. Why has it not proved popular?

4. Undertake a search at the Bank Negara in Malaysia (www1.bnm.gov.my). Why has Malaysia rejected SET?

5. Prepare a report on smart cards examining:
   (a) privacy issues and smart cards
   (b) anonymity and smart cards
   (c) technology that protects and/or enhances privacy for smart card users.

FAQ ON CREDIT CARDS ON THE INTERNET

Accepting Credit Card Payments on the Internet
by K. KERR

Answers are provided to questions that new Internet sellers will have regarding costs, risks and process steps needed for receiving and authorising credit card payments on line.

Core topic
Emerging Payment Systems — Industry Applications

Key issue
What challenges will organisations face in the emerging payments industry?
Enterprises that are new to e-commerce, be they Internet-only or existing brick-and-mortar firms, will need to accept credit cards — the dominant payment method for e-purchases — for Internet sales to consumers and small businesses. Several common questions are addressed to guide the formation of a payments implementation.

If I already have a merchant account and a connection to a payment processor for retail store sales, what else do I need to begin accepting payments on the Internet?
A seller needs to acquire an Internet merchant account separate from its in-store merchant account and establish a gateway connection from its web site or storefront to the processing networks if authorisations are to be accomplished in real time. Some enterprises capture and then rekey payment information into in-store payment systems, bypassing the need for an Internet gateway connection. That method is inefficient and expensive with any significant level of transactions, and is not advised for most merchants. Gateway connections can be made by purchasing and installing software solutions, by developing in-house solutions or by contracting with an outsourced gateway provider.

What will it cost to process credit card payments on the Internet?
A seller will pay a discount rate — a percentage of each transaction — that will typically be in the 2 per cent to 3 per cent range. A set transaction fee of about 30 cents also will be paid for each sale. Some acquirers will charge an initial setup fee of several hundred dollars, and some charge monthly minimums. The discount rate quoted by most acquirers for Internet credit card transactions is often the same as for mail order/telephone order (MO/TO) catalogue sales, which is significantly higher than for in-store transactions. In-store discount rates are typically in the 1.5 per cent to 1.75 per cent range, with about a 30 cents transaction fee. Merchants will be charged a fee in the $10 to $15 range for each payment chargeback. This is a concern for merchants selling goods that attract online credit card fraud perpetrators. Fees for fraud protection and tax calculation services, assessed by the payment gateway services, are also charged on a per-transaction basis.

Isn't the credit card company that authorises payment liable for chargebacks for online sales?

No, Internet sales are similar to MO/TO sales, and are treated as card-not-present transactions. Because only the credit card number (rather than the card itself) is presented at the time of purchase, the fraud risk is greater, and the transaction risk switches to the seller, who is wholly liable for all chargebacks for Internet-based sales (see Note 1). While card issuers and merchant acquirers (banks or processors) are not liable for fraudulent or other chargeback transactions on the Internet, they incur significant handling expenses for chargebacks, which explains the higher discount rate. Acquirers will stiffen terms or cancel an Internet merchant's account if chargebacks remain at a high level.

Note 1: Awareness of liability

A recent survey conducted by CyberSource of business management, senior corporate officers and IT personnel drawn from its own customers revealed that 41 per cent of the respondents were not aware that merchants are liable for online fraud.

How important is it to receive real-time authorisations when customers try to purchase on line?

Customers are given real-time authorisations for in-store purchases and will expect the same immediate acceptance of their transactions on the Internet. With rising Internet fraud rates, real-time connections to the processing networks also give merchants access to systems (i.e. fraud detection services and digital certificate networks) used to authenticate buyers. One of the biggest struggles that Internet sellers face is converting online visitors from shoppers to buyers. Industry studies indicate that even when potential customers reach the payment page during the purchase cycle, they abandon purchases nearly two-thirds of the time. Not finalising payment authorisation at the time of purchase further jeopardises the closing of an online sale.

Legitimate payment attempts will fail to be authorised when incomplete or incorrect information is entered by the customer. These authorisations, however, can often be gained by querying the customer. When this is done in real time, the sales loss rate will be minimised. When done off line, customers must be contacted later, sometimes with difficulty; and some customers will reconsider the purchases (particularly impulse buys) and may not complete the transactions. Many customers might be annoyed with the transaction delay, which could damage a brand image.

SOURCE: Gartner Interactive, 24 January 2000, www4.gartner.com/Init.

Questions

1. Prepare a list of advantages and disadvantages of accepting credit cards on the Net for merchants and for customers.
2. Do some research to prepare a report on:
   - online credit card fraud
   - offline credit card fraud.

SUGGESTED READING

Centre for Electronic Commerce 1996, 'Smart Cards and the Future of Your Money', Report for the Commission for the Future, Monash University.

Churchman, P. 1987, *Electronic Payment Systems*, Basil Blackwell, Oxford, UK.

Emmelmainz, M. 1990, *Electronic Data Interchange: A Total Management Guide*, Van Nostrand, New York.

Furche, A. and Wrightson, G. 1996, *Computer Money: A Systematic Overview of Electronic Payment Systems*, dpunkt, verlag für digitale Technologie GmbH, Heidelberg, Germany.

Gattorna, J. and Walters, D. 1996, *Managing the Supply Chain: A Strategic Perspective*, Macmillan, London.

Hammond, R. 1996, *Digital Business: Surviving and Thriving in an On-line World*, Hodder and Stoughton, London.

Kalakota, R. and Whinston, A. 1996, *Frontiers of Electronic Commerce*, Addison-Wesley, Cambridge, MA.

McKeown, P. and Watson, R. 1996, *Metamorphosis: A Guide to the World Wide Web and Electronic Commerce*, John Wiley & Sons, New York.

Tran, V. G. 1995, 'EDI: Good for what ails the healthcare world', *EDI World*, September, pp. 28–30.

Tyree, A. 1997, *Digital Money*, Butterworths, Sydney.

END NOTES

1. This document is (pro tem) at www.xamax.com.au/AIIA/CrCards.html.

2. http://help.netscape.com/kb/consumer/19971208-6.html.

3. Deitel, H. M., Deitel, P. J. and Nieto, T. R. 2000, *E-business and E-commerce: How to Program*, Prentice Hall, New Jersey.

4. See 'How Credit Cards Work', at www.howstuffworks.com/credit-card.htm?printable=1.

5. Definition at http://whatis.techtarget.com/WhatIs_Definition_Page/0,4152,283970,00.html.

6. See www.ecml.org.

7. Jones, Russ 2001, 'Prepaid Cards: An Emerging Internet Payment Mechanism', www.commerce.net/research/ebusiness-strategies.

8. Michael Aaron 1997, 'Internet Payments: Opportunities and Status', IBM Computer Money Day, April, Sydney.

9. Kalakota and Whinston 1996.

10. Hyndes, M. et al. 1999, 'Creating a Clearway on the New Silk Road: Annex 1 — Impact of the Internet on Business Efficiency', Department of Foreign Affairs and Trade, Australia.

11. Fu, Shiwa; Chung, Jen-Yao; Dietrich, Walter; Gottemukkala, Vibby; Cohen, Mitchell and Chen, Shynkwei 2001, 'A Practical Approach to Web-Based Internet EDI', Proceedings of the 19th International Conference on Distributed Computing Workshop, www.research.ibm.com/iac/papers/icdcsws99/index.html.

12. See www.xmlsolutions.com.

CHAPTER

8

TECHNOLOGY OF SECURE ELECTRONIC TRADING

Learning objectives

You will have mastered the material in this chapter when you can:

- appreciate the need for security in electronic trading
- list the important security principles for data and network security
- describe and debate the differing encryption technologies
- understand and describe security protocols
- understand how to implement web server security technology
- understand and describe the technologies behind data security
- confidently describe security strategies based on the principles in this chapter.

'Welcome to thebusinessworld.com. It's digital: information is more readily accessible than ever. It's inescapably connected: businesses are increasingly — if not totally — dependent on digital communications. But our passion for technology has a price: increased exposure to security threats.'

Bruce Schneier 2000, *Secrets & Lies: Digital Security in a Networked World*, John Wiley & Sons, New York.

INTRODUCTION

A 2001 CommerceNet survey on the 'Barriers to eCommerce' drew responses from 1000 people in 36 countries.[1] The survey found that the uncertainty of information security and data integrity (encryption), the fear that a company's technological infrastructure might not withstand attacks, and uncertainty about the true identity of communicating parties (user authentication) were major barriers to implementing e-commerce technology.

In reality, current security techniques for Internet commerce are stronger than techniques for faxing orders to commercial enterprises or ordering goods over the telephone. In fact, given today's security methods (such as 128-bit Secure Sockets Layer (SSL), discussed in chapter 7), it would take a $100 million computer system 10^{16} years to break the code.[2]

Nonetheless, although the perception of vulnerability is stronger than the reality, digital threats do need to be taken seriously. Security breaches enable criminals to 'scam' huge numbers of credit cards over the Internet. Security fears have also been fuelled by publicity surrounding the massive spread of computer viruses, the destructive attacks made by computer hackers and crackers and the disabling of computer networks through distributed denial-of-service attacks.

The security of data held in huge e-commerce databases is one area of concern. For example, a credit card database may contain information about a person's spending or shopping habits. Indeed, some e-commerce ventures that failed in early 2000 realised that their major (often their only) asset was their customer database. Not only are data plundered; they are combined and cross-referenced and placed on public networks.[3] In January 2000 a California woman started legal proceedings against DoubleClick, accusing the online advertising company of unlawfully obtaining and selling consumers' personal information.[4]

WHY SECURITY IS IMPORTANT

If it is to survive and prosper, the Internet business must be aware of the threats and attacks that can be used against it. Businesses need to be on guard against information theft, espionage and liability. They also need to set up as many deterrents and defences as possible. The first part of this chapter will identify the types of attacks that an organisation must guard against and suggest possible threat mitigation tactics. In 2000 Cisco Secure Consulting Service analysed 33 midsize and large customer sites over a period of six months and found vulnerabilities in *all* the customer sites. Most problems could be traced to outdated software or lax systems administration maintenance.[5]

TYPES OF ATTACKS

The following section will examine the types of attacks that can threaten an Internet commerce business and will suggest ways to mitigate the threat.

DENIAL OF SERVICE AND DISTRIBUTED DENIAL OF SERVICE

Early in 2000 several high-powered Internet commerce sites such as Amazon, Yahoo! and eBay were overwhelmed by what has been called a *distributed denial-of-service (DdoS)* attack. A **denial-of-service (DoS) attack** occurs when a user or organisation is deprived of the services of a resource to which they would normally expect to have access. This loss of service might affect a particular network service, such as email, or it might involve the temporary loss of all network connectivity and services. In the worst cases, web sites accessed by millions of people can be forced temporarily to cease operation. A denial-of-service attack can also destroy programs and files in a computer system.[6] Denial-of-service attacks are particularly dangerous if the operating system is out of date and the system administrator has not downloaded patches and fixes, since DoS attacks rely on weaknesses in the system itself.[7] In a **distributed denial-of-service attack**, the perpetrator scans systems to attack and, once inside the client system, installs handler system software to scan for, infect or otherwise compromise other agent systems. The agent systems are loaded with remote control attack software and respond to the client when it issues commands to handler systems that control agents in a mass attack.[8] The victim's bandwidth is quickly eliminated and customers can no longer access the site.

In September 2000 the web site of one of the world's largest money traders was disabled in what appeared to be a deliberate attack.

technical INSITE

WESTERN UNION WEB SITE HACKED

BY STEVEN MUSIL

'Human error' allowed a hacker to copy the credit card and debit card information of about 15 700 customers from Western Union's web site, the company said today.

The money-transferring company first learned of the hacking Friday. A Western Union spokesman said the vulnerability was caused when 'performance management files' were left open on the site during routine maintenance, allowing the hacker access. He did not know when the maintenance began or how long the site had been left unprotected.

'We are still in the due diligence period,' said Peter Ziverts, a spokesman for the Englewood, Colorado–based company. 'But this wasn't an architectural problem; this was due to human error.' Ziverts said that he did not know how long the site would be out of service, indicating that it would be 'at least a few days'.

Company representatives began contacting customers during the weekend via email and telephone.

One customer reported learning of the hacking from an answering machine message left by someone identifying himself as a Western Union president.

'Sounds like a big (mistake) on someone's part at a site you'd expect to be locked down tight,' the customer said.

Western Union, a subsidiary of First Data, said no instances of credit card fraud had been reported to the company.

As CNET News.com reported earlier, American Express announced last week that it will offer disposable credit card numbers for safer online shopping, part of a bid to address privacy and security issues analysts say have slowed the growth of e-commerce.

(continued)

Online money transfer accounts for an 'absolutely minuscule' portion of the company's total transactions, Ziverts said. He would not say how much online business the company has lost because of the problem.

The main page of the company's web site was replaced this weekend with a message saying the site was out of service. The message also directed customers to call a toll-free number to reach a company agent.

The company is investigating the breach, but Ziverts declined to provide further details about the probe or to say what agencies were involved.

SOURCE: http://news.cnet.com/news/0-1005-200-2743344.html, 10 September 2000.

EXERCISES

1. The attack on the Western Union web site sounded an alarm throughout the e-commerce community. Can you identify any ways in which e-businesses have responded to meet this threat?

2. How can an organisation like Western Union protect itself from attacks of this kind? Check the case study on page 266.

VIRUSES

The *fear* that **viruses** can affect business operations, systems and transactions, and communications between businesses and between businesses and customers, can cause as much or more damage than the actual virus. The management problem for businesses is to set up controls to trap and eliminate computer viruses, and to disseminate information about appropriate software so that a distinction between normal control structures and viruses is available to users of business systems. Online and electronic commerce are very susceptible to virus damage because of the complexity of the Internet connections network and the availability of sites where hackers and virus creators can hide and load their software. The oldest forms of interference are called **worms**. They may be distinguished from viruses in that worms propagate and exist independently; they do not have to attach themselves to another program or part of the operating system.

A computer virus is defined by its ability to replicate itself. A virus cannot replicate itself independently; it requires some form of carrier or 'host'. A computer virus damages the computer system it 'infects' either accidentally or deliberately. Computer viruses can occur anywhere in a PC's software — as boot blocks, in file allocation tables, in .EXE and .COM files, or in ordinary files masquerading as functional files. These programs seek out unused resources and use them to resolve master program problems or tasks. *Cracks* are programs that have been copy protected and have been illegally penetrated. **Macro viruses**, such as Melissa, attach themselves to files that contain macros (programming routines that may be repeated automatically) and are then activated every time the macro runs in any file that uses it. Such viruses are particularly worrisome for word processing and spreadsheet software.[9] The Melissa virus (1999) and the ILoveYou virus (2000) cost organisations billions of dollars in repairs.[10]

Computer viruses are classified according to their mode of infection, the path used to replicate the virus and the type of system infected. Boot viruses infect the boot block on a floppy or hard disk. These computer viruses usually replace the boot block with all or part of a virus program. The virus files hide in memory and the virus moves the boot block on the disk to another location. File viruses infect ordinary .EXE or .COM files. Usually they simply attach the virus code to the file. A multipartite virus infects both boot blocks and executable files. Being opportunistic, they find available files at random. A systemic virus attacks the system files necessary to run DOS. These files control the allocation of system resources such as directories. Polymorphic viruses attack the integrity of the operating system used in business system computers and servers. Stealth viruses can modify file structures to conceal additional coding. The newer viruses, metaviruses, use metalanguages embedded in powerful programs like MS Word to cause damage to existing files and new files as they are created.

Virus infection is not always obvious in business organisations and may grow exponentially. Initially, the viruses spread and multiply quickly, slowing only when a saturation point is reached. Any infection can go undetected for months. In most cases, damage caused by the virus will be widespread before the problem is recognised. In business organisations it is therefore essential that infection is detected as early as possible. The earlier it is detected, the easier it is to stop.

Another problem for businesses engaged in electronic commerce is that the original virus can set off multiple infections, all with different paths of infection. Virus detection becomes increasingly important in organisations as they come to rely heavily on computer systems for their management and operations and for trading. The more reliant a business is on computer systems, the more vulnerable it is to damage caused by computer viruses. A strong company policy against illegal software is one simple step in preventing virus infection.

It is impossible for computer viruses to be created accidentally. They are invariably introduced into business systems by contact with infected disks, or through downloads from web sites or Internet commerce transactions. Software bugs that cause virus-like damage can be created accidentally, but such bugs are not viruses, since they are not created specifically to cause malicious damage, they do not propagate, and they can be easily tracked and rectified.

DEALING WITH VIRUSES

Businesses engaged in e-commerce must ensure that their networks are secure from external or internal accidental or deliberate damage caused by computer viruses.

Virus infections must be dealt with quickly using expert knowledge. Lack of understanding of the location of the virus or the nature of the virus can be catastrophic for a business. Properly designed computer virus repair software must be used, since attempts to clean up supposed viruses can often create more damage than could be caused by the viruses themselves. Most anti-virus programs keep a database of virus footprints or bits of code known to be parts of viruses. When the anti-virus software identifies a similar 'footprint' in a file, it is able to confirm that the file has been infected.[11] The software must then disinfect the file.

TROJANS, VANDALS AND SPAM

Trojan programs are designed to hide themselves inside apparently harmless applications until triggered. In a network environment, for example, a Trojan may steal an online service password and send the stolen information to the author of the Trojan. A **vandal** is an applet that downloads via a web browser and then attempts to destroy anything from a file to a key part of the computer system itself. **Spam** refers to unsolicited, nuisance electronic mail that can overwhelm storage space and take up valuable computer time.

HUMAN SECURITY ISSUES

E-commerce has attracted the attention of **hackers** — computer enthusiasts who attempt to demonstrate their technical skills by gaining access to other people's computer networks and systems. They threaten e-commerce businesses by accessing commercially or personally sensitive data. Hackers like to claim that they act with no criminal intent — indeed that they perform a public service, warning organisations of weaknesses in their electronic security systems. In this, they seek to distance themselves from crackers. A **cracker** also breaks into someone else's computer system, often on a network, bypassing passwords and ignoring licences in computer programs, intentionally breaching computer security. A cracker may do this for profit, out of malice, for some nominally altruistic purpose or cause, or simply for the challenge. Such breaking-and-entering has been done ostensibly to point out weaknesses in a site's security system.[12] The ethics of such actions are questionable.

Dissatisfied staff are known to have caused havoc to computer systems — for example, a sacked system administrator might have embedded a trojan program in the network that will overwhelm it six months after his dismissal. J. P. Morgan Chase & Co., in New York, uses a cross-departmental approach in tackling computer crime. The company has teams around the globe dedicated to managing information security; incident response teams include senior managers, a fraud division, the human resources department in cases where an employee is involved, auditors if there's a breakdown in controls, as well as legal and corporate staff.[13]

A profile of a typical computer criminal might include the following characteristics[14]:

- male
- mid-thirties and of no particular ethnic background
- good information technology skills
- works in a management or supervisory position, which gives him superior understanding of the workings of the system
- a skilled business person who can make use of the fruits of crime and invest them wisely.

Forensic accountants and specially trained police staff are now employed to track down serious computer criminals, as is illustrated in the following technical insite.

COMPUTER FORENSICS

BY KAREN DEARNE

When anonymous Hotmail emails containing defamatory remarks about senior staff began circulating within a large company, management decided to get tough and called in the forensic accountants. Computer forensics is the application of computer investigation and analysis techniques to determine potential electronic evidence, according to Graham Henley, a Price-WaterhouseCoopers associate director.

Case study #1

A study of Hotmail email headers identified the Sydney-based ISP to which the suspect was connected when the defamatory messages were sent. A search of the company's PABX system identified a call made to the ISP at the time the last Hotmail message was sent and the data port was located. Six computers in this area were forensically imaged and a series of keyword searches identified, one containing a reference to the Hotmail account. The computer had recently been defragmented in a bid to destroy potential evidence but data fragments were reconstructed and viewed. Further analysis provided detailed evidence and the suspect was later sacked.

SOURCE: Based on a PriceWaterhouseCoopers case file, related in 'Cybersleuths get on e-crime trail', *The Australian*, 22 May 2001, pp. 41 and 44, australianIT.com.au.

EXERCISES

1. Investigate the types of work that computer forensic analysts do and prepare a portfolio of some of the techniques they use to track down potential suspects.

2. Investigate what companies and organisations employ computer forensic experts. What type of background do these experts have — for example accounting, computing science, military, police? Make a chart that lists the above information.

ELEMENTS OF COMPUTER SECURITY

Transaction security is of the utmost importance in an online environment. Trading partners and consumers alike must have sufficient confidence in the system to buy and sell goods and services electronically. To minimise security concerns and protect the data being exchanged by trading partners, the e-business system must address four security areas. These issues are described below.[15]

CONFIDENTIALITY AND PRIVACY

There is little doubt that as the e-business grows, communication with trading partners and the use of online private information will increase in the course of daily operation. As the community becomes more dependent on the e-business as a conduit of vital and sensitive information, community members will increase their demands that these transactions be kept confidential and the privacy of members' information ensured.

The threat of unauthorised monitoring of this information (called **packet sniffing**), where unauthorised people 'hack' into systems to monitor and interpret communications, presents a real danger to the Internet community today. With the right equipment and skills, hackers can readily gain access to business networks and even compromise the systems of trading partners connected to the e-business. In a classic case, two hackers gained access to telephone carriers, including MCI, and sold 50 000 credit cards and phone numbers to Europeans, who then used the data to make free long-distance calls using these accounts.[16]

SECURITY SAFEGUARDS

Personal information should be protected by reasonable safeguards against such risks as loss, unauthorised access, destruction, use, modification or disclosure. Access to personal information should be limited to those within the organisation with a specific need to see it.

ACCOUNTABILITY

Someone within the organisation — say, the chief information officer or an information manager — should be held accountable for ensuring full compliance with its privacy policy. Privacy audits to monitor organisational compliance should be conducted on a regular basis, as should employee training programs.

ENCRYPTION AND AUTHENTICATION

The transmission of information in an unprotected (or raw) form across the Internet presents a genuine security concern for an organisation. Whether the information is of a highly sensitive nature or considered public knowledge, what is important to an organisation is its reliable, secure transmission. **Encryption** (the use of secret codes) is the first line of defence in securing transmission of data across the public network of the Internet.[17] The goal of encryption is to convert information crossing the Internet into a form that renders it unintelligible and useless to anyone except the valid recipient, who holds a special 'decryption key' (figure 8.1).

Two main types of encryption technique are available today. One is called secret-key or symmetric encryption. The more recent method is called public-key or asymmetric encryption.

SECRET-KEY (SYMMETRIC) ENCRYPTION

Secret-key encryption, also known as **symmetric encryption**, allocates to the sender and the receiver of information a single key, which they share. Using this method, both transmitter and receiver employ the same key to encrypt and decrypt the information being sent across the network. One widely adopted implementation of secret-key encryption is **Data Encryption Standard** (usually called simply DES).

Although secret-key encryption is fast and useful in many cases, it has limitations owing to its 'one key' architecture.[18]

- Both parties must know and trust each other.
- Both parties must protect the key and ensure it is not publicly known.
- Management of the key is inherently insecure — the key must be generated, distributed and stored.
- The single-key system is not well suited to an open network used by large numbers of unknown parties (the Internet).

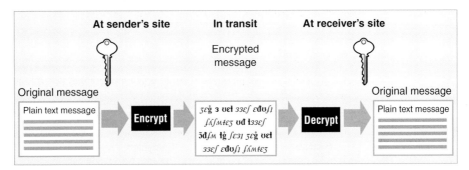

FIGURE 8.1: Encryption

TRIPLE DES

Concerns over the DES key length have led many organisations to use a variant of DES known as Triple DES. **Triple DES** uses a three-key approach; it is essentially a three-stage DES encryption system that follows the steps outlined below.[19]

1. Each 64-bit block is encrypted by the first secret key (as in standard DES).
2. The block from the first step is decrypted using the second secret key. In fact, the same algorithm is applied in reverse direction to scramble the data, which can be unscrambled only by using the same encryption key.
3. The block from the second step is encrypted again with the first key.
4. At the receiver's end, the message is decrypted by the first key, encrypted again by the second key and decrypted again by the third.

As can be seen, Triple DES requires substantially more processing than simple DES. However, organisations continue to employ Triple DES because of the extra levels of security it offers.

PUBLIC-KEY (ASYMMETRIC) ENCRYPTION

Public-key encryption, also known as **asymmetric encryption**, uses two encryption keys. One key is used to encrypt the message at the transmission end. A second key is used to decrypt the message at the receiver's end. The two keys are mathematically related so that information encrypted with one key can be decrypted only by the other key — hence the term *key pair*. Public-key encryption uses this pair of keys for each party involved in the transmission. One of the two keys is a 'public' key; the other is 'private'. The public key can be made known to anyone; the private key must be kept confidential.

One well-known public-key encryption technique is **RSA**, named after its inventors, Ron Rivest, Adi Shamir and Leonard Adleman. In this method, each party holds two keys — one public, one private. When sending a message, the transmitter encrypts the message using the public key. The receiver decrypts the message using a private key, which is known only to that person. Since only the real author of the message has knowledge of the private key, this method verifies the identity of the sender and ensure data integrity.

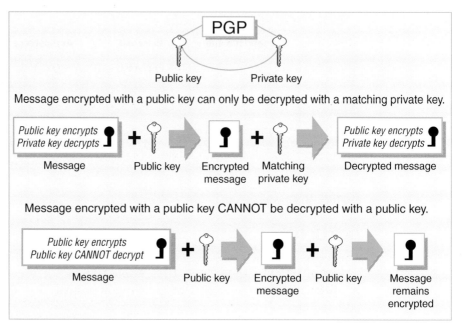

FIGURE 8.2: Public-key encryption

SOURCE: A. Dahl and L. Lesnick 1996, *Internet Commerce*, New Riders, Indianapolis, IN, p. 129.

PRETTY GOOD PRIVACY (PGP)

Pretty Good Privacy (PGP) uses a combination of encryption techniques to provide military strength security for email and other types of files sent over the Web (see figure 8.2).[20] Now called PGP Security, a Network Associates business, the company specialises in products and services that focus on solving privacy and data confidentiality issues, and has a strong history of setting security industry standards. PGP Security's security products, including firewall, encryption, intrusion detection, risk assessment and VPN technologies, address the full range of security and privacy issues anywhere information is transmitted or stored. PGP Security's products include several of the industry's well-known security brands, such as Gauntlet Firewall and VPN, PGP Data Security, CyberCop Scanner and PGP e-ppliances. PGP Security's COVERT research team identifies and works to resolve serious vulnerabilities before attackers are able to exploit them. The findings are incorporated into the product offerings, ensuring protection from the latest threats as they surface.[21]

The following table summarises the common types of encryption that can be used to secure electronic trading.

TABLE 8.1	COMMON ENCRYPTION ALGORITHMS	
TYPE OF ENCRYPTION	**ALGORITHM AND HOW IT WORKS**	**WEB SITES OR EXAMPLES**
Symmetric	DES (Data Encryption Standard), created by IBM, uses 56-bit key. Fast — used to encrypt large amounts of data at one time	www.itl.nist.gov/fipspubs/fip46-2.htm
Symmetric	Triple DES — encrypts a block of data three times with three keys	http://csrc.nist.gov/cryptval/des.htm
Symmetric	RC2, RC4, RC5, RC6 — variable key size for very fast bulk encryption RC2 can be used in place of DES. RC4 can be as much as 10 times faster than DES. Proprietary systems	www.rsasecurity.com/rsalabs/faq/3-6-2.html www.rsasecurity.com/rsalabs/faq/3-6-3.html www.rsasecurity.com/rsalabs/faq/3-6-4.html
	IDEA (International Data Encryption Algorithm), created in 1991, offers 128-bit encryption. Proprietary system	www.ascom.com
Asymmetric	RSA, invented by Rivest, Shamir and Adleman at MIT in 1977, supports variable key length and large amount of text.	www.rsasecurity.com/rsalabs/faq
Asymmetric	Diffie-Hellman, invented by Diffie and Hellman at Stanford University in 1976 — the first public key encryption	www.106.ibm.com/developerworks/eeng/library/crypt03ac.htm
Asymmetric	DSA (Digital Signature Algorithm), developed by National Institute of Standards and Technology in the US, set cryptographic standards for the US government.	www.itaa.org/infosec
	PGP (Pretty Good Privacy) — used to encrypt email messages and files	www.pgp.com www.web.mit.edu/network/pgp.html

SOURCE: Based on D. Kosiur 1997, *Understanding Electronic Commerce*, Micosoft Press, Redmond, WA, p. 78.

DIGITAL SIGNATURES

As in the physical world, a signature in the virtual world is used to verify the origin and contents of a message. Advancing the functionality of pure encryption, this digital signature allows the recipient of a message to verify the identity of the sender of the data — that is, it allows the recipient to *authenticate* the sender.

Digital signatures, using the public-key encryption method, ensure that the message is not tampered with during transmission. Moreover, digital signatures mean that the sender cannot deny having sent the information. Digital signatures work by combining the private key of the sender with the document to be sent, then performing a calculation on the composite so as to generate a unique number — called a digital signature, or fingerprint (see figure 8.3).

Other types of digital signature use biometric technology.[22] Biometrics involves the identification and authentication of a person using inherent biological properties, such as fingerprints or eye or speech patterns. Biometric signatures are obviously more 'human' oriented but have technological shortcomings. Peripheral devices are required to cater for the encryption and decryption of information.

The ability of this technology to provide secure and authenticated transmission of information makes it highly suitable for the world of e-commerce. The technology does, however, have several drawbacks.

STEPS SHOWING HOW DIGITAL SIGNATURES WORK

The e-commerce client wishes to send sensitive information to the bank. It is important that the bank knows that the information is being sent in a secure manner and is not tampered with in transit.[23]

- The client types banking details such as account number and PIN number into an email message.
- Special software generates a message hash (mathematical summary) of the details.
- The client then uses a private key that has been previously obtained from a public–private key authority to encrypt the hash.
- The encrypted hash becomes the client's digital signature of the message. (Note that it will be different each time the client sends a message.) At the other end, the client's bank receives the message.
- To make sure it's intact and authentic, the bank generates a message hash of the received message.
- The bank then uses the client's public key to decrypt the message hash or summary.
- If the hashes match, the received message is valid.

Some security experts are concerned about the security issues involved in the effort to keep digital signatures safe from theft. Cyber criminals, it is believed, may decide that the potential gains from breaking digital signatures are worth the computing effort involved.

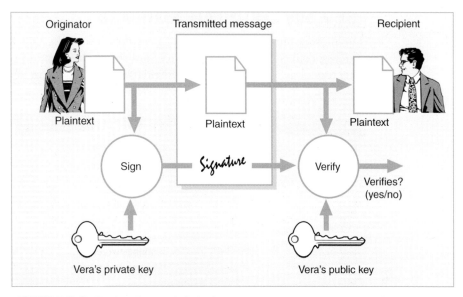

FIGURE 8.3: Technology of digital signatures

SOURCE: W. Ford and M. Baum 1997, *Secure Electronic Commerce,*
Prentice Hall, New Jersey, p. 111.

DIGITAL CERTIFICATES

Digital certificates offer yet another level of authentication for an organisation. Still exploiting the advantages of public-key encryption, digital certificates utilise the services of a trusted third party to authenticate the owner of a public key. In this way, both sender and receiver use the third party (or Certificate Authority) to verify the owners of the public keys, ensuring two-way authentication. Transmissions between parties are thus encrypted using public keys, but are digitally signed by the Certificate Authority. Digital certificates offer the highest level of authentication and represent, as Kalakota puts it, 'the heart of secure electronic transactions'.[24]

Chevron Canada considered many security alternatives when designing its new electronic document transfer intranet.[25] 'Having an ID and password for network access is not secure for us,' commented James Eaton, network specialist at Chevron. Chevron considered token-based cards, but found that **PKI (Public Key Infrastructure)** offered a more cost-effective and secure solution. By using an in-house Certificate Authority to generate certificates and a virtual private network (VPN), Chevron Canada can now tap into the corporate network to access inventory applications that capture the required information directly, instead of relaying documents to various departments. (We should note, however, that Schneier (2000)[26] does not believe that PKI is the answer, arguing that 'Digital certificates provide no actual security for electronic commerce; it's a complete sham'.)

THE X.509 CERTIFICATE STANDARD

The most common standard used in certifications is the OSI **X.509** certificate, which specifies the directory service and the authentication service using the directory. The digital certificate begins with a number of required fields, as shown in table 8.2.[27]

TABLE 8.2	REQUIRED DIGITAL CERTIFICATE FIELDS
FIELD	**DESCRIPTION**
Version number	Version number of the X.509 standard
Serial number	Each digital certificate issued by the certificate authority is given a unique serial number
Signature algorithm identifier	Identifies which digital signature algorithm will be used to sign the digital certificate
Issuer	Name of the certificate authority in X.500 name syntax
Valid period	Certificates are valid for a limited time. At the end of this period, companies must update their certificate or apply for a new one.
Subject	Name of the certified company in X.500 format
Public key information	This field has two pieces of information: the public key algorithm used by the subject company, and the subject company's public key.

SOURCE: R. Panko 1999, *Business Data Communications*, 2nd Edition, Prentice Hall, New Jersey, p. 391.

ELEMENTS OF INTERNET SECURITY

The ability to transact in a secure environment is a fundamental requirement in e-commerce. The protection of business data and personal records such as credit card information is of the highest priority in the online world. How does an organisation ensure secure web transactions? The three common standards used are:

• Secure Sockets Layer (SSL) protocol
• Secure HTTP (S-HTTP)
• Secure Electronic Transaction (SET).

Each of these standards is used to protect data on the Internet. Figure 8.4 illustrates three ways these web security standards may be used in networks.

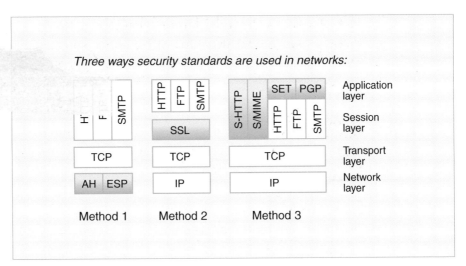

FIGURE 8.4: Web security standards used in networks

SOURCE: D. Kosiur (1997), p. 83.

SECURE SOCKETS LAYER (SSL)

The **Secure Sockets Layer** protocol (SSL) was developed initially by Netscape in the early 1990s and is still commonly used by organisations wishing to transact securely on the Internet. SSL manages authentication, message integrity and encryption in the one process.

SSL is a low-level encryption scheme used to encrypt e-commerce communications and transactions in higher-level protocols such as HTTP, Network News Transfer protocol (NNTP) and FTP. The SSL protocol can authenticate servers (verify the server's identity), encrypt data in transit and verify client identity.

SSL is available on several browsers, including Netscape Communicator, Secure Mosaic and Microsoft's Internet Explorer. This software is also available on a number of servers including those from Netscape, Microsoft, IBM and Quarterdeck. SSL uses public-key encryption to exchange a session key between the server and the client accessing the server. This session key is used to encrypt the HTTP transaction. A different session key is used for each transaction, so that if a hacker manages to decrypt a message or transaction, the key protecting all of the data remains secure. To decrypt another transaction will require the same amount of effort.

S-HTTP

Another security protocol has been developed that operates with HTTP, the highest-level protocol most commonly used on the World Wide Web. **S-HTTP** (Secure HTTP) works only with the HTTP protocol.

S-HTTP operates differently from SSL. SSL executes a negotiation protocol to establish a Secure Sockets Level connection, whereas S-HTTP is integrated with the HTTP protocol and provides authorisation and security of documents. S-HTTP security services are negotiated through the headers and attributes attached to each information block.

SECURE ELECTRONIC TRANSACTION (SET)

Refer to page 220 for details on SET. Further information may be found at www.setco.org.

CRYPTOLOPE

A recent development in security protocols is **cryptolope**, IBM's trademark for its *crypto*graphic enve*lope* technology. Cryptolope objects are used for secure, protected delivery of digital content and can be compared to secure servers. Both use encryption to prevent illicit interference or theft of content. Both use digital signatures to offer the end user a guarantee that the content is genuine. However, IBM argues that cryptographic envelopes go further.

- A single envelope can incorporate many different, but interrelated, types of content — for example text, images and audio — and keeps the package intact.
- A cryptolope object is a self-contained and self-protecting object that can be delivered in any way that is convenient. For example, cryptolope objects can be placed on CD-ROMs, mirrored to different FTP sites or even passed casually from user to user — all without compromising the underlying security.
- A cryptolope object ties usage conditions of the content (for example price) to the content itself. You might specify that viewing of the content be restricted to a special receiver, or that data can be delivered only to a system that is capable of applying a digital watermark. Because the cryptolope object is digitally signed, usage conditions cannot be tampered with without invalidating the cryptographic envelope.

All the cryptolope components are written in Java, and the 'envelope' is nothing more than a JAR (Java archive) file. The opener is simply a program that causes the cryptolope object to begin execution. This allows maximum flexibility in applying cryptolopes to an application.

NETWORK SECURITY TECHNOLOGY

The goal of network security is to allow authorised users access to information and services while preventing unauthorised users from gaining access to and possibly corrupting the network. But there is a trade-off between network security and network performance — increased security often decreases the efficiency of the network.[28]

FIREWALLS

A **firewall** is a set of related software programs located on a network server that provides a protective layer between the resources of a private network and users from other networks.[29] Firewalls are often installed on special computers logically separated from the rest of the network so that external entities cannot access private information directly.

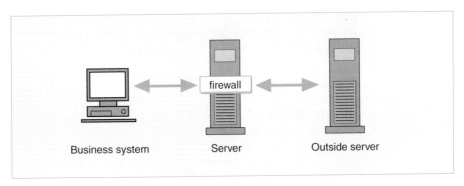

FIGURE 8.5: Firewall and internal protection

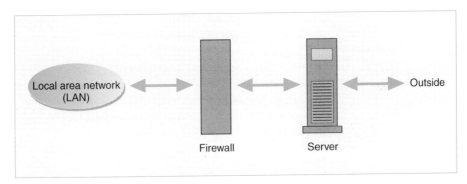

FIGURE 8.6: Firewall allowing external access

A firewall system should have the following characteristics.
- All traffic moving from inside the corporate network to outside the network, and vice versa, must pass through it.
- Only authorised traffic, as defined by the local security policy, is allowed to pass through it.
- The system itself must be immune to penetration.

Data packets sent to a firewall by a network *router* are examined and the firewall determines whether the packets should be forwarded to the intended destination. The firewall may check the packets in several ways. A simple method is to check that the source domain name and IP address of the packet are acceptable to the network.

MODES OF OPERATION

Firewalls may operate in several modes, as outlined below.

Static mode

A firewall can allow all traffic to pass through the system except what is explicitly blocked by the firewall as designated in a security policy. This is called the *default permission* use of a firewall to control Internet or network traffic.

A second static mode denies all traffic except that which is explicitly allowed by the firewall security policy. This is sometimes called a *default deny* system of firewall operation. The default deny mode is considered to be more secure than default permission.

Dynamic mode

Dynamic firewalls manage security in a more fluid fashion. They allow both denial and permission of any service to be established for a given time period.

TYPICAL FIREWALL COMPONENTS

When building a firewall to protect and secure Internet commerce, it is essential that certain functionality be built into the operations of the firewall. Elements of the firewall solution should include proxy servers and packet filtering.

Proxy servers

Proxy servers are application-specific programs that take the place of another program. Typically, firewalls act as proxies for certain network services. When internal users use telnet, for instance, to connect to a host on the other side of the firewall, the proxy service accepts the telnet request and forwards it to the real telnet service.

To the user, proxy servers are invisible. All Internet requests and returned responses appear to be lodged directly with the addressed Internet server. An additional advantage of a proxy server is that it can cache (store) frequently used information for users. Frequently requested Internet sites are likely to be stored in the proxy's cache. Storing information in the cache means that the proxy does not need to access the original source of the information on each request, which improves user response time.

Packet filtering

Packet filtering is the firewall's most important functionality. Every packet passed to the firewall is examined and either forwarded to its intended recipient or rejected. Many third party firewall software packages provide traffic filtering at the IP and transport levels, and provide application-level protocol checking — for example for FTP, HTTP or telnet.

A firewall can act as a security agent in protecting the resources within the network behind the firewall by sorting all incoming packets of data. This is particularly useful in combatting IP spoofing (when an attacker disguises the identity of the originating host server or router). If filtering is well planned, all manner of attacks, including IP spoofing and virus attacks, can be minimised and unwanted data kept from entering the network.

NEW FIREWALL APPLICATIONS

NASA's Ames Research Center in California is the site for an Extranet called Darwin that links aircraft designers in other NASA offices in the United States with industry partners such as Boeing and McDonnell Douglas Corporation. Darwin provides real-time remote access to NASA's supercomputer-based wind tunnel analysis. It uses industrial strength security to ensure that unauthorised users are kept out and that authorised users do not access one another's data. Most organizations that allow third parties past the firewall create a demilitarised zone (DMZ), a staging area between the public Internet and the intranet that contains data detached from corporate repositories. Authentication is achieved using security certificates, IP addresses are checked for all users logging in and there is further screening at the database level.[30]

New security products are being released that will help ensure fraud-free transactions. CertifiedMail.com has developed a 'round trip' means of tracking and securely replying to transactions employing an embedded SSL web link built into the transaction by using Extensible Markup Language. The IP addresses of senders and receivers are recorded by a system that is synchronised with an atomic clock. This enables CertifiedMail to locate online transactions exactly and establish where the transaction was opened and from what computer.[31]

ACCESS CONTROL LISTS

Access control lists (ACLs)[32] are lists of instructions that are applied to a router's interface and tell the router what kinds of packets to accept or deny. Acceptance and denial can be based on certain specifications, such as source and destination address. These lists allow the network manager to:
- manage traffic
- scan specific packets — any traffic going through the interface is tested against certain conditions that are part of the ACL
- filter network traffic by controlling whether routed packets are forwarded or blocked at the router's interfaces
- filter the packets that flow in or out of router interfaces.

PASSWORDS

One of the most serious security issues in Internet commerce is user authentication. An operating system bases much of its protection on knowing:
- who a user is
- the relationship of the user to the system.

Compare a physical business to a cyber business. In a bricks-and-mortar business, the owner is able to make a physical connection with the client. There is a known organisation with a known address. Sellers physically transport goods and services to that known address, and complete payment through a bank. In the world of Internet commerce, many of these processes are now done electronically in real time, so sellers and business partners need to be able not only to authenticate the messages and the information, but also to verify the speed at which the messages are being delivered. This means that an Internet business needs an authentication process that is much faster and more accurate.

The most common way this is achieved is through the use of passwords — even the simplest credit cards, telephone systems and computers use some form of password for authentication. These passwords are fairly straightforward. A network manager, for example, can usually read all the passwords used by those on a particular network, and while passwords are secure in 99 per cent of cases, there will always be those who seek to break in and change them, as we discussed earlier in the section on hackers and crackers.

PASSWORD RULES

Hackers use any of the following techniques to uncover passwords. They may:

- try to access the system list of all passwords
- test all passwords they can. For example, people tend to use short passwords, usually of three or four digits or letters. Hackers might try out simple words like 'enter', 'day' or 'night' or the user's name. Some actually use spell-checkers as a source of potential passwords to scroll through.
- focus on the user. It was common practice in banks in the 1980s and early 1990s to ask customers to nominate a security name, but the range of choices was usually limited. Most commonly, they asked you for your mother's maiden name.
- use a random number or random letter generator to mount an exhaustive attack. It is generally believed that about 15 per cent of passwords are words from a dictionary, and that about 86 per cent of passwords could be uncovered with about one week's worth of 24-hour-a-day testing. The use of faster computers and more sophisticated random number and letter generators will reduce that time period significantly each year.

Here are some simple rules to follow regarding passwords. (It would also be useful at this stage to reread the technical insite on page 12 in chapter 1.)

- Do not use easily guessed passwords such as your birthday or your car registration number.
- Change your password regularly. (A password change procedure should be in force.)
- Keep your password secure.
- Use mixed case letters (e.g. EmL) and non-alphabetic characters (such as %BmK*).
- Passwords should provide multi-level access — allow access only to the resources people need.
- Passwords should be stored in a separate, encrypted file.

A recent innovation in security has been the development of one-time passwords. Here the user generates a password each time it is needed, so instead of assigning a particular phrase or number set, you assign a mathematical function or formula that will generate a new password every time it is created. However, if you know the formula, it is very easy to breach the password.

How does an Internet business improve authentication and use it as a security measure? The most common way is by limiting the number of times that any organisation, trader or access point (such as an ATM) allows someone to log onto a system. Everyone makes mistakes when typing passwords into a computer system; many people forget or misspell their password. In an e-commerce environment it is important that the security system permits three to five attempts before the system logs itself out and the user has to attempt to log on again. This takes time, and frustrates those trying to break into the Internet or attack an e-business. Sources points of exchange in Internet commerce can also slow down the log-on process by creating a number of loops or processes as part of the password authentication exchange. This process means that you are able to stop the attacker who is working against the clock using a random number generator.

However, there are some problems with this. When using the Internet, misspelling a password can produce undesirable outcomes. It is common knowledge on the Internet that many of the more objectionable web sites have been named so as to attract people who misspell domain names. Well-known domain names are often misspelt, usually because we type too fast, or are distracted in the typing process. What is important is that there is absolute security in the initial e-commerce communication and that a number of processes ensure authentication.

Routers may act as a firewall and integrate standards-based encryption, authentication, tunnelling and firewall security in a single device. Such routers may combine the functions of a router, a Virtual Private Network (VPN) server, an encryption device and a remote access server (RAS) in one box. Firewalls should rely on several layers of security including packet filters and encryption, such as Simple Key Management of IP (SKIP), developed by Sun Microsystems, Inc.

technical
INSITE

CHANGING PASSCODES

The RSA SecurID® system is the world's leading two-factor user authentication solution, relied upon by thousands of organisations worldwide to protect valuable network resources. Used in conjunction with RSA ACE/Server®, an RSA SecurID authenticator functions like an ATM card for your network, requiring users to identify themselves with two unique factors — a PIN or password and a unique SecurID-generated access code — before they are granted access. More than 7 million people around the world use RSA SecurID authenticators to securely access web servers and applications, network operating systems and more — in both remote and local networking applications.

FIGURE 8.7: Credit card-sized devices with changing codes
SOURCE: www.ptr.co.uk/products/rsaauthenticators.htm

EXERCISES

1. Visit www.ptr.co.uk/products/rsaauthenticators.htm and prepare a short report on the advantages and disadvantages of these systems.
2. Write a report on the encryption techniques used by such systems.

THREAT-MITIGATION TECHNIQUES

The following table identifies some threat-mitigation procedures that organisations may use to assist them.

TABLE 8.3	THREAT-MITIGATION TECHNIQUES	
TECHNIQUE	**WHAT CAN BE DONE**	**EXAMPLES**
Good system administration	Updating software patches Logging access to computers Strong or one-time passwords Encryption	See the following resources: *The Site Security Handbook* (http://info.internet.isi.edu/in-notes/rfc/files/rfc2196.txt) *Useful User's Security Handbook* (http://info.internet.isi.edu:80/in-notes/rfc/files/rfc2504.txt)
Server security	Concerns how personal information is stored Creating secure infrastructure protecting mission-critical data from external and internal threats	Set up a demilitarised zone (DMZ) with two logical firewalls (one firewall protects the DMZ from the outside world, while the other, configured with more restrictions, protects the internal system from the DMZ).[35] The following sites are useful first ports-of-call for security/ virus/worm issues. www.cert.org www.auscert.org.au
Intrusion detection systems	Look for security errors such as a high rate of failed log-ins that might indicate a hacker trying to get into the system.	Intrusion detection functions include: • monitoring and analysing both user and system activities • analysing system configurations and vulnerabilities • assessing system and file integrity: ability to recognise patterns typical of attacks; analysis of abnormal activity patterns; tracking user policy violations.[36] www.sei.cmu.edu/publications/documents/99.reports/99tr028/99tr028abstract.html Use a protocol analyser — hardware and software that captures network traffic and creates reports that may indicate when an unauthorised user is acting as an authorised user.[37]
Access control lists	Allow access to systems and information using firewall technologies	*Encyclopedia of Computer Security* (www.itsecurity.com) Firewall technologies: secureNet, SunScreen, Cisco Routers, Raptor Family (formerly Eagle), Firewall 1, The Wall, Cyberguard, Gauntlet, Cybershield (with DG/UX B2)
Service provider filtering	Service provider can provide the filtering software and/or hardware	Security Search Net (www.securitysearch.net) World Wide Web Security FAQ (www.w3.org/Security/Faq)
Network auditing tools	Network managers may use Simple Mail Management Protocol (SMMP)	A protocol that enables computers and network equipment to gather standardised data about network performance Information Security Forum (www.securityforum.org/menu.htm) Institute of Information Security (www.instis.com)
Specific filtering	Packet filtering routers, proxy servers	Internet Security Review (www.isr.net/index.html)

Viruses, worms, trojans, vandals	Anti-virus software must be kept up-to-date Consistent anti-virus software across all machines	www.trendmicro.com www.macafee.com Symantec at www.norton.com
Forensic computing expertise	Unhappy staff may sabotage your organisation's network. Untrained staff may make genuine errors that bring down the network.	Put in place staff training. Ensure staff are aware of acceptable user policies. Warn staff if monitoring is in place (see chapter 10 for details on legal issues). Stop Internet access for people leaving your employ. Ensure your IT staff have regular rotation of duties. Separate staff duties — e.g. the web site developer should not operate the applications.

SOURCE: Based on Powerpoint slides by B. Fraser 2000, *Deploying Secure Networks*, Networkers 2001, March 28–30, Brisbane.

SUMMARY

This chapter discussed the vexed issue of security in an electronic world. We indicated why security is important and set out the essential elements of computer security. We discussed Internet security protocols such as SSL, SET and S-HTTP. The technology behind web servers has revealed the need for firewalls, demilitarised zones and access control lists. We looked at the importance of good system management and password control and put forward a table of useful threat-mitigation techniques that may be used by e-commerce practitioners.

key terms

access control lists	firewall	Secure Sockets Layer
asymmetric encryption	hacker	S-HTTP
cracker	macro viruses	spam
cryptolope	packet filtering	symmetric encryption
Data Encryption Standard (DES)	packet sniffing	Triple DES
denial-of-service (DoS) attack	PKI (Public Key Infrastructure)	Trojan
digital certificates	proxy server	vandal
distributed denial-of-service (DdoS) attack	public-key encryption	viruses
	RSA encryption	worms
encryption	secret-key encryption	X.509

QUESTIONS

1. Do some research on the use and current status of digital certificates. Do you agree or disagree with Schneier's statement that 'Digital certificates provide no actual security for electronic commerce; it's a complete sham'[38]?

2. Write a report on information and identity theft.

3. Prepare a set of security guidelines that you could give your IT staff to sign.

4. Prepare a report on any recent computer hacks and/or denial-of-service attacks.

5. Do some research on the following items:
   (a) ping of death
   (b) Stacheldraht attack
   (c) port redirection attacks.

A YEAR AFTER MELTDOWN: NO SILVER BULLET FOR DDoS

BY ELLEN MESSMER AND DENISE PAPPALARDO

A year after distributed denial-of-service attacks blasted the likes of Yahoo!, eBay and E-Trade Group, no one has found an easy way to defend against a flood of unwanted IP packets.

In fact, everyone's still pretty much in the dark — literally, in one case — when it comes to finding a silver bullet.

A recent meeting of the DDoS Working Group, a forum organised last year to plot network defences, was conducted solely by the light of laptops after KPMG International's Silicon Valley office was visited by one of California's rolling blackouts. In the ghostly glow could be discerned John Zent, manager of risk management for Yahoo!, and Allen Yousefi, information security officer at eBay, along with representatives from security vendors eager to woo these top e-commerce firms.

The talk was no brighter than the lighting. According to several attendees, Yahoo! and eBay are more than just dismayed by the slow pace of finding technical defences to denial-of-service attacks and the even more nefarious distributed denial-of-service attacks, which let an individual launch IP attack streams from hundreds, or even thousands, of compromised computers.

Web site operators are frustrated by the apparent inability of ISPs and Web-hosting providers to quickly filter out denial-of-service attack traffic when it pours into their routers and servers. Whether a low-grade nuisance or the kind of multi-barrelled assault that upended Microsoft's sites for three days, this 'bad' traffic is eating up bandwidth and at times blocking legitimate traffic to the most prominent e-commerce sites.

'People are getting a little radical about it,' said one attendee. For companies such as Yahoo! and eBay, 'it's a service-level agreement [SLA] issue with the ISPs and collocation providers.' He predicted this year will see lawyers battling over whether distributed denial-of-service traffic should have to be filtered out to satisfy SLAs.

Despite the gloom, there are many efforts under way to cope with all manner of denial-of-service threats, and rays of hope are visible.

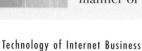

- Service and software providers have united to share information and forge common defences.
- Promising security start-ups focusing on the problem are attracting big-name backers.
- Law enforcement groups — working with both the network industry and its customers — are nailing the bad guys.

The DDoS Working Group is doing what it can to spur cooperation among ISPs. The group plans to publish recommendations for automated distributed denial-of-service defences by the end of March.

'There are political issues and technical issues,' says Tom Clare, a product manager for Check Point Software Technologies and a DDoS Working Group member.

The document is expected to define a common intrusion-detection method for collecting and measuring the percentage of bandwidth being consumed and a flow tag to identify traffic and other Layer 2 data collected from the packets. A firewall or other network device that implemented the DDoS Working Group specification would be able to report the start of an attack to the ISP, and other ISPs using compatible equipment would be able to share the information.

But it's uncertain whether ISPs can interact smoothly even if equipment makers support a common security specification, which may leave this as yet another security proposal that never got off the drawing board.

ISPs in the middle

This much is clear: ISPs play the critical role in the distributed denial-of-service endgame against attackers, who are heavily armed with denial-of-service 'malware', software posted at hacker sites for free use. And most of the intrusion-detection analysis and filtering that ISPs do is manual and difficult.

'We can't be held responsible for attacks on our customers,' says Amir Moujtahed, director of systems engineering and corporate security at Epoch Internet, an ISP. 'But if customers give us the IP addresses [of the source], we will block them.' Epoch has intrusion-detection equipment from NFR Security on its external and internal networks, and Epoch engineers watch the logs closely for evidence of attack signatures. But it's a labour-intensive process.

Moujtahed says ISPs are trying to do their part by installing anti-spoofing filters and cooperating with competitors through informal agreements hashed out in the ISP Service Consortium, which meets monthly.

'This is all part of the lesson learned after what happened last year,' Moujtahed says. 'ISPs like Genuity, UUNET and AOL compete, but we are working together on this.'

It's small comfort to the high-tech industry that the 16-year-old perpetrator of last February's incidents, a Canadian hacker nicknamed Mafiaboy, pleaded guilty to single-handedly attacking Amazon.com, eBay, Yahoo!, Charles Schwab & Co., CNN and eTrade, among others.

Mafiaboy carried out his distributed denial-of-service spree using attack tools available on the Internet that let him launch a remotely coordinated blitz of IP packets from servers compromised by agent attack 'zombies'.

Mafiaboy awaits sentencing, but it's expected he won't get much more than two years in a juvenile detention centre.

Those attacks forced most of the victimised e-commerce sites offline for about three hours. In the heat of battle to block the blitz of IP packets, ISPs did what they could through filtering bad traffic and claimed victory when it ended. But security experts familiar with what occurred agree that this filtering accomplished little and that relief came because Mafiaboy simply stopped his attacks after three-hour intervals.

'The attacks happened Monday to Wednesday, and those guys were still working Friday and Saturday to figure out what happened,' says Frank Huerta, CEO of Recourse Technologies, which makes security gear to detect and trace denial-of-service attacks.

Like many experts, Huerta says the work ISPs did manually filtering bad traffic didn't stop Mafiaboy's attacks. And though law enforcement officials did extensive work bringing him to justice, one reason they succeeded was that he bragged about his exploits in an Internet chat room.

Microsoft became one of the latest high-profile victims of a distributed denial-of-service attack, though no one seems to be bragging about causing it. The software giant lost MSN.com, Carpoint.com, Expedia.com and other Web properties for a day, hours or minutes over the course of a week. Microsoft declined to explain its response to the attacks, other than to say it was working with the FBI. However, CIO Rick Devenuti acknowledges that Microsoft 'accepts full responsibility' for the inconvenience to its Web users. He says the company hadn't applied 'sufficient self-defence' by using third-party products at the front end of its core network.

There are stopgap measures that Web sites can take to shore up defences, such as using as many load-balancing and high-speed pipes as they can, as well as intrusion-detection systems that can indicate suspicious activity is suddenly on the radar screen.

And that is better than nothing. Fidelity Investments and Bear Stearns reportedly deployed Top Layer Networks' AppSwitch with its intrusion-detection features after last February's attacks on e-commerce sites.

Overall, there's a more sober-minded assessment of the problem among vendors than a year ago. Cisco Systems claimed that making use of ingress filtering in routers, a technology described in IETF draft RFC 2267plus, would stop denial-of-service attacks. But the router manufacturer has abandoned that stance.

'There is no silver bullet for a [denial-of-service] attack,' says Lance Hayden, a manager with Cisco's consulting services team. But Cisco and a number of venture capital firms are investing in start-ups that are promising to develop comprehensive defence systems for distributed denial-of-service attacks. So, too, are established security vendors, including Internet Security Systems (ISS). Allen Wilson, director of emerging technologies at ISS and a DDoS Working Group member, says tracing this type of attack remains 'very manually intensive and time-consuming. For ISPs, it's one hop at a time, and you need to get hold of people and let them know that your network is attacking theirs.'

Finding a cure

ISS claims to be developing technologies that depend on what it calls 'the moving target defence'. The idea is that if an attack is launched at a Web site, the victim and ISP work together to identify the source and then create a 'black hole for the IP address', Wilson says.'You drop the packets but don't kill the connection, which helps trace back the attackers.'

At the same time, you create a temporary IP address for your site that gets broadcast out to enable legitimate traffic to still find you.

Quantifying the denial-of-service problem is not easy. Whenever a Web outage occurs, security experts always suspect denial of service, even if the business blames internal screw-ups. Online auction vendor eBay has suffered several Web outages in recent months that many security experts suspect were denial-of-service attacks, something eBay vehemently denies. However, it was clearly a denial-of-service attack that disabled much of the Undernet, part of the Internet Relay Chat network, in early January.

After the February 2000 attacks, the Clinton administration asked the IT industry what it could do to help combat what everyone suddenly realised was a dangerous situation on the Net.

It took 11 months to come forward with a plan, but 19 high-tech corporations recently formed an organisation called the IT Information Sharing and Analysis Center (IT-ISAC), which will run a so-called 'virtual centre' to share information about denial-of-service attacks and software vulnerabilities in general. Founding members are paying almost $1 million for the privilege, although general membership fees, which won't include access to all the information, drop as low as $5000.

The organisation's database of shared information, which will be managed by ISS, is intended to help solve security problems, so vendors accessing this sensitive information have agreed not to use it as a marketing weapon.

Those who expected ISPs to roll out new technologies or services to help stop these attacks in the past 12 months have surely been disappointed. ISPs are essentially using the same spot-filtering and monitoring techniques today as a year ago. Nevertheless, ISPs claim heightened awareness and vigorous monitoring have helped reduce damage.

'We regularly see attacks, but nothing at the level of last year's on multiple, highly visible customers,' says Kelly Cooper, security engineer at Genuity.'If we were to offer filtering and monitoring services to our customers for an extra charge, that would sort of be like blackmailing them.'

Genuity expects new capabilities from router and switch vendors that will integrate IP address filtering directly into the operating system of the device. One of the most common reasons why ISPs are not setting up IP address filtering is because it can slow the network. However, if filtering is integrated into network devices, performance should not be hurt, Cooper says.

Vint Cerf, senior vice president of Internet architecture and technology at WorldCom, says that standard load-balancing and content-distribution techniques that many Web-hosting service providers use reduce the negative impact of these attacks.

'Load sharing across multiple servers helps reduce the impact of classic [distributed denial-of-service] attacks because there are multiple versions of a

Web site operating across the Internet,' Cerf says. In addition to distributing legitimate traffic, load balancing and caching distribute rogue distributed denial-of-service packets so one server is not crumbling under the weight of an attack.

ISPs also see hope in specifications being developed by the Internet Engineering Task Force. I-Trace is one preliminary technology that will allow ISPs to quickly find where a distributed denial-of-service attack originates. Once the ISP recognises the source of an attack it can immediately set up a filter.

But this technology is very much in the early stages of development. All in all, it certainly seems like the industry will experience at least another year of being in the dark on distributed denial of service.

SOURCE: E. Messmer and D. Pappalardo 2001, www.nwfusion.com/news/2001/0205ddos.html. © Network World.

Exercises

1. Prepare a research report on load sharing as a method of reducing classic distributed denial-of-service attacks.

2. Visit the Internet Engineering Task Force web site (http://www.ietf.org) and report if any progress has been made on I-Trace.

3. Do some research to find out what happened to Mafiaboy. Debate the ethics of what he been accused of doing.

SUGGESTED READING

Bayles, D. 1998, *Extranets: Building the Business to Business Web*, Prentice Hall, New Jersey.

Dahl, A. and Lesnick, L. 1996, *Internet Commerce*, New Riders, Indianapolis, IN, p. 128.

Deitel, H., Deitel, P and Neito, T. 2000, *E-business and E-commerce: How to Program*, Prentice Hall, New Jersey.

Fink, D. 1998, *E-Commerce Security: Hands-on Solutions: E-Commerce*, CCH Publications, Sydney.

Kalakota, R and Whinston, A. B. 1997, *Electronic Commerce: A Manager's Guide*, Addison-Wesley Longman, Reading, MA.

Kosiur, D. 1997, *Understanding Electronic Commerce: How online transactions can grow your business*, Microsoft Press, Redmond, WA.

Panko, Raymond 1999, *Business Data Communications and Networking*, Prentice Hall, New Jersey.

Pfaffenberger, B. 1998, *Building a Strategic Extranet*, IDG Books, Foster City, CA.

Schneier, B. 2000, *Secrets & Lies: Digital Security in a Networked World*, John Wiley & Sons, New York.

Tittle, E. and Johnson, D. 1998, *A Guide to Networking Essentials*, Course Technology, Cambridge, MA.

END NOTES

1. www.commerce.net/barriers_study/study.html.
2. Kosiur 1997.
3. Schneier 2000, p. 19.
4. Gray, D. 2000, *DoubleClick Sued for Privacy Violations*, IDG Books, 28 January 2000, www.thestandard.com/article/0,1902,9234,00.html.
5. Frazer, B. 2001, 'Deploying Secure Networks', Networkers 2001, March 28–30, Brisbane.
6. www.whatis.com.
7. Cisco Systems pamphlet: 'The Easy Guide to Network Security: An introduction to the key issues for the ecommerce economy', www.business.cisco.com.au.
8. Frazer 2001.
9. Cisco Systems pamphlet: 'The Easy Guide to Network Security'.
10. Deitel, Deitel and Nieto 2000, p. 201.
11. Schneier 2000, pp. 153–4.
12. www.whatis.com.
13. Patrick Thibodeau, 'IT urged to work with corporate legal staff to fight computer crime', 4 April 2001, www.computerworld.com/cwi/story/ 0,1199,NAV47_STO59238,00.html.html?OpenDocument&~f.
14. Fink 1998, p. 40.
15. Kalakota and Whinston 1997, p. 136.
16. Kalakota and Whinston 1997, p. 136.
17. Kalakota and Whinston 1997, p. 138.
18. Kalakota and Whinston 1997, p. 139.
19. Panko 1999, p. 393.
20. Dahl and Lesnick 1996, p. 128.
21. Press release: Tuesday, 17 April 2001, 'PGP Security Delivers Mac Client Support for Intel VPN Products',www.pgp.com/aboutus/press/ pr_template.asp?PR=/PressMedia/ 04172001.asp&Sel=935.
22. Borasky, D. 1999, 'Digital Signatures: Secure transactions or standards mess?', *Online* 23 (4), p. 47.
23. http://whatis.techtarget.com/definition/0,289893,sid9_gci211953,00.html.
24. Kalakota and Whinston 1997, p. 143.
25. Mendel, Brett 1999, 'Sorting out Security', *InfoWorld* 21 (32), p. 33.
26. Schneier 2000, p. 239.
27. Panko 1999, p. 390.
28. Deitel, Deitel and Nieto 2000, p. 215.
29. www.whatis.com.
30. Pfaffenberger 1998, p. 307.

31. Fonseca, B. 2000, *Keeping Internet Business Fraud in Check*, Security Watch, *Information Age*, April 2000. p. 13.

32. Odom, W. 2000, Cisco CNNA Exam #640-507: Certification Guide, Cisco Press, Indianapolis, IN, p. 640, www.ciscopress.com.

33. www.betanet.co.uk/secureid.htm.

34. Bayles, D. 1998, *Extranets: Building the Business to Business Web*, Prentice Hall, New Jersey, p. 129–30.

35. Schneier 2000, p. 193.

36. www.whatis.com.

37. Tittle and Johnson 1998, p. 292.

38. Schneier 2000, p. 239.

CHAPTER 9

DEVELOPING A SECURITY POLICY FOR ELECTRONIC COMMERCE

Learning objectives

You will have mastered the material in this chapter when you can:

- define the nature and purpose of a security policy
- explain what is meant by trust and the importance of trust in Internet commerce
- evaluate the nature of risk in Internet commerce
- explain how risk can be overcome and managed in a policy context
- write and develop a security policy
- describe how a security policy would be implemented and evaluated.

'The biggest threat to business security comes not from outside, but from within the company. The first step to securing the corporate environment is to ensure the perimeter of internal networks is secure. This can be done by installing technological solutions such as firewalls, access control, and anti-virus software, but above all by ensuring that a workable security policy is in place.'

Elspeth Wales 2000, 'Security begins with a policy', *Business Online*, June supplement, p. 10.

INTRODUCTION

Security is one of the most fundamental concerns of organisations and individuals engaged in e-commerce and e-business across the world. This is especially the case in Asian countries where there is a deep distrust of the use of credit cards for business to consumer e-commerce purchases. In the realm of business to business e-commerce the situation is different. Payment mechanisms like credit cards are not an issue since banks act as intermediaries in the invoice/payment process. Banks are traditionally perceived as secure and trustworthy organisations, and businesses trading with each other call on that trust when dealing with security issues and payments.

However, the adoption of information technologies, and more especially web technologies, in business has highlighted the need to address security at the organisational level. Organisations have traditionally built, developed and implemented policy as a means of creating frameworks to enable them to run effectively and efficiently. With new technologies comes the need to deal with security. This chapter concentrates on the creation, and the reasoning behind the creation, of such policies.

TRUST AND ELECTRONIC COMMERCE

Trust has always played an essential role in business. As a fundamental prerequisite to commerce, trust is embodied in all market structures and processes. Electronic commerce, however, has dramatically changed these structures and processes, and the nature of trust itself is also being transformed. It is therefore important that Internet businesses consider:
• the impact of the transformation of trust on an emerging new marketplace
• the impact on companies of redefining structures and processes for the new marketplace.

In previous chapters we have discussed emerging perspectives on how trust is being transformed in e-commerce, and how it can be fostered and enhanced in the online medium. With an understanding of the origins of trust, we can better identify what appropriate language, models and frameworks engender trust and increase confidence in online communities. Further, we can identify those trust strategies that are defining new business models.

WHAT IS TRUST?

Trust is a dynamic process that deepens or weakens according to experience. Individuals first look for clues or 'forms' that signal 'trustworthiness'. Over time, individuals perceive the 'character' underlying the forms. Certain forms of trust are used on web sites — for example 'seals of approval' such as the TRUSTe, VeriSign, Visa or MasterCard symbols. At stake is the credibility of the company and its reputation. Its brand is the key issue for sales and for trading. Figure 9.1 shows the home page of MasterCard, a major player in the trust-building business.

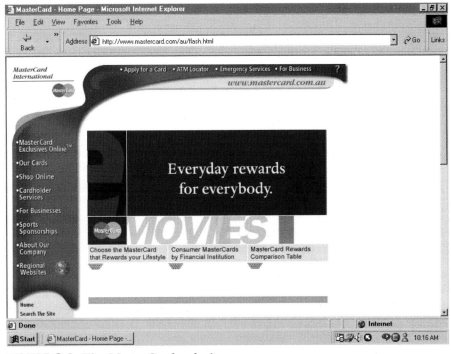

FIGURE 9.1: The MasterCard web site

There are several key elements in achieving trust in an Internet commerce relationship. These are set out in table 9.1.

TABLE 9.1 BUILDING TRUST	
KEY ELEMENT	**WHAT IT MEANS**
Fulfilment or delivery mechanisms	Can consumers or trading partners get what they want when they want it? This relates to ease of ordering, delivery and recourse policies. See www.fedex.com; www.ups.com.
Presentation, ethical business practices and disaster recovery procedures	• Correct, timely, professional site design • Design attributes that signify quality and professionalism • Organisational controls • Clear, easily accessible information about the e-business • Fair, open pricing • Sufficient balanced product information[1] • Appropriate use of personal information See www.informationweek.com/825/ethics.htm and chapter 10

However, there are some concerns that have to be addressed, and these will be discussed in the following sections.

BUILDING TRUST

The consumer's control over his or her personal information is essential in trust-building. Major concerns include:

- consumer choice about how personal information is used
- that personal information, once released, is hard to reclaim and protect.

Other forms of trustworthiness will follow once control has been established and security and privacy concerns addressed. The risk of personal information being accessed illegally tends to create fear and a reluctance to participate in e-commerce. Indeed, the perceived threat from hackers is substantially greater than concerns about misuse by institutions (companies, marketers, advertisers or politicians). There is little faith that the legal system or the government can offer protection.

In Internet commerce, security signifies the control of information, but that security can exist only when both trading partners trust in the Internet commerce transaction. As we have seen in previous chapters, successful Internet transactions require an element of mutual trust in each of the partnerships.

PROBLEMS

There are a number of obstacles to achieving this relationship of trust. These include:

- the rapid growth rate of the Internet
- the explosion of information on the Internet
- security weaknesses
- difficulties associated with the control of the information
- the viability of any form of trusted relationship in such a rapid growth arena
- disputes over intellectual property rights on the Internet — that is, who owns and controls the information (see chapter 10 for more details).

At the simplest level, a company exposes itself on the Internet to having its data stolen or changed, and therefore its integrity questioned. A **security policy** should enable the technology to protect the information, data and transactions over the Internet, and safeguard the trust relationship.

Currently, the law is not able to protect the Internet trust relationship adequately. This is illustrated in the following technical insite.

technical INSITE

ELECTRONIC TRANSACTIONS BILL TO PROVIDE VITAL LEGAL FRAMEWORK FOR E-COMMERCE

BY STEPHEN REVILL AND MALCOLM WEBB

There's little doubt that one of the key inhibitors to the widespread take-up of e-commerce by New Zealand business is the lack of an unequivocal legislative framework within which to operate.

One of the fundamental elements of commerce is the establishment of a contract between the parties to a transaction to regulate the dealings between those parties. A core constraint with e-commerce is the difficulty of applying existing law to the fast-moving information technology which is the Internet's defining feature.

This can lead to areas of ambiguity and an over-reliance on principles of law sometimes established many years before the Internet became a commercial reality.

Which is why the forthcoming Electronic Transactions Bill — currently in the consultation phase — is so important to New Zealand. The Electronic Transactions Bill (ETB) must bridge the gap between the new and the old — time-established legal principles which have applied to business for centuries need to be reshaped and reconsidered to address the legal framework for an entirely new, but increasingly prevalent, way of conducting business in the twenty-first century.

The legislation's role is clear. It must seek to address the form in which a 'transaction' takes place and make it clear that the legal validity and effect of a transaction is not undermined simply because it took place in electronic form.

The aim is simple — be technology neutral and avoid unnecessary ambiguity and costs.

Similarly, the government's key objectives are to:
• facilitate the use of new technology by removing legislative impediments currently preventing its use for communications
• remove uncertainty surrounding the legal status of electronic communications and related technologies.

In that sense, the ETB will seek to be similar to the Australian *Electronic Transactions Bill 1999*.

At this stage it's envisaged that ETB will apply to all requirements under New Zealand law for the use of writing signatures, recording information, retaining information and producing documents, unless those requirements are expressly excluded. Likely exclusions could include wills, affidavits, statutory declarations and negotiable instruments.

And central to the legislation will be the precondition that both parties in the transaction (particularly the recipient) agree to the use of electronic communications in an agreed format.

The key features of the new legislation are still being fine-tuned, but the most important issues being raised are as follows.

Validity of electronic communications
New Zealand law is currently silent on the legal validity of electronic transactions, but it is proposed ETB follows the Australian legislation and stipulates that electronic transactions will not be invalid merely because they involve one or more electronic communications.

Requirements for 'in writing'
Many statutes relating to traditional commerce require documents and communications to be 'in writing'. The ETB proposes that those requirements are satisfied by electronic communications where:
• those communications are accessible so as to be useable for subsequent reference
• the recipient has agreed to receive the information electronically

Signatures
Signatures are often required under New Zealand law, but there is no statutory definition of a 'signature' in New Zealand. In the past, the courts have permitted a variety of marks or symbols — whether written, printed or stamped.

(*continued*)

An e-signature will have the same legal effect as a hand-written one if:
- a method is used to identify the person and indicate his or her approval of the information communicated
- the method satisfies the ETB's (yet to be defined) reliability criteria
- the person receiving the signature gives his or her consent to receiving that signature in electronic format and by electronic means.

Work is continuing on the way in which the 'reliability criteria' will be determined. This work is likely to be strongly influenced by developments in Australia and the recent UN report on electronic signatures.

Production of documents

It is proposed that the ETB contain a provision that allows a document to be produced in electronic form where:
- the integrity of the information is maintained
- the information is readily accessible so it can be used for future reference
- the recipient consents to that document being produced in electronic form.

Retention of documents

Much of New Zealand law places heavy emphasis on keeping records and retaining documents. It is proposed that the ETB contain a provision which allows information to be recorded and retained electronically, providing, again, it can be readily accessible for subsequent reference. It is also important that it can be generated and retained in a manner which provides a reliable means of assuring the integrity of the information.

SOURCE: S. Revill and M. Webb, *Topics*, September 2000, p. 26.

EXERCISES

1. Why are the Electronic Transaction Bills so important?
2. List several issues concerning legislation on e-commerce and illustrate them using real-life examples.
3. Under what conditions will New Zealand law consider that an electronic signature has the same legal effect as a written one?
4. What provisions allow a document to be produced electronically?

THE MANAGEMENT OF TRUST IN E-COMMERCE

One of the essential components of trust pertains to the management of the relationship between any organisation and individuals who trade on the Internet. In the previous chapter we discussed encryption. The technology behind symmetrical or asymmetrical encryption has no impact on relationship trust. The following issues do have an impact, however:
- management of the cryptographic keys
- control of secret keys.

A number of specific methodologies (for example PGP, or 'pretty good privacy') have been developed to enable cryptographic trust. The idea is to create a relationship of trust between those who take advantage of the trading relationship, and build up trust over time. This mirrors the trust built up in the world of paper or plastic cards, where the identification of a Visa or

MasterCard, for example, automatically inspires trust in a retailer. Over time digital certificates and digital signatures will also create trust. For example, a Medicare card, a Medibank (health insurance) card or a social security card automatically evokes a trust we understand. When digital signatures, verifiable and authenticated, are used more commonly throughout the world, they too will automatically inspire a sense of trust. This trust relationship must then be managed.

Internet commerce relationships are based on technical processes — for example, one web site may send another web site a cookie, a stream of digits that automatically identifies the web site the next time it is opened. The receiving computer or server stores the cookie so that the process of opening up the business relationship will evolve quickly. But there must be a sense of confidence that the cookie will cause no damage and will do exactly what it is supposed to do — namely, act as a relationship holder. Again, this requires trust. The following diagram illustrates the hierarchy of trust in e-trade.

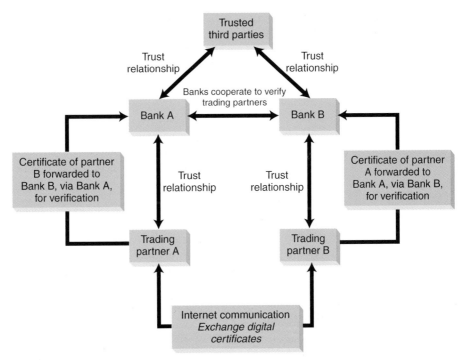

FIGURE 9.2: Trust hierarchy

SOURCE: B. Murphy and R. Booth 2000, 'HSBC: A Treasurer's Guide to E-Commerce: Digital Certificates — Enhancing the Ability to Compete', www.treasury-management.com/TOPICS/00ecom/00ec7.pdf.

ANONYMITY

The issue of anonymity in this form of business relationship is also important. Is it necessary for the process of exchanging information on the Internet to be completely anonymous? In the real world, anonymous business relationships are extremely rare. Business is nearly always open and transparent. On the

Internet the same should apply. The problem with the Internet is that we can use aliases or pseudonyms, which can itself erode trust. A security policy can overcome the problem of aliases or pseudonyms. While privacy must be protected in a B2B or B2C relationship, it is nonetheless essential that the true nature and status of each partner in the relationship has been identified and verified.

DATA MINING

In B2C businesses a lot of customer information is collected. For example, many supermarkets use credit point systems such as 'Fly Buys'. Credit points are registered against the owner of the 'Fly Buys' card, and all their purchases are continually collated and monitored. This enables **data mining** (the analysis of data for relationships that have not been previously discovered), which in turn facilitates strategic marketing. The question is, can we still speak of a trust relationship when the company uses customer information in this way? It is important in a trust relationship that companies that solicit information from their customers ensure that this information is maintained securely so that the nature of their relationship is not passed on to other parties.

However, there is increasing evidence of databases being built, sold on and used by other companies to capture information about the way consumers behave. Online customers may reveal information about themselves such as their wealth, gender and shopping habits. Creating and maintaining trust is difficult when e-consumers are giving out information that they expect will be kept private between them and the online store. These consumers might believe the relationship is confidential when in reality it is not.

SET AND TRUST

The importance of the trust relationship can be illustrated using an example of the SET protocol in a relationship between a customer, a seller and an intermediary (usually a bank or other financial institution). A trust and security policy is inherent in the SET protocol. In any SET transaction 10 distinct steps are required for the trust relationship to exist; each of these steps should be secure in its own right and maintain the security, privacy and trust of those involved.

1. The customer initially requests a transaction,
2. which the merchant then acknowledges.
3. The customer then will present a purchase order,
4. which will be verified by the merchant.
5. At that point the customer will make a payment
6. and that payment will be verified by the bank.
7. The customer will then make a status query,
8. and the merchant or seller will send back purchase status information. (In an EFTPOS transaction, the EFTPOS outlet or point of sale sends a query to the bank about the status of the card being used.)
9. There is then a request for payment
10. and that payment is verified.

Each of these 10 steps is essential to the process. Unfortunately, SET[2] has not proved popular, since it requires special software on both the client and the server side; it is also expensive, and transactions are more time-consuming than under other protocols such as SSL.

TRUST AND E-COMMERCE RELATIONSHIPS WITH GOVERNMENT

Business to government (B2G) and consumer to government (C2G) business are other significant areas of Internet commerce. The governments of Hong Kong, Singapore and New Zealand, for example, have been developing and stimulating e-commerce for five years. Governments need to develop the same trust relationship with their electronic business partners and citizens. These days, for example, most companies in Australia and New Zealand have to submit their annual report and annual statement of accounts to the Securities Commission electronically. People collecting pensions, paying car licences or claiming social security benefits must have a trust relationship between themselves and the specific government departments.

Governments must maintain trust with their citizens and business partners, and ensure the integrity and security of the data they maintain. Governments need the data for the purposes of risk management and dispute resolution. For example, the Australian Taxation Office (ATO) maintains all of its relationships with wage earners in Australia in an electronic format. In any dispute between an individual and the ATO, it is very important that the data be well managed so that they can be released at the appropriate time. Immediate recording of the data is therefore an essential part of the trust relationship.

In the same way, banks must have confidence in clearing houses throughout the Australian and New Zealand banking systems and those of many other countries around the world. Money is transferred from one bank account to another in various banks at the end of each trading day, or in real time during the trading day. It is therefore essential that the data be maintained correctly and managed securely. The banks themselves must therefore have a trust relationship with each other, especially when huge sums of money are being transferred electronically.

Governments must ensure that:
- data collected by government are secure
- privacy concerns are addressed
- clients understand the need for data collection — to justify expenditure or the costs of running a particular organisation or department for example.
- they have data with which to operate, especially for purposes of economic management.
- they collect the data to perform legitimate functions, such as keeping statistics on unemployment and pension recipients, and for social and economic policy planning.

The purpose of the security policy is to protect the data collected so that the community as a whole trusts how the government manages all this information.

WHEN TRUST FAILS

In certain circumstances the trust relationship between two parties engaged in Internet commerce may fall apart.

BUSINESS FAILURE

Businesses sometimes fail. Large corporations collapse; small companies are bought by larger companies; small banks are absorbed by larger ones. Many of the companies that existed on the Web in 1997 no longer exist today. Some of them failed, some of them were absorbed by other companies, and some of them simply changed their names. Such events may damage the trust relationship between customers and business.

CRYPTOGRAPHIC FAILURE

Another circumstance that can destroy the trust relationship is cryptographic system failure. This usually follows the theft or exposure of the private key or secret key.

FRAUD

Trust can also be lost when fraud becomes widespread. For example, there is a great deal of evidence of credit card fraud both on and off the Web. Credit card numbers are 'scammed' or credit cards themselves are stolen. Some companies are now refusing to take credit card numbers over the telephone.

NETWORK FAILURE

A fourth cause of loss of trust is associated with the Internet itself — namely network failure. In 2000 the fibre optic cable providing high-speed Internet connection between Singapore and Australia was cut, and the Internet went down for a period of time. Servers, electricity supplies, switches, routers, and of course home computers, are all subject to breakdowns. Such network problems intensify any existing lack of trust.

Businesses, such as Dell (www.dell.com), depending on the Internet to sell goods on a real-time basis, need a permanent, reliable, 24-hour network service. If the network fails, the trust relationship with their clients disappears. To secure that relationship, it is essential that the security policy established by the company (as by all e-businesses) covers all the possible contingencies.

TRUST SEALS

Trust seals are becoming an important visible symbol of a secure trading relationship, especially in B2C Internet commerce.

Seals of approval offer some reassurance of the organisation's control over the necessary security systems. Research comparing 1999 with 2000 suggests the perceived trustworthiness has increased for all five widely used seals tested — particularly for TRUSTe, Visa and BBBOnline. Seals of approval have different acceptance rates in different cultures. Security symbols inspire greater confidence than credit card symbols in the United States, where TRUSTe ranks highest. In Latin America, on the other hand, Visa appears to be the most trusted symbol. There are two possible reasons for this. First, financial institutions are generally 'trusted' and security seals are not well recognised in Latin America. Second, VeriSign may have rated higher than TRUSTe because of associations with the Spanish word *verdad*, meaning truth. Seals of approval symbols appear to be more important than the content of written policies. Very few respondents read the privacy statements associated with seals. How 'valid', then, are the policies on web sites today? The US Federal Trade Commission (FTC) (May 2000) found 45 per cent of the most popular sites display a privacy seal.

FIGURE 9.3: VeriSign — a visible symbol of a trust relationship in Internet commerce

The most trusted web sites are those with strong brand presence in the online world. Research has found that e-brands have already succeeded in winning over consumers relative to their physical world competitors. This suggests that consumers are more likely to visit Amazon's virtual store than a physical branch of Barnes and Noble! However, while ordering books over the Web can be easy and satisfying, there are situations even in that industry where browsing capabilities are more relevant. Searching the contents of an art book, for instance, is not that easy in a web environment.

Trust is sometimes overlooked in technical areas, with the result that:
- network sniffers can access information and data not intended for untrusted sources
- Domain Name Services are subject to flooding or spoofing
- the Routing Internet Protocol (RIP) trusts information that affects the routing of IP packets even if it does not know the source.

THE TRUSTe STORY

The TRUSTe seal is designed to assure the consumer that the site will disclose:
- what personal information is gathered about you
- how information will be used
- with whom the information will be shared
- choices as to how information is used
- safeguards to protect your information from loss, misuse or alteration
- how you can update or correct inaccuracies in your information.

It also has a WatchDog page. As part of the self-enforcement program, users can complain about privacy violations or misuse of trustmark, or specific privacy concerns pertaining to a member web site. TRUSTe increased its recognition in the US by almost 60 per cent between 1999 and 2000, from 500 licensed web sites to more than 1200 sites in a variety of industries. BBBOnline has 450 sites. In May 2000 the FTC informed the US Congress that self-regulatory enforcement initiatives could not ensure that the online marketplace emulated the standards of industry leaders. The FTC recommended that Congress enact legislation that, in conjunction with continuing self-regulatory programs, would ensure adequate protection of online consumer privacy. The search for trust must result in the development and implementation of policy.

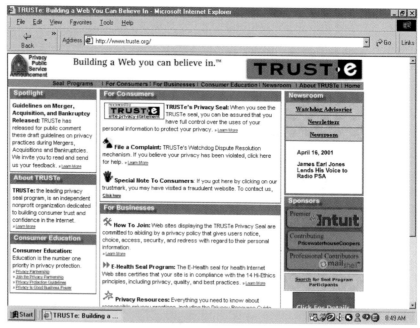

FIGURE 9.4: The TRUSTe web site

EXERCISES

1. Do some research on how trust seals are viewed in your country. Investigate the reasons behind the attitude.

2. *Self-regulation will ensure adequate protection of consumer privacy on line.* Debate this statement.

SECURITY BEGINS WITH POLICY

BY ELSPETH WALES

Seventy-three per cent of security breaches come from inside a company's network, says the FBI. Internal security is the first step to business security.

The biggest threat to business security comes not from outside, but from within the company. The first step to securing the corporate environment, according to experts such as James Luke, information warfare specialist at IBM, is to ensure the perimeter of internal networks is secure. This can be done by installing technological solutions such as firewalls, access control and anti-virus software, but above all by ensuring the a workable security policy is in place.

'It is important for a company to look at its information as a whole and to understand where the risks are, as the majority of security breaches emanate from inside the organisation,' says Luke, who advises businesses on making their networks secure. 'So you have to start with basics. It's no good putting in security systems if you don't vet your staff. So you have to deal with softer issues too, such as creating an environment where you can report a security fault.'

Luke points out that corporations are increasingly protective of their customers' data, and no one will conduct e-business with a company that does not support security.

A security policy is a wide-ranging document which is about managing the entire company, managing it securely and doing so to protect the corporation's key asset — its information.

Mike Graves, a marketing manager at Hewlett-Packard Internet Security Division, says that a business is in trouble if it is unable to answer two questions:

• what is our security policy?
• what will happen to me if I do not follow the policy?

Ideally, he says, a policy should be written to cover the coming five years and should be compiled by a senior executive at director level with responsibility for security. It can be inappropriate for IS staff to draft a security policy because their view of security might not reflect that of the senior management.

'It has to be relevant, to protect the business adequately, and the staff must be made aware of the policy and the consequences of failing to follow,' he advises.

A security policy defines which employees are allowed into specific categories of networks and access to applications, which external companies' staff are allowed into which parts of the enterprise networks, and places restrictions on access to sensitive applications such as financial forecasts and strategic plans.

Above all, a security policy must be easy for the staff to use and should not hinder their work. If they have to know 10 different passwords to gain access to a system, they will before long find a way around the system, thereby making the entire security policy worthless.

HP's Graves points out that the growing popularity of rented applications presents another security consideration. If companies take this route, they must make sure that the supplier renting out the applications can also provide the necessary level of security to accompany them and be sure that the supplier knows what their security responsibilities are, he says.

'People may overlook this aspect of renting applications, assuming security will be provided as a matter of course. If it's not explicitly covered from the outset, it's your fault not the outsourcer's,' he warns.

Luke stresses that business must realise that security is not the responsibility of an individual.

'Security and management of information across the enterprise is the responsibility of every individual in the organisation. That means there needs to be education about it across the enterprise and policies and procedures need to be set up so they are naturally easy to use.'

SOURCE: *Business Online*, June 2000 supplement, p. 10.

EXERCISES

1. List several security problems caused from the inside of an organisation.
2. What issues should be considered when making a security policy?
3. What security concerns does growing popularity of rented applications present?
4. How would an organisation pursue an integrated approach to corporate security?

DEVELOPING A SECURITY POLICY

All organisations engaged in Internet commerce need a well-established, well-planned and well-written security policy. To develop such a policy it is essential that the security requirements of the business are determined, written down and specified. Once this process has begun the security policy itself will emerge.

DEVELOPING A SECURITY REQUIREMENTS REPORT

The six stages in the development of a security requirements report are outlined in the following table.

TABLE 9.2	SIX STAGES IN THE DEVELOPMENT OF A SECURITY REQUIREMENTS REPORT	
STAGES	**CHECK**	**COMMENTS**
1. Identification of business-related security issues	• For data essential to the operation of the business • For any data, business process or information worth stealing • For any security weaknesses in the operations of the business • How much information the business can afford to lose • How much the business can afford to spend on network and business security	It is very important that the business outline clear priorities concerning these issues.

2. Analyse the threats and vulnerabilities of the business system and assess the security risks.	• Data that must be kept secure, such as market research, invoices, network documentation • The network itself	Evaluate what is worth protecting.
	• The importance of the business system's competitive advantage • For unauthorised modems used in the organisation • Whether employees are using unsolicited and unsecured software	It is important to identify all threats, vulnerabilities and security risks, and establish measures to protect the organisation from them.
	• The process and design of the network architecture in the organisation • That a secure architecture and a secure business process are related to one another	It is important that the technology does not drive the business process, but rather the business process drives the architecture, which will provide the security for the business process.
	• The level of functionality required to make the business work • The business processes that need to be monitored • The monitoring of those processes	In all businesses there are expensive solutions and simpler solutions, and sometimes solutions somewhere in between. The business has to determine which is the most appropriate and cost-effective for its circumstances.
3. Understand how a technology and process implementation for security can occur.	• Whether the architecture design can be understood and replicated if personnel leave the company • Each piece of technology, network software and user software covered by the system • That every person in the company is aware of the need for security	All employees must be clearly informed about the need for Internet and business process security, and the competitive advantage that can be gained through security.
4. Implement ongoing educational processes.	• Educational objectives and training solutions for all personnel	This is important so that any new activities, business processes or ideas coming into the company are protected, and any security changes are made clear to all personnel.
5. Undertake an audit of the impact of the security measures on business processes, and identify exceptions.	• That the policy is being implemented properly. It is important that the technologies in place are meeting the goals of the organisation.	Exceptions include different levels of access, or more secure access, for different personnel. Anyone dealing with financials, or with new products, will need a different level of authentication to work within the system, and the security system must reflect this.
6. Implement ongoing evaluation.	• That ongoing evaluation is established • That the policies are adjusted as necessary	The technologies used to secure data, business processes or competitive advantage must be changed to reflect any modifications to policy.

The following technical insite illustrates how one bank has dealt with the issues outlined in table 9.2.

BANK DATA SAFE AS HOUSES

BY ALICIA CAMPHUISEN

One of the biggest advantages of data storage is the ability to have the latest information available any time, particularly when access can mean the difference between keeping a pleased customer and losing a dissatisfied one.

Suncorp Metway, Australia's seventh largest bank, is heeding this lesson to maintain its own internal mandate of having a higher level of customer satisfaction than its competitors.

To help meet this target, the bank has steadily rolled out a Storage Area Network (SAN) to connect its system of isolated servers.

Suncorp Metway processes transactions for more than 2.5 million customers, and over its three years the organisation has amassed a data repository of more than four terabytes (TB), which were stored on the bank's multiple Hewlett-Packard servers.

The problem with this situation was that staff could not freely share information across this network, said Suncorp Metway manager of enterprise technical services Howard Charles.

'We need to have free and constant access to our information all of the time,' he said. 'This is part of what a financial institution needs to have to establish credibility.'

The bank was also steadily increasing its data, and servers could only fit a limited number of the tape drives it used before another server had to be introduced. This costly exercise was exacerbated by the fact that at some times the bank had storage capacity in other parts of the server environment, but the bank could not readily move storage arrangements to utilise this capacity. This meant some storage capacity was simply going to waste.

SAN solution

The twin issues of being unable to share data and not having room to grow, prompted Suncorp Metway to opt for a networked solution. The bank wanted to use a SAN, as it could provide redundancy for disaster recovery as well as high availability.

'The main thing we have to have is high availability of our data,' said Mr Charles. 'The equipment for this may have come at a slight premium, but the resulting 24/7 availability is certainly a trade-off. Our data is our business.'

The bank also wanted a SAN as it could provide cross-platform access to data; however, this proved easier in theory than in practice.

Mr Charles said the bank intended to integrate Hitachi drives with HP hardware, but interoperability issues eventually forced it to seek another solution.

Self-taught

As Suncorp Metway tested each SAN system before purchasing it, Mr Charles discovered that many inter-vendor server/drive/SAN combinations did not operate as well as the bank wanted.

He also learned that while storage vendors were aware of interoperability issues, many of these issues around operating standards had not been developed by the time of the bank's implementation. Because of this, Suncorp Metway decided on a solely Hitachi SAN solution, which was implemented for tape backup in October 1998.

As the bank had trouble finding SAN implementation expertise at the time, IT staff became more familiar with networked storage throughout the testing process.

Mr Charles, whose background is in mainframe systems, said that the key to making this situation work was understanding the main problem they wanted to solve. In Suncorp Metway's case, the ability to share storage capacity and have high data availability were the primary criteria to meet.

The bank has already recorded dramatic improvements in access after the implementation. 'There has been a 300 per cent improvement in the processing times of our Unix applications, an increase in data availability, and a better backup capability,' said Mr Charles.

'We can also reuse infrastructure by utilising spare storage capacity in the mainframe, mid-range and NT environment. We're not wasting this space.'

Mr Charles said the SAN has also become easier to manage under the bank's storage scheduling and capacity plan. The bank's robotic tape libraries, in conjunction with the direct access to storage servers that the SAN permits, have increased its response time when restoring data, and has completely removed manual intervention from the process.

The bank must still introduce more servers as its data repositories grow, but the ability to move storage around as needed has made this a less expensive, less frequent and more easily manageable exercise.

Where to now?

Now, 14 months into the implementation, Suncorp Metway uses its Fibre Channel SAN to connect 25 Unix servers on two sites four kilometres apart that store a total of 1.6TB of data. The bank uses a combination of disk and central tape libraries for its backup.

The SAN rollout is continuing, with the bank planning to move 1.7TB of data from its NT servers over to its Unix environment. Mr Charles expects the SAN to hold more than 3TB of data in the next 12 months, including account information, transaction records, testing data, mail and internal data from its People-Soft enterprise system.

After going through the implementation, the bank has also realised the value of its information resources.

'Storage is more important than processors,' said Mr Charles. 'We can replace a CPU, but not our data.'

SOURCE: *Image and Data Manager,* March/April 2000, p. 79, www.idm.net.au.

EXERCISES

1. What were the twin issues faced by Suncorp Metway when opting for their network solution?

2. How did Suncorp Metway deal with the problem of lack of SAN implementation expertise?

3. Outline some of the improvements that Suncorp Metway experienced after the implementation.

4. Summarise the experience of Suncorp Metway after the implementation and explain your understanding.

In summary, a security policy requires five major steps.

1. Identify the assets of the company and identify the comparative business advantage of the company.
2. Identify the threats to that competitive advantage and the threats to the data.
3. Identify those points in the system, in the architecture and in the business process that are vulnerable.
4. Consider all the risks involved. What level of security do you need to achieve?
5. Implement the policy by taking protective measures.

The key is to ensure that the level of security is appropriate to:

- the level of business activity
- the level of protection needed.

Some organisations place greater emphasis on increasing the productivity of their workers than on security. The Internet and the business processes are open so that employees can access them continually and work quickly as a result. Such a business strategy, although it may appear economical, is highly risky. Employees may feel respected and act creatively in such organisations. However, such a pleasant workers' environment could change quickly once security features are put in place. This could actually lead to a loss in productivity as workers begin to fret about new security implementations.

At the other extreme is the overly protective security system. In essence, this may also decrease productivity because of the time absorbed by the implementation of protective measures, such as obtaining passwords and maintaining levels of security. It will certainly increase the cost of running the system and restrict employees' creativity and use of the Internet. The ultimate aim of a company developing a security policy should be to find a balance between these two extremes. One solution is to adopt the International Organization for Standardization (ISO) model for security in organisations called ISO7499-2.

THE POLICY DEVELOPMENT PROCESS

The security policy should be developed in collaboration with those who use the policy. All organisations have marketing, operational and competitive policies. In Internet commerce, security and network operation policies are adjuncts to these processes, complementing them in order to achieve the corporate goal of competitive advantage in the marketplace. **Policy development** is a key responsibility of senior management.

ACCEPTABLE NETWORK AND COMPUTER USE

Any security policy must incorporate acceptable use of networks and computers in the organisation. A password policy, for example, will determine how passwords are created, how often they are reviewed and how frequently they should be changed. An acceptable, fully understood policy on email use should also be instituted. Many organisations now put a limit on the amount of private email employees can engage in at work. More details on email usage are discussed in chapter 10.

PHYSICAL ACCESS

Policies on physical access to computer rooms, servers, offices and special equipment rooms are also required. Access modes, such as keys, swipe cards, passwords and PINs, must be specified. Policies on the use of smart cards for access to physical environments and/or bank accounts should also be considered.

LEGAL POLICIES

Next, policies on software licensing and usage must be developed. These should address actions to be taken when employees load onto the organisation's system or computers illegal or non-business software such as games or any form of software that might interrupt or change an operating system. Multilingual users should know whether they may use, say, a Thai, Russian or French operating system. Microsoft, for example, manufactures all of these products, so a multilingual policy that is clear and unambiguous about the use of such software will be needed.

INTERNET ACCESS

A clear policy on access to the Internet is, of course, fundamental. Many organisations are concerned about employees 'surfing' the Web for irrelevant information. Pornography, hate sites or sites that defame people in the organisation are usually banned and often filtered out (see chapter 10 for more details). However, as we have noted, open access to the Internet may often improve the creativity of employees by allowing them access to other sources of information, and this in turn may improve productivity. Policies on Internet access for virtual teams and remote or teleworkers must also be developed.

VIRUS AND DENIAL-OF-SERVICE ATTACK POLICIES

Finally, the policy must incorporate protective measures against viruses and other forms of intrusive attacks, including Trojans, denial-of-service attacks, address spoofing, or any sort of activity whose intent is to destroy or change data or informational process within the business.

The policy should consider:
- what anti-virus software is to be installed on every machine
- updating time frames for virus software
- responsibility for cleaning out viruses
- responsibility for notification about virus attacks.

In 2000 the Love Bug virus caused an enormous amount of damage to many organisations unprepared to deal with the consequences of a virus entering a mail server via email. They had virus detection software, but nothing that dealt with attacks via email. Keeping up to date with virus detection software is vital, but because the attacks come from many different sources, organisations must be constantly on the alert for new forms of attack. It is essential to monitor such sites as www.cert.org to keep up with the problems that could affect Internet businesses.

SECURITY MEASURES
THE GOOD, BAD AND FRUSTRATING

BY MARK BROATCH

New Zealand IT managers are nervous about security. This year, they regularly put security into their top two or three concerns, along with IT costs and availability of in-house skills, according to International Data (IDC). Australian IT is worried too, but slightly less so. This may have something to do with another survey's finding that, per capita, they were second only to the US in the number of secure servers they had access to. But what are we so worried about, and does our concern put a crimp on e-commerce plans?

We've been Love Bugged to death, so we are all a little wiser there — perhaps. And everyone's heard of the disgruntled employee who puts the boss's salary on the Internet as a leaving gesture, the clever cracker proving a point, and the thick-skinned spammer who clogs the network. Perhaps you've also heard of the business competitor who taps into your intranet to steal your company's budget figures. But they are all real.

A joint survey by the FBI and the Computer Security Institute (CSI) reported that breaches in computer security cost 163 large US companies and government organisations US$124 million in 1998. And that's just the tip of a Titanic-smashing iceberg, as few companies report security breaches. No one likes to advertise their vulnerability. It makes account holders, customers, shareholders, managers and staff nervous. Despite this, most companies spend less than 1 per cent of their operating budgets on security, according to yet another study, by Gartner Group.

There are at least 40 000 computer viruses and other malicious logic programs in existence. In July last year, WarRoom Research, a US security and intelligence consultancy, released a study of 320 Fortune 500 companies spanning 27 industries. It found that 67 per cent reported some level of confirmed hacking activity in 1997 and 1998, more than 32 per cent reported breaches from competitors in both domestic and foreign markets, and more than 40 per cent reported incidents linked to internal employees or consultants in trusted positions.

Maybe malcontents are less interested in small-fry Kiwi companies, but nonchalance is a dangerous game. The successful denial-of-service attacks on several huge US web sites earlier this year prove no one is immune. The Pentagon reportedly detects as many as 100 hacks on its systems in a typical week. President Bill Clinton has proposed spending US$1.46 billion this year — an increase of 40 per cent — to protect the country's critical infrastructure, and on recruiting super-cyber-experts to respond to future computer crises. He has recognised the threat to a knowledge economy, but whether we have got the message is another question.

But let's be realistic. You've got a bullet-proof firewall around your intranet or extranet, you've instigated staff security policies. What else can you do? Complex security procedures interfere with productivity, efficiency and, thus, profitability. Multiple, complex, frequently changed log-ons and passwords are tough for hackers to guess — and for employees to remember. Curtailing email use to limit virus threats irritates staff and limits communication internally, and externally with customers. And firewalls slow network traffic as the software inspects content and authenticates users. Security is further complicated by the proliferation of devices that staff want to use to access the network.

Companies must make policies on who gets access to data and what types of email attachments are allowed, say security specialists. But too much security can also stand in the way of the business units' desire to do e-business with customers, partners and suppliers. A partner may eventually prefer a more access-friendly company.

The route to resolving the conflict, security experts say, is for everyone in the enterprise to view security as a strategic imperative with shared responsibility between IT and business. Security can't just be shoved onto IT. It can provide policies and guidance, but users own the data and have a responsibility to take care of it. Getting users to understand and accept some responsibility is essential. Encryption software is useless if the laptop user disables it before dialling into the network. Users should also be regularly reminded — though not harassed, or they will begin to ignore security e-missives — that electronic communication may involve legal issues such as defamation and confidentiality.

Technology may help matters to some degree. Digital certificates — smart cards that contain embedded authorisation information — allow people to move from application to application without having to re-enter passwords or IDs, while single sign-on (SSO) technology promises users will need only to identify themselves once before simultaneously accessing several different systems. Post-it notes with multiple passwords pinned to the cubicle are no substitute.

SOURCE: *CIO*, June 2000, p. 59.

EXERCISES

1. What makes security one of the top concerns for IT managers?
2. What kind of security problem is especially pertinent to New Zealand companies, and why?
3. How does a firewall work?
4. How can technology help with the security problems?

PENALTIES AND SECURITY BREACHES

A security policy needs a very clear statement about penalties for violations of that policy. There must be a clear statement of penalty in the event that a member of the organisation:

- imports a virus
- hacks into restricted parts of the system
- inadvertently accesses restricted areas
- interferes with data or changes data deliberately.

POLICY IMPLEMENTATION PROCESS

Once policies have been developed, they have to be implemented. All members of an organisation must know who is responsible for each aspect of security for Internet commerce. Guidelines should establish who is responsible for **policy implementation** and for evaluation of personnel using the policy.

Key concerns for policy administrators include:

- continual **policy evaluation**
- emphasis on security as the key element in the business processes within an organisation
- prioritisation of security awareness of the threat of network, computer and virus attack
- development of a security culture in the organisation
- a clear, coordinated, well-written security policy of which every employee is aware
- promotion of security in a team environment in the organisation. Computer networks in companies represent a distribution of responsibility; it is no longer the case that each employee is responsible for his or her own work alone. Operating on a computer network requires that people be responsible not only for their own computers and their own part of the network, but for anyone else connected to the network.

AUDITING

As we have noted, a continual auditing process should take place. Such a process will attempt to understand:

- what the computer networks are being used for
- how they are being used
- how often they are being used
- what particular machines are being used for.

Servers in the twenty-first century have network operating software and data files sophisticated enough to provide reports on a weekly, daily or monthly basis. Such reports enable network managers to continually monitor use of the Internet, email, downloading of files, downloading of middleware and shareware from the Internet, downloading of video and audio files and so on. Unusual activities are monitored and recorded. A **security audit** process must be maintained on a continual basis. Feedback should be provided in reports not only to management but also to employees, so that they are also kept fully informed. (See chapter 10 for more details on monitoring issues.)

MANAGING SECURITY POLICY IMPLEMENTATION

To make Internet security policies work, a senior manager or a number of managers must take responsibility for their implementation. These executives responsible for Internet security policy must make sure that:

1. a policy is written
2. the policy is acceptable to all users in the organisation
3. the policy meets the competitive demands of the organisation.

It is also important that employees understand the real value of the organisation's assets. Information and knowledge have an increasing intrinsic, measurable value. In many cases, information will become as much a key asset of the organisation as its physical products, processes, equipment and capital. In the future, businesses will need to find a way to measure the intrinsic value of information itself. Security will therefore play an increasingly important role in protecting this asset.

HOW SENIOR MANAGEMENT CAN ASSIST

Senior management need to demonstrate continually and positively the importance of the security policy and be able to express that importance not only in terms of employee use of the Internet but also in terms of increased productivity as a result of having secure processes in operation. Table 9.3 outlines senior management's responsibilities.

TABLE 9.3	SENIOR MANAGEMENT ROLES
SENIOR MANAGEMENT ROLE	**HOW**
Training	Training should occur as a natural part of security policy implementation. Everyone needs to understand what is going on, what changes are taking place and why, and what impact they will have on their work processes.
Auditing the audits	It is essential that management audit the audits. Managers must examine the audits on a weekly or even daily basis in very secure organisations. They must take responsibility for the impact of these audits, and they must deal with any breaches that occur.
Leading by example	Managers should use the network and the security policy; they must organise it, audit it and keep training up to date at all times.

SUMMARY

Security policy must meet the internal needs of the organisation so that it can maintain its competitive advantage. If it is to grow, the business's processes and operations have to be secure. The successful business relationship in Internet commerce is built on trust. A properly designated security policy will help the development of trust. Business relationships in Internet commerce are fundamentally based on trust:

- that what is put up for sale is really for sale
- that the transaction will occur in a secure environment
- that the credit card number is legitimate
- that the delivery of the goods will occur within the time period stated.
- that there will be a positive and mutually satisfactory business relationship between two people, two companies or two organisations, as in a bricks-and-mortar exchange.

Trust in Internet commerce can be confidently relied upon only once business processes and technology have been securely established. That trust is built upon a security policy that:

- meets the needs of the organisation's assets
- identifies threats, vulnerabilities and risks
- adopts a series of protective measures that will guarantee e-business security.

QUESTIONS

1. What is a trust relationship in business?

2. Why is trust so crucial to Internet commerce?

3. How does trust in the business relationship in Internet commerce differ from that in traditional bricks-and-mortar commerce?

4. How can a business involved in B2B commerce establish trust with its trading partners?

5. How can trust be established in a web site like www.alibaba.com?

6. What are the key elements of a security policy for Internet commerce?

7. How could a security policy be developed for an aggregator site like http://www.mySimon.com?

8. Why would any web business want a detailed, written security policy?

UNUSUAL SUSPECTS

By SUE BUSHELL

In Australia business and regulatory authorities warn that the potential for fraud to cross borders and for international shysters to 'eat into the Australian economy' is higher than ever, partly because of the trend towards e-commerce. According to the report *Taking Fraud Seriously: Issues and Strategies for Reform*, fraud costs Australia more than $3.5 billion a year and adds $21 to the cost of each insurance policy. Written by the Australian Institute of Criminology for the Institute of Chartered Accountants Fraud Advisory Council, the report notes the global electronic village has brought about a significant growth in fraud opportunity through new products, services and service delivery channels.

Yet there's been no concomitant improvement in detection and prosecution. Fraud control, detection and prosecution techniques are all being run at national levels, rather than under an international approach. Technology-induced global-isation compounds the problem. 'This is no more apparent than in the financial sector,' the report says. 'Bonnie and Clyde no longer have to turn up at a branch in order to rob the bank. Indeed, if they did, they would be severely limiting their potential "take". They would now be more likely to try to rob the bank through a technology-assisted approach, from the other side of the world.'

Internet fraud is becoming so serious the Australian Securities and Investment Commission (ASIC) recently established a dedicated electronic enforcement division, while police everywhere admit they simply haven't the resources to deal adequately with the problem. Detective Inspector Phil

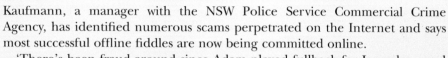

Kaufmann, a manager with the NSW Police Service Commercial Crime Agency, has identified numerous scams perpetrated on the Internet and says most successful offline fiddles are now being committed online.

'There's been fraud around since Adam played fullback for Jerusalem, and there is always going to be. People will always want other people's money with minimal exposure to themselves,' he says.

Credit card fraud

To quantify the fraud cost of e-commerce, Kaufmann approached several leading Australian banks in February 1999. One bank reported 70 per cent of all credit card 'charge backs' (where the merchant is left footing the bill for a fraudulent credit card transaction) were Internet related. Credit card fraud remains the most insidious Internet fraud perpetrated in Australia. Perpetrators either rely on credit-card generator programs found on the Internet, hack into users' or merchants' computers to obtain stored credit card details, or else use invasive 'Trojan horse' programs to gain legitimate credit card details from PCs.

There are plenty of credit-card generation applications, bank-identification system guides and instructions for 'carding' or for using stolen cards available online. Criminals frequently use stolen credit-card numbers to ring up online purchases — most typically of high-ticket electronic items or downloadable products like software, music clips and images — and stick online merchants with the tab.

In some cases, fraudulent transactions have reportedly accounted for 20 per cent or more of web merchants' sales, until managers took action and installed anti-fraud software. Other avoidance measures include outsourcing credit-card verification to third parties with sophisticated neural-net anti-fraud software, or developing anti-fraud systems in-house. Some organisations even take verification procedures offline and check cards manually.

Other types of e-commerce fraud include theft of money, the compromising of trade secrets, the theft of intellectual property and customer data, the misrepresentation of business identity, not getting paid and the deliberate misrepresentation of data. Cramming — billing companies or consumers for services they never ordered — is also booming. Authorities overseas have identified a range of Internet scams from 'work-at-home' businesses, through services purporting to improve one's credit rating, to investments in exotic products like coconut plantations.

E-commerce fraud devastating

Bruce Schneier, president of Minneapolis-based Counterpane Systems, writes in the electronic newsletter *Risks-Forum Digest* that there are three features of electronic commerce that are likely to make online fraud more devastating than non-technical fraud.

First is the ease of automation. The same automation that makes electronic commerce systems more efficient than paper systems also makes fraud more efficient. 'A particular fraud that might have taken a criminal 10 minutes to execute on paper can be completed with a single keystroke, or automatically while he sleeps. Low-value frauds that fell below the radar in paper systems become dangerous in the electronic world. No one cares if its is possible to

counterfeit nickels [US five cents]. However, if a criminal can mint electronic nickels, he might make a million dollars in a week.'

Second is the difficulty of isolating jurisdiction. In an electronic world without geography a criminal doesn't have to be anywhere near a system he is frauding — he can attack Citibank in New York from St Petersburg.

The speed of propagation creates a further risk. News travels fast on the Internet. If someone figures out how to defraud an electronic commerce system and posts a program on the Internet, a thousand people could have it in an hour, a hundred thousand in a week.

Electronic extortion

Electronic payment systems create security vulnerabilities that lead to instances of fraud being perpetrated on the Internet and funds being stolen electronically, says Australian Institute of Criminology research analyst Dr Russell Smith. Telephone and computer home banking expose other vulnerabilities.

Yet while e-fraud is a growing problem, senior Australian criminal investigators concede off the record that companies have to find a balance between spending too much money combating fraud and not doing enough. 'The level of compliance these days has, unfortunately, got to take an acceptable level of fraud as a cost overhead in the business structure. It's whatever is acceptable to you — we believe it is nil, but the practicalities of it aren't that clear,' one investigator says.

Kaufmann admits it is impossible for any company to achieve 'zero tolerance' to e-fraud prevention, but argues that adopting a combative approach at least gets the message out to the public and staff that the company is reliable and committed to fraud reduction. 'The lack of proper policies is half the problem anyway. You've got to be a responsible member of the business community and of the wider community and stop crime,' Kaufmann says. 'I'm the manager of the risk assessment and prevention area. What we're trying to put across is you've got to have an ethical company structure and then you find it easier to put together a control plan and have your staff and personnel acting ethically as well.'

Electronic commerce systems should have the goal not of preventing crime, which is impossible, but of detecting and fingering the guilty, Kaufmann says. Preventing fraud on the Internet would involve the use of both conventional approaches like risk awareness raising exercises and user education, as well as novel technological approaches such as those that can secure cards and hardware. If such measures can't entirely prevent Internet fraud then the aim should be to at least identify the presence of fraudulent transactions quickly in order to reduce the extent of any losses suffered or repeat occurrences.

SOURCE: *CIO*, September 1999, pp. 63–9.

Questions

1. Describe the difference between Internet fraud and common fraud.

2. List several types of e-commerce fraud.

3. Why is fraud in Internet commerce more devastating than other fraud?

4. What should a company do in order to best reduce the possibility of e-fraud?

SUGGESTED READING

Ahuja, Vijay 1997, *Secure Commerce on the Internet*, Ap Professional, Boston, MA.

Bernstein, T., Bhimani, A., Schultz, E. and Siegel, C. 1996, *Internet Security for Business*, John Wiley & Sons, New York.

Camp, J. 2000, *Trust and Risk*, MIT Press, Boston, MA.

Ford, W. and Baum, M. 1997, *Secure Electronic Commerce*, Prentice Hall, New Jersey.

Furche, Andreas, and Wrightson, Graham 1999, *Computer Money: A Systematic Overview of Electronic Payment Systems*, dpunkt Verlag, Heidelberg, Germany.

Ghosh, Anup K. 1999, *E-commerce Security*, John Wiley & Sons, New York.

Greenstein, M. and Feinman, T. M. 2000, *Electronic Commerce: Security, Risk Management and Control*, Irwin McGraw-Hill, New York.

Minoli, D. and Minoli, E. 1997, *Web Commerce Technology Handbook*, John Wiley & Sons, New York.

Norris, M., West, S. and Gaughan, K. 2000, *eBusiness Essentials*, John Wiley & Sons, New York.

Parker, Donn B. 1999, *Fighting Computer Crime*, John Wiley & Sons, New York.

Pfleeger, Charles P. 1996, *Security in Computing*, Prentice Hall, New Jersey.

Vacca, John 1997, *Intranet Security*, Charles River Media, Hingham, MA.

END NOTES

1. Neilsen Norman Group 2000/2001, 'E-Commerce Usability, User Experience World Tour', presented by Rolf Molich, Dialog Design, Denmark, molich@dialogdesign.dk, www.dialogdesign.dk.

2. Deitel, H. M., Deitel, J. and Nieto, T. R. 2000, *E-business and E-commerce: How to Program*, Prentice Hall, New Jersey, p. 210.

CHAPTER 10

THE IMPACT OF LAW AND ETHICS ON TRADING USING ELECTRONIC COMMERCE

Learning objectives

You will have mastered the material in this chapter when you can:

- identify the problems associated with determining which legal jurisdiction applies to international transactions conducted via the Internet
- assess the applicability of traditional, real-world law on e-commerce
- identify Internet regulation issues relating to e-commerce
- appreciate the potential for fraud and other criminal activities using the Internet
- understand how copyright and defamation laws may be infringed by making information freely available over the Internet
- understand how privacy of the individual and company records may be breached by users of the Internet and what safeguards are required to preserve that privacy
- appreciate how the Internet may be regulated as a consequence of government concerns over such matters as censorship and consumer protection
- understand Internet taxation issues
- identify potential technical and legal solutions to the various e-commerce issues.

'If people choose to cruise the Internet, it is a free-for-all territory at the moment. It's not really governed by anything ... it's the Wild West. And if people can take advantage of the Wild West, then let them do it. That's what I believe.'

Greg Lasrado, Australian Internet millionaire named by US authorities over a web-jacking incident, quoted in R. Guilliatt 2000, 'No Way Out', *Sydney Morning Herald*, *Good Weekend*, 22 July, p. 24.

INTRODUCTION

As the opening quotation illustrates, the Internet is equated by some to a lawless territory where the fast movers can make a killing (or a fortune), and rebels and anarchists can act with impunity and move on before the legal process can catch up. How does the Internet resemble the Wild West? It is a vast unexplored (cyber-) territory that is being opened up by agile pioneers, who move in quickly to stake their claims and test the **laws** that might restrict their activities. Think about some of the questionable online activities that have gained recent publicity, such as domain name squatting, hijacking of web sites, piracy, **defamation**, theft of **copyright** material and blackmail.[1] But in the business world there must be, and there are, regulations and controls, and it is becoming apparent that appropriate regulations and laws must be devised to cover Internet-based payment methods and new communication technologies.

Commercial transactions are subject to a comprehensive system of controls based on:

- the common law
- **legislation** at State, federal and international levels
- industry codes of practice.

These controls have been established in an ad hoc fashion over time in response to the need to provide a high degree of certainty in contractual relationships and to give consumers confidence that they will obtain 'a fair deal' in any dispute. Both of these are necessary ingredients in the promotion of trade and commerce upon which modern economies depend. The controls have evolved and have been adapted to new technologies as they arise, although there is always a time lag before the controls 'catch up' with the latest technology.

We are still at an early stage in establishing controls over commercial transactions on the Internet, despite the large volume of transactions taking place daily. Unique features of the Internet compared with earlier technological changes are:

- its rapid proliferation
- the multiplicity of communication channels
- the enormous volume of information and range of services available
- the ease and speed with which trans-border transactions can be conducted.

These developments pose a unique set of problems. Although international agreements for the regulation of international trade do exist, they are not keeping pace with commercial realities. The principal problem is that existing agreements, and even many of those proposed, deal only with business or trade transactions. They do not deal with consumer purchases, which are responsible for the huge growth in transactions over the Internet.

Naturally, responsible e-businesses know the value of satisfied customers and the dangers of dissatisfied ones, who can very quickly damage a cyberbusiness's reputation.

Generally speaking, if there is a dispute over a failed payment transaction, responsibility rests either with the seller or with the customer, depending on the mechanism used — credit card transactions favour the customer, while a Secure Electronic Transaction (SET) favours the merchant.[2] An 'Agreement of Terms' must be explicitly addressed by an e-commerce vendor. The following technical insite gives some pointers that might assist.

technical
INSITE

FROM SHRINKWRAP TO CLICKWRAP

Chris Shine, a partner with Blake Dawson Waldron, argues that e-businesses should make clear all terms and conditions of sale on their web sites and require customers to click on an 'I acknowledge' or 'I accept' button before buying. In fact, sellers of software over the Internet have set up their sites so that potential buyers must follow a set procedure of pressing a prominent acceptance button, signalling their agreement to the terms and conditions of the licence, before they can proceed to download the software. These agreements, commonly known as 'clickwrap' agreements, are the online equivalent of the shrinkwrap or seal around a physical software product. Paul May believes that providers of services can benefit from examining the way in which software vendors work. The following table illustrates some of the lessons to be learned.

TABLE 10.1	APPLYING REAL-WORLD PRINCIPLES TO THE WORLD OF E-SERVICES	
REAL-WORLD SOFTWARE VENDORS	**WHAT THIS MEANS**	**PROVIDERS OF ONLINE SERVICES**
Sell rights to use software	Vendors retain IP rights — customers pay a fee to use the software.	Can use similar model
Every software licence specifies the bounds of the vendor's liability.	Vendors insert disclaimers relating to liability.	A clickable statement of liability can be used to put disclaimers in place.
Software licences set out the legal **jurisdiction** that will be used in any dispute relating to the agreement.	Usually, but not always, the home jurisdiction of the vendor	Agreements should specify a jurisdiction — there is no accepted default court of law for online transactions.

Other important technical and legal points, such as those that follow, should be considered.

1. Make sure the agreement text is clearly written — seek assistance from a lawyer if you are unsure.
2. Keep a dossier of all electronic and paper-based changes to the agreement — that is, maintain strong version control of the agreement.

3. Use an agreement text with an acceptance button to implement a set of disclaimers relating to the product or service.
4. Emails and electronic newsletters from corporate accounts should contain a standard disclaimer that reflects the company's association with the text of the message. Below is an example.

Disclaimer: Neither internet.com nor the writers of this newsletter makes specific trading recommendations or gives individualized market advice. Information contained in this newsletter is provided as an information service only. Internet.com recommends that you get personal advice from an investment professional before buying or selling stocks or other securities. The securities markets are highly speculative areas for investments and only you can determine what level of risk is appropriate for you. Also, users should be aware that internet.com, its employees and affiliates may own securities that are the subject of reports, reviews or analysis in this newsletter.

Although internet.com obtains the information reported herein from sources that it deems reliable, no warranty can be given as to the accuracy or completeness of any of the information provided or as to the results obtained by individuals using such information. Each user shall be responsible for the risks of their own investment activities, and in no event shall internet.com or its employees, agents or affiliates be liable for any direct, indirect, actual, special or consequential damage.[3]

---

5. Employees should be encouraged to send emails from personal rather than corporate accounts.
6. It might be worthwhile for a corporate web site to deny responsibility for any sites to which it links or that link to it. It is appropriate to deny any business connection to a reference site that has not obtained permission to so link. In strategic alliances or subcontracted delivery arrangements in which part of the relationship involves linking to each other's sites, include a web linking clause in the agreement.
7. If someone else requests that you link to them, or will pay you a fee to link to them, use a web linking agreement.[4]

SOURCES: Adapted from P. May 2000, *The Business of E-Commerce: From Corporate Strategy to Technology*, Cambridge University Press, Cambridge, UK, p. 232; and K. Nicholas 1999, 'Sellers may be strolling into a legal maze', *Sydney Morning Herald*, 2 September, p. 30.

EXERCISES

1. Investigate the legal position of *clickwrap* agreements in your country. Report on any cases that have gone to court.
2. Investigate the legal ramifications of linking to other sites. In particular, research cases that have gone to court over what is known as *deep linking* — that is, linking to another web site well beneath their main page. Investigate the use of software measures to prevent deep linking.
3. Search out cases that have dealt with the issues of using frames that hide the addresses of sites to which a corporate web site links.

Other major concerns include how security of commercial transactions over the Internet can be maintained and how the consumer's interests can be protected, including the individual's rights to **privacy**. Added to this are issues associated with protecting a society's values, exemplified by government's role in controlling content on the Internet, particularly in relation to **censorship**.

CONTROL OF INTERNET CONTENT

A first step in trying to establish a legal framework for any new technology is to classify it so as to establish how existing legislation may be made to fit the new technology. Although the Internet service provider (ISP) is now the major focus for attempts at legislative controls, there is a wide variation between each country's approach.[5] Singapore, for example, has classified ISPs as broadcasting media, requiring them to be registered. It thereby exercises control by allowing access only to authorised web sites. In the United States, the *Telecommunications Act (1996)* considers the ISP to be a telecommunications carrier. The US Supreme Court struck down the *Communications Decency Act*, which would have restricted indecent material on the Internet, as unconstitutional and an attack on free speech.

An international working group, the Internet Content Rating Association (ICRA), supported by such computer industry heavyweights as Microsoft, has been formed to establish worldwide standards for content rating.[6]

In Australia, a Senate select committee report[7] argued that Internet content should be treated in the same manner as that on a broadcast medium such as television. One outcome of the report was to make the Federal Government's Telecommunications Industry Ombudsman available to hear complaints from users of the Internet.[8] The more significant outcome, however, was the enactment of the *Broadcasting Services Amendment (Online Content) Act*, 1999. This Act is intended to regulate Internet content hosted both within Australia and offshore by restricting the use of the Internet for transmission of objectionable material, especially pornography, and by promoting measures to protect children from viewing such material.

The Act requires ISPs and Internet content hosts (ICHs) to comply with guidelines based on pre-existing film and video classifications, and encourages the industry to adopt a code of practice or suffer the introduction of mandatory standards by the Australian Broadcasting Authority (ABA),[9] which is charged with the responsibility of implementing the Act. The ABA can initiate investigations into Internet content on its own initiative or as a result of a complaint from the public, and can issue notices requiring ISPs or ICHs to take down or deny access to prohibited content. The Act was introduced in the face of prolonged opposition by industry groups[10] who consider that measures of control are impractical, costly and represent an invasion of privacy of users.

The *Australian Online Services Act* of January 2000 requires ISPs to supply software filters, but research has shown that less than 2 per cent of people are using them.[11] In the first six months of operation of the Internet censorship scheme, the ABA received 201 complaints and rejected more than half of them. Ninety-five items of content were referred either to the Australian Federal Police or to overseas authorities.[12]

Software — for example Cybersitter at www.cybersitter.com, Surfwatch at www.surfwatch.com and Net Nanny at www.netnanny.com[13] — allows parents to block incoming material using key words or phrases and other indicators. Blocking and filtering technologies allow users to decide what material can and cannot be accessed on their browsers, but they lack refinement. Typical examples of blocked words and letters include 'xxx', which blocks out Superbowl XXX sites; 'breast', which blocks web sites and discussion groups about breast cancer; and the consecutive letters 's', 'e' and 'x', which block sites containing the words 'sexton' and 'Mars exploration', among many others.[14] In the United States this software could potentially be considered a violation of First Amendment rights in that the user is never in control of what can and cannot be viewed.[15] Alternatives to such filtering and blocking software include:

- setting up acceptable use policies. Many sites (e.g. http://teams.lacoe.edu/documentation/places/policies.html) offer guidelines to follow.
- education for parents and children. In the United States, Safe Kids Online is a brochure published by the National Center for Missing and Exploited Children that is available on line (www.safekids.com/child_safety.htm) as well as in printed form. The brochure:
  - provides parents with accurate information about risks that children and teenagers may be exposed to on the Internet
  - encourages parents to educate their children to be 'street smart' rather than to restrict their Internet access
  - includes a set of guidelines for parents
  - includes a section for young people called 'My Rules for Online Safety'.[16]

Figure 10.1 shows the home page for Cybersitter.com, one of the many software solutions available for people who wish to block access to certain sites.

FIGURE 10.1: Home page of Cybersitter.com

SOURCE: Solid Oak Software, Inc.

The Personalization Consortium (www.personalization.org) is an international advocacy group formed to promote the development and use of responsible one-to-one marketing technology and practices on the World Wide Web. The consortium encourages the growth and success of e-commerce that delivers the benefits of personalised electronic marketing while articulating best practices and technologies that protect the interests of consumers. Tracking devices that may threaten privacy include[17]:

- *ID cards* that allow information to be sent to your computer from a web site; the site needs the numerical address of the consumer's PC on the Internet, the browser and the operating system to send information
- *click-through advertisements*, which allow advertisers to learn what sites generate the most sales
- *web bugs or clear GIFS* that are embedded in an image on the screen. Web sites hide these information-collecting programs (used by affiliates to gather consumer information) in various parts of the sites. These tags help web sites and advertisers to track users' whereabouts on line. Each time a user goes to a web site, the bug sends a ping or call back to the server, announcing its identity and its whereabouts on the Web. The US White House ordered its drug policy office to stop using web bugs on its anti-drug site, http://freevibe.com. It also issued strict guidelines regulating technology use by the US government.[18]

technical INSITE

LITTLE WEB BUG IS WATCHING YOU

A web bug is a graphic on a web page or in an email message that is designed to monitor who is reading the web page or email message. It can also track users of newsgroups. Web bugs are often invisible because they are typically only 1 pixel × 1 pixel in size. The Internet **advertising** community also calls them 'clear GIFs', '1-by-1 GIFs' and 'invisible GIFs'. Invisible GIF files are also used on web pages for alignment purposes. A web bug will typically be loaded from a different web server than the rest of the page, so they are easy to distinguish from alignment GIF files. They are represented as HTML IMG tags. For example, here are two web bugs found on Quicken's home page (www.quicken.com).

```
<img src="http://ad.doubleclick.net/ad/
pixel.quicken/NEW" width=1 height=1 border=0>
```

```
<IMG WIDTH=1 HEIGHT=1 border=0 SRC="http://
media.preferences.com/
ping?ML_SD=IntuitTE_Intuit_1x1_RunOfSite_A
ny&db_afcr=4B31-C2FB-
10E2C&event=reghome&group=register&time=1999.
10.27.20.5 6.37">
```

These two web bugs were placed on the home page by Quicken to provide 'hit' information about visitors to DoubleClick and MatchLogic (preferences.com), two Internet advertising companies.

A web bug can reveal the following types of information to its related server:
• URL of the web bug
• IP address
• host name
• browser version
• operating system and version
• web browser cookie (optional).

A web bug can be found by viewing the HTML source code of a web page and searching for IMG tags. It will typically have its height and width parameters in the IMG tag set to 1. Also, for the tag to be a bug, the image should be loaded from a different server than the rest of the web page.

SOURCES: The Web Bug FAQ, http://www.tiac.net/users/smiths/privacy/wbfaq.htm; Richard M. Smith (rms2000@bellatlantic.net), 11 November 1999, version 1.0; P. Ching 2000, 'Cookie Monster?' *Communiqué*, November 2000, p. 28.

EXERCISES

1. Do some research on ways to remove web bugs and cookies, and write a formal report on your methods.
2. Discuss the following proposition: *The use of web bugs is unethical.*

COOKIES

Although security measures can provide some protection for the information transmitted over the Internet, they cannot hide the trail created by each transaction. A web server is able to send a program called a 'cookie' over the Internet to be deposited on a user's hard drive without disclosure or consent. The cookie was introduced as part of Netscape's web technology. When a web browser requests a page from a web server, the server sends back to the browser not just the requested page, but also an instruction to write a cookie (i.e. a record) into the client computer's storage. Once a cookie is written into storage, users can be identified each time they visit the same site, thus allowing a profile of each user to be established based on usage patterns. Some online newspapers store user names and password in a plain text cookie file. To examine a cookie folder on a personal computer, use *Find* on the Start menu and search for cookies or cookies.txt or MagicCookie in the browser directory/ folder. The cookies may be read using Notepad.

This arrangement could have advantages for both sellers and online consumers, since the seller is able to offer a customised, personalised service for the user. The main objections to the cookie are that:
• it is introduced to a user's hard drive without disclosure or consent
• the information collated could become accessible to other organisations, including government.

To overcome such objections a user could be:

- informed if and when the cookies were to be placed
- told of the uses to which the cookies would be put
- given the choice as to whether to proceed or not.

However, the seller is under no legal obligation to do this. Currently, if users turn cookies off on a browser, they are bombarded with queries as to whether they wish to accept a cookie. This slows down the interaction and annoys users, who often turn cookies back on.

In Australia the *Commonwealth Privacy Act 1988* provides privacy safeguards that Federal Government departments must observe in collecting, storing and using personal information. The Act was amended in 1990 to include credit providers, but private companies remain unregulated. Since then, as a result of pressure from various quarters, the Federal Government has announced that it is preparing national legislation. The proposals are for 'light touch' data protection built around a self-regulatory model that allows individual industries to adopt their own privacy codes, with legislative provisions applying if an industry code is not adopted.

However, because of the international nature of the Internet many national regulations may not apply to foreign companies. Furthermore, it is not always possible to determine in which country the company is located, so that enforcement of privacy provisions may be impossible.

Although guidelines have been prepared by such bodies as the United Nations, they carry no legal authority. The most influential provision to date is the European Union (EU) Council Personal Data Protection Directive, which was formally adopted in July 1995.[19] This established a set of legal principles for privacy protection applicable to both public and private sectors, and national legislation has since been enacted by all EU member states[20] modelled on the Directive.

Although these legal principles apply only in the EU, their effect is far reaching. This is because the Directive also prohibits the transfer of data from the EU to countries that do not have adequate data protection laws. Conversely, the import of data from such countries may also require the importer to abide by the EU Directive. This is one of the factors putting pressure on countries such as Australia to improve their privacy protection laws.

technical INSITE

TREASURY'S WEB SITE 'BREACHED PRIVACY LAWS'

BY TONI O'LOUGHLIN

TREASURY'S GST Assist web site had lax security measures which breached privacy laws, the Federal Privacy Commissioner, Mr Malcolm Crompton, has found.

Mr Crompton's findings follow his investigation into the student who illegally downloaded the banking details of 20 000 individuals and businesses last June. The investigation revealed the GST Assist Internet site had failed to provide even the most basic security mechanism, a firewall, because of deficiencies in the **contract** used to hire the firm that designed the web site.

Web site security checks were 'limited' and did not address the need to protect the 20 000 Bank/State/Branch and bank account numbers from illegal access, Mr Crompton said.

'Someone found a staggeringly simple way of getting [into] the site as a result,' he said. All that needed to be done was to change the site's internal web address, which was exposed to the public, to open the database. The breach 'illustrates the need for government departments and organisations to develop rigorous privacy protection measures as they move operations and services on line,' Mr Crompton said. While unauthorised, no charges have been laid against the student who downloaded the information and then distributed to each business and individual their own bank details to prove the site was insecure.

Mr Glenn Carlos, project manager for the GST Start Up Assist Office, a Treasury agency that runs the GST Assist site, said the site's security was fixed immediately after the breach.

Privacy protection mechanisms had not been installed because the information was not considered private. 'The information on there was BSB and account numbers, the same stuff that's on the bottom of your cheque,' Mr Carlos said. There was also a need to install the most efficient system to allow businesses and individuals to register as GST Assist providers, he said. Mr Crompton said government departments needed to put more effort into protecting personal information on line. In particular, more care was needed in writing contracts when work was outsourced. It is the third time this year that a government department has breached the privacy laws.

The Tax Office broke the privacy laws with its plan to make publicly available, and sell, the private details of people who are required to have Australian Business Numbers under the GST. The Australian Electoral Commission also breached privacy rules when it handed over the voting roll to the Tax Office.

SOURCE: *Sydney Morning Herald*, 18 October 2000, p. 8.

EXERCISES

1. Write a technical report that outlines what security measures must be put in place before a government web site goes on line.

2. Develop a policy document that provides guidelines to technical staff developing a government or business online site that sets out how to ensure privacy for those using the site.

3. Debate the following proposition: *Outsourcing IT development of web sites is a potential legal minefield.*

MONITORING EMPLOYEES

Cyberbludging[21] (using the Internet at work to play games, gamble or do your shopping etc.) means lost productivity and raises questions about responsibility. Employees using work computers to download pornographic material expose themselves and their employer to sexual harassment liability should someone take offence at pornography in the workplace. Xerox used 'reactive monitoring', in which a comprehensive log of Internet sites visited every month was scanned for 'red flags' — or sites deemed inappropriate for workplace access — and subsequently fired 40 of its workers for 'inappropriate use of the Internet'.[22] Table 10.2 outlines monitoring methods.

TABLE 10.2	MONITORING METHODS		
METHOD	**HOW IT WORKS**	**COMMENTS**	**EXAMPLES**
Internet Access Control (IAC) software	Keeps database of objectionable sites maintained by the manufacturer and updated periodically	Not able to restrict everything Commonly used for home users	Net Nanny
Internet Access Management (IAM) software	Allows IT managers to select types of sites to be blocked Reports attempts to visit restricted sites by users	Commonly used in corporate sites	Websense, SurfControl, WebSpy, I-Gear
LANguard	Scans network traffic for content and can display report, log and alert IT managers	Allows for viewing of sites as they are visited by staff Also monitors other connections (e.g. Internet Relay Chat (IRC)) Protects against Internet misuse, password cracking, Trojan horses, and hackers	www.languard.com

SOURCE: Adapted from F. Williams 2000, 'Get back to work, Cyberbludging Corporate IT', *Australian Personal Computer*, November, pp. 116–24.

INTELLECTUAL PROPERTY

For owners of **intellectual property** the law provides well-established protection that covers many areas of human and corporate endeavour. The Internet provides increased opportunities for eroding that protection in regard to three types of intellectual property — copyright, **patents** and **trade marks**.

COPYRIGHT

Copyright protects a wide array of creative work including writing, artwork, music, film and computer programs; it also extends to broadcast material, covered quite separately from the copyright on the original work.[23] The copyright automatically belongs to the creator, or owner, from the time of creation of the work. International treaties such as the Berne Convention provide for protection of Australian copyright owners overseas, and vice versa, although the rights vary from country to country according to the material. The copyright symbol © is not required for protection in Australia.

Copyright owners have the right to use their material in a variety of ways, and rights may be assigned or leased with or without limitations or conditions. Use of copyrighted material, usually by copying without the permission of the owner, will be an infringement of copyright, except in certain circumstances — for example copying a limited portion of a book for study purposes (the 'reasonable portion' test).

The *Copyright Amendment (Digital Agenda) Act 2000* came into effect in March 2001. The right of communication applies to 'active communication', such as broadcast or cable transmission, and to 'passive communication', such as making material available to be viewed or downloaded (e.g. on a web site). There are criminal penalties and civil remedies for making, importing or commercially dealing in devices and services that circumvent technological copyright protection measures such as decryption software. (There are, however, 'permitted purpose' exceptions, such as for governments and decompilers of software.) Liability of carriers and ISPs for infringing copyright is also dealt with. Factors to be taken into account when determining whether a person is liable for authorising or infringing copyright are based on existing case law. For full details, see www.copyright.org.au.

DIGITAL WATERMARK TECHNOLOGY

Digital watermarking, sometimes called 'fingerprinting', allows copyright owners to incorporate into their work identifying information invisible to the human eye. When combined with new tracking services offered by some of the same companies that provide the watermarking technology, copyright owners can, in theory, find all illegal copies of, say, their photographs and music on the Internet and take appropriate legal action. For webmasters, digital watermarking can help ensure that only lawful image and audio files are used, protecting webmasters against the dangers of copyright infringement.[24]

The following technical insite raises some important questions on how technology is challenging copyright holders and law-makers. As we explained in chapters 8 and 9, security and trust are vital components in Internet commerce transactions. The development of technologies to protect corporate assets is vital — the problem is in keeping abreast of the technology used to sabotage corporate security.

OF NAPSTER, GNUTELLA, MP3, INTERTRUST AND WEBNOIZE

Table 10.3 outlines some of the technologies that are currently challenging lawmakers and copyright owners and some legal responses.

TABLE 10.3	TECHNOLOGY VERSUS THE LAW		
NAME OF TECHNOLOGY	**HOW IT WORKS**	**LEADING PLAYERS**	**LEGAL CHALLENGES**
MP3	A type of software compression used to copy music from CDs to computers; provides high-quality, small-sized audio files	Diamond Multimedia — released the RIO MP3 portable player, which meant users were no longer chained to PCs	Recording Industry Association of America (RIAA) filed suit saying the RIO did not comply with the Audio Home Recording Act — defeated June 1999 (see www.mp3.com.au)
Napster	Users log onto central server, search computers of other connected users for MP3 files. Peer-to-peer trading of files then initiated.	Napster.com	RIAA filed suit in December 1999 alleging infringement of US copyright and state laws. Metallica band filed suit alleging copyright violations in April 2000. Napster states it will start charging.
Secure Digital Music Initiative (SDMI)	Embeds watermarking into future audio CDs for identification purposes. Two watermarks on a track — if transmitted over the Internet, one is designed to break.	RIAA and International Federation of Phonographic Industries and Federation of Music Producers Japan	Hackers challenge the technology — a coalition of researchers from Princeton and Rice Universities and Xerox claimed they had beaten the technology.

Gnutella	Peer-to-peer networking without a centralised server — difficult to track people file sharing. Includes Bearshare and Limewire	http:// gnutella.wego.com
Digital Rights Management	Encryption technology for the music industry — for example, if people pay a certain amount they have unlimited rights to music; if they pay less they may rent some music.	InterTrust Webnoize

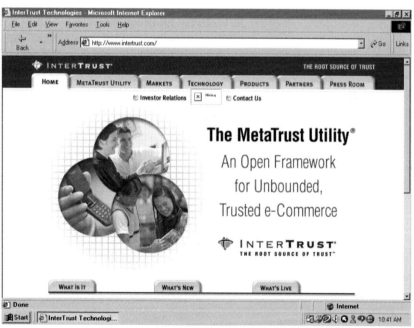

FIGURE 10.2: The InterTrust home page

SOURCES: Shane Nichols, 'Can't stop the music', *Australian Financial Review*, 23 September 2000, p. 4; D. Fallon, 'The day the music died', *ICON*, *Sydney Morning Herald*, 10 March 2001, p. 9; D. Gardine, Online Music Feature, *Australian Personal Computer*, March 2001, p. 59.

EXERCISES

1. Write a report on the history of the legal action against Napster.com.
2. Explain the technology and software underpinning the service that is offered by Napster.com.
3. Explain the technology and software that underpins the service offered by Gnutella.
4. Debate the following proposition: *Swapping music files on the Net is stealing.*

PATENTS

A patent is a right granted for any device, substance, method or process that is new, inventive and useful. A patent must be applied for at the Patent Office, and once granted is legally enforceable and gives the owner exclusive right to commercially exploit the invention for the life of the patent.[25] There is no such thing as a 'world patent'; separate applications must be made for each country. Patents covering software or programming related to web sites are the fastest growing sector at the US Patent Office.[26] US Internet companies have been lodging patent applications for online business models since a 1998 US court ruling that business methods could be patented. Amazon.com, for instance, patented a one-click system of e-commerce in September 2000, as well as an online affiliate program system. Priceline.com pioneered the reverse auction model of asking consumers to nominate how much they would pay for goods and services, such as airline tickets and hotel rooms, after which Priceline sought vendors who would accept the bid. Priceline was able to obtain a patent from US authorities. Such patents have been criticised for stifling Internet competition.

Applying for patents can take a long time and become expensive. Figure 10.3 shows the home page of PatentWizard.com, which sells PatentWizard 2.0, a software tool designed by a patent attorney (Michael S. Neustel) to assist businesses and inventors in drafting and filing their own 'provisional' patent application with the United States Patent and Trademark Office (USPTO).

Questions and exercises

1. Do some research to find out what other patents related to Internet commerce have been granted, either in your country or in the United States.
2. Debate the issue of whether it is reasonable to patent a business method.
3. Has Amazon.com been able to extend its patent for '1-Click' shopping to Australia or to your country?
4. Is there any evidence that patent restrictions are being bypassed by moving operations to other countries where the patents do not apply?

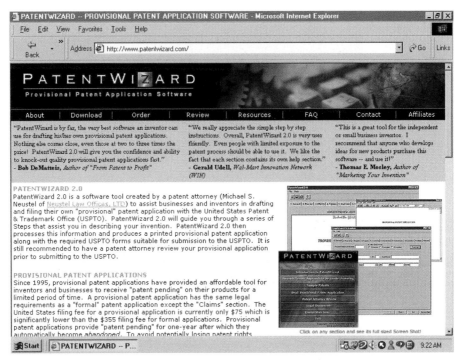

FIGURE 10.3: Home page of PatentWizard.com

TRADE MARKS

A registered trade mark gives the owner exclusive legal rights to use, license or sell it for the goods and services for which it is registered[27] under the provisions of the *Trade Mark Act*. A trade mark can cover not only words and pictures but also sound and even smell. The law provides penalties for infringing a trade mark either by using it or by showing something similar to the trade mark. Trade mark infringement has occurred through 'metatagging', whereby a word is incorporated into a site in order to increase the chances of a search engine returning the site. An interesting early case was *Oppedahl & Larson v Advanced Concepts*, Civ. No. 97-Z-1592 (D.C. Colo., 23 July 1997). The defendants had no clear reason for using the name of Oppedahl & Larson, a law firm that has dealt in domain name disputes, in their metatags. The defendants apparently hoped to capture traffic that would gain them domain name registration fees or web site hosting clients. The court banned them from using the name without authorisation.[28]

There are many legal web sites that offer comments, analysis and background on cases involving attempts to use other businesses' trade marks illegally — for example http://searchenginewatch.com. Of course, different countries apply different laws concerning trade marks within different legal environments, and it is important that e-businesses check the global legal ramifications when trading over the Internet.

Table 10.4 catalogues a number of lawsuits relating to metatagging.

TABLE 10.4	LAWSUITS AND METATAGGING		
FILED/SETTLED (mm/dd/yy)	**CASE**	**VENUE**	**OUTCOME**
07/23/97 02/06/98	Oppedahl & Larson v Advanced Concepts	US District Court, Colorado	Permanent injunction
07/01/97 08/27/97	Insituform Technologies v National Envirotech	US District Court, Louisiana	Settlement and permanent injunction
09/08/97	Playboy v Calvin Designer Label	US District Court, San Francisco	Preliminary injunction (issued on filing)
? 04/22/98	Playboy v AsiaFocus and Internet Promotions	US District Court, Virginia	$3 million award
? 04/23/98	Playboy v Terri Welles	US District Court, Los Angeles	Denied preliminary injunction; appeal rejected
01/4/99	Terri Welles v Playboy	US District Court, San Diego	

SOURCE: Meta Tag Lawsuits, http://searchenginewatch.com/resources/metasuits.html.

CRIMINAL ACTIVITIES

Electronic banking, particularly when operating from 'bank secrecy' jurisdictions, offers the criminally inclined opportunities to launder illicit funds. There have also been several cases of financial **fraud** by online 'banks' against their customers, as illustrated in table 10.5.

TABLE 10.5	EXAMPLES OF ILLEGAL ACTIVITIES AMONG ONLINE BANKS		
ONLINE BANK	**PROBLEM**	**OUTCOMES**	
Netware International Bank	Netware Bank officers charged with bank fraud, mail fraud and money laundering (1997).	May 1999 — guilty pleas entered in two of the three cases, 5:99 CR6 (US v Bear) and 5:99 CR7 (US v Skeen).	

First Bank of Internet (March 1995) announced it was initiating transaction processing services for Internet electronic commerce.	Not a chartered or lending institution, therefore not a bank. It was a Visa ATM card site used for purchasing products over the Internet.	After warning from government authority, it closed its operations in April 1995.
European Union Bank — started in 1995, collapsed in August 1997	Co-founders allegedly absconded with US$8 million to US$10 million in depositors' funds.	Registered offshore in Antigua and Barbuda Government officials are seeking the bank's co-founders, reportedly two Russian nationals with links to organised **crime**.

SOURCE: US Department of the Treasury Financial Crimes Enforcement Network (FINCEN), A Survey of Electronic Cash, Electronic Banking and Internet Gaming, August 2000, pp. 36–7, www.treasury.gov.

ONLINE BANKING AND TAXATION ISSUES

A major growth market will be found in servicing and securing the global information flows of the mobile rich, who are taking their businesses offshore. It is estimated that 60 per cent of the world's private banking is held in trust in offshore, unsupervised tax havens.[29] Grand Cayman, a tiny tax haven in the Caribbean, has become the fifth largest banking centre in the world, with 500 banks and nearly 3000 registered companies.[30] The Internet is changing so fast that tax officials are becoming frustrated with the time it takes to change existing inflexible tax rules. Bishop (2000) has quoted one vexed taxman as saying, 'They can move millions of dollars at the click of a mouse, and five years later, when we've changed the rules, they've come up with another scheme.'[31]

HACKERS AND CRACKERS

Although most people use the term 'hacker' to refer to anyone who attempts to break into computer systems or networks, for others it simply identifies a clever programmer or engineer with sufficient technical knowledge to understand the weak points in a security system.[30] As discussed in chapter 8, a 'cracker' will also break into someone else's computer system, often on a network, bypass passwords or licences in computer programs, or in other ways intentionally breach computer security. A cracker, however, is more likely to be doing this for profit or out of malice rather than for some perceived altruistic purpose or cause, or simply for the challenge. Hackers are said to deplore cracking. However, as Eric Raymond, compiler of *The New Hacker's Dictionary*, notes, journalists often still ascribe break-ins to 'hackers',[31] and the terms are frequently used interchangeably.

Some frightening statistics are set out below.

- Between 200 and 300 computer network viruses are released every month.
- An Internet-connected computer is broken into every 20 seconds.
- Some malicious registered end users may have the ability to breach e-business environments if they have the ability to reverse-engineer the application.[32]
- In October 2000 Microsoft admitted trade secrets had been stolen directly from its own computer systems over the Internet. The thieves may have had access to Microsoft's corporate network for more than six weeks.[33]
- In February 2000 a large number of e-business sites, including CNN, Yahoo! and eTrade, were shut down or seriously debilitated as a result of a massive denial-of-service attack. In April 2000 a 15-year-old Canadian who used the nickname 'Mafiaboy' was arrested in connection with the February attacks on major web sites.
- The Love Bug, released in May 2000, affected countless networked computers and cost an estimated $10 billion in lost work hours. The virus originated in the Phillipines, but authorities there were unable to bring charges as they did not have the technical expertise to gather sufficient evidence.

COMBATING HACKERS AND CRACKERS

The computing community works tirelessly to improve security, but obviously the problem is not going to go away. As long as there are computer networks there will be people who will try to break into them. Indeed, it could be said that it is a human problem — there will always be those who seek to challenge the system. Below are outlined some of the responses currently in use.

- IBM has assembled a team of highly skilled computer scientists to assess the vulnerability of any Internet environment and report on potential problems and solutions.
- The Computer Emergency Response Team (CERT), organised by Carnegie-Mellon University, may be consulted by organisations that believe their Internet environments have been compromised. Australia has AusCERT, operating out of Queensland University of Technology.
- The Australian Securities and Investment Commission (ASIC) formed the Electronic Enforcement Unit, which relies on automated search tools to keep up with Internet-enabled financial fraud. One case to investigate in Australia is *ASIC v Matthews*. Matthews operated a web site called www.chimes.com.au where reports on shares were posted by him and by third parties. Matthews was not licensed by ASIC as an investment advice business. He maintained he was not 'publishing information' but merely held an 'electronic sandwich board'. An injunction was granted but ignored as further reports were posted to the site. Matthews was held in contempt and given a two-month suspended jail sentence.[36]
- The Users' Security Handbook is found at http://info.internet.isi.edu:80/ in-notes/rfc/files/rfc2504.txt; the Site Security Handbook is found at http://info.internet.isi.edu:80/in-notes/rfc/files/rfc2196.txt.

DOMAIN NAMES

Domain names are administered on a national basis around the world. Any name may be registered as a domain name provided it has not been previously registered by another company or individual.[37] Registration of a domain name is not backed up by legislation and, like the registration of a business or company name (which does, however, have a legislative basis), does not automatically give the registrant the right to use that name as a trade mark. However, the registrant can also register their domain name as a trade mark, providing it meets the requirements of the *Trade Marks Act*.

One aspect of domain names that has prompted legal redress is domain name squatting, whereby individuals have registered famous or significant names in the hope that the owners of the names would be prepared to pay considerable amounts of money to purchase the domain names. While names such as wallstreet.com reportedly have been sold for US$1 million or more[38], court action by well-known companies to protect domain names has been successful where the domain name is in fact a trade mark, and some success has also been had in protecting well-known names where no trade mark existed. Action has succeeded under the legal designation of 'passing off' when the name has been used to induce readers into believing that they are dealing with the real entity. Legal proceedings have also been taken against domain name owners who have registered misspellings of a popular name to catch browsers who mis-type the name they are searching for, as in, for example, www.amazom.com instead of www.amazon.com.

A '.com' can be registered for up to 10 years, but '.com.au' domain names can be registered for only two years. It is important to renew the registration, since there have been several cases of domain names being snapped up by competitors or cybersquatters after the web site owner failed to renew. The Internet Corporation for Assigned Names and Numbers (ICANN), which oversees the domain name system, has recently established an international system for mediating cybersquatting disputes. The arbitration process provides an alternative to the courts for a company that alleges that a holder of a domain name has no legitimate interest in the name. In January 2001 ICANN announced a series of new top-level domain names. The new domains, launched during 2001, are .biz, .info, .name and .pro.

JURISDICTION

Every country has its own network of laws governing most aspects of private and commercial life according to its particular social, political and commercial circumstances. A few legal systems prevail across groups of countries. Australia, together with most English-speaking countries, has inherited the 'common law' system from England. However, although this leads to some general affinities, any dispute may receive a different interpretation and have a different outcome depending on which State of Australia the events occurred in. Laws established at international forums have been adopted by many national governments, but these represent only a small part of each country's legislative base.

There is a large body of law called Conflict of Laws, which is directed towards identifying which jurisdiction's law is to be applied in any dispute — that is, whether a State, national, foreign or international law should apply, and which is the most suitable court (or 'forum') in which the dispute should be heard.

In order for a court to hear a matter with a trans-border dimension, various tests have to be applied to determine the appropriate jurisdiction. A key consideration is that one party to the hearing or the subject matter of the hearing must have some connection with its jurisdiction — for example that a contract was signed within the jurisdiction. However, all manner of complications can occur. The other party may be resident overseas and may decide not to appear to defend the proceedings. In that case, even if the court were to make a judgement in the plaintiff's favour, the court might not be able to enforce the judgement. It is possible to enforce judgements outside Australia in only a limited number of countries (such as the United Kingdom) under reciprocal arrangements.

Alternatively, the aggrieved party may have to take action in the defendant's jurisdiction by commencing new proceedings. The other party may even initiate counter proceedings in a foreign jurisdiction. Further complications arise when evidence required for the hearing is outside the court's jurisdiction and it may not be possible to compel the party to make the evidence available, which would effectively bring the action to a halt.

These sorts of problems occur in conventional commercial transactions. They are increasingly likely to occur also with transactions conducted over the Internet, because much e-trading is conducted outside the existing legislative framework.

 # DEFAMATION

The print and broadcasting media are obliged to monitor their outputs carefully to avoid litigation by individuals or companies protecting their interests. Web site owners and bulletin board participants must also be careful. Consider, for example, the following situation in the United States.

After making allegations on his web site (www.drudgereport.com) concerning a White House aide, Matt Drudge faced a potentially ruinous defamation suit. According to one newspaper article, 'the Internet has turned anyone with a mouth and a modem into a global publisher'.[39] However, it is important to note in this example that Mr Drudge clearly identified himself, and both the parties were resident in the same country, the United States. Therefore United States law could be applied. The situation would have been more complicated had Mr Drudge:

• resided in another country
• posted the information on a web site located in a third country

- used an ISP in a fourth country
- chosen to remain anonymous or used a fictitious name.

All of these would be quite feasible on the Internet, and would make it exceedingly difficult, if not impossible, for the offended party to obtain a legal remedy. An illustration of some of these difficulties is provided by a decision in the 'Macquarie Bank' case in the Supreme Court of NSW.[40]

It is important to note that email transmissions can also give rise to defamation proceedings. Anything written in an email, or included in an email attachment, that is likely to injure the reputation of another person may be defamatory if it is 'published' to a third party. Publication does not need to be intentional but can arise even if you accidentally forward a copy of a defamatory email. Since publication will occur in every jurisdiction in which defamatory email is received, the sender could be the subject of multiple court proceedings!

technical INSITE

JUDGE REFUSES BANK'S PLEA TO CLOSE 'DEFAMATORY SITE'

BY ANNE LAMPE

MACQUARIE Bank has failed in a bid to shut down an Internet site which it claims is defaming it and an executive director Mr Andrew Downe. Justice Caroline Simpson yesterday ruled that Australian courts had no jurisdiction to restrain the publication of material over the Net.

In the process, the case has highlighted the limitation of sovereign laws when dealing with the Internet.

Macquarie last Friday sought an interim injunction seeking to shut down the Website, macquarieontrial.com, which includes material relating to the drawn-out litigation between a former employee of a MB subsidiary, Mr Charles Berg, and the bank.

Mr Berg and a colleague, Mr Michael Bell, are seeking about $30 million in damages from MB for alleged unfair termination of an employment contract.

The case has been bogged down in the NSW Industrial Relations Commission, with Macquarie Bank arguing that Australian courts have no jurisdiction to hear disputes over employment contracts entered between the two men and its Hong Kong subsidiary.

Mr Berg now resides in the US and says he and Mr Bell have spent $300 000 on litigation but have not had their grievances aired in court.

On May 24 material in relation to the litigation began to appear on macquarieontrial.com. MB said the material was defamatory and Justice Simpson agreed.

But, she said: 'Any order made by this court would be enforceable only if the defendant were voluntarily to return to NSW. He cannot be compelled to do so for the purpose of enforcement.'

Justice Simpson added that the most significant factor mitigating against the orders being sought was the nature of the Internet itself.

'It is reasonably plain, I think, that once published on the Internet, material is transmitted anywhere in the world that has an Internet connection. It may be received by anybody, anywhere, having the appropriate facilities.

'Once published, material can be received anywhere, and it does not lie within the competence of the publisher to restrict the reach of the publication.'

(continued)

She added: 'It is not to be assumed that the law of defamation in other countries is coextensive with that of NSW and indeed, one knows that it is not. It may very well be that, according to the law of the Bahamas, Tadjikistan, or Mongolia, the defendant has an unfettered right to publish the material. To make an order interfering with such a right would exceed the proper limits of the use of the injunction power of this court.'

SOURCE: *Sydney Morning Herald*, 3 June 1999, p. 28.

QUESTIONS

1. Have there been any further cases where a defamation action has failed owing to want of jurisdiction?
2. Have any courts in other countries, faced with similar circumstances, reached a different verdict?

ETHICS

Anyone engaging in business activities should pay regard to the obligations imposed on them by legislation and industry codes of practice. However, in the absence of legislation or codes, which as we have seen may often reflect the situation in Internet business, what should be the guiding principles in establishing and operating the business? It is here that ethical considerations play a part. They may be thought of as the moral dimension of business. Most professional bodies have established codes of **ethics** to regulate their dealings with their employer, members of the public or clients to ensure that their respective interests are safeguarded.[41]

Below are listed the 'Ten Commandments of Computer Ethics' posted at www.cpsr.org/program/ethics/cei.html by the Computer Ethics Institute.[43]

1. Thou shalt not use a computer to harm other people.
2. Thou shalt not interfere with other people's computer work.
3. Thou shalt not snoop around in other people's computer files.
4. Thou shalt not use a computer to steal.
5. Thou shalt not use a computer to bear false witness.
6. Thou shalt not copy or use proprietary software for which you have not paid.
7. Thou shalt not use other people's computer resources without authorization or proper compensation.
8. Thou shalt not appropriate other people's intellectual output.
9. Thou shalt think about the social consequences of the program you are writing or the system you are designing.
10. Thou shalt always use a computer in ways that insure consideration and respect for your fellow humans.

If you are proposing to conduct business on the Internet and you are uncertain that what you are proposing is appropriate, you should ask yourselves these questions.[43]

• Are you hiding certain facts because you fear disapproval?
• Are you purposely colouring facts to bias your message?

- If what you were doing was done to you, would you feel upset?
- Could anyone object to your action as unfair?
- Will anyone be harmed by your action?
- Do you feel the need to rationalise your behaviour?
- Could a destructive practice or trend evolve?

If the answer to any of the above questions is yes, then you should reconsider your proposed action.

SUMMARY

There are currently very few legislative controls on the Internet, although efforts are being made in various countries and internationally to draw up a suitable legal model and guidelines.

Current laws and industry self-regulation have some applicability to Internet transactions within the State or nation. Consumer protection laws provide protection against misleading advertising and faulty goods. However, problems arise in trans-border transactions in determining which country's laws apply and which country's courts have jurisdiction. Problems are exacerbated if the parties to a transaction cannot be determined. This is possible owing to the anonymity the Internet can provide, especially through the use of hyperlinks, and the ease of establishing and closing down web sites in a short space of time.

A major challenge is to provide security over Internet communications to prevent fraud. Encryption techniques are being developed to secure monetary transfers and ensure that messages are not corrupted, accidentally or deliberately, by third parties. Hand in hand with the question of security is the question of protecting the privacy of the Internet user, who leaves a 'trail' that can be followed and recorded every time he or she uses the Internet.

Also, there is the question of who controls the content on the Internet. Countries are adopting different approaches to this issue, depending upon their societal and cultural values.

This chapter has reviewed some of the technologies and strategies that are being implemented to help develop customers' trust in Internet commerce. It remains to be seen whether proposed legal remedies can move at Internet speed to assist in such trust-building.

key terms

advertising	ethics	mousetrapping
censorship	fraud	pagejacking
contract	intellectual property	patents
copyright	jurisdiction	privacy
crime	law	trade marks
defamation	legislation	

QUESTIONS

If you were in the process of establishing a commercial web site in Australia:

1. What issues would you address in order to safeguard your operation from any legal disputes?

2. How would you provide users with confidence that transactions conducted with your site would protect their privacy?

3. Would you need to investigate the bona fides of linked site(s) if you provided hypertext links to other web sites? Could you protect yourself from legal disputes arising from users who gained access to the linked site through your own? If so, how?

4. Would your answers be any different if you were establishing your site in (a) Europe or (b) the United States? If so, how?

---

case study | PAGEJACKING AND MOUSETRAPPING: THE REAL COST

By ANTHONY ABRAHAM

Definitions of 'pagejacking' and 'mousetrapping'

These two terms refer to recent techniques used by scammers to divert Internet users from their intended web destination (**'pagejacking'**) to the scammers' site, from which the user is unable to leave using his or her browser's 'back', 'forward' or even 'close' buttons (**'mousetrapping'**).

How do scammers pagejack and mousetrap?

To pagejack, scammers make digital copies of certain web pages, including metatags. Metatags are hidden text in web pages that inform the Internet's search engines about the subject matter of a site and permit the search engines to properly categorise the site. The scammers then insert one change to the copy of the web page by adding a command to 'redirect' any user intending to go to a legitimate site to a pornographic site.

For example, to find an innocent site like 'wedding services', the unsuspecting Internet user would type in 'wedding services' in the appropriate search engine field. The search results would list a number of sites including the copied site, which the user would assume is legitimate. Once the user clicks on the copied site, he or she would be rerouted to the offending site by virtue of the added 'redirect command'.

Once at the offending site, the user would be mousetrapped. The offending site has been programmed to redirect the user to another site. Each time users depress the 'back' button of their browser, they go back to the initial page of the offending site, which then redirects them to another offending page. This creates a loop out of which users will be unable to break using the browser 'back' button.

The scammer is able to program a web page to redirect the user with the use of either JavaScript, a popular Internet programming language, or the insertion of HTTP-EQUIV, a line of coding in the metatags. (*Note:* The 'back' button on Internet Explorer 5 is not vulnerable to this type of programming since it will not record instructions that send the user forward when the 'back' button is depressed. As such, the 'back' button can be used to exit the offending site using Internet Explorer 5.)

How does pagejacking and mousetrapping benefit the scammer?
The scammer can make money pagejacking and mousetrapping by:
- increasing the advertising revenue at his site since the scammer is paid for each new visitor that comes to the site. Each redirection to the site resulting from the user's attempt to leave counts as a new visit, and hence gives more money to the scammer.
- referral fees to other offending sites. Sometimes the redirection is to another pornographic site that pays the scammer for each referred visitor. Furthermore, the other pornographic site owner makes advertising revenue in the same manner described in the preceding paragraph.
- increasing advertising revenue by charging premium advertising rates. Busier sites can command higher advertising rates.
- offering visitors other pornographic material for a price
- using the scheme to inflate the value of the domain names or web addresses of their sites by increasing the numbers of visitors to those addresses. The scammers would then try to auction or sell their sites or the domain names of their sites on the Internet at many multiples of their original cost.

What are the real costs of pagejacking and mousetrapping?
- Users lose time trying to get out of offending sites.
- Users lose a sense of security and control when surfing the Net.
- Children can be exposed to offensive material. One cannot quantify the damage to a child by his or her being subjected to this kind of material at a young age, and their frustration in trying to escape the offending pages.
- Parents lose a sense of security in letting children surf the Net alone.
- The legitimate web site owner loses customers and/or credibility when visitors are redirected to a pornographic site. For business sites, this results in lost customer sales and lost advertising revenue, and reduces the value of the site if the business tries to sell it to another company.
- Search engines can become tools for scammers and become less effective. Without search engines, the ability to find desired web sites becomes a difficult if not impossible task.
- Advertisers pay more than would be otherwise required because of inflated numbers of visits to a site.

What can users do to prevent pagejacking and mousetrapping?
- Disable the JavaScript function of your browser before you surf the Net. This will allow you to exit the scammer site where the type of programming used in the metatags is JavaScript. Certain users will not like this, since many sites use JavaScript to enhance the visual and audio 'feel' of a site.
- Obtain Internet filtering software that filters pornographic and other offending material. This should help in avoiding being redirected to the pornographic site. Ensure that your filtering software is constantly updated.
- If you find yourself at the scammer site, manually enter a new URL (web site address) or choose a new site from your Favourites folder.

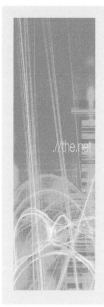

- Talk to your children to prepare them for what they might encounter on the Net and how to handle the situation if they find themselves being pagejacked and mousetrapped.
- Depress the triangle on the 'back' button of both Netscape and Internet Explorer, and choose the second last URL (web address).

Pagejacking and mousetrapping are prohibited under the *Federal Trade Commission Act*, which prohibits unfair or deceptive practices affecting commerce, since these techniques involve the improper diversion of consumers away from web pages they were intending to visit. If you encounter pagejacking or mousetrapping, report it to the Fraud Bureau's Complaint Centre and to the Federal Trade Commission.

SOURCE: Adapted from Consumer Aid Education Center, www.consumeraid.org; www.woodcox.com/pagejacking.htm.

Exercises

1. Investigate other types of scam on the Internet, select one and prepare a report.
2. Debate the following proposition: *Just as commerce is global, law enforcement must be too.*

SUGGESTED READING

Adam, Nabil R. 1999, *Electronic Commerce; Technical, Business and Legal Issues*, Prentice Hall PTR, www.phptr.com.

Lawson, Jerry 1999, *The Complete Internet Handbook for Lawyers*, American Bar Association, New York.

Lessig, Lawrence 1999, *Code and Other Laws of Cyberspace*, Basic Books, New York.

O'Shea, Peter (Ed.) 2000, *E-mail for Business Handbook*, The TMTE Group, Sydney, www.ecommercetoday.com.au/emailhandbook.

Schneier, Bruce 2000, *Secrets and Lies*, John Wiley & Sons, New York.

END NOTES

1. Allen, Mark 1998, 'The Wild West of the Web'. Paper presented at UTS course on electronic commerce on the Internet, by Mark Allen, Partner at Henry Davis York Lawyers, Sydney.
2. May, P. 2000, *The Business of E-Commerce: From Corporate Strategy to Technology*, Cambridge University Press, Cambridge, UK, p. 231.
3. Internet.com's Internet Advertising Report, with contributions from the InternetNews.com staff, News Update, 1 August 2000.
4. Newcomb, S. 2000, 'The Web Link to Liability', *ACS Newsletter*, October 2000, p. 21.
5. For current news on national approaches to this and other Internet issues, see Global Internet Liberty Campaign, www.gilc.org.
6. Internet Content Rating Association, www.icra.org.
7. www.aph.gov.au.
8. Telecommunications Industry Ombudsman, www.tio.com.au.

9. Australian Broadcasting Association, www.aba.gov.au.

10. Internet Industry Association, www.iia.net.au; Electronic Frontiers Australia, www.efa.org.au; Internet Society of Australia, www.isoc-au.org.au.

11. Dearne, K. 2000, 'Censorship law's joke', *The Australian*, 24 October 2000, p. 24, www.australianIT.com.au.

12. Kidman, A. 2000, 'Net censorship: $4,700 a site', Newswire, *Australian Personal Computer*, November 2000, p. 15.

13. American Civil Liberties Union 1998, 'Censorship in a Box, Cyber-Liberties', www.aclu.org/issues/cyber/box.html#blocking.

14. Deitel, H. M., Deitel, P. J. and Nieto, T. R. 2000, *E-business and E-commerce: How to Program*, Prentice Hall, New Jersey, p. 174.

15. American Civil Liberties Union 1998.

16. Deitel, Deitel and Nieto 2000, p. 164.

17. Deitel, Deitel and Nieto 2000, p. 164.

18. Ching, P. 2000, Cookie Monster? *Communiqué*, November 2000, p. 28.

19. European Union Directive on the protection of individuals with regard to the processing of personal data and the free movement of such data, http://europa.eu.int/eur-lex/en/lif/dat/1995/en_395L0046.html.

20. For example, see the UK's *Data Protection Act 1998*, www.hmso.gov.uk/acts/acts1998/19980029.htm.

21. Williams, F. 2000, 'Get back to work', Cyberbludging CorporateIT, *Australian Personal Computer*, November 2000, pp. 116–24.

22. Williams 2000, pp. 116–24.

23. For resources on copyright, see the Australian Copyright Council, www.copyright.org.au.

24. Doug Isenberg (no date), 'Digital Watermarks: New Tools for Copyright Owners and Webmasters', http://www.webreference.com/content/watermarks/tracking.html.

25. For further information, see www.ipaustralia.gov.au.

26. Anonymous, 'Amazon's one-click suit', *Sydney Morning Herald*, 25 October 1999, p. 41; reprinted from the *New York Times*.

27. For further information, see www.ipaustralia.gov.au.

28. See Meta Tag Lawsuits, http://searchenginewatch.com/resources/metasuits.html.

29. Angell, I. 2000, *The New Barbarian Manifesto: How to Survive the Information Age*, Kogan Page, London, p. 88.

30. Angell 2000, p. 90.

31. Bishop 2000, p. 11.

32. Definition from www.whatis.com.

33. www.whatis.com.

34. Fellenstein, C. and Wood, R. 2000, *Exploring E-commerce: Global E-business and E-societies*, Prentice Hall, New Jersey, p. 39.

35. Higgin, D. 2000, 'Secrets safe-ish, say Microsoft, as invaders breach Fortress Gates', *Sydney Morning Herald*, 30 October 2000, p. 3.

36. Allen, Mark 1999, 'Legal Aspects of Electronic Commerce'. Lecture given at UTS in 1999.

37. For rules and policies on registration, see www.internetnamesww.com.au.

38. Anonymous 1999, 'What's in a name? Big bucks', *Sydney Morning Herald*, 24 August, p. 28, reprinted from the *New York Times*.

39. Kurtz, Howard 1997, 'New media, old rules', *Sydney Morning Herald, Icon*, 23 August 1997, p. 14.

40. *Macquarie Bank Limited and Anor v Berg* [1999] NSWSC 526 (2 June 1999), www.austlii.edu.au/do/disp.pl/au/cases/nsw/supreme_ct/1999/526.html.

41. For example, see Australian Computer Society Code of Ethics, www.acs.org.au/national/pospaper/acs131.htm.

42. Computer Ethics Institute, 11 Dupont Circle NW, Suite 900, Washington DC 20036, ph: 202-939-3707, fax: 202-797-7806.

43. Based on Parker, Charles C. 1996, *Understanding Computers Today and Tomorrow*, Dryden Press, p. SOC 2-22.

CHAPTER
11

MANAGING THE TECHNOLOGY OF INTERNET BUSINESS

Learning objectives

You will have mastered the material in this chapter when you can:

- define the role of managers in the solution of Internet business problems
- explain the various component parts of managing technology for Internet business
- explain why businesses must use an integrated solution for management of Internet business technologies
- understand why outsourcing and the use of Application Service Providers (ASPs) are important for the management of Internet business technologies.

'A modern enterprise consists of multiple business units and, in many instances, overlapping business functions: administrative, manufacturing, marketing, support, and so on. To successfully drive e-business, an organization must have a mechanism that enables it to cut across all these functions, taking responsibility for business initiatives spanning different operating units.'

A. Hartman and J. Sifonis (with J. Kandor) 2000, *Internet Ready: Strategies for Success in the E-conomy*, McGraw-Hill, New York, p. 13.

INTRODUCTION

The technologies of Internet business as they are applied in e-commerce and e-business solutions provide an advantage for business and government organisations only when measurable economic or strategic benefits can be created. Developing and understanding a strategy is essentially a managerial rather than a technical function within an organisation, and is one of the most crucial elements in understanding the need to adopt information technology (IT) and web technologies in business.

Management needs to understand the sequence of decisions that have to be made in business to enable the effective integration of all elements of an organisation — operations, accounting, finance, marketing, supply chain and logistics, IT and human resources. Without effective management, any adoption of IT could be as much a risk as a benefit to the organisation. IT does not necessarily solve problems at all. Indeed, it can sometimes create greater problems, if other systems are not changed at the same time. Applying existing systems to an IT environment without change and review would be a disaster, and far more costly than any proposals for the adoption of web technologies.

WEB ADOPTION AND ITS SIGNIFICANCE FOR MANAGING ORGANISATIONS

Following the dramatic rise of the influence of the Internet and the Web as media of business exchange, e-commerce and e-business have become an integral and growing part of many business activities across the world. The competitive importance of IT to organisations is illustrated in figure 11.1. These diagrams illustrate clearly the critical significance of relationship as a fundamental management issue in the world of e-business. A recognition of the importance of competitive advantage emerged out of the need for business to become more strategic. With this evolutionary process has come the responsibility in the new era of e-business to focus on the importance of building customer relationships and improving supply chain management — all relationship- and process-oriented items.

However, with this growth have come changes to the nature of business itself. E-business is not essentially the same as conventional business. It has introduced increased complexity in business organisations. The nature of this complexity for managers and the evolution of the complexity of IT adoption in business organisations is shown in figure 11.2.

The diagram shows the trends that managers have had to deal with over the past four decades. Each era featured changes in the nature, diversity, range and conceptual basis of the technologies. In the late 1990s and into 2000 this complexity increased with the adoption of Internet technologies, **ASP**, and the integration of network technologies based on the Internet in business configurations and management processes.

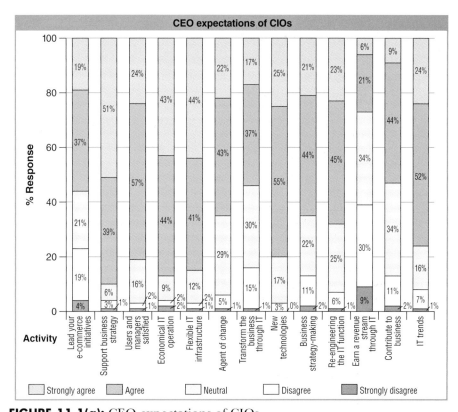

FIGURE 11.1(a): CEO expectations of CIOs

SOURCE: Compass World IT Strategy Census 2000. Reproduced in *CIO*, October 2000, p. 38.

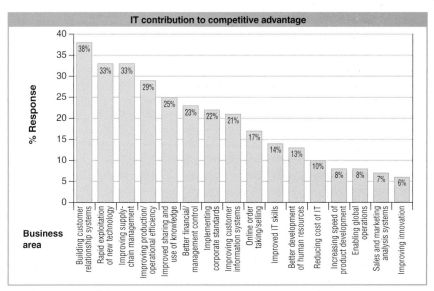

FIGURE 11.1(b): IT contribution to competitive advantage

SOURCE: Compass World IT Strategy Census 2000. Reproduced in *CIO*, October 2000, p. 34.

The following abbreviations appear in a box within the figure:

- **RAID** redundant array of independent disks, for storing the same data in different places
- **CASE** computer-aided software engineering
- **HIPPI** high performance parallel interface

Information technology complexity (vertical axis)

1960s	1970s	1980s	1990s	2000s
Mainframe Magnetic tape master files Batch-oriented systems	Minicomputer Structured programming techniques Hierarchical DBMS Character-based terminals Online transaction processing	Desktop (PC class) Relational DBMS Computer-aided software engineering Artificial intelligence Graphical user interfaces LAN work groups	Desktop (workstation class) Object-oriented DBMS Integrated CASE Heterogeneous networks RAID disk architecture HIPPI interfaces Fibre optic networks Client/server architecture International systems Cooperative distributed processing Parallelism Natural language interfaces Neural networks Scalable hardware architectures	Peer-to-peer network Human-computer interaction

	1960s	1970s	1980s	1990s	2000s
Control	Senior management	MIS management	Department management	Users	Users
Delivery method	Centralised	Departmental	Desktop	Distributed	Distributed
Investment criteria	Labour/capital trade-off	Flexibility through technology gains	Strategic planning	Organisational effectiveness	

FIGURE 11.2: Evolution of information technology

SOURCE: Adapted from R. A. Burgelman, M. A. Maidique and S. C. Wheelwright 1996, *Strategic Management of Technology and Innovation*, 2nd Edition, Irwin, Boston, MA, p. 92.

IT also introduces a new dimension into the management spectrum of organisations. The traditional modes of management are now better supported by the intelligence additions of IT. Initially, Decision Support and Expert Systems were developed to enable better management and decision making in organisations. Today data warehousing has filled that role and managers have access to a greater range of smart tools. Organisations and businesses are now entering an era of the intelligent enterprise. Quinn (1996)[1] argues that manufacturing industries in the late twentieth and early twenty-first centuries accept that investment in intelligence provides more financial and managerial security for business organisations than investment in 'bricks and mortar'. As a result, the following business trends have emerged in creating an 'intelligent organisation' rather than a financially strapped entity trying to maintain traditional business practices. The 'intelligent organisation' features:

- a service- or knowledge-based strategic focus
- a more market-driven strategy
- a recognition that global networks dominate inter-business communications and trading
- an acceptance that networks have created more competition for services and supply of goods as part of the supply chain.

In this era of new business and IT-supported management it is essential that organisations consider all the pathways they have at their disposal to facilitate better management. Management has to ask if the organisation is 'Internet ready'. Traditional management concepts and theories are being challenged as organisations drive into the new e-business era. Hartman and Sifonis[2] argue that management in business organisations needs to think beyond traditional methods and see that e-business is a new model that needs new ways of thinking and new ways of doing business. They suggest that 'net readiness is a combination — unique to each organisation — of four drivers (leadership, governance, competencies and technology) that enables enterprises to deploy high-impact Web-enabled business processes that are focused, accountable, and measurable'.[3] To attain this level of 'Internet readiness', organisations need to establish an e-business architecture that supports business goals (the product of leadership and governance) with sound foundation technologies and staff competencies from the CEO down. 'Internet readiness requires an architectural foundation that encompasses a standards-based, enterprise-wide technology platform, on top of which the organisation can deploy a variety of value-added applications and networks'.[4] This architecture is illustrated in figure 11.3.

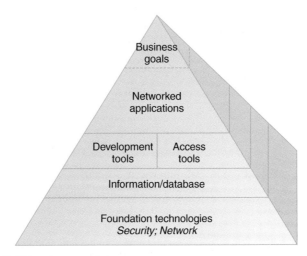

FIGURE 11.3: E-business architecture

SOURCE: Hartman and Sifonis (2000), p. 27.

To enable the building of such technology architectures for e-business, management of all organisations now must consider the significance of the digital future. What support mechanisms are now available? How can they best be used to ensure IT and subsequently e-commerce work for the growth and profitability of the business enterprise? In the new world of e-business, managers have to deal with a new set of forces that optimise the leverage of technology in creating business value. Deregulation of competition throughout the world, deregulation of financial markets coupled with globalisation of communications, organisations, financial markets and international trading, along with digitisation, have created a new set of forces for managers to work with. New technology, especially the Internet, has provided a super-fast realignment of inter-organisational trading relationships, which has created new, more challenging time frames for managerial decision making. Only an understanding of these new frameworks and the creation of a supporting **IT architecture** for e-business will enable the leverage of business value for the organisation seeking to compete to its greatest potential in the twenty-first century. There is a need for the gifted geek in the management of IT-savvy organisations.

Given these fundamental changes, today's business managers must reassess their objectives. What are they trying to achieve in their enterprise? How are they going to adapt to the e-commerce revolution? How will they set objectives that maintain core business and at the same time enable the adoption of current and prospective e-commerce practices? Will their organisation/enterprise succeed in the new era of e-commerce? Weill and Broadbent (1998)[5] argue that managing the IT portfolio in organisations requires executives to address four sets of objectives (see figure 11.4). These issues may equally be applied to the adoption and management of e-commerce in any organisation.

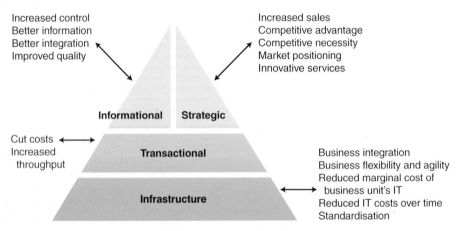

FIGURE 11.4: Management objectives for the IT portfolio

SOURCE: P. Weill and M. Broadbent 1998, *Leveraging the New Infrastructure*, Harvard Business School Press, Boston, MA, p. 26. © 1998 by the President and fellows of Harvard College

Each of these sets of objectives must frame the actions of managers when dealing with the adoption, implementation and continual evaluation of e-commerce as a strategic decision. Weill and Broadbent argue that the higher-order objectives of increased control, better information, better integration and improved quality, together with strategic business positioning, rely on a base of infrastructure management that addresses key management decisions related to the management of the technologies that underpin business operations. Managing the integration of technology, enabling flexibility of technology use and establishing standards are key components in enabling effective IT and e-commerce adoption. It is worth looking initially at the strategic formulation managers need to address to enable the **IT infrastructure** for e-commerce to provide the basis for effective management.

AN E-SAVVY STRATEGY FOR E-COMMERCE

What do e-savvy CEOs need to know to develop and implement sound e-commerce solutions for their business? In a business world challenged by dramatic change, driven by hype about the business benefits of the Internet, seduced by a technology-led stockmarket, how do CEOs used to doing business in a particular way cope? What must they do to make e-commerce work for their business, whether small, medium or large?

Businesses need to plan diligently for e-commerce. They need to be dynamic. They need to learn, grow and change to meet new challenges and do business better. Business is becoming potentially more global. How do we meet that challenge? Strategy focuses the challenges of change. Strategy enables learning and growth. Strategy creates the framework for sustained and profitable growth. Developing a strategic plan is an essential and important process for all business. What are the challenges in making a plan in the age of e-commerce? Let's look at the 3.5.7. approach.[6]

---

3 steps to a better focus

5 strategies to evaluate the potential of the Web

7 tactics to use as a framework for building specific plans

What new focus is needed in e-business? According to the 3.5.7 model, the following three points highlight why most Internet businesses have not yet made millions, but why they should persevere.

- The Internet is not a sales transaction tool — yet. Its acceptance will take time, as did the acceptance of ATMs, for example.
- Communication is where the money is. Business should realise that the potential of e-commerce lies largely in cheap communication costs.
- E-commerce needs new thinking, new strategies and a new approach.

What is the potential of e-commerce? E-commerce can be better served by strategic innovation in the following five areas:

- *communicating with existing customers.* The e-savvy business opens itself to its customers. It invites comments to its web site about quality, customer service and the functionality of products or services. It is also good practice for the e-savvy business to respond to its customers. When it doesn't, as much evidence from the United States suggests, disgruntled customers will set up alternative web sites to advertise the fact!

- *providing service and support.* The e-savvy business will have a simple, well-constructed web site that enables the user to find what they want quickly and that gives them the opportunity to talk to someone directly. The e-savvy business site provides the phone and fax numbers and email address of a person in the company designated to communicate with customers. An option such as enquiries@stupidcompany.co is not enough.
- *communicating with prospects.* The e-savvy business sees growth as a natural extension of the adoption of e-commerce. It seeks to understand how a different medium can be utilised by different suppliers and different customers.
- *augmenting traditional business communication.* The e-savvy business advertises its web site and works with clients and customers to encourage them to use it. It adopts and builds extranets with suppliers and forges stronger strategic alliances with these suppliers. It uses these extranets to make the business relationship more transparent.
- *internal communications.* The e-savvy business adopts intranets to make internal communications transparent. Knowledge is power, and empowering employees with business knowledge and an understanding of what customers want and need can facilitate better business and improved productivity.

Finally, the e-savvy business can profitably adopt seven tactics to make e-commerce work successfully. It can:

- build brand awareness and loyalty
- adopt direct response promotions
- participate in and positively foster education of the marketplace
- enable product demonstration on the Web and ensure effective distribution
- create a positive public and press relations program
- maintain effective research and product development
- ensure that effective and timely service and support are available to all clients, suppliers and customers.

However, such change has to be well led. It is essential, then, that the CEO is also e-savvy. Dramatic change such as the adoption of e-commerce cannot be left to the IT department or the marketing department. It must be an integral and institutionalised part of the whole organisation from the CEO down. What, then, should the e-savvy CEO do?

Seven effective habits for the e-savvy executive are to:

- kill the old systems and think only in terms of the new. E-commerce is not maintaining existing practices and structures and merely putting them on the Internet.
- help people help each other to understand the potential of the Internet for business. CEOs should encourage new ideas and new processes and encourage staff to work in ways that enable them to better understand the potential of e-commerce for their organisation.
- encourage openness by giving all staff access to customer feedback and to plans developed for e-commerce adoption. If staff know what is expected early on and can participate in the development process, there will be increased returns for the business.

- send a regular message to all staff, keeping them up to date with what is happening
- build a knowledge management system that will facilitate effective business communication and management both within the organisation and with clients. Adoption of intranets and extranets must be a key concern of the e-savvy CEO.
- fix the organisational chart and follow the reporting structures to ensure that the CEO is as much a part of e-commerce adoption as any other manager
- institutionalise learning as a key issue in the organisation. An e-savvy CEO will set time limits for staff with a problem before seeking assistance. An e-savvy CEO will encourage staff to inform him or her of any problems. An e-savvy CEO will encourage new ways of thinking and facilitate their adoption as part of business improvement.

So what is new? The relationships with customers, suppliers and intermediaries are now different. The traditional supplier and customer were kept at 'arm's length'. Intermediaries were separate entities, operating in their own business realm. In the new digital age of business the relationships are much closer and the business process far more integrated (see table 11.1).

TABLE 11.1	RELATIONSHIPS WITH CUSTOMERS, SUPPLIERS AND INTERMEDIARIES		
	CUSTOMERS	**SUPPLIERS**	**INTERMEDIARIES**
Traditional	• Some communication with original manufacturer • Mix of voice response, phone access, hard copy information	• Arm's length relationships • Mix of phone, fax, mail and EDI orders, invoices and payments	• Stand-alone entities, separate processes • Mix of manual and real-time information exchange
Digital age	• Direct access to manufacturer • Electronic access to product information, rating and customer service	• Electronic relationships • Electronic payments, orders and invoices • Use extranets	• Extended enterprise links, shared processes • Real-time information exchange

One industry example will illustrate the new integrated world of e-business integration and exchanges.

LIGNUS is a managed electronic business platform for the timber industry that is centred around a secure e-marketplace for the exchange of wood and timber-related products and services. LIGNUS utilises the power and reach of the Internet to facilitate market discovery, eliminating the barriers of time, distance and market knowledge. LIGNUS members communicate, negotiate and conclude the sale and purchase of wood products with other companies either within their own country or internationally. The system allows for the administration of a sophisticated affiliate partner program through which wood industry associations can use the LIGNUS system to augment their support to members and be rewarded based on member performance.

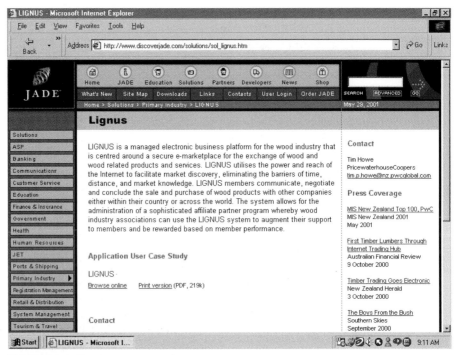

FIGURE 11.5: The LIGNUS home page

SOURCE: www.discoverjade.com/solution/sol-lignus.htm.

MANAGING TECHNOLOGY

E-commerce is not just a web presence for an existing company. It is a new way of thinking, requiring new strategic planning, more openness and better strategic business relationships and strategic partnerships. Above all, e-commerce needs to be well thought out and planned before it is adopted. There are many success stories in the world of e-commerce and many, many failures. Avoiding failure requires effective business modelling and thinking in a new way about your business.

STRATEGY DEVELOPMENT

The primary driving force behind managing technology in any business organisation is the **business strategy** developed to frame decision making and the direction of the business. A strategy can be understood as:

- a plan for the future
- setting a goal and the steps to reach it
- a method of facing competition
- a mission
- a path
- a set of integrated decisions
- a battle plan.

In essence, a strategy is the pattern behind a stream of decisions focusing on a recognised goal.

WHY DO BUSINESSES NEED A STRATEGY?

Below are some of the reasons behind the importance of a business strategy.

- Businesses need to plan.
- Businesses need to be dynamic. They need to learn, grow and change to meet new challenges and do business better.
- Business is becoming potentially more global. How do you meet that challenge?
- Strategy focuses the challenges of change.
- Strategy enables learning and growth.
- Strategy creates the framework for sustained, profitable growth.

This strategy must be applied at three levels within the organisation. It is essential that the core business activity of the company is clearly recognised so that any introduction of e-commerce and the technologies to enable it will focus on that corporate-level strategy. This will enable the business to gain a competitive advantage from adopting e-commerce in the first place by translating the strategies into operation and making them work.

The three levels of strategy within an organisation are:

- *corporate strategy:* a set of explicit or implicit decision rules that determines what business(es) a company will be in and will not be in, and how it will allocate resources among them
- *business strategy:* how a company develops and sustains a competitive advantage within an industry
- *functional strategy:* the set of decisions made in marketing, operations, finance, research and development, and human resources that support the business strategy.

It is essential that all businesses are able to identify and use these three levels of strategy. Without a clear understanding of the focus of the business, without an ability to assess relative competitiveness and without a clear set of applications at the operational end of the business, any attempt at adoption or later management of an e-business strategy would be futile.

In a recent evaluation of e-commerce strategy, Siegel and House (1999)[7] suggest five steps to success, all of them related to management. They are:

- define the vision
- coordinate your internal resources
- establish partnerships
- coordinate your data
- measure the effectiveness.

Another approach focuses on whether the organisation is 'Internet ready'.[8] The Internet ready organisation is driven by four key elements, all of which relate to management and the management of technology. They are *leadership, governance, competencies* and *technology.*

Hartman and Sifonis (2000) argue that a business is more likely to be ready to launch successfully into e-commerce when it is well led by a CEO with a new attitude and perspective, who does not leave the process to the CIO or the IT department. The qualities of a good leader for IT are outlined in figure 11.6.

Net Ready leaders need qualities that enable them to thrive in an environment in which the sheer number of opportunities can overwhelm any strategy and in which the stakes and fast-moving pace of business leave no margin for error.

Traditional CEO	Net Ready CEO
'Do as I say'	'Do as I do'
'Get out of my way'	'Get on my team'
Focused on strategy	Focused on execution
Constrained by money	Constrained by time
Encouraging	Evangelizing
Cautious	Paranoid
Gets to 'yes'	Is able to say 'no'
Concerned with the long term	Concerned with the short run
Has a preference for comfort	Insists on truth
Market driven	Customer driven
Intolerant of ambiguity	Welcomes ambiguity
Sequential	Multitasking
Focused on retention	Focused on recruitment

FIGURE 11.6: Qualities of Net Ready leadership

SOURCE: Hartman and Sifonis (2000), p. 6.

LEADERSHIP ISSUES

A great deal of recent research on the roles of CEOs and CIOs in managing IT, information systems and e-commerce in organisations points to five basic objectives in that process. These are:

• reducing cost
• leveraging investments
• enhancing executive and managerial decision making
• enhancing products and services
• reaching the customer better and making the customer relationships longer lasting.

In attaining these goals, management is able to achieve better organisational effectiveness and control, and as a result has a better chance of staying in business and making money.

The business processes must be well managed and well integrated. The skills and competencies of those in the organisation have to meet the demands of e-commerce, and training from the CEO down becomes absolutely essential. Finally, the technology itself has to be well managed, and it is to that serious issue that this chapter now turns.

MANAGING THE INFRASTRUCTURE (PLANNING AND INSTALLATION OF E-COMMERCE TECHNOLOGIES)

The management of e-technologies in organisations is a multi-component task for managers. The process is not simple, since it relies on managers not only making decisions about the types of hardware and software that need to be used, but also being able to manage the integration of such components. This process is represented in figure 11.7.

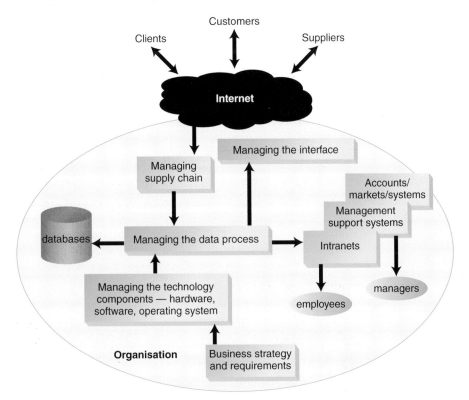

FIGURE 11.7: Multi-component tasks in IT and e-commerce management

Managing technologies for the adoption of e-commerce in a business organisation requires management of each specific component shown in figure 11.7. In the first instance, it requires managers to understand the business strategy and therefore their requirements in adopting e-commerce. Once these are clearly established and understood, the business can then make decisions about the technologies to be used.

MANAGING THE TECHNOLOGY COMPONENTS

The strategy that has been determined by the business will frame all decisions about the components needed to make the technology work for that business. The requirements of the type of e-commerce to be undertaken must drive the decisions about what hardware, software and operating systems the business will choose to use and install. This will mean significant decisions about the size and type of servers, about the type of links that will be needed within the organisation's network, what areas the network needs to cover, the operation of that network, types of routers, location of firewalls, cabling routes and type of cable. In addition, the business has to decide what operating system is most suitable. This is difficult for business managers today, since they have to choose between the more established Unix and NT systems and the emerging Linux systems, for example. These decisions should be guided almost entirely by the requirements of the organisation. Choosing what operating system to use for business to business e-commerce is a different proposition than for an e-shop where the operations involved are less complicated. Purchasing technology components is a major investment for business, so careful evaluation of alternatives must remain an integral part of that process.

MANAGING DATA AND BUSINESS PROCESSES

All e-commerce, including B2B, B2C, C2C and B2G transactions, requires that operational decisions be based on accepted business processes, with access to sound databases. These processes form the second level of management decision making in e-commerce. Business managers require business processes in place to enable the technologies to support their decision making. They must also ensure that the databases will enable the business operations to be grounded on reliable and accurate data. These databases support not only the business processes (buying, selling, invoicing, storage of accounts and so on), but also planning practices that enable forecasting, business planning and the revision of strategy as business fluctuations naturally occur. To maintain this level of technology management within an e-business demands proper management of the databases. This requires that management has made well-considered decisions about database software to be used, and established what that software will do. Can it support the types and frequencies of decisions to be made? Can it be integrated with other decision-making processes in the business? Can the databases support multiple transactions simultaneously? Will the database integrate with the Net interface in a way that enables smooth real-time operations? Will the databases support business data warehousing and any demands for data mining? Will the database support data quality management and auditing?

To enable the most effective use of these databases it is essential that the human resources component of the business has the requisite skills and training. These individuals must also be aware of the accepted standards and practices of the business, which are adopted with the installation of the underlying technologies and operation of specific database software. This requires full integration of the component parts of the systems in operation. Managers must ensure that the system integrates with user PCs, databases, other information services and system administration (see figure 11.8).

E-commerce essentially relies on a distributed system whose components must be integrated in ways that overcome the inefficiencies when decentralised processes are put in place. In the late 1990s large software component manufacturers developed software packages for business organisations which they argued would provide organisation-wide integration of all services. These **enterprise resource planning (ERP)** systems provide managers with management processes and structures that enable the integration of business processes, strategies and operations. Examples of ERP systems include SAP (http://sapinfo.com), PeopleSoft (www.peoplesoftassist.com), Baan (www.baanassist.com), Oracle (www.oracleassist.com), Prologic CIMS (www.procims.com), JBA (http://system21.geac.com) and Pivotpoint (www.pivotpoint.co.uk). An example of how this integration problem was resolved in one business is given in the following technical insite.

FIGURE 11.8: Integration of e-commerce management processes

ONE FOR ALL, ALL FOR ONE: STUDY OF CEREBOS FOODS

BY THOMAS LEE

Does ERP implementation in multiple sites give you the chills? Cerebos Pacific — manufacturer of food products such as instant coffees, gravies, sauces and nutritional drinks — installed a financial solution in four locations.

Yukito Nishitani, its vice president for IT, will tell you the task required massive work and delicate planning. Probe further and it becomes apparent that a rallying cry used by seventeenth-century literary characters still retains its relevance in the modern world of IT today.

Cerebos essentially adopted a 'one for all, all for one' approach in its 1997 implementation of a J. D. Edwards solution for financial, manufacturing and distribution. Nishitani says, 'We have operations in nearly every country in the Asia–Pacific region but we decided, for a start, to concentrate on four locations — Thailand, Singapore, Malaysia and Taiwan — where our main markets are.'

Each of those business units, though of different size, operates in similar ways. The idea was first to build and implement a 'model' system based on a single site. Once implementation had been completed there, implementation would begin on the other sites simultaneously.

Meeting of minds

Recalling the 'all for one' segment, Nishitani says, 'I gathered all the financial and factory managers throughout the region to discuss what a "model" system would be like for our operations throughout the territory. We got together and mapped out the current processes we use and how we can improve on them.'

This step is important because there must be agreement from all territories on what the common processes are. The meeting of minds was good for another reason: 'It was the first time that some of the senior managers from various territories got the chance to meet their counterparts from the other Asian operations of the company,' says Nishitani. One particular manager who has been with the company for five years had told him so. 'There was also a lot of exchange of ideas between managers which I think was very valuable as a whole.

(continued)

'For the finance module, we started with Singapore as the pilot site to implement the model system,' he says. 'Of course, during the implementation we had to put in all the required "local flavour" to meet local requirements.' Completion in Singapore led to the 'one for all' segment. 'After Singapore, we brought the model system to Thailand and Malaysia for implementation at the same time.'

The same methodology was applied to the manufacturing module implementation. 'We started with building up a model system first. We took our Thailand factory as our standard, to develop and implement this. Then later we implemented in the other places,' Nishitani says.

The Thai factory was chosen because it is Cerebos's largest factory in Asia. In terms of customisation, Nishitani says the large staff headcount of the Thai operations meant that the solution had to accommodate a reporting procedure with more management levels. 'We also had to take into account Thailand's Value Added Tax system (VAT) during customisation.'

But regardless of how well thought through the implementation methodology was, obstacles still stood in the way. 'Our biggest problem was the shortage of resources, in particular staff,' says Nishitani.

'The implementing teams consisted of our own managers or assistant managers — all of whom continued to shoulder the day-to-day responsibilities of their normal jobs in their respective countries. That means, of course, that we cannot concentrate 100 per cent on the project,' he says.

Their daily tasks ranged from the closing of monthly accounts at the beginning of each month to the preparation of detailed budgets. 'With all that work being done by the same people, you can imagine it required quite a lot of effort. We sometimes had to work till midnight!'

A clear sign of this task-juggling that regional Cerebos managers had to do: 'They were always on the phone while they were here in Singapore, because they had to periodically call their own local operations to ensure things were proceeding smoothly,' recalls Nishitani.

Mammoth workload

Despite the mammoth workload, however, he isn't complaining. 'We just worked the longer hours.' The reality is that the situation was a fait accompli — something even the hiring of additional staff couldn't have alleviated — because the bulk of the work involved business process re-engineering that only the managers and project team members could have done.

Nishitani kept managers motivated throughout by ensuring they got a week's break from the implementation every fortnight. During this period, they would usually return to their base operations to do normal work, and more importantly, see their families. 'Everyone would then fly back to meet together again after one week,' he explains.

In sharp contrast to the frenzied pace of implementation work, however, was the vendor selection and evaluation phase of the ERP project. Nishitani says, 'We took quite a long time for this.' The project started in late 1994 when Cerebos contacted a few likely vendors. Evaluations took place in early 1996. 'Then we decided on JDE in August 1996.' It was, in all, almost two years before the project got off the ground.

Momentum

Nishitani advises against this procrastination because it affects the project's overall momentum. 'Making things happen fast is important. For instance, when you are selecting the product or vendor, do not take too much time. Start the project fast. Our project started in 1994 with discussions on how to go about it. We invited many vendors to demonstrate their products but nothing happened.'

To other IT managers about to embark on similar projects, he says, 'You need to discuss concrete examples. Otherwise, if you just discuss a product — what it can do and what it provides — it can only be general comments. You must get down to it. Even if you make the wrong decision, starting is more important than just waiting for everything to happen because if you implement something, you will then know what progress you need to make.' His logic is that mistakes can be corrected, whereas no work means there is no forward progression — only status quo. 'It just remains as talk.'

Key components

The factors that helped JDE clinch the deal over two other close rival bids, according to Nishitani, were numerous. First and foremost was the region-wide support issue. Cerebos wanted a solution it could roll out in several Asian countries with assurance of local support.

'The other concern was flexibility of the system because business dynamics change very quickly. Our business was growing very quickly at that time together with the strong Asian economies, so our requirements of the system would be changing very fast too,' he says.

'During that time we configured the system based on our operations running three shifts, 24 hours a day. Now, with the crisis, it's two shifts, or 18 hours.'

In final evaluations, Nishitani reveals that it boiled down to the vendor meeting requirements such as 'quality of consultants, functionality of the solution and some specific user needs'. Elaborating, he says, 'It emerged that the knowledge of JDE consultants was most suitable. They also had the better system. The other two were not so strong.'

He also points out: 'Ours is process, rather than assembly, manufacturing. JDE systems, though not quite purpose-built for process, are flexible enough for our use.' Process manufacturing is when the final product is derived via synthesisation. Assembly manufacturing refers to 'piecing together' a product. 'The other offered solutions would have required a lot of modification and special setting-up,' explains Nishitani.

Consequently, even though the JDE solution was the most expensive offering of the lot, Cerebos went ahead with the almost S$5 million deal. 'Their price was about 10 to 20 per cent higher compared to other packages. But I think it is still value for money. The important thing is that the system meets our requirements,' says Nishitani.

Knowing the limits

As for consultants, he believes those who know their limits are better than unthinking 'yes men'. 'The JDE consultants, if they couldn't do something, would admit so. They would tell us to consider alternative strategies. This attitude is good. I have met many other consultants who will tell you "everything is possible" and "we have a solution". Even when they cannot do it, they will say they can.'

Two months ago, the Singapore Stock Exchange–listed Cerebos completed installation of the manufacturing solution in Taiwan, marking the end of the whole implementation project. It took, in all, two and a half years for four countries. Nishitani says Cerebos wants to roll out the same or similar systems to all its other offices and operations in Asia.

'We still have so many things to do. Our next target territories are China and Indonesia. An evaluation of our China operations will be completed shortly and we will decide on implementation there.'

But the company's IT plans don't end with an ERP solution. 'Our next step will be a higher level IT system for executives. ERPs are more for day-to-day operations and transactions. Top-level decision-makers, however, need an Executive Information System to provide details on things like sales performance.'

(continued)

Such a system would enable Cerebos to compare sales figures by product and by territory; and also to analyse products in profit-and-loss terms — 'and to do that at great speed', says Nishitani.

He adds: 'We are already looking at the various vendors offering such solutions, like data warehousing systems, for example. We will establish them in the next few years.'

SOURCE: *MIS Australia*, June 1999, Vol. 8, Issue 5, pp. 59–62.

QUESTIONS

1. What does Cerebos manufacture?
2. Is this a form of dispersed manufacturing?
3. How did Cerebos implement its ERP?
4. What management impact has there been with the adoption of the JDE system?
5. Has the adoption been successful? Why?
6. How is this ERP adoption an example of integration?

WAP

It is important that these business processes are adaptable to the latest technologies and business applications of technology. In the new millennium the benefits of wireless application protocol (WAP) technology is becoming more apparent. This protocol is the de facto world standard for the presentation and delivery of wireless information and telephony services on mobile phones and other wireless terminals. The technology details and standards for WAP are elaborated in the WAP White Paper, which can be found at the WAP Forum web site (www.wapforum.org). This type of technology enables managers to operate from any geographic location. There will be no need for a formal office. All organisational communication can be carried out in real time through mobile phones for messaging, graphic display, email and telephony. Business can be managed from any location.

MANAGING THE BUSINESS INTERFACE

Business and technology must coexist in e-commerce. The links between decision making by managers and CEOs and their use of technology must be enabling, not constraining. Technology must be seen as the servant, not the driver, of business and there must be clearly understood pathways for business to be improved through the employment of technology. One of the key elements in managing this business interface lies in managing the supply chains that support business operations, especially in a B2B e-commerce environment.

SUPPLY CHAIN MANAGEMENT

Supply chains provide the essential business links between businesses and the goods and services they need in order to operate. Businesses need component parts, services, information and sometimes raw materials to facilitate their core business. They also need other sorts of supplies, such as office equipment, photocopiers and printers, that are not a core part of the business but nonetheless support the core business. All organisations set up supply chains to manage the ordering and delivery of both sets of products and services. In the modern company, ERP systems are used to manage the selection and operation of these goods and services. Such ERP systems create an integrated management system, which makes decision-makers more effective. Databases attached to the ERP system enable quick retrieval of information and better management of the ordering process and inventories of preferred suppliers. The Honda Motor Company in Japan have a managed, automated supply chain linked to a designated group of suppliers to whom they are committed at an established price and level of quality. They do this to ensure continual supply, stable prices and the maintenance of quality. General Motors in the US, however, have not adopted a similarly stable supply chain. They prefer their suppliers to be more competitive, and are willing to change suppliers if prices and quality control can be maintained.

New solutions to the management of the business interface are becoming better established. **Outsourcing** of management and business functions has been an accepted part of business for some time. However, the outsourcing of applications and computing services is a more recent phenomenon and one that is becoming more and more common.

DEVELOPING MORE INTEGRATED SOLUTIONS

In implementing IT and web technologies, managers have to be able to deal with the complex impacts that result. This requires substantial attention on how all of the functionalities in the business organisation can be integrated.

OUTSOURCING AND ASPs

One innovation available to businesses seeking to better manage their technology is the application service provider (ASP), through which they can outsource all their technology management and operations. The ASP provides all of the functionality required within the organisation for business processes and technology management. IT is somewhat similar to 'thin client' computing, but the supply of software and applications, and managing those processes, may be outsourced rather than managed from within the business organisation. However, such an approach means a clear change in direction and management style. New trust relationships with the outsourcing organisation would have to be established, along with new ways of thinking about the use of technology. (We alluded to these new ways of thinking and approaches to leadership earlier in the chapter.)

An example of a recently established company that provides managerial services for technology management is JADE Direct. This organisation enables hospitals and businesses to meet their needs in managing information systems and the technologies that support them. This web-based function provides the opportunity for businesses to address other business issues, such as costs, without having to deal with the problem directly. This has the added advantage that new technology changes can be utilised more effectively given the limited infrastructure investments needed by the business. The ASP becomes both the provider and the enabler. Below are the main advantages of an ASP.

- All files are stored in a secure facility.
- No more file backups should go wrong.

- Only a minimum specification PC and Internet connection are required.
- Printing is simple and may be done at your local PC.

JADE Direct's services can be viewed at their web site (figure 11.9).

FIGURE 11.9: The JADE Direct web site (www.discoverjade.com)

Johnson and Johnson resolved their 'management challenge' by using outsourcing. The Johnson and Johnson story appears in the following technical insite.

technical INSITE

CUT RATE CALLS

BY MANDY BRYAN

Johnson and Johnson has simplified its telecommunication accounts and cut costs through outsourcing.

Deregulation of Australia's telecommunications market might give IT managers more providers to choose from, but for some, such as Johnson & Johnson's Paul Yaortis, there has been a downside. Rather than dealing with a single supplier, Yaortis found himself managing 200-odd accounts with several providers.

Other pressures further rendered inhouse telecommunications administration an uphill battle — demand for greater bandwidth from the business, increased mission criticality of linkages, the challenge of recruiting and retaining specialist staff and the ever-present pressure to shrink costs, he says.

The health and beauty products manufacturer has for the last three years — along with its affiliate, Johnson & Johnson Medical — outsourced the billing administration headache. More recently, though, it extended its outsourcing contract to include telecommunications facilities management.

More with less

Among the first to move to this type of niche service, Yaortis feels it helps IT help the business units to do more with less. 'It is becoming more and more apparent that IT is becoming the underlying foundation of all these disciplines,' he says. 'As we move to more Web-enabled tools of business, telecommunications becomes more and more critical to our business.'

To date, the manufacturer has an intercontinental backbone for its Lotus Notes application, intranet access, and e-mail service that links Johnson & Johnson globally. Hong Kong, Japanese and Chinese affiliates are soon to start accessing its newly implemented SAP ERP via a second 128Kb link to its Botany-based servers in Australia.

As it ramps-up tools enabling business change and efficiency, the IT department is under the very same business pressure to contain its costs — thus the decision to extend the outsourcing deal that it had formed in 1996 with telecommunications reseller and services company Macquarie Corporate.

Deregulation

Three years ago, at the advent of deregulation, the vendor took ownership of the 200 lines and services that the individual carriers were formerly providing the manufacturer, consolidating these down to one monthly bill complete with pre-prepared and customised analysis.

'We have in excess of 200 different kinds of accounts and invoices coming through on a monthly basis and to process that by a single person assigned to telecommunications within Johnson & Johnson would have been a nightmare,' he says. It also gives him a snapshot view of company telecommunication activities rather than trying to analyse all that himself.

On the downside, it did take an unexpectedly long time for those billings to actually go across to Macquarie, he says. 'We had to look after Macquarie, look after Optus and look after Telstra and it was a juggling act trying to maintain all these billings. It took five months before we could say, "OK we have nothing to do with Telstra or Optus".'

As one of the first to take on a service like this, problems with the carriers' old churn processes (movement between suppliers) was a major contributor, says Yaortis.

Regardless, by 1997 Johnson & Johnson Medical also saw the benefits the service offered the Botany operations and climbed aboard.

When the lone communications staffer at the Botany plant left last year, Yaortis was very open to the opportunity to also offload its internal voice communications facilities, allowing it to do away with day-to-day management of its PABX mobile fleet, voice mail, 1800 and 1300 numbers, new lines, number changes and procurement.

More for less

For an annual telecommunications spend of around $600 000, Johnson & Johnson's Botany plant gets consolidated telecommunications services with account management services and facilities management services thrown in as a value-add. The vendor, Yaortis notes, gets its cut from the carriers by reselling services it has bought at a wholesale rate.

The service therefore saves the company an estimated 20 per cent on inhouse administration costs as the outsourced services do away with two staff positions, one to administer the 200 telecommunications accounts and another dedicated to facilities management.

(continued)

Aside from the cost benefits, access to a range of expertise makes navigating the maze of protocols, standards and regulations a less hazardous process. 'They become our eyes and ears of the industry, we have monthly meetings with account management and we hope that they bring the latest innovations and standards that the different communications carriers are offering in terms of services,' he says.

Yaortis laments that he would like to take more advantage of the technical aspects of consultancy that the outsourcer offers. Itching to redesign the whole typology of its WAN to form a virtual private network, Yaortis admits he is wheel-clamped by corporate policy. 'I have one arm tied behind my back because the corporate dictates these kinds of innovative options.

'We did a pilot from Botany to the New Zealand office of voice-over-frame and that proved successful but we got gazumped on it. We could not move with it because the corporate directive was no voice-over-frame. That's the global village.'

And when the cutting edge projects aren't there, highly skilled telecommunications staff are even harder to recruit and retain. Yaortis also believes it is getting harder to find one person who specialises in all critical areas and the scale of Johnson & Johnson's voice facilities doesn't merit a team. Outsourcing this function therefore enables the 12-strong IT team to 'grab bits and pieces of expertise'.

In this deal, Johnson & Johnson can identify the area in which it wants expertise and the outsourcer mixes and matches staff according to the need. Currently, one outsourcer works onsite two days a week.

Johnson & Johnson keeps an internal LAN/WAN administrator to look after its routers and switches and hubs and desktops, file servers, data management and storage are all manned by the inhouse team.

The only disadvantage with the outsourcing model Yaortis has identified so far is not having access to a full-time staff member to deal with unforeseen events. 'If we can't wait for them to come in next time, we have to take care of it in some other way,' he says. In an emergency, though, resources can be sourced through the outsourcer.

Regardless, Yaortis is certain that under no circumstances will Johnson & Johnson bring these functions back inhouse.

SOURCE: *MIS Australia*, June 1999, Vol. 8, Issue 5, pp. 51–2.

QUESTIONS

1. What was the 'management challenge' in Johnson and Johnson that created the need for outsourcing?
2. What did Johnson and Johnson decide to outsource? Why?
3. What has been the impact of the outsourcing process on costs?
4. Has this been an effective management decision? Why?

EMERGING TRENDS IN MANAGING INTERNET COMMERCE TECHNOLOGIES

What, then, are the emerging trends that will impact on managing e-technologies in the new century? The main ones are outlined below.

• The extended enterprise concept of electronically networking customers, suppliers and partners is now a reality, is worldwide and is growing at a rapid rate.

- The Internet is forcing companies to transform themselves by rethinking their business strategies, organisational structure and processes, and their business models.
- New channels are changing market access, branding and market structures — in short, the entire customer experience — and causing disintermediation in traditional channels.
- Businesses can now build real-time, intimate relationships with their customers, often cutting out 'middlemen' — improving service, strengthening customer relationships and reducing costs at the same time.
- The balance of power in the business relationship is shifting to the customer.
- With the unlimited access to information afforded by the Internet, customers are becoming much more demanding than their non-wired predecessors. Customers are challenging businesses to supply almost everything on the Web, from cars to fruit and vegetables. Greengrocer.com.au (see figure 11.10) in Australia was established to meet demand for the latter and has flourished since. The Ford Motor Company has taken on the challenge of Internet commerce and provides a safe and well-managed environment in which to get information about cars, and has established a new way of buying them, directly from Ford (see figure 11.11).

Many universities support research centres to assist businesses in coming to grips with the strategic role of information systems technology to achieve and maintain competitive advantage. One example is at Brunel University in the United Kingdom (www.brunel.ac.uk/cs/research/csis).

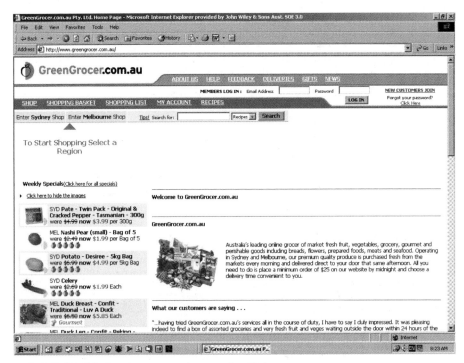

FIGURE 11.10: Buying groceries on the Web

SOURCE: Reproduced courtesy of GreenGrocer.com.au.

FIGURE 11.11: Buying a car on the Web

SOURCE: www.ford.co.uk.

- *True customer loyalty is much harder to build.* Access to the Internet has meant loyalty is maintained for as long as access to information remains unchanged. (i.e. not very long). Customer service becomes a critical element in maintaining loyalty in the new era of digital business. This must be carefully managed.
- *The face of competition is changing fundamentally.* The Internet has pushed business, initially anyway, towards a more perfectly competitive market. There are now large numbers of buyers and sellers, offering the best possible competition for all goods and services. New small companies emerge daily and present challenges to existing suppliers. Innovative e-businesses are creating new markets and expanding the domains of business not only locally but internationally.
- *The pace of business is accelerating to warp speed.* Customers expect delivery on time even from across the globe. Managing a new e-business must reflect the adoption of new integrated **supply chain management** systems and create effective outlets for delivery of products or services.
- *Planning horizons, information needs and the expectations of customers and suppliers are now reflecting 'Internet time'.* Business now faces the challenge of the 24-hour, seven-day every day trading regime. Locking the office at 5 p.m. in the afternoon is no longer a reality in the digital world where customers may be both local and international.
- *The Internet is pushing enterprises past their traditional boundaries.* Old businesses are doing new business in new ways.
- *Traditional enterprise boundaries between companies and their suppliers are a thing of the past*, as are internal boundaries separating processes, functions and

business units. The development of exchanges and aggregators is integrating e-business into the world of business within new business models and in new business associations.

- *Knowledge is becoming a key asset and source of competitive advantage.* Knowledge is the foundation of e-business. The old forces of labour, land and capital are now both dominated by and framed by knowledge and time.
- *No longer can corporations account for intellectual capital as merely 'goodwill'.* We are rapidly becoming a knowledge-based global economy. Accounting procedures are beginning to revise the measures of knowledge and incorporate them into the assets of organisations.
- *The Internet represents a seismic shift in how companies structure their operations, share knowledge, empower employees and get things done.* Change is now both rapid and fundamental. Incremental change is no longer an option.
- *It is not a matter of seeing what an enterprise can do on the Web, rather of how the Web can be used to improve business processes.* All business can be done in an innovative way, adapted to the Internet and the new ways of doing business.

The importance and impact of these trends will be discussed more fully in the final chapter on future trends. However, their application in modern business practice is illustrated in the analysis of examples that have emerged from the successful adoption of e-commerce and e-business in the Republic of Ireland, where there has been a concerted national and business strategic focus on making best use of new technologies in business. The web sites illustrated below and overleaf are exemplars of best practice and strategy in adopting and then managing e-business across a wide variety of business types and sizes. This is clearly illustrated in the case studies available on the Enterprise-Ireland web site (figures 11.12 and 11.13).

FIGURE 11.12: Enterprise-Ireland.com (1)

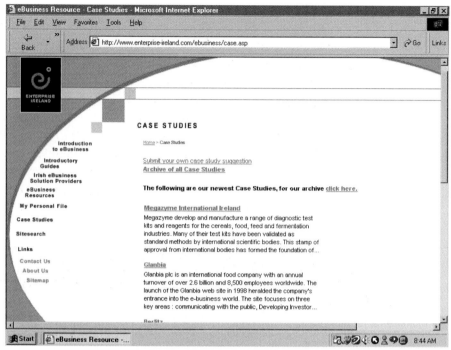

FIGURE 11.13: Enterprise-Ireland.com (2)

SUMMARY

This chapter has argued that making e-commerce work for business improvement and growth relies on effective management. It is imperative that **IT management** be based on a clear understanding of the architecture developed and implemented to drive the e-commerce solutions proposed, and that this architecture be based on sound practices derived from lessons learned from IT management. To this end, organisations have the opportunity either to choose to manage the IT function of an e-business from within the organisation, or to develop it by outsourcing to an application service provider, thereby gaining access to more cash reserves and improving the efficiency of the IT function driving and supporting their business. This approach can be supplemented by using integrated software packages such as ERPs to support supply chain efficiency and ensure the business runs effectively from the initial production process to the delivery and service of the product or service to the customer.

key terms

application service provider (ASP)	enterprise resource planning (ERP)	IT management
business strategy	IT architecture and infrastructure	outsourcing
		supply chain management (SCM)

QUESTIONS

1. Why is the business component in e-commerce more significant than the technology it uses?

2. How can any business effectively manage the complexities of technology and yet ensure it is well integrated within the business?

3. Read Hartman and Sifonis (2000), chapters 3 and 9. Why do the authors suggest that a company like Cisco (www.cisco.com) or Fruit of the Loom (www.fruit-of-the-loom.com) can be so successful at e-commerce?

4. What impact do you think WAP technologies will have on managing technology for e-commerce (see www.wapforum.com)?

5. What do the proponents of the XML format claim will be its advantage for managing technology integration in business (www.w3.org/XML and www.oasis-open.org/cover)?

---

case study

TAKING FLIGHT — THE QANTAS EXPERIENCE

By BRAD HOWARTH

Qantas passengers will enjoy a smoother journey thanks to a unique team approach used to create its new network.

One of the dangers of being a pioneer in adopting new technology is choosing a path that the rest of industry fails to follow. The airline industry fell into this trap when it began developing its wide area networks in the mid-1960s.

In their rush to implement global reservation and departure control systems, airlines built networks based on customised and proprietary standards that were eventually superseded by the mass adoption of standardised TCP/IP networks.

Now, $250 million later, Qantas has joined the modern connected world, thanks to a global network rollout in conjunction with Telstra and the telecommunications provider SITA.

Qantas's executive general manager for corporate services, David Burden, says the payoff for the airline of its new network, dubbed QIPNet (Qantas Internet Protocol Network), will come through greater reliability and a range of new applications.

The new TCP/IP-based network connects more than 1200 workstations in 56 locations around 30 countries. It replaces a proprietary system that was the backbone for everything from weather reports and flight planning to maintenance procedures.

Burden says the old system created some unusual problems for Qantas. 'If you only have six bits per character, you don't have enough different characters to handle things like upper and lower case, accents and all the rest of it. To this day, when you look at a boarding pass, you'll notice that all the text is printed in upper case.'

Merging expensive networks

The idea for a revamped system presented itself in the early 1990s when Qantas merged with domestic carrier Australian Airlines. There was an

immediate need to link the airlines' networks, which Burden describes as two of the most complicated telecommunications networks in Australia.

'The fundamentals of the two networks were different — Qantas had gone with a router network, while Australian Airlines had a bridged network,' Burden explains. 'So by the early 1990s we had an incredibly complex network infrastructure, and a very expensive one to operate because we were buying a lot of point-to-point telecommunication lines.'

Mounting costs, problems with network outages and the sheer limitations of the networks' capacity led Qantas to start looking for alternatives. Market momentum around TCP/IP dictated it was the most logical foundation for a new network.

'In 1995–96 we looked at what was the right way forward, and we came to the conclusion that it wasn't going to be feasible to modify the existing network to absorb TCP/IP and use the new technologies,' says Burden. 'The only solution was to move to a brand new network. We wanted to move to TCP/IP, but we also wanted to use much better transport mechanisms like asynchronous transfer mode and frame relay. We wanted to take advantage of faster bandwidth and we wanted to get out of the legacy protocols and a lot of the legacy hardware.'

'We also realised that we didn't want to keep doing what we had done previously — design a network, buy a bunch of equipment, and then operate the thing,' he adds.

It would have cost several hundred million dollars in upfront purchase costs for the hardware alone, before implementation and running costs, and there was no guarantee that the network wouldn't be superseded within a few years. A decision was taken to go with a network service provider.

Business priorities

In late 1997 Qantas created a technical specification that focused on business needs and asked for proposals from all suppliers with expertise in this area.

'The key requirement was to try to define it in business terms,' says Burden. 'We tried to construct a description of various levels of network service, in terms of what was relevant to the business units — conditions such as what level of reliability and what length of response time were necessary.'

The units were presented with the costings and asked to justify their requests. 'For our most important sites, like the major airports and the major reservation offices, we've gone for the top level of performance. For some of the smaller, outlying stations we've gone for lower levels.'

The request for information identified three suitable candidates, who were issued with a formal request for a proposal. In January 1998 two suppliers were chosen, Telstra for the domestic network, and telecommunications provider SITA for the international network.

Burden says the two were selected on price and on the quality of their physical infrastructure, including reliability and redundancy. The SITA contract will see it continue to manage Qantas's global networking infrastructure for six years at a cost of $90 million. A similar $150 million contract was won by Telstra.

Building the team

Rather than operate the project as a regular client/supplier relationship, Qantas opted to bring its staff together with those from Telstra and SITA as a single team located together under program director Paul Payne. At its peak, the project team numbered around 200 staff from the three companies.

'The design was done jointly between our team, Telstra and SITA. A lot of it involved carrying this on the other two companies' backbone infrastructure, but a lot of it also involved peculiarities concerning our legacy protocols and the linkages to some of our internal and external organisations.'

Burden says the management experiment worked beautifully. 'There was a single project office that was responsible for all of the critical path and analysis of task completion, and they really ran it as a single project team. In about three months the whole mindset of the project shifted away from being supplier/customer to being a team of people working together to produce something that would serve the flying public.

'To get that level of mutual respect and to get everyone to socialise and feel that they were part of one project team was a major achievement on the part of the program director,' he says.

With the decisions on networking partners made, the project team began the task of establishing the connections to Qantas's various business operations. This took 18 months and involved linkages to 400 communication rooms and 600 sites around the world, and virtually rewiring Qantas's entire infrastructure.

Cutover to the new network started in December 1999. Burden says that while everyone on the new network is happy with its performance, simply having a new network doesn't mean that the applications themselves are any different, as many continue to use the old protocols.

'In some cases it was piggybacked on the new network,' says Burden. 'And as long as that exists there will be intrinsic problems. But apart from a few issues, the basic network has run very well; it's fast, and much more reliable than what we'd had.'

Documenting change

After just six months of operation, the return on investment in the network is above the original predictions of 25 per cent.

'I'm very pleased,' Burden says. 'It was a huge infrastructure project, and it cost a lot of money, even with the rates of return, but going in and fixing the plumbing is not viewed as exciting.'

A further benefit has been a higher level of quality documentation on the network itself. Burden says the old infrastructure had simply been allowed to grow as and when necessary. People would solve a particular problem and move on.

'We've implemented some strict documentation processes, so any change to any part of the network requires documentation, and we often photograph the work. So whenever a change is made to a communications room anywhere in the world, one of the required steps is a before and after digital photo,' he explains.

'Like most large companies, our networks have a horrible habit of growing in a way that is not properly documented.'

Burden says poor documentation combined with the sheer technical complexity of the old network probably produced the greatest number of issues for the project team.

'With the hundreds of communication rooms located around the world and the topological complexity of the network, we had around 35 000 network devices connected,' Burden says.

'With any merger you inherit different administrative systems, and the record keeping is never good. We kept finding new communication rooms and new devices that had to be connected, or new external services that had to be linked up.'

Managing risk

Moving entirely to the new infrastructure will also increase the reliability of the network. Burden cites a recent power blackout in the Sydney CBD as an example of a situation that would have crippled the old network. He says the new network continued functioning without interruption.

'Over the past five years we, like all of our colleagues in the business, have become far more dependent on IT systems. Five years ago it was quite acceptable to operate with one per cent downtime. Today, anything less than 100 per cent availability is unacceptable,' he says.

'The more you use the technology to make things convenient and fast for the customer, the more dependent you become on the technology actually working. And it's got to work 100 per cent. This was one element of a concerted strategy to create an environment that is 100 per cent reliable for Qantas's IT infrastructure.'

Burden says customers should expect to see a much lower probability of service outages in a reservation office or an airport. 'It is difficult to imagine circumstances under which we would lose all communications into a place,' Burden says.

By far the greatest benefit for customers will be through the new broadband applications that Qantas will be able to support on its network. He says the most important task now is to migrate as many of the legacy applications as possible onto modern technologies, while also starting to implement the next generation applications that take advantage of multimedia.

Customer benefits

'Instead of being limited to very low volume, green screen transactions, we can move images around, we can give people Internet access, and we can have them using far more sophisticated mail systems and corporate applications,' says Burden.

'Eventually, we'll be able to provide very sophisticated applications at check-in points. In the future, we could be able to show our customers a picture of the interior of the aeroplane so they could choose their seat. We are using it in the maintenance and engineering areas, where we can move digital images of components and data on diagnostics.

'There are so many exciting things that can be done with Web-based applications that we just couldn't do under the old protocols. We're beginning to see a great deal of creativity, because until now Qantas staff were limited by what the networks were able to perform.'

Burden explains that the new network has also delivered some productivity improvements through faster operation of booking terminals, leading to faster check-in and reduced response time for phone queries. 'Those things are relatively small individually, but big in aggregate,' Burden says.

As the top 20 global airlines tended to grow and develop at roughly the same pace, most have found themselves dealing with the same problems that have made Qantas's network upgrade necessary. Burden believes Qantas is one of the first to take on such a dramatic overhaul. British Airways has just completed a similar project, while American is going through that process now.

'Of course, both of those companies have much larger networks than even we do, but I think what we've implemented is as good as what anyone has anywhere else in the world,' Burden says.

SOURCE: *MIS*, November 2000, pp. 42–4.

Questions

1. Why was the move from the use of wide area technology to web-based integrated systems developed by SITA and Telstra strategically important for Qantas?

2. What benefits for Qantas customers were expected from the adoption of this new technology?

3. What is QIPNet?

4. What processes did Qantas use to integrate and manage their systems with the new technology?

5. How did they deal with the risks involved?

SUGGESTED READING

Aldridge, M. D. and Swamidass, P. M. (Eds) 1996, *Cross-Functional Management of Technology: Cases and Readings*, Irwin, Boston, MA.

Burgelman, R. A., Maidique, M. A. and Wheelwright, S. C. 1996, *Strategic Management of Technology and Innovation*, 2nd Edition, Irwin, Boston, MA.

Downes, L. and Mui, C. 1998, *Unleashing the Killer App: Digital Strategies for Market Dominance*, Harvard Business School Press, Boston, MA.

Hartman, A. and Sifonis, J. (with Kandor, J.) 2000, *Internet Ready: Strategies for Success in the E-conomy*, McGraw-Hill, New York.

Loveridge, R. and Pitt, M. (Eds) 1992, *The Strategic Management of Technological Innovation*, John Wiley & Sons, Chichester, UK.

Siebel, T. and House, P. 1999, *Cyber Rules: Strategies for Excelling at E-business*, Currency/Doubleday, New York.

Siegel, D. and House P. 1999, *Futurize Your Enterprise: Business Strategy in the Age of the E-Customer*, John Wiley & Sons, New York.

Weill, P. and Broadbent, M. 1998, *Leveraging the New Infrastructure*, Harvard Business School Press, Boston, MA.

END NOTES

1. Quinn, J. B. 1996, 'The Intelligent Enterprise', in Irwin, R. D., *Cross-Functional Management of Technology: Cases and Readings*, Times Mirror Books, USA, pp. 118–31.

2. Hartman and Sifonis 2000.

3. Hartman and Sifonis 2000, p. 3.

4. Hartman and Sifonis 2000, p. 27.

5. Weill and Broadbent 1998.

6. Adapted from Lawrence et al. 1998, *Internet Commerce: Digital Models for Business*, 1st Edition, John Wiley & Sons, Brisbane.

7. Siegel and House 1999, p. 228.

8. Hartman and Sifonis 2000, pp. 3–34.

CHAPTER 12

THE FUTURE OF E-COMMERCE TECHNOLOGIES

Learning objectives

You will have mastered the material in this chapter when you can:

- identify some new technology trends in e-business
- understand the terms *pervasive* and *ubiquitous computing*
- appreciate the movement towards nanotechnology
- comprehend the issues surrounding nanotechnology
- explain bandwidth trading
- understand advances in e-publishing.

'IT is no longer a set of back office support systems but a vital part of a [business's] ability to deliver goods and services and, for an increasing number of companies, both an important competitive advantage and an integral component of the products they are offering.'

PriceWaterhouseCoopers Technology Forecast 2000, *From Atoms to Systems: A Perspective on Technology*, PriceWaterhouseCoopers, Technology Center, California, p. 3.

INTRODUCTION

Throughout this book we have seen how the technology of the Internet is transforming the way in which business is being carried out. During the evolution of the Internet, many pundits have claimed that the 'e' in e-business and e-commerce will soon become redundant — most business will be done electronically without question.

It is difficult to forecast the future, but in this final chapter we will offer some predictions and take up some ideas from commentators and journalists about what shape the future might take. Trends we have identified include:

- pervasive e-business
- miniaturisation
- wireless trends
- voice technology
- bandwidth management
- electronic publishing and electronic paper.

By now, we appreciate that the Internet presents itself to business as uncharted territory, forcing firms to seek new strategies in an ever-changing technological and economic environment. Those firms who wish to succeed in Internet commerce have had to address three unique characteristics: ubiquity, interactivity and speed.[1]

The main drivers in the business acceptance and uptake of Internet commerce appear to be:

- continued global expansion or globalisation
- convergence of media and communications technologies
- increasing awareness and familiarity among consumers and business users of Internet tools
- easier-to-use Internet interfaces (browsers, directories, search engines)
- new business opportunities in new forms.

PERVASIVE E-BUSINESS

Pervasive e-business implies that all appliances will one day be able to connect to the Internet (this was discussed in chapter 1 under the term *Ultranet*). Everywhere on the Internet is accessible to users on what is essentially an unlimited and equal basis — this is what we mean by the term 'ubiquity'. The user can go anywhere on the Net with a minimum of effort; there is no technological reason for the user to start at a specific spot or web site. Exciting new forms of Internet-based interactivity have developed. Software is distributed and tested on line, information is exchanged and modified more easily, data are stored on line, and virtual organisations can operate more effectively through interacting on a global basis at any hour of the day or night.

UBIQUITOUS COMPUTING

Ubiquitous computing refers to the idea that computing power will come to be embedded in most of the appliances and devices used by people in the course of their everyday leisure and work. PriceWaterhouseCoopers has developed a table showing the requirements for research to make ubiquitous computing a reality.

TABLE 12.1	RESEARCH REQUIREMENTS FOR UBIQUITOUS COMPUTING
RESEARCH AREA	**UBIQUITOUS COMPUTING NEEDS**
Low power	Researchers are aiming to design new chips that work in parallel with lower clock speeds running at lower voltages.
Low cost	Trend towards low-cost devices that connect to the Internet — perhaps even disposable devices
Transparent networking	Networks that support mobile applications — e.g. Bluetooth
Mobile applications	Applications that automatically migrate between computing devices

SOURCE: PriceWaterhouseCoopers Technology Forecast 2000, p. 47.

Ralph Merkle, from the Xerox Palo Alto, has predicted that by 2050 there will be devices that have the computing power of roughly a billion Pentium computers.[2]

MINIATURISATION AND MOBILE COMMERCE

Two of the leaders in mobile devices, Palm and Nokia, have shown that their brand of m-commerce will be somewhat different from traditional surfing the Web. Palm and Visa have combined to show how the Palm Pilot is able to beam credit card data to a point-of-sale terminal using the infra-red port on the top of the Palm.[3] The credit card terminal beams back data, such as a digital receipt, coupons and so on, to the Palm.

Nokia is testing a smart card, made by a company called 2Scoot, that will be moulded into the shape of a phone faceplate and will snap onto the front of the phone. The idea is that the consumer touches the phone to a pad near the door of a takeaway restaurant, for example, to place an order. Before leaving, the customer touches the phone to a pad attached to the cash register to have the meal charged to his or her credit card.[4] Figure 12.1 shows the home page of new technology company 2Scoot.

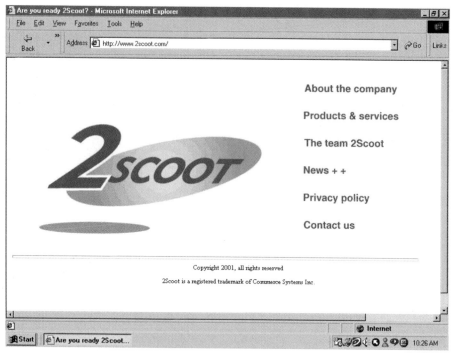

FIGURE 12.1: Home page of 2Scoot.com

NANOTECHNOLOGY

Nanotechnology refers to the design and fabrication of molecular-sized devices and machines. The United States government has identified it as a key area for research in the twenty-first century.[5] **Nanobots**[6] are the work-horses of the nano-manufacturing world. They are nanometer-scale (one one billionth of a metre) robots that use tiny arms to pick up and move atoms and tiny electronic brains to direct the process. There are two basic types of nanobots: general assemblers and a special class of assemblers known as self-replicators.[7]

ASSEMBLERS

These cell-size robots may be equipped with fingers for manipulating matter, probes for distinguishing one atom or molecule from another, and programs to tell the robots what to do.

SELF-REPLICATORS

Most assemblers will need the additional ability to make copies of themselves. To make a skyscraper, for example, a handful of assemblers would first clone themselves into an army of trillions of tiny robots, then start building.

WHAT THIS COULD MEAN IN THE E-BUSINESS WORLD

The following technical insite presents a nightmare scenario of what such technology could mean in the future.

THE NANOTECHNOLOGY OF CYBER CRIME

BY CHRISTINE CANABOU

Futurist

Tom Talleur, 52, is a managing director in forensic and litigation services at KPMG. He founded NASA's network and advanced technology crimes division, which investigates national and international cyber attacks against NASA's communication systems.

Scenario

'Technology is feverishly re-creating our physical reality. As we begin to coprocess the virtual world and the physical world, integrating technology into every support device of our lives, we're learning to tolerate a greater threshold of cyberattacks. Tomorrow, we will put up with e-crimes the way we tolerate allergies today. The current biological warfare will be trumped by cyberlogical warfare. E-crimes will exploit us in very personal ways as cyberchips are embedded into our bodies. We will learn to accept the side effects of such invasions, in much the same way that we deal with the effects of drugs and vaccinations.'

So what?

'Our society will be running around like a dog chasing its tail as our physical reality becomes crafted at the subatomic level by self-replicating *nanobots*. E-crimes will become adaptive, predatory and morphological, driven by entities that exist solely to destroy entire communication networks. Cyber-illnesses will become so pervasive that entire service brownouts will delay global communication and B2B commerce, which in turn will create tremendous opportunities for further abuses in the marketplace.'

Futurology decoder key

'Cybercrime won't stifle the expansion of e-commerce — it will accompany it. As technology becomes more sophisticated, entire markets will be created for cyberwarfare entities and then for counter entities. And the focus will be on defending the individual. Clinical psychologists of cyberspace will help people cope with the new reality of integrated virtual and physical worlds, where we'll experience unprecedented exploitations. Widespread identity thefts will follow. We'll see cases of permanent identity loss by 2015.'

SOURCE: Christine Canabou, 'Life of Crime', *Fast Company*, 1 April 2001, p. 60, found at www.fastcompany.com/online/45/futurist.html.

EXERCISES

1. Investigate the incidence of identity theft and prepare a report on it and the ways in which it might be thwarted.
2. Discuss the proposition that e-crimes will become adaptive, predatory and morphological.

Software in the twenty-first century has to be easy to use, multipurpose and compatible across a wide variety of platforms. The World Wide Web has transformed the user interface for many types of software, and we are now seeing operating systems with browser-type interfaces. Another challenge for software developers is to make software that takes into account the small size of the personal digital assistants (PDAs) that are becoming increasingly popular. Natural language will enable users to interact more naturally with computer software and talking head–type user interfaces will start to appear. Research on human computer interface is expanding (see www.hcibib.org).

MOBILE WALLETS

The Ericsson Wireless Wallet concept has generated great interest, demonstrating that a Bluetooth-enabled Wireless Wallet could provide a simple and efficient way to manage the variety of smart cards that people carry around. The industrialisation of the Wireless Wallet for volume production will be carried out together with Ericsson partners. Ericsson is focusing on the core technology used in the Wireless Wallet, the WAP over Bluetooth module named the WCM or Wireless Core Module.[8]

GEOLOCATION SOFTWARE

Despite the fact that the Internet has always been called a frontierless environment, **geolocation** software is being developed to work out where people are the instant they access a particular web site.[9] Geolocation software works by:
- conducting real-time analyses of web traffic
- attempting to determine the country, State or even city of the web surfer.

The implications of such software are far-reaching. If it is used in conjunction with blocking software, governments will be able to control what material is accessible over the Internet — for example, countries could control access to gambling and pornography sites. China keeps its citizens behind the Great Firewall, using software to block access to sites with proscribed content.[10]

USER INTERFACE

Companies are developing talking-head interfaces to make **voice recognition** more realistic.[11] Intelligent agent software will improve — already we are familiar with some of the work intelligent agents do in the Office 2000 package, such as correcting text as you type it.

COLLABORATIVE COMPUTING SOFTWARE

Collaborative Product Commerce is a software product suite designed to help Internet users communicate and collaborate. This type of software will take advantage of the Internet to enable people, from all over the globe, involved in product design to provide vital input throughout a product life cycle.[12] This is being promoted by Sun Microsystems as a way of coping with increased consumer demand for tailored products.

INTERACTIVE TELEVISION

Industry consultants Strategy Analytics predict that 625 million people around the world will have access to online services on their TV sets by 2005, including online shopping, banking, games, information and interactive entertainment services.[13] These conclusions are presented in a study entitled 'Interactive Digital Television: Worldwide Market Forecasts' published recently by Strategy Analytics within its strategic advisory service, The Interactive Home. Table 12.2 shows the situation at the start of 2001 and a prediction for the end of 2001.

TABLE 12.2	INTERACTIVE TELEVISION RESEARCH REPORT FINDINGS				
WORLDWIDE (START OF 2001)	WESTERN EUROPE	ASIA–PACIFIC	NORTH AMERICA	LATIN AMERICA	WORLDWIDE (END OF 2001)
20 million homes • 74 per cent use satellite • 21 per cent use cable • 5 per cent use terrestrial	62 per cent of audience	10 per cent of audience	18 per cent of audience	1 per cent of audience	38 million homes

SOURCE: Stratetgy Analytics (28 February 2001).

The most advanced market in the world is the UK, where 40 per cent of homes will have interactive digital television by the end of 2001. All Britain's major digital platforms — satellite, cable and terrestrial — offer a wide range of interactive services, such as interactive sports coverage, television commerce (t-commerce), games, email and walled garden Internet.[14]

COMMUNICATIONS

Much work is being done to ensure that packet-switched networks achieve the same quality of service as that offered by circuit-switched networks. Table 12.3 offers some forecasts for communications technologies in the twenty-first century. Useful technical forums for further research include the Open Group (www.opengroup.org), a vendor- and technology-neutral consortium offering a wide range of resources, products and services, and opportunities for collaborative problem solving; and Protocols.com (www.protocols.com), a free information service for the data communications and telecommunications industry.

TABLE 12.3 · THE FUTURE OF COMMUNICATIONS TECHNOLOGIES

TECHNOLOGY AND SERVICE	DETAILS	WEB SITES
Voice-over IP (VoIP)	Offers efficient use of bandwidth	www.protocols.com www.protocols.com/voip/standards.htm
Optical wavelength switching	Carriers will be able to lease out entire wavelengths of their fibre optic networks.	www.allayer.com/opticaltech.html
Web-based customer self-service tools	Web-based interfaces for billing information	www.discovercard.com
SMS to dominate the growth in mobile data services	SMS (Short Message Service) is a service for sending messages of up to 160 characters to mobile phones that use Global System for Mobile (GSM) communication. GSM and SMS service is primarily available in Europe. SMS is similar to *paging*. However, SMS messages do not require the mobile phone to be active and within range and will be held for a number of days until the phone is active and within range. SMS messages are transmitted within the same cell or to anyone with roaming service capability.[15]	www.whatis.com
Adoption of WAP for wireless personal digital assistants		www.wapforum.org
Interference among Bluetooth, 802.1 and HomRF	Could limit deployment — not apparent until deployed	www.bluetooth.org

SOURCE: PriceWaterhouseCoopers Technology Forecast 2000, p. 378.

The following technical insite provides background information on the increasing popularity of the communication technology called **Digital Subscriber Line (DSL)**. This technology is set to revolutionise small and medium-sized business and home access to the Internet.

FAST ACCESS TO THE INTERNET OVER COPPER WIRES

Digital Subscriber Line is a technology for bringing high-bandwidth information to homes and small businesses over ordinary copper telephone lines. xDSL refers to different variations of DSL, such as **Asymmetric Digital Subscriber Line (ADSL)**, **High Bit Rate DSL (HDSL)** and **Rate Adaptive DSL (RADSL)**.

Assuming your home or small business is close enough to a telephone company central office that offers DSL service, you may be able to receive data at rates up to 6.1 megabits (millions of bits) per second (of a theoretical 8.448 megabits per second), enabling continuous transmission of motion video, audio, and even 3-D effects. More typically, individual connections will provide from 1.544 Mbps to 512 Kbps downstream and about 128 Kbps upstream. A DSL line can carry both data and voice signals and the data part of the line is continuously connected. DSL installations began in 1998 and will continue at a greatly increased pace through the next decade in a number of communities in the US and elsewhere. Compaq, Intel and Microsoft, working with telephone companies, have developed a standard and easier-to-install form of ADSL called G.Lite that is accelerating deployment. DSL is expected to replace ISDN in many areas and to compete with the cable modem in bringing multimedia and 3-D to homes and small businesses.

. . .

Digital Subscriber Line is a technology that assumes digital data does not require change into analog form and back. Digital data is transmitted to your computer directly as digital data and this allows the phone company to use a much wider bandwidth for transmitting it to you. Meanwhile, if you choose, the signal can be separated so that some of the bandwidth is used to transmit an analog signal so that you can use your telephone and computer on the same line and at the same time.

SOURCE: www.whatis.com, a property of Tech Target Inc.

EXERCISES

1. Explain the differences between ADSL, HDSL and RADSL.
2. Prepare a report on the uptake of xDSL in your country.

INTERNET2

In 1996 a project known as Internet2 started in Chicago, involving more than 154 American universities together with representatives from a few high-tech and telecommunications companies. The project aims to establish Gbit-per-second points of presence nationwide on a Very High Performance Backbone Network (vBNS). It will give people more control over how their information is used, and since it will be more secure it will be of great interest to Internet commerce companies. Once the wide bandwidth represented by Internet2 moves from academia into the corporate world a set of new, powerful web applications will appear.

In February 1999 Internet2 went live on the Abilene fibre-optic network developed by the University Corporation for Advanced Development, Indiana University and corporate partners Cisco Systems Inc., San Jose, California; Nortel Networks Corp., Toronto; and Qwest Communications International Inc., Denver. The three companies have invested an estimated US$500 million in this superior Internet. With speeds up to 2.4 Gbits per second, Abilene is potentially 85 000 times faster than a standard 28-Kbit-per-second connection. The research effort is concentrated on higher bandwidth with the aim of making a large pipe available to everyone, including end users in their homes. That is going to enable a new set of services and applications for home and business use.[16]

Southern Illinois University connected to **Internet2** (I2) in March 2001 through Illinois Century Network.[17] One use of the high-speed Internet connection is multicasting between the universities involved. Live, interactive lectures will be available in classrooms for courses in the sciences, education, engineering and agriculture. When I2 is up and running, almost all departments throughout the university will have applications. I2 will allow such teaching applications as broadcast television quality videoconferencing, which will help professors at universities across the country run collaborative courses. I2 has been used already in such fields as telemedicine and music. It has allowed physicians to diagnose diseases from across the country and orchestras to perform concerts of music generated simultaneously at two locations.

AUTOMOBILE INTERNET

In 2001 the fastest-selling items in automobile media are MP3, DVD and the Internet.[18] Commuting time can be used effectively, thanks to voice-recognition technology. By the end of the twentieth century Pioneer was retailing a $499 VR system that could pick any of 80 CD titles spoken by its user. Drivers can ask the car to download their emails and read them. If a user wants to reply or send a new message, he or she simply starts dictating — fingers need never leave the wheel. Currently, 7 per cent of cars in the US have email access. The automotive computer technology market turned over US$1 billion last year, and by 2005 it is expected to be worth eight times that.[19]

Other technologies for the car include:
- **satellite radio**, bringing you up to 100 channels of interference-free, CD-quality radio. Delphi expects to have it in the US next year and predicts there will be 28 million satellite radio–capable cars by 2005.
- **telematics**, a technology that combines voice and data to provide location-specific security, information and entertainment. A telematics system will notify call centre operators if your airbag deploys (so they can send help), unlock the car if you've locked the keys in, give you turn-by-turn instructions if you're lost, track your car if it's stolen and even update sports scores. The biggest supplier of telematics is Motorola, whose next-generation iRadio system will add a raft of new services, allowing drivers to capture music on demand, download spoken books, access email and listen to real-time traffic reports, then be guided around the trouble spots.[20]
- Microsoft predicts that very soon every car will have a web address, bringing in far more than just email.

TELEWORKING

E-commerce may force some business service organisations to reconfigure the way in which they conduct their business. This may result in a change in the compilation of the sector's inputs, as some are reduced while others are increased. For example, the use of teleworking may reduce office space costs (which are about 15 per cent of business service organisation costs).[21]

> Significant reductions in both bandwidth costs and infrastructure accessibility seem likely to occur in the 2000–2005 timeframe, which will lead to very large, and perhaps ubiquitous, adoption of very high bandwidth services, certainly in the larger professional service organizations. Although teleworking (and the paperless office) have been touted as one of the most visible manifestations of the information economy for many years, it seems probable that this period will see much more user-friendly and acceptable home work environments (such as effective video conferencing) and is likely to lead to the creation of teleworking scenarios that offer a genuine and long term alternative to traditional office-based work. As this happens, there will be a downward pressure on salaries and real estate costs which presently account for approximately 25 per cent and 15 per cent of professional services organisations' gross costs, respectively.[22]

Internal efficiencies that e-commerce would create within the business services sector could mean that approximately five per cent less labour would be required to carry out current business functions. It was also expected that there would be a reduced need for consumables, such as paper, as information products are stored and delivered electronically.[23]

> It is likely that 20 per cent of all legal services will be delivered electronically by 2005 and probably 40 per cent by 2010. Examples abound in the consumer market in the areas of conveyancing, debt recovery, financing transactions and registrations. Many of these services will be provided in the normal course without any human involvement. Larger legal service providers will also utilize electronic preparation and delivery of services and are likely to be best placed to spend the significant amounts required on research and development of these services and products.[24]

BANDWIDTH TRADING

Predicting how much bandwidth is required has proved very difficult, given the phenomenal growth in use of the Internet since 1994. The need for speedy access is critical to the future of e-business. Communication speeds, both wired and wireless, are doubling every 12 months.[25]

John Du Pre Gauntt, of PriceWaterHouseCoopers, argued in 1999 for the idea of trading bandwidth.[25] He put forward the following query:

> If a customer accesses the site of a seller, then the customer is paying for the communication. If the customer then decides to make a purchase of the product or service, should the final price of the item include the customer's communication costs — especially for bandwidth hungry audio and video files?[26]

According to his argument, if we accept that the transaction model for e-commerce is electronic networks, and the price for bandwidth is a central business cost, it is feasible that bandwidth could be capitalised and traded in a public setting.

Several problems must be solved before this can be done — notably, modelling network demand (see www.telegeography.com) and modelling price changes over time. Figure 12.2 shows the home page of TeleGeography, which maps Internet traffic.

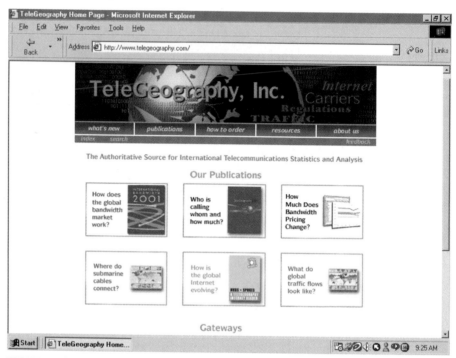

FIGURE 12.2: The TeleGeography home page

One company, Band-X, is using the Web to enable buyers and sellers of international minutes or bandwidth capacity to browse multiple bids and offers. Figure 12.3 shows the home page of this company.

According to Du Pre Gauntt, the keys to the future of bandwidth trading lie in:

• how systems such as Band-X scale
• how they can aggregate, analyse and integrate price and volume information into workable risk models.

For an e-business to thrive, it is essential to discover the types of bandwidth-intensive communications that will be conducted on the network. To calculate transmission time, use File size/Bandwidth; for throughput, use File size/Download time. Throughput is affected by other variables such as connection speed and other traffic on the network.

FIGURE 12.3: Home page of Band-X

SOURCE: Band-X Ltd, www.band-x.com.

E-PUBLISHING

Digital or e-publishing will have a tremendous impact on the delivery of education — indeed, already Cisco Systems has set up a worldwide academy with online learning to deliver material to allow people to prepare for certification as network administrators throughout the world. Many libraries will become online libraries. We have already seen the arrival of the ebook. Software that allows users to convert Word documents to Microsoft Reader format means people are able to create e-books with technology that makes it easy to read text on screen.[27] An e-book can hold up to 150 books' worth of text.

Much research is being done at MIT's Media Lab to develop electronic paper and ink. The technical insite on the next page describes the work. The take-up of e-books has been hampered by people's unwillingness to give up the traditional paper book. As a result, some researchers are working to create an e-book that resembles a traditional book in as many respects as possible — for example by enclosing the e-book inside a leather cover. The increasing popularity of personal digital assistants may encourage the adoption of electronic books — Compaq's iPAQ Pocket PC, for example, incorporates Microsoft Reader.

E-PAPER AND E-INK

Electronic Paper

Books with printed pages are unique in that they embody the simultaneous, high-resolution display of hundreds of pages of information. The representation of information on a large number of physical pages, which may be physically turned and written on, constitutes a highly preferred means of information interaction. An obvious disadvantage of the printed page, however, is its immutability once typeset. We are currently developing electronically addressable paper-page displays that use real paper substrates. This effort includes the development of novel electronically addressable contrast media, microencapsulation chemistry, and desktop printing technologies to print functional circuits, logic, and display elements on paper or paper-like substrates, including interconnecting vias and multi-layer logic.

SOURCE: Joseph M. Jacobson; Barrett Comiskey; Patrick Anderson, and Leila Hasan 2001, 'Electronic Paper Books and Electronic Books', www.media.mit.edu/micromedia/elecpaper.html.

E Ink, Philips Announce Agreement

E Ink's technology uses an electrical current to gather tiny globules of electrically charged ink into shapes and characters on a screen. E Ink Corp., which makes a type of *electronic ink* that it says makes computer screens as easy to read as paper, announced an agreement with Philips Components on Tuesday to put the screens on handheld devices and electronic books. The companies said they plan to develop a prototype by June, and expect to have them available to consumers by 2003.

SOURCE: AP Online, 27 February 2001.

QUESTIONS

1. What is the current situation with regard to:
   (a) e-paper
   (b) e-ink.
2. Discuss the effect of electronic publishing on traditional book publishers.

BLUESKY FORECAST

Some predictions by Kurzweil (2000)[29] are reproduced here for your consideration and discussion.

1. Personal computers will disappear by 2009.
2. Visual information will be written directly into our retinas by devices in our glasses or contact lenses.
3. Ubiquitous very high bandwidth wireless connection to the Internet will be standard at all times.
4. A web site visit will take the form of a virtual reality experience.
5. By 2009 we will have billions of nanobots travelling through our brains, communicating directly with our biological neurons.
6. People will web-beam their lives to enable others to share the full sensory experiences through the Web.

Internet commerce still has a long way to go. Building the infrastructure to do business on the Web will ultimately lead to a more mature, methodical approach to exploiting this new sales, marketing and customer-service channel. Meanwhile existing channels will continue to be nurtured and developed. Successful companies will create web-based efficiencies that customers will embrace, even though power will be transferred to those customers in the process.[30]

Technological innovation and the global expansion of commerce are the forces combining to contribute to the further growth of Internet commerce, particularly in the developing nations. The most important innovation to be introduced by Internet commerce will be in the ways businesses and people interact with one another and the ways in which products and services will be offered. Aggregators, e-auctions and online exchanges, running on broadband, wireless or mobile appliances, will be the electronic marketplaces of the future.

Differentiated and customised products will offer more choices than mass-produced goods, for which firms with sufficient economies of scale will have the cost advantage.

Internet commerce will provide countless opportunities and challenges to our economies and societies. Traditional institutions, such as banks, universities, established business intermediaries, the media and publishing houses, are now finding it necessary to redefine their roles in the new global commercial environment.

key terms

Asymmetric Digital Subscriber Line (ADSL)	High Bit Rate DSL (HDSL)	Rate Adaptive DSL (RADSL)
Digital Subscriber Line (DSL)	Internet2	satellite radio
	nanobots	telematics
geolocation	nanotechnology	ubiquitous computing
	pervasive e-business	voice recognition

QUESTIONS

1. Write a report on one of the following:
   (a) mobile e-commerce
   (b) interactive television e-commerce
   (c) bandwidth management.

2. How has nanotechnology advanced since this book was published? What effect, if any, has it had on e-business?

3. Prepare a paper on the future of e-publishing.

4. Stegangraphy (hiding messages within seemingly harmless documents or graphics) will allow spies to embed intelligence messages in common web sites. Discuss.

MANAGEMENT DISCONTENT

By DAVID WALKER

Buying the wrong software to manage a Web site can be an expensive mistake.

As Internet technology advances, new things suddenly become possible. Take content management. Just five years ago, it was almost impossible to waste a million dollars building a Web site.

But modern, twenty-first-century Internet technology means that any medium-sized organisation with Web ambitions can now pour a seven-digit sum straight down the hole almost instantly. And one of the easiest and most efficient ways to do this is to buy the wrong Web content management system, or CMS.

Web content can be articles, pictures, products, email archives, Flash presentations, streaming audio, whatever. This content needs a lot of things done to it. You may need systems for creating the content (authoring), describing it (metadata tagging), changing and updating it (editing), letting several people edit it together (collaboration), letting the right people do the right things to it (workflow), stopping the wrong people from manipulating it (security), keeping track of how it has changed (versioning), deciding when to display it (scheduling), displaying it in the right standard format (templating), allowing it to be displayed by others (syndication), allowing it to be displayed differently to different visitors (personalisation), and more.

Your system may start as a couple of junior staff with HTML editors and the Windows file system. But that solution doesn't scale. The average large organisation's Web site has anywhere between 10 000 and 10 million pieces of content. At which time the organisation has a Web content management problem.

But when you go looking for software to fix this problem, you'll find yourself like a shopper in some exotic bazaar, besieged by a hundred CMS vendors all promising to fix your problem. And whichever solution you choose, you've a good chance of ending up out of pocket and unhappy. Most of today's CMS offerings simply don't work the way they should. Many people in the nascent Web content management community have suspected this for a year or more. But now an established technology research firm, Forrester Research, says the same thing.

Forrester has examined a dozen commercial CMSs, including well-known solutions from Vignette, Broadvision, nCompass and Interwoven. Forrester's winner, Open Market Content Server, scored a mere 3.0 out of five. In a report titled 'Managing Content Hypergrowth', Forrester concludes that today's CMS offerings are 'immature', that none adequately addresses all needs, and that the vendors all have very different visions of how the CMS will evolve. It also warns that organisations that have bought a CMS are going to run into problems maintaining and customising it and that they are likely to discover nasty mismatches between their CMS and other software, such as application servers and outside systems. 'Owner satisfaction will be short-lived,' Forrester concludes bitingly.

Oh, and by the way, Forrester estimates that putting in place a 'basic content management system' will cost you more than $1 million, and a fancy solution will cost much more.

Scape.com, the most extreme example of an expensive Australian content start-up, has spent a reported $23 million on a Vignette-driven Web site (and packed it full of barely readable text but that's another story). Faced with the prospect of spending $1 million plus on a CMS that won't cover business needs or integrate with other systems, what's a large CMS buyer to do?

Forrester warns firms to dodge vendors trying to lock them into a proprietary technology; it recommends the few tools that integrate well with other software, like Interwoven's TeamSite, or use standard platforms, such as Open Market's Java-compliant Content Server.

Forrester also encourages firms to spend more time describing and organising their data so that it can be used with whatever CMS they eventually choose. There's a school of thought that says most firms are better off building their own CMS, and that in buying an off-the-shelf CMS solution you sacrifice too much business flexibility. Forrester rejects this argument. At the same time, it gives organisations a seven-digit reason to remain nervous about Web content management.

SOURCE: *Sydney Morning Herald*, Computers section, 13 February 2001, p. 3.

Exercises

1. Prepare a report on the use of Content management software.
2. Select several web companies and conduct a survey on their experiences with content management software.

SUGGESTED READING

Comiskey, B., Albert, J. D., Yoshizawa, H. and Jacobson J., 1998, *Nature* 394 (6690), pp. 253–5.

Jacobson, J., Comiskey, B., Turner, C., Albert, J. and Tsao, P. 1997, *IBM Systems Journal* 36 (3), pp. 457–63.

Ridley, B. A. Nivi, B. and Jacobson, J. M. 1999, *Science* 286 (5440), pp. 746–9.

Singh, S. 1999, *The Code Book*, Doubleday, New York.

END NOTES

1. Kenney, Martin and Curry, James 1999, *Implications for Firm Strategy and Industry Configuration*, The E-conomy Project, Berkeley Roundtable on the International Economy (BRIE).
2. Shelly, G. B., Cashman, T. J. and Vermaat, M. E. 2001, *Discovering Computers 2001: Concepts for a Connected World*, Course Technology, Cambridge, MA, p. 14.40.
3. Fortt, J. 2001. 'A Glimpse of future commerce on hand today', *Sydney Morning Herald*, IT section, 23 January 2001, p. 6.
4. Fortt 2001.
5. PriceWaterhouseCoopers Technolgy Forecast 2000, p. 24.
6. Visions 21, 'Our Technology: What is Nanotechnology?', *Time*, 19 June 2000, www.elibrary.com.

7. *Time*, 19 June 2000.

8. www.ericsson.com/wirelesswallet.

9. Guernsey, L. 2001, 'Suddenly the Frontierless Internet is running up against real borders', *Sydney Morning Herald*, 16 March, p. 10.

10. 'Stop signs on the Web: The internet and the law', *Economist*, 13 January 2001, pp. 19–23.

11. Shelly, Cashman and Vermaat 2001, p. 14.40.

12. Gengler, B. 2001, 'Shot in the arm for product collaboration', *The Australian*, 13 February 2001, p. 44.

13. Strategy Analytics 2001, 'Interactive digital TV will reach 625 million viewers by 2005', 28 February, www.itvreport.com/news/0201/022801strategy2.htm; www.strategyanalytics.com.

14. Strategy Analytics 2001, 28 February.

15. www.whatis.com.

16. Wilcox, Joe 1999, 'Expanding the Information Highway', *TechWEb*, 6 July 1999.

17. Hemphill, Carly, 'New technology to enhance research, teaching at Southern Illinois U.', *Daily Egyptian* (U-WIRE), Carbondale, IL, from http://www.elibrary.com.

18. Easdown, Rod, 'Not-so-hard driving', *Sydney Morning Herald*, Motoring section, 23 February 2001.

19. Easdown, *SMH*, 23 February 2001.

20. Easdown, *SMH*, 23 February 2001.

21. Commonwealth of Australia 2000, *E-commerce Beyond 2000*, Department of Communications, Information Technology and the Arts, Canberra, p. 123.

22. Duncan Giles, Blake Dawson Waldron, 20 July 1999, in Commonwealth of Australia, p. 123.

23. Commonwealth of Australia 2000, p. 123.

24. Duncan Giles, Blake Dawson Waldron, 20 July 1999, in Commonwealth of Australia, p. 123.

25. Kurzweil, R. 2000, 'Dear PC: R.I.P.' *Business2.0* magazine, 26 September, http://business2.com/content/magazine/indepth/2000/09/15/18865.

26. Du Pre Gauntt, J. 1999, 'The Network is the Market: Financing Internet Bandwidth', OntheInternet, January/February, 1999, p. 23.

27. Du Pre Gauntt 1999, p. 24.

28. Ziffer, D. 2001, 'Start', *Communiqué*, April, p. 4.

29. Kurzweil 2000.

30. Kindel, Stephen 1999, *Reassessing e-Commerce*, GartnerGroup, Feb/March, ee-Online, www.gartnergroup.com.

glossary

access control lists: refers to mechanisms and policies that restrict access to computer resources. ACLs specify what operations different users can perform on specific files and directories.

Active Server Pages (ASP): HTML pages that include one or more scripts (small embedded programs) that are processed on a Microsoft web server before the pages are sent to the user

ActiveX: a set of technologies that enable software components to interact with one another in a networked environment regardless of the language in which the components were created

advertising: the act or practice of bringing anything, such as business activity, to the attention of the public

advertising-supported model: a business model based on offering advertising space on web pages to obtain revenue

applet: an application with limited features that is usually portable between operating systems

application service provider: a third-party entity that manages and distributes software-based services and solutions to customers across a wide area network from a central data centre. In essence, ASPs are a way for companies to outsource some or all aspects of their information technology needs.

Asymmetric Digital Subscriber Line (ADSL): uses the frequency spectrum between 0 kHz and 4 kHz for the telephone service and 20 kHz to 2.2 kHz for data transfer over the copper line in a standard telephone line. This line provides asymmetric transmission of data, with 265 Kbits to1.5 Mbits downstream (to the user) and up to 256 Kbits/s upstream, depending on line length and line/loop condition. This is many times faster than existing PSTN modems (56 Kbit/s) and ISDN (64 to128 Kbits) services.

asymmetric encryption: a cryptographic system that uses two keys — a public key known to everyone and a private or secret key known only to the recipient of the message. When John wants to send a secure message to Jane, he uses Jane's public key to encrypt the message. Jane then uses her private key to decrypt it.

asynchronous: digital exchange that occurs out of time sequence (e.g. a transfer of funds might be made in a retail shop using EFTPOS,. which is then confirmed. However, the actual transfer of funds may be batched together and the transaction completed some hours later.

attachment: data files, such as word-processed or spreadsheet files, that are sent along with an email

authentication: a means of countering the threat of impersonation. Online data and information transmission in electronic form requires that the message sent reach only the intended recipient.

back channel: a channel used for sending data in the opposite direction to the primary channel. Back channels are frequently used to send control information. Using back channels, information can still be delivered even though the primary channel may be malfunctioning. Also called backward or reverse channel

banner advertisements: small rectangular billboard-style advertisements displayed on web pages. *See also* click-through advertising

behaviour oriented: In object-oriented programming objects exhibit behaviours — for example, a window object may have an alert method (behaviour) that allows the program to display a message in a separate window.

Bluetooth: Bluetooth wireless technology is a de facto standard, as well as a specification for small-form factor, low-cost, short-range radio links between mobile PCs, mobile phones and other portable devices.

browser: a software application that allows the user to navigate the Web and view various Internet resources, move to other documents via hypertext, view images, listen to audio files etc.

business strategy: a deliberate sequence of decisions and plans of action to initiate and implement business objectives for the competitive advantage of that business

censorship: the suppression of material in public media, such as books, films etc., that is deemed to be objectionable on moral, political, military or other grounds

click-through advertising: advertising on a web page that links an Internet user to the site of the advertiser. By clicking on the advertisement, the user is routed to the advertiser's URL.

client/server: network configuration comprising a host machine (server) and a machine requesting data or services (client)

client/server computing: form of computing in which both client computers and server computers contribute to the processing within a system. Clients and servers communicate over a network, with clients requesting services from servers, and servers providing responses to these requests.

ColdFusion: middleware product designed to allow a web page to be used as an interface to a database. ColdFusion makes use of scripts that are embedded inside standard HTML to provide web page templates.

Common Gateway Interface (CGI): specifies a standard mechanism for a web server to communicate with a script or program running on the same server in order to pass data between them

Common Object Request Broker Architecture (CORBA): allows applications to communicate with one another no matter where they are located or who has designed them. With CORBA, users gain access to information transparently, irrespective of the software or the hardware platform it resides on, or where it is located on an enterprise's network.

compressing: running a data set through an algorithm that reduces the space required to store it or the bandwidth required to transmit it

content management systems: provide an infrastructure for creating and maintaining web site assets, including text content, images, sound files and application components.

contract: agreement between two or more parties creating obligations that are enforceable or otherwise recognisable by law

cookie: file that a web server stores on a user's computer when a web site is visited. A cookie gathers information about the user.

copyright: the exclusive right, created by law, to make copies of, or otherwise control, a literary, musical, dramatic or artistic work for a certain number of years. Copyright is included in the all-embracing term 'intellectual property', which provides protection to patents, investments, trade marks and industrial designs.

cracker: a person who tries to access a computer system illegally

crime: an act, a failure to act or other conduct that is prejudicial to the community, rendering the person responsible liable to a fine or other punishment

cryptolope: IBM's trademark for its cryptographic envelope technology. Cryptolope objects are used for secure, protected delivery of digital content and can be compared to secure servers.

customer relationship management (CRM): incorporates an integrated system of methodologies, processes and software (typically Internet capable) that brings together servicing of customers in terms of sales, marketing, accounts, orders and ongoing support

data encryption standard (DES): a popular symmetric-key encryption method developed in 1975 and standardised by ANSI in 1981 as ANSI X.3.92. DES uses a 56-bit key.

data mining: analysis of data for relationships that have not previously been discussed

data-oriented systems: data systems whose focus is on the supporting database.

data warehouse: an integrated collection of transaction data specifically structured for querying and reporting, and catalogued for retrieval and analysis

defamation: the act of publishing a false or derogatory statement about another person without lawful justification

denial-of-service (DoS) attack: In a denial-of-service attack, a network is flooded with useless traffic, blocking normal services. Many DoS attacks, such as the Ping of Death and Teardrop, exploit limitations in the TCP/IP protocols. For all known DoS attacks, system administrators can install software fixes to limit the damage. But, as with viruses, new forms of attack are constantly being dreamed up by hackers.

design specifications: specifications determined for any new or remodelled system that result from a requirements analysis for a systems project

digital certificates: a digital document issued by a certification authority. The digital certificate includes the company's name, public key, serial number, expiration date and the signature of the trusted certification authority — e.g. Verisign.

Digital Subscriber Line (DSL): a set of digital communication protocols designed to enable high speed data communication over copper telephone lines

directory: an approach to organising information. On the Web, a directory is a subject guide, typically organised by major topics and subtopics. In computer file systems, a directory is a named group of related files that are separated by the naming convention from other groups of files. In computer networks, a directory is a collection of users, user passwords and, usually, information about what network resources they can access.

Distributed Component Object Model (DCOM): a Microsoft protocol that enables distributed software components to communicate over a network in a reliable and secure manner. DCOM serves a similar purpose to CORBA, but is restricted to Windows-based systems.

distributed denial-of-service attack: In a distributed denial-of-service (DDoS) attack, a multitude of compromised systems attack a single target, thereby causing denial of service for users of the targeted system. The flood of incoming messages to the target system essentially forces it to shut down, thereby denying service to legitimate users.

Document Object Model (DOM): Application Programming Interface (API) specification for HTML and XML documents

Document Type Definitions (DTDs): schemas that specify the valid tags and document classes within an XML document

Dot Com: In a Dot Com economy, Dot Com companies are those specifically formed to do business almost entirely on the Internet — i.e., they generally have no physical shopfront or outlets, and they conduct business by trading information, services or products on line.

ebXML (extensible business Extensible Markup Language): a new standard that focuses on creating a set of consistent components with which to conduct global business to business electronic commerce.

e-cash: digital cash

EDIFACT: (Electronic Data Interchange for Administration, Commerce and Transport), a standard for EDI transactions

electronic catalogue: electronic version of a print catalogue; usually a collection of representations (photographs, sketches) of products which can be used for sales promotion or information

Electronic Data Interchange (EDI): computer to computer exchange of business information, such as orders and invoices, between customers and vendors

electronic funds transfer (EFT): the exchange of money electronically; e.g. the electronic transfer of funds from one bank account to an account in another bank

electronic funds transfer a point of sale (EFTPOS): the electronic transfer of value at the checkout in a shop, supermarket or other service provider

electronic malls: a web site that brings together a large number of e-shops accessible to any logged-in users

electronic payment system (EPS): an information system designed to record, transfer, store and process data about goods and services purchased

electronic procurement: the use of the Web to enable large-scale purchasing by governments or any business organisations. The process normally entails supplying companies putting in quotes for the supply of defined products.

electronic purchasing: the use of any electronic technology to buy goods, services or information

encryption: the process of enabling information/data/knowledge to be coded in such a way that it cannot be read without a decoding system or key

enhancements: a change to a product that is intended to improve it in some way — e.g. give it new functions, or make it faster or more compatible with other systems. Enhancements to hardware components, especially integrated circuits, often mean they are smaller and less demanding of resources..

enterprise application integration (EAI): a business term for the plans, methods and tools aimed at modernising, consolidating and coordinating the computer applications in an enterprise

enterprise resource planning (ERP): an integrated software package that enables separate business processes such as finance, marketing, control systems, logistics and human resources management to create an environment of cooperation to improve business efficiency and profitability

environment variables: predefined variables that contain information about the client, server and the current request; an essential component of the Common Gateway Interface

ethernet: a communications standard commonly used in local area networks for transmitting data among computers on a network

ethics: a system of moral principles by which human actions or proposals may be judged good or bad, right or wrong

Extensible Markup Language (XML): a metalanguage — i.e. a language for defining other languages. It is used to define text markup so the text can be used and interpreted by different applications, including those that present information to people. XML allows developers to develop custom tags such as product-number, product-name etc. Will allow for rich searches and for transaction processing tasks to be implemented by browser and web server. Derived from SGML, XML retains SGML's power while reducing its complexity. Unlike HTML, XML allows the developer to create new tags that describe the data, and optionally create a set of rules called Document Type Definitions (DTDs). Any standard XML parser can read, decode and validate this text-based, self-describing document, extracting the data elements in a platform-independent way so that applications can access the data objects through yet another standard called Document Object Model (DOM).

extensible style language (XSL): the layout or presentation of an XML document may be defined by XSL

extranet: a collaborative network that uses Internet technology to link businesses with their suppliers, customers or other businesses that share common goals.

file transfer protocol (FTP): provides simple means of exchanging files between computers on the Internet.

firewall: both the software and hardware that stand between the Internet and a corporate network for security access control

forms: a mechanism within HTML that lets users enter data to be sent to the server. Form elements include text boxes, check boxes, radio buttons and submit buttons

fraud: obtaining material advantage by unfair or wrongful means. It involves the making of a false representation knowingly, without belief in its truth or recklessness.

functional design specification: presents a formal statement of services to be provided by the system. It may replace the less detailed requirements definition if the project is a small enhancement and/or maintenance effort, or supplement a formal requirements specification for a large project. This document will act as a contract between the developer and the customer, and should be understandable by both customer (functional) and developer (technical) staff.

geolocation: web site owners often want information on user demographics — including geographic location or business ties — to support their sales and marketing goals. Content owners may provide content only if a site can guarantee that it goes only to users in a particular geographic location. These financial dynamics have helped the emergence of geolocation technologies, which may make it technically possible for a company such as Yahoo! to determine the physical location of each person who accesses its site.

GET: one of the commands within the HyperText Transfer Protocol. A GET is a request for the server to return the specified document.

groupware: an application that allows many people to interact together. This software is often used to run virtual meetings.

hacker: either 'a clever programmer' or someone who tries to break into computer systems illegally.

hidden fields: a type of form element that can contain a value but is not visible on a web page. Used to store values that the user cannot change. These values are passed back to the server at the same time as user-entered data. Hidden fields are useful for storing state information when transactions involve two or more web pages.

High Bit Rate DSL (HDSL): a form of DSL, providing T1 or E1 connections over two or three twisted-pair copper lines, respectively. Used mostly to replace traditional T1/E1 connections, such as connecting PABXs

hypertext: software technology that allows for fast and flexible access to information. Users browse and retrieve information by following hotlinks rather than by following a linear structure.

Hypertext Markup Language (HTML): a page description language used to compose and format most text links between documents. It is a subset of Standardised General Markup Language.

Hypertext Transfer Protocol (HTTP): a multimedia transport protocol used in communications between browser clients and web host computers

information-systems: a set of processes, people and/or data that collects, alters, transforms, integrates and communicates information in an organisation

integration: enables different components to relate or 'talk' to each other

intellectual property: an all-embracing term covering copyright, patents and trade marks. Describes those rights that protect the product of a person's or corporation's work by hand or brain against unauthorised use or exploitation by others

Interactive Mail Access Protocol (IMAP): allows for better control over the way messages are delivered. When a user connects to a mail host, the user is able to see a one-line summary of each message. Allows selective downloading or deletion of email messages.

interactivity: interaction between a user (such as a consumer) and a web site or organisation

Internet: an international network of computer networks. It permits public access to information on a huge number of subjects, and allows users to send and receive messages and obtain products and services. It relies on agreed rules and protocols about how information is exchanged.

Internet auctions: bring together many buyers and sellers on a web site. They emulate traditional auctions by providing trading mechanisms for negotiating price, delivery and other terms.

Internet exchanges: also referred to as electronic marketplaces and B2B portals, they provide a range of B2B services for buyers and sellers to trade with each other. These services include supply chain management platforms, electronic procurement services, electronic catalogues and auctions.

Internet Explorer: popular HTML browser created by Microsoft

Internet search engines: databases of web links, often comprising millions of web pages, which can be searched via the Web using keywords to find sites providing the information, services or products of interest to the searcher

Internet2: a project to establish gigabit-per-second points of presence nationwide. Internet2 went live in late February 1999.

intranet: a locally operated hypertext environment generally using TCP/IP architecture and services delivered to browse software on networked PCs and desktop workstations. It is privately developed and operated within a business or organisation; like the Internet but can usually be accessed only from within the organisation.

IPSec: protocol that provides security for transmission of information over unprotected networks such as the Internet.

IT architecture and infrastructure: In information technology and on the Internet, infrastructure is the physical hardware used to interconnect the computer and users, along with the software used to send, receive and manage the signal that is transmitted. Architecture applies to both the process and the outcome of thinking out and specifying the overall structure, logical components and logical interrelationships of a computer, its operating system or a network.

IT management: Since computers are central to information management, computer departments within companies and universities are often called IT departments. Some companies refer to these departments as IT management.

Java: a programming language used as a software development tool for the Internet

Java Database Connectivity (JDBC): an Application Programming Interface developed by Sun Microsystems to facilitate generic communication between programs and databases. JDBC is similar to ODBC in that it acts as an intermediary between the program and the database, translating the application's data queries into commands that the database engine will understand.

JavaScript: a scripting language originally developed by Netscape and now available on most browsers. Designed to coexist and interact with HTML source code, thus facilitating client-side tasks such as interactivity and validation of user-entered data

Java Virtual Machine: a program that emulates a computer designed specifically to run Java bytecode. Can be run on any computer platform for which the virtual machine is available

Jini Initiative: a new idea that Sun Microsystems calls 'spontaneous networking'. Using the Jini architecture, users will be able to plug printers, storage devices, speakers and any kind of device directly into a network, and every other computer, device and user on the network will know that the new device has been added and is available.

Joint Application Development (JAD): a process in which a group of users and/or team members interact, learn from one another and discuss problems for resolution. A structured workshop can be used to define requirements and design system externals.

jurisdiction: the power of a court or judge to hear an action, petition or other legal proceeding, and the district or limits within which the judgement or orders of a court can be enforced

just-in-time (JIT): systematic management process for the delivery of component parts at the time they are needed in the production process

L2TP: an open standard protocol for creating virtual private networks with multi-vendor interoperability and acceptance

law: the body of rules that a State or community recognises as binding on its members or subjects

legacy system: existing company databases (which often have been developed in third-generation languages such as COBOL) or back-end systems, such as EDI. Developing e-commerce systems often requires integrating them with legacy systems that hold critical corporate data.

legislation: the body of laws enacted by the legislature.

logistics: supply chain organisation and management

Lynx: a keyboard-oriented text-only web browser.

macro virus: a computer virus that 'infects' a Microsoft Word or similar application, causing a sequence of actions to be performed automatically when the application is started or something else triggers it. Macro viruses tend to be relatively harmless. A typical effect is the undesired insertion of some comic text at certain points when writing a line. A macro virus is often spread as an e-mail virus. A well-known example is the Melissa virus, released in March 1999.

message queuing: system or architecture able to manage the transmission of information efficiently

metalanguage: a language able to describe other languages

middleware: software that operates between an application, such as a database or email program, and the transport layer that performs the services and hides the details of that layer. In a database situation, for example, a client program might send a request message, and the database middleware program passes the request to the database middleware on the server machine. This then puts the request in whatever format is needed to get the desired data. These programs are useful for linking database servers to traditional legacy database programs (e.g. written in COBOL).

money: unit of value used in exchange

mousetrapping: on a web site, a trap is a page that does not allow the reader to move back to a previous page (the Back button on the toolbar is inoperable). A few web site creators apparently use this technique to hold the reader and force them to read the page or to encourage them to visit other pages on their site.

MP3: (MPEG-1 Audio Layer-3), a standard technology and format for compression of sound while preserving the original level of sound quality when it is played

multi-organisational electronic service delivery: a business model that involves the integration of related services provided by two or more organisations. Involves developing a single entry point, often via the Web, where customers can obtain services without having to understand the structure or relationships of the organisations providing these services, and without having to deal with each organisation individually

Multipurpose Internet Mail Extensions (MIME): facilitates the exchange of different kinds of data files on the Internet

nanobots: a microscopic robot built by means of nanotechnology. As yet, this technology is only speculative. Also called a nanoagent

nanotechnology: a hypothetical fabrication technology in which objects are designed and built with the individual specification and placement of each separate atom.

Netscape: a computer software company that markets Internet and web software, including Netscape Navigator and Netscape Communicator

network effect: a world governed by networks that is rewriting the rules for how to build companies, market products and create value. So-called 'network effects' are the basis for the new approach to marketing business involving different markets, different business models and entirely different business strategies.

online fee-for-service model: a business model based on providing services such as education and web development via the Internet for a fee

online fee-for-transaction model: a business model based on providing bookings and other online transactions via the Internet for a fee

online marketplace: Internet-based site allowing businesses and industries to communicate, collaborate and trade products and services

online payment: electronic payment for goods and services purchased on line using the Web.

online subscription: a business model in which customers pay a subscription fee in order to access online information

Open Database Connectivity (ODBC): an Application Programming Interface developed by Microsoft to facilitate generic communication between programs and databases. ODBC acts as an intermediary between the program and the database, translating the application's data queries into commands that the database engine will understand.

order fulfilment: the process of ensuring that goods and services purchased on the Web can be paid for and are actually delivered

outsourcing: giving responsibility for any business function within one organisation, often IT management, to another organisation.

packet filtering: also referred to as static packet filtering. Controlling access to a network by analysing the incoming and outgoing packets and letting them pass or blocking them based on the IP addresses of the source and destination. Packet filtering is one technique, among many, for implementing security firewalls.

packet sniffing: monitoring data travelling over a network using a program or device. Sniffers can be used both for legitimate network management functions and for stealing information off a network. Unauthorised sniffers can be extremely dangerous to a network's security because they are virtually impossible to detect and can be inserted almost anywhere. This makes them a favourite weapon in the hacker's arsenal.

pagejacking: stealing the contents of a web site by copying its pages, putting them on a site that appears to be the legitimate site, then inviting people to the illegal site by means of deceit — e.g. by having the contents indexed by a major search engine whose results in turn link users to the illegal site. Once they have moved enough of a web site's content as well as the page descriptor information within each page, pagejackers can submit the illegal site to major search engines for indexing. Users of the search engine sites may then receive results from both the illegitimate and the legitimate site, and can easily be misled into linking to the wrong one.

patents: government grants to inventors giving them the sole right to make use of and sell such inventions for a limited time.

peer-to-peer (P2P): on the Internet, peer-to-peer (referred to as P2P) is a type of transient Internet network that allows a group of computer users with the same networking program to connect with each other and directly access files from one another's hard drives

Perl: a programming language designed specifically for processing text. Perl is freely available for a wide variety of computer systems and has become one of the most commonly used languages for writing CGI scripts.

personal digital assistant (PDA): handheld computer, often supporting personal information management (PIM) applications

personalisation: the act of recognising a customer, subscriber or visitor as an individual and modifying actions based upon information known about this customer

pervasive e-business: when e-business becomes so common that it is accepted as the main way of doing business

PHP: a freely available, server-side scripting language that facilitates database access and dynamic generation of web page content. Derived largely from Perl, it is designed to be embedded in HTML in a similar manner to ASP and ColdFusion scripts.

plug and play: hardware or software that, once installed ('plugged in'), can immediately be used ('played') — as opposed to hardware or software that requires configuration

Point-to-Point Protocol (PPP): a protocol that provides a method for transmitting packets over serial point-to-point links. A standard for telephone modem communication between a user's personal computer and an Internet service provider (ISP)

policy development: the development of a set of strategies and ideas that will frame a policy document to structure organisational development and planning

policy evaluation: the process of assessing the outcomes determined within a policy document

policy implementation: the process of implementing the strategies and plan framed in a policy document; the action stage of the policy process.

portal: a web site designed to offer a variety of Internet services from a single convenient location. The goal of the portal is to be designated as your browser's startup page. Most portals offer certain free services such as a search engine; local, national and worldwide news, sports and weather; reference services such as yellow pages and maps; shopping malls; and email.

POST: one of the commands within the HyperText Transfer Protocol. A POST is a request for the server to accept the received data as input to a script.

Post Office Protocol (POP): a TCP/IP protocol used in electronic mail that allows users working on intelligent devices such as personal computers to work on local devices. POP may also refer to 'point of presence', which is a site with a collection of telecommunications equipment, usually digital-leased lines and multi-protocol routers.

PPTP: a tunnelling protocol sponsored by Microsoft for connecting Windows NT clients and servers over remote access services (RAS). Often used to create virtual private networks

privacy: the right to not have one's private life intruded upon or unjustifiably brought into the public arena. The issue of privacy is imperfectly recognised in many legal systems.

process oriented: when processes are easy-to-define and well-understood business policies and procedures, they can be thought of as the mission-critical business processes.

project management: planning, scheduling and controlling the activities during the system development life cycle.

prototype: working model of proposed system

proxy server: a firewall component that sits between a client application, such as a web browser, and a real server. It intercepts all requests to the real server to see if it can fulfil the requests itself. If not, it forwards the request to the real server.

public-key encryption: in public-key encryption, a public key, combined with a private key, is used to effectively encrypt messages and decrypt digital signatures. The use of public and private keys is known as asymmetric cryptography. A system that uses public keys is called a Public Key Infrastructure.

Public Key Infrastructure (PKI): a system of digital certificates, certificate authorities and other registration authorities that verify and authenticate the validity of each party involved in an Internet transaction. PKIs are currently evolving and there is no single PKI nor even a single agreed-upon standard for setting up a PKI. However, nearly everyone agrees that reliable PKIs are necessary before e-commerce can become widespread. A PKI is also called a trust hierarchy.

rapid application development: development of software throughout the system development process. A common approach in RAD is prototyping, which is the development of a working model of the proposed system.

Rate Adaptive DSL (RADSL): a variation of ADSL in which the modem can adjust the speed of the connection, depending on the length and quality of the line

Rational Unified Process (RUP): a software development process that emphasises quality through best practice, minimises risk, reduces time-to-market through an interactive approach, provides standard templates and employs rapid development methodology

resource definition format (RDF): facilitates accessing of resources through the use of a highly flexible indexing system

return on investment (ROI): a measure of a project's or corporation's profitability.

RSA encryption: A public key encryption technology developed by RSA Data Security, Inc. The RSA algorithm is based on the fact that there is no efficient way to factor very large numbers. Deducing an RSA key, therefore, requires an extraordinary amount of computer processing power and time.

satellite radio: use of orbiting satellites to relay data between multiple earth-based stations. Satellite communications offer high bandwidth and a cost that is not related to distance between earth stations, long propagation delays or broadcast capability.

search engines: *see* Internet search engines

secret-key encryption: In cryptography, a private or secret key is an encryption/decryption key known only to the party or parties that exchange secure messages. In traditional secret key cryptography, a key would be shared by the communicators so that each could encrypt and decrypt messages to and from the other.

Secure Hypertext Transfer Protocol (S-HTTP): an extension to the HTTP protocol that incorporates inbuilt security to support sending data securely over the Web.

Secure Sockets Layer (SSL): a protocol originally developed by Netscape to facilitate the secure transmission of documents to and from web browsers. SSL uses a form of public key encryption to encrypt data for transmission. Web pages that make use of SSL start with https instead of http.

security: concerned with protection of information systems and operating systems from illegal or unauthorised access or interference

security audit: process of checking that the procedures determined for security of a network or for IT use within an organisation are being followed

security policy: set of required processes (framed in a document) that deal with organisational security issues

Serial Line Internet Protocol (SLIP): is a TCP/IP protocol used for communication between two machines configured for communication with each other. For example, your Internet server provider may provide you with a SLIP connection so that the provider's server can respond to your requests, pass them on to the Internet and forward your requested Internet responses back to you.

server: a special-purpose device within a LAN that performs a specific function. For example, the file server will provide access to the shared files for all LAN users. The file server is usually a computer that has no other function in the network.

session ID: a unique identifier used by web browsers to manage security and scripting functionality

SET: a protocol aimed at providing an Internet payment mechanism that protects the stakes of every participant in the current credit card system — banks as well as credit card companies

shopping trolleys: the online or web-based versions of physical trolleys (or carts) used by shoppers in supermarkets and department stores

S-HTTP: an extension to the HTTP protocol to support sending data securely over the World Wide Web. Not all web browsers and servers support S-HTTP; another technology for transmitting secure communications over the Web — Secure Sockets Layer (SSL) — is more prevalent. However, SSL and S-HTTP have very different designs and goals, so it is possible to use the two protocols together. Whereas SSL is designed to establish a secure connection between two computers, S-HTTP is designed to send individual messages securely.

Simple Mail Transfer Protocol (SMTP): a protocol used to transfer electronic mail between computers, usually over an Ethernet connection.

smart card: a credit card–sized card containing a computer chip that is capable of receiving, processing, storing and transmitting monetary information

spam: electronic junk mail or junk newsgroup postings. Some people define spam even more generally as any unsolicited e-mail. However, if a long-lost friend finds your e-mail address and sends you a message, this could hardly be called spam, even though it's unsolicited.

Standardised General Markup Language (SGML): a protocol that defines documents in plain text using tags embedded in the text to specify the definition

standard input: the defined path to a computer program. The standard input path is usually the keyboard. In the case of CGI scripts, the web server provides input data to the script; thus, standard input in this case is actually an output stream from the web server.

standard output: the defined output path from a program. The standard output path is usually the monitor screen. In the case of CGI scripts, the output from a script becomes an input to the web server. The web server teats this input as if it was reading a web page from a file.

stateless: stateless operation means that a system is unable to store transaction or state information between communication sessions. HTTP operates in such a way that each page access is treated as a separate communication session without any link being maintained to previous communication sessions. Web applications such as shopping trolleys often need to link information that is entered over a number of pages. This is often done through the use of techniques such as cookies, hidden fields or session IDs.

stored value card (SVC): a card storing information about value that can be used in exchange for goods and services

Structured Query Language (SQL): a standard fourth-generation programming language for relational database systems

supply chain: the network of relationships that an enterprise maintains with its suppliers and trading partners

supply chain management (SCM): the structure and/or process used in bringing together components in a production process. It is the staged process of sourcing, producing, and distributing goods and services.

support: to have a specific functionality. For example, a word processor that supports graphics is one that has a graphics component.

symmetric encryption: encryption in which the same key is used to encrypt and decrypt the message. This differs from asymmetric (or public key) encryption, which uses one key to encrypt a message and another to decrypt the message.

synchronous: action taking place on the Web in real time — i.e., as an event happens the exchange takes place

telematics: the broad process of using computers in concert with telecommunications systems. Includes dial-up service to the Internet as well as all types of networks that rely on a telecommunications system to transport data

thin client: a user interface where most of the computing is done on a powerful back-end server

timeboxing: a method of controlling scope applied during analysis or construction that imposes an immovable deadline on the completion of a task, activity, stage or system by strictly controlling functionality.

TRADACOMS: a recognised brand of EDI software.

trade marks: signs or symbols used or intended to be used to distinguish goods or services provided in the course of trade by a person from goods or services provided by any other person. These symbols could be letters, words, names, signatures, numbers, devices, brands, or even a smell or scent.

transactions: typically involve the exchange of documents such as orders, bookings, invoices etc. between two parties

Transmission Control Protocol/Internet Protocol (TCP/IP): a set of commands and communications protocols used by the Internet to connect dissimilar systems and control the flow of information. The protocol allows users of the Internet to find information, use email, interact with other businesses, find personal details of people who have developed their own home pages, exchange business information and data, or download software from the Internet.

Triple DES: uses a three-key approach and is essentially a three-stage DES encryption system. Each 64-bit block is encrypted with the first secret key (as in standard DES). The block from the first step is decrypted with the second secret key. (In fact, the same algorithm is applied in reverse to scramble the data, which can only be unscrambled by the encryption process using the same key.) The block from the second step is encrypted again with the first key. At the receiver's end, the message is first decrypted with the first key, then encrypted with the second and decrypted again with the third. The processing time required makes it slow for many environments.

Trojan: (or Trojan Horse), a computer program that carries within itself the means to allow its creator access to the system using it. Unlike viruses, Trojans do not replicate themselves, but they can be just as destructive. One of the most insidious types of Trojan horse is a program that claims to rid your system of viruses but instead introduces viruses into your computer.

trust: the qualified reliance on received information. Trust in e-commerce involves a willingness to rely on an exchange partner, with an expectation of trustworthiness based on past performance or report.

ubiquitous computing: a speculative concept that looks to a time when computers will be placed in every appliance and device we used

Ultranet: a speculative term describing the super-network that will develop once all devices are connected

Unified Modelling Language (UML): a standard notation for the modelling of real-world objects as a first step in developing an object-oriented design methodology. Its notation is derived from and unifies the notations of three object-oriented design and analysis methodologies.

Use Case modelling: a methodology used in system analysis to identify, clarify and organise system requirements. The Use Case comprises a set of possible sequences of interactions between systems and users in a particular environment and related to a particular goal.

user requirements document: a document that outlines business needs and best software solutions (*see* page 123)

value-added network (VAN): an online service that provides proprietary software to communicate with firms registered with the service

value-added services: specialist services that a customer values highly, so that they are more likely to do business with an organisation offering those services

vandal: an applet that downloads via a web browser then attempts to destroy files or other computer components

very-high-speed backbone network service (vBNS): a spine or backbone that allows very-high-speed interaction for the next-generation Internet

virtual communities: groups of people with similar interests who communicate and interact in an electronic or online environment

Virtual Private Network (VPN): utilises a public network, such as the Internet, to transmit private data. An emerging form of extranet implementation that may become a viable replacement for traditional wide area networks (WANs)

virtual storefront: a full information service designed to include the marketing of a business's services, products, online purchasing and customer support on the Internet

viruses: programs that copy themselves into other programs and spread through multiple computers; often designed to damage a computer by destroying or corrupting its data

voice recognition: the ability of a machine or program to receive and interpret dictation, or to understand and carry out spoken commands. Also called speech recognition

VPN tunnel: a secure pathway between entities using VPN

web portals: a business model that provides a central point on the Web intended as the first place a user will go when they start using the Web. Offer such services as web searching, free email and information services such as news, sports, stock market, television and weather resources

Wireless Application Protocol (WAP): an industry open standard to facilitate the easy access to information by handset users. It was engineered with the low bandwidth of current mobile technology, which uses small monochrome screens. WAP is a specification for a set of communication protocols to standardise the way that wireless devices, such as cellular telephones and radio transceivers, can be used for Internet access, including email, the Web, newsgroups and Internet Relay Chat (IRC).

work flow management: allows an enterprise to manage the quality of work produced

worms: programs that replicate themselves and are self-propagating. Unlike viruses, worms are meant to spawn in network environments. Network worms were first defined by Xerox in March 1982. The Internet worm of November 1988 is perhaps the most famous; it successfully propagated itself on more than 6000 systems across the Internet.

X.25 protocol: an international standard for connecting devices to a packet-switching network

X.400 protocol: a family of open systems interconnection (OSI) protocols used to deliver messages between electronic mail hosts and to specify message structure

X.500 protocol: a standard that describes how to create a directory containing all the electronic mail users' names and their addresses

X.509 protocol: used for public key digital certificates. Used by the Secure Sockets Layer (SSL) protocol as part of a two-phrase handshake protocol for server and client authentication

XLINK: specification allowing elements to be inserted into XML documents in order to create and describe links between resources

XML/EDI: provides a standard framework to exchange different types of data so that the information — be it in a transaction, exchanged via an Application Program Interface (API), web automation, database portal, catalogue, a work flow document or message — can be searched, decoded, manipulated and displayed consistently and correctly by first implementing EDI dictionaries and extending the vocabulary via online repositories to include business language, rules and objects.

XML schemas: *see* document type definitions

XPATH: specification created to provide a common syntax for querying and addressing the contents of XML documents

XPOINTER: Xpointer, which is based on the XML Path Language (Xpath), supports addressing into the internal structures of XML documents.

yellow pages model: The yellow pages marketing model reflects a multiple-listed, ubiquitous online directory of all relevant sites and businesses for ease of access by the user. In essence, it is the application of the advertising model used in telephone yellow pages, in which businesses advertise by category or type of business, to the Web.

index

access control lists (ACLs)   261
accountability, computer security   250
Active Server Pages (ASP)   99, 102–5
ActiveX   107
   and security   108
ActiveX controls, creating and using   107–8
adapters   237
advertisements, click-through   306
advertising-supported models   45–50
Application Program Interface (API)   98–9, 152
application service providers (ASPs)   330, 347–50
assemblers   364
asymmetric encryption   251–3
asynchronous communication   130, 131
Asymmetric Digital Subscriber Line (ADSL)   369
attachments to email   30
auditing e-commerce   142
automobile Internet   370
Automotive Network Exchange (ANX)   173–4

back channel   128
back-end database system   236
bandwidth trading   371–3
banner advertisements   45, 47
behaviour-oriented perspective   118
Berners-Lee, Tim   78
binary numbers   85
BizTalk   159–61
bluesky forecast   374
Bluetooth   19–20
Boehm's Spiral Model   139–40
browsers   21, 27
business failure   282
business interface   346
business models   127–30
   e-commerce   44–69, 135–7
business process management   342
business strategy   338, 339–40
business to business (B2B)   10, 13–14
   and extranet   162–3
   and XML use   159–61
   e-procurement, case study   188–90
   electronic payment systems   228
   integration   178–205
   Internet auctions   66
   transformation   150–1
   virtual communities   64

business to consumer (B2C)   11–12
   case study   109–10
   electronic payment systems   213–16
   security of transactions   110
   virtual communities   53–4
business to government (B2G), and trust   281

Cascading Style Sheets (CSS)   153
cataloguing   183–4
censorship   304–5
Cerebos foods, case study   343–6
Cisco Systems   37–40, 140
clear GIFS   306–7
click-through advertising   45, 47, 306
clickwrap agreements   302–3
client/server architecture   21
client/server computing (web-based)   76–86
   extending to perform transactions   86–96
client/server models   130
ColdFusion   99, 100–2
collaborative computing software   366
collaborative e-business models   129
Common Gateway Interface (CGI)   27–8, 91
   interaction with a web browser   91–6
Common Gateway Interface (CGI) scripts   98
Common Object Request Broker Architecture
      (CORBA)   87, 88, 132
communication technology, future
      directions   367–9
company based models of e-commerce   50–7
component-based approaches   119
computer ethics   322–3
computer forensics   249
computer security   249–50
   digital signatures   254–5
   encryption and authentication   250–3
computing history   4–7
confidentiality and privacy   249–50
   extranet   166
consumer to business (C2B)   15
   Internet auctions   66
consumer to consumer (C2C)   15
consumer to government (C2G), and trust   281
content management systems   185–7, 376–7
cookies   96–7, 307–9
copyright   301, 311, 312–13
corporate strategy   339
corProcure   188–90

crackers   248, 317–18
credit cards on the Internet   213–14
   case study   240–1
   how they work   214–16
criminal activities   316–17, 365
   see also fraud
cross-functional applications   198–9
cryptographic failure   282
cryptolope   258
cyberbludging   309
CyberCash   219
cybercrime   365

Data Encryption Standard (DES)   250
data management   342
data mining   280
data-oriented perspective   118
data warehousing   134
database integration   134–5
database management systems   133–7
defamation   301, 320–2
denial-of-service (DoS) attack   245–6
   security policy   291–3
design specification   124
DigiCash   219
digital cash   219–20
   security issues   220–1
digital certificates   255–6
digital currency products   221–3
digital economy   9
Digital Rights Management   313
digital signatures   254–5
Digital Subscriber Line (DSL)   368
digital watermarking   311
direct link EDI   230
directory   22
Distributed Component Object Model
   (DCOM)   87, 88, 132
distributed denial-of-service (DDoS) attack   245
   case study   266–70
distributed function client/server model   86, 87
Document Object Model (DOM)   152
Document Type Definitions (DTDs)   151,
   152–3
domain names   319
Dr Shewart's PDCA Life Cycle   138–9
duplex mode of transmission   24, 25
Dynamic Systems Development Method
   (DSDM)   122–4, 140, 141

e-business
   architecture   333
   managing the human factor   195–9
   pervasive   362
e-business leader   197

e-business team   197
e-cash   55, 219
e-commerce
   advent of   8–10
   and information systems   31–2
   and trust   274–82
   as management tool   32–4
   building blocks   23
   business models   44–69, 135–7
   e-savvy strategy   335–8
   history   2–4
   management   338–54
   risk assessment   142
   types of   10–16
e-ink   374
e-paper   374
e-publishing   373–4
e-software development, case study   125–6
e-wallets   218
EAI see enterprise application integration
ebXML (electronic business Extensible Markup
   Language)   159
EDIFACT   232
electronic catalogues   54, 55
electronic cheques   217–18
Electronic Commerce Modelling Language
   (ECML)   218
Electronic Data Interchange (EDI)   8, 131, 150,
   229
   communications channels   229–30
   Internet   234–7
   standards   231–2
   traditional   229, 232–3
   see also XML/EDI
electronic funds transfer (EFT)   8, 228
electronic funds transfer at point of sale
   (EFTPOS)   8, 217, 228
electronic malls   48, 63–4
electronic monitoring   168
electronic negotiations   58
electronic payment systems (EPS)   213
   B2B   228
   B2C   213–16
   credit cards on the Internet   213–16, 240–1
   digital cash and prepaid cards   219–21
   digital currency products   221–3
   e-wallets   218
   EFTPOS   217, 228
   electronic cheques   217–18
   electronic funds transfer   228
   smart cards   227–8
electronic procurement   58–9
electronic purchasing   239
Electronics Transaction Bill (NZ)   276–8
email   30–1

email address   31
embedding script to produce web pages   99–105
embedding session information in a URL   87
encryption and authentication   250
   common algorithms   253
   public-key encryption   251–3
   secret-key encryption   250–1
   Triple DES   251
enhancements   124
enterprise application integration (EAI)   178
   application technology components   183–8
   architecture   180
   capital cost reduction   201
   checklist   187–8
   cost of investment   199–200
   increased revenue   200–1
   inventory management   201–2
   middleware technology   181–3
   process simplification   201
   reasons for   178–9
   return on investment   199–204
   technologies   179–80
enterprise integration   130
enterprise resource planning (ERP)   130, 179, 342
environment variables   91, 93–4
ethernet connections   24
ethics   322–3
Evolutionary Development Model   138–9
Extensible Markup Language (XML)   3, 79, 131, 151–2
   and B2B infrastructure   159–61
   benefits of   154–5
   see also XML/EDI
Extensible Style Language (XSL)   153
extranet   17–18, 129
   and B2B e-business   162–3
   and the knowledge factory   163–4
   architecture   165
   benefits of   164
   confidentiality and privacy   166
   data and network security   167–8
   data integrity   168–9
   definition   162
   security   166–7
   VPN   169–71
extreme programming (XP)   142

fat client/thin server   86, 87
file transfer protocol (FTP)   27
financial services, use of m-commerce   10
firewalls   165, 258–9
   applications   260–1
   modes of operation   259–60
   typical components   260
forms   83, 88–90

fraud   282, 296–8, 316
functional design specification   138
functional strategy   339

geolocation software   366
GET   83, 89, 91
glossary   379–89
Gnutella   313
going on line   121
government to business (G2B)   15, 58
government to consumer (G2C)   15
government to government (G2G)   15
groupware   17–18

hackers   245–6, 248, 317–18
half-duplex mode of transmission   24
hidden fields   97
High Bit Rate DSL (HDSL)   369
hotlinks   26
hub and spoke model   234–6
human factors, in transition to e-business   195–9
human security issues   248–9
hyperlinks   26
Hypertext Markup Language (HTML)   3, 27, 76, 77–9, 151
   development   78–9
   limitations   151
Hypertext Transfer Protocol (HTTP)   3, 19, 26, 27, 76, 82–4
   sending data via   90–1

ID cards   306
information services, use of m-commerce   10
information systems, and Internet commerce   31–2
information technology
   architecture   333–4
   competitive importance   330
   evolution   332
   management   332–5, 354
infrastructure management   340–2
intellectual property   52, 310–13
intelligent agent software   366
inter-organisational models of e-commerce   57–62
Interactive Mail Access Protocol (IMAP)   30–1
interactive television   128, 367
internal security   285–6
Internet
   access   29
   definition   16
   history   6–7
   inappropriate use   309–10
   operation   22–7
   protocols   24–7
Internet auctions   48, 64–6

Internet business technologies and standards 130–2
Internet content, control of 304–5
Internet EDI 234
  components 236–7
  hub and spoke model 234–6
Internet exchanges 66–8
Internet Explorer 21
  VBScript 80
Internet fraud 296–8
Internet Inter-ORB Protocol (IIOP) 132–3
Internet Protocol (IP) 84, 85, 86
  see also Transmission Control Protocol/Internet
    Protocol
Internet security 256–8
Internet service providers (ISPs) 23, 28
Internet2 369–70
Intranets 16–17
IPSec (IP Security) 171

Java 21–2, 80, 105–7
  and security 107
Java applets, creating and using 105–7
Java Database Connectivity (JDBC) 87, 88
Java Virtual Machine 105
JavaBeans 135
JavaScript 79–82
Jini Inititative 19
Johnson and Johnson, case study 348–50
Joint Application Development (JAD) 31, 118,
    120–1
  personnel 121
just-in-time (JIT) 60, 61, 179, 192

knowledge factories 163–4

L2TP (Layer 2 Tunnelling Protocol) 171
law 301
  and jurisdiction 319–20
  and online transactions 302–3
  and privacy 306–7
leadership 340
legacy systems 119
legislation 301
leveraging Internet technology 195
leveraging knowledge management 196
LIGNUS 337–8
Livelink 129
logistics companies 56
Lynx 21

m-commerce 9–10, 128
  and miniaturisation 363
macro viruses 246
mail repository 236

management (e-commerce) 335–8
  emerging trends 350–4
  infrastructure management 340–6
  leadership issues 340
  outsourcing and ASPs 347–50
  strategy development 338–40
management (information technology) 330–5
message queueing 179
metalanguage 151
middleware 134
  infrastructure components 130–1
  technology 181–3
miniaturisation, and m-commerce 363
mobile commerce see m-commerce
mobile wallets 366
models of e-commerce 44–68
  advertising-supported 45–50
  case study 135–7
  company-based 50–7
  inter-organisational 57–62
  third party 63–8
monitoring employees 309–10
mousetrapping 324–5
MP3 4, 312
multi-organisational electronic service delivery
    (MESD) 53, 59–60
Multipurpose Internet Mail Extensions (MIME) 27

nanobots 364
nanotechnology 364–5
Napster 312
Netscape Navigator 21
  JavaScript 80
network effect 117
network failure 282
network security 258–63
  access control lists 261
  firewalls 258–61
  passwords 261–3
networked economy 117–18

OBI standard 237
object-oriented approaches 119
online advertising models 44–9
online banking and taxation issues 317
online fee-for-service model 52–3
online fee-for-transaction model 53
online marketplaces (OLMs) 13–14
online payment 55–6
online procurement systems 58
online subscription 50–2
open buying on the Internet (OBI) 237–8
Open Database Connectivity (ODBC) 87–8
'Open Skies' airline reservation system 113–14
Oracle's database integration 135

order fulfilment, virtual storefront companies   56
order processing   184
Orica Chemicals, case study   206–9
outsourcing   347–50

packet filtering   260
packet sniffing   250
pagejacking   324–5
passwords   261
   rules   262–3
patents   314–15
payment systems   184–5
   electronic   213–39
payments to virtual storefront merchants   55–6
peer-to-peer networks (P2P)   10
Perl (programming language)   94, 99
personal digital assistants   2, 9
personalisation   48, 187
pervasive e-business   362
PHP   99, 105
PKI (Public Key Infrastructure)   255
plug and play   179
Point-to-Point Protocol (PPP)   24
policy development   290–3
policy evaluation   294
policy implementation   293–5
pornography   304, 309–10
POST   83, 89, 90
Post Office Protocol (POP)   25, 26
PPTP (Point-to-Point Tunnelling Protocol)   171
prepaid cards   220
Pretty Good Privacy (PGP)   252
privacy   166, 249–50, 304, 306–7
   and cookies   307–8
   laws on   308–9
private networks   230
process-oriented perspective   118
Procter & Gamble, case study   70–1
product calatogues   54, 55
programming the web model   98–110
project management   138–41
prototype   118
proxy servers   260
public-key encryption   251–3

Qantas, case study   355–9
Quick Response (QR)   60, 61

Rapid Application Development (RAD)   31, 118, 140–1
   definitional framework   141–2
Rate Adaptive DSL (RADSL)   369
Rational Unified Process (RUP)   125–6
Remote Method Invocation (RMI)   132
resource definition format (RDF)   22

return on investment from EIA   199–204
risk assessment, e-commerce   142
RSA encryption   252

satellite radio   370
search engines   22
   advertising on   45–6
secret-key encryption   250–1
Secure Digital Music Initiative (SDMI)   312
Secure HTTP (S-HTTP)   3, 110, 257
Secure Sockets Layer (SSL)   110, 170, 257
security   274
   and ActiveX   107–8
   and Java   107
   and standards   130
   B2C transactions   110
   computer security   249–50
   digital cash   220–1
   digital certificates   255–6
   digital signatures   254–5
   encryption and authentication   250–3
   human security issues   248–9
   importance of   244
   Internet security   256–8
   network security   258–63
   threat-mitigation techniques   263–5
   types of attacks   244–8
security audit   294
security policies   274
   development   286–93
      acceptable network and computer use   290
      Internet access   291
      legal policies   291
      penalties and security breaches   293
      physical access   291
      virus and denial-of-service attack
         policies   291–3
   implementation process   293–5
      auditing   294
      management   294–5
   internal security   285–6
   trust and e-commerce   274–82
   trust seals   282–4
security safeguards, computers   250
self-replicators   364
SEPP   220
Serial Line Internet Protocol (SLIP)   24, 25–6
servers   27
service/retail, use of m-commerce   10
session ID   97
SET (secure electronic transaction)   220–1, 258
   and trust   280–1
'shopping trolleys'   54
Simple Mail Transfer Protocol (SMTP)   27
simplex mode of transmission   24, 25

smart cards   223–8
software developments   366
spam   248
SSW System Development Methodology   123–4
Standard Generalised Markup Language
    (SGML)   27, 79, 151
standard input   91, 93–4
state information   96–7
stateless operation   96
stored value cards   223–6
    advantages and risks of   227–8
    types of   227
Structure Query Language (SQL)   88, 134
STT   220
supplier sourcing   58
supply chain   190
    traditional inefficiencies   191
supply chain integration models   191
    integrated make-to-stock   192
    just-in-time manufacturing   192
    Vendor Managed Inventory (VMI)   192, 193–4
supply chain management   56, 60–2, 191, 346–7,
    352
support   124
symmetric encryption   250–1
synchronous communication   130–1
system development methodologies
    background   118–19
    dynamic systems development method   122–4
    Rational Unified Process   125–6
    web development methodologies   119–20
systems development life cycle   32, 120

technology convergence   130–2
telecommunications, use of m-commerce   10
telematics   370
television, interactive   128, 367
teleworking   371
tendering   58
thin client/fat server   86, 87
third party models of e-commerce   63–8
timeboxing   140
TRADACOMS   232
trade marks   315–16
translator   236
Transmission Control Protocol (TCP)   84, 85
Transmission Control Protocol/Internet Protocol
    (TCP/IP)   19, 23, 26, 76, 84–6
Triple DES   251
trojans   248
trust
    and anonymity of the Internet   279–80
    and e-commerce   274–82
    and e-commerce relationships with
        government   281

and SET   280–1
failure of   282
management   278–9
what is it?   274–8
trust seals   282–6
TRUSTe story   284

ubiquitous computing   363
Ultranet   18–19
Unified Modelling Language (UML)   118
Uniform Resource Locators (URLs)   20–1
    embedding session information in   97
Use Case modelling   125
user requirements document   124

value-added networks (VANs)   230–1
value-added services   47, 48
vandals   248
Vendor Managed Inventory (VMI) model   192,
    193–4
very-high-speed backbone network service
    (vBNS)   28
virtual communities   48
    B2B   64
    B2C   53–4
virtual credit card   216
virtual organisation   195–9
Virtual Private Network (VPN)   169–71
    extranet technology   171
virtual storefront   54–7
    building, case study   135–7
virtual storefront companies
    order fulfilment   56
    payment to   55–6
virtual teams   197–8
Virtual Vineyards, case study   144–6
viruses   246–7
    dealing with   247
    security policy   291–3
voice recognition   366
VPN tunnel   170

waterfall method   138
web adoption and its significance for managing
    organisations   330–8
web browsers   21, 27
interaction with CGI script   91–6
web bugs   306–7
web client/server model   76–7
    extending to perform transactions   86–96
    programming   98–110
    three-tiered systems   87–8
    two-tiered systems   87, 88
web content management systems   185–7, 376–7

web development methodologies   119–20
web-object architectures, evolution   132–3
web portals   22, 47–8
web servers   27, 237
Wireless Application Protocol (WAP)   9–10, 346
work flow management   185
World Wide Web   2–3, 26
    architecture   27–30
    history   6–7
worms   246

X.25 protocol   232
X.400 protocol   232
X.500 protocol   232

X.509 certificate   256
X.509 protocol   237
XHTML   79
XLINK   154
XML *see* Extensible Markup Language
XML schemas   153
XML/EDI framework   155–7
XML/EDI trading system   158–9
XPATH   154
XPOINTER   154
XSL *see* Extensible Style Language

yellow pages model   49–50